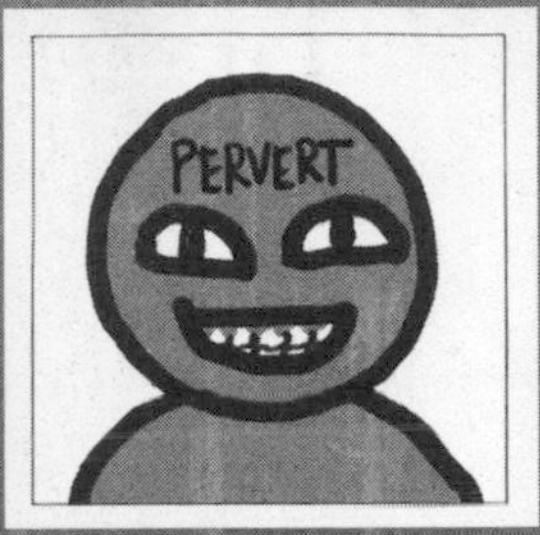
PERVERT

ABOUT ME, PART 2: MY TASTES IN WOMEN

WHEN I TELL PEOPLE I LIKE SHIZUKA KUDO (POP IDOL) AND ASAMI KOBAYASHI (SINGER/ ACTRESS), THEY SAY I HAVE VERY NARROW TASTES. THAT'S NOT COMPLETELY TRUE. I LIKE TOMOMI NISHIMURA (TV PERSONALITY), TOO. AND SHIMA IWASHITA (ACTRESS). AND CHIHARU KAWAI (ACTRESS). AND MASAMI HISAMOTO (COMEDIAN). AND ERIKO NAKAMURA (ANCHORWOMAN). AND CLARISSE DE CAGLIOSTRO (FICTIONAL ANIME CHARACTER). AND MAKI WATASE (OF THE BAND LINDBERG). AND NAE YUKI (ACTRESS). AND DUMP MATSUMOTO (PRO-WRESTLER). IN OTHER WORDS, MY TASTES HAVE A WIDE RANGE.

—YOSHIHIRO TOGASHI, 1992

Born in 1966, Yoshihiro Togashi won the prestigious Tezuka Award for new manga artists at the age of 20. He debuted in Japan's WEEKLY SHONEN JUMP magazine in 1988 with the romantic comedy manga **Tende Showaru Cupid**. His hit comic **YuYu Hakusho** ran in WEEKLY SHONEN JUMP from 1990 to 1994. Togashi's other manga include **I'm Not Afraid of Wolves!**, **Level E**, and **Hunter x Hunter**. **Hunter x Hunter** is also available through VIZ Media.

YUYU HAKUSHO VOL. 12
The SHONEN JUMP Manga Edition

This manga contains material that was originally published in
English in **SHONEN JUMP** #48-52.

STORY AND ART BY
YOSHIHIRO TOGASHI

English Adaptation/Gary Leach
Translation/Lillian Olsen
Touch-up Art & Lettering/Elizabeth Watasin
Design/Courtney Utt
Editor/Urian Brown

Managing Editor/Frances E. Wall
Editorial Director/Elizabeth Kawasaki
Editor in Chief, Books/Alvin Lu
Editor in Chief, Magazines/Marc Weidenbaum
Sr. Director of Acquisitions/Rika Inouye
Sr. VP of Marketing/Liza Coppola
Exec. VP of Sales & Marketing/John Easum
Publisher/Hyoe Narita

Printed in the U.S.A.

Published by VIZ Media, LLC
P.O. Box 77010
San Francisco, CA 94107

SHONEN JUMP Manga Edition
10 9 8 7 6 5 4 3 2 1
First printing, May 2007

www.viz.com

THE WORLD'S
MOST POPULAR MANGA

www.shonenjump.co

SHONEN JUMP MANGA

Yu Yu HAKUSHO ™

Vol.12
The Championship Match Begins!!

STORY AND ART BY
YOSHIHIRO TOGASHI

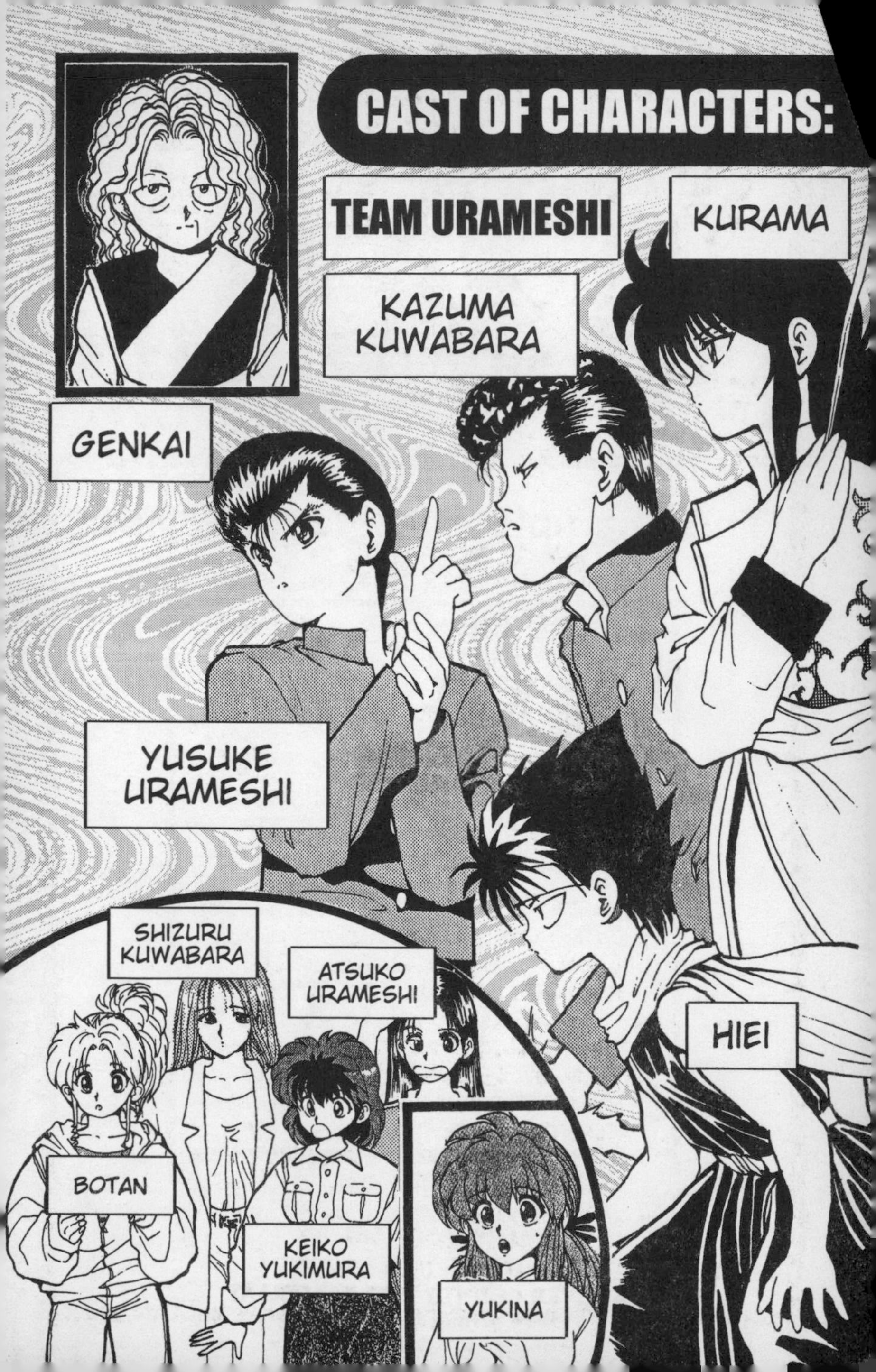
CAST OF CHARACTERS:
TEAM URAMESHI
KURAMA
KAZUMA KUWABARA
GENKAI
YUSUKE URAMESHI
HIEI
SHIZURU KUWABARA
ATSUKO URAMESHI
BOTAN
KEIKO YUKIMURA
YUKINA

TEAM TOGURO

- TOGURO (YOUNGER)
- TOGURO (ELDER)
- BUI
- KARASU
- SAKYO

The Story So Far

THIS IS THE STORY OF YUSUKE URAMESHI, A HAPLESS YOUTH WHO WAS HIT BY A CAR WHILE TRYING TO SAVE A CHILD AND SO BECAME A GHOST. PUT THROUGH A NUMBER OF ORDEALS BY KING ENMA, YUSUKE EARNED HIS WAY BACK TO LIFE. HE NOW WORKS AS AN UNDERWORLD DETECTIVE, WITH ALL SORTS OF DEMONS YEARNING TO SEE HIM DEAD AGAIN.

YUSUKE AND HIS FRIENDS HAVE BEEN ENTERED IN THE DARK TOURNAMENT, WHERE THEIR TEAM HAS ADVANCED TO THE FINALS. THEY'RE NOW UP AGAINST THE ATROCIOUS AND FORMIDABLE TEAM TOGURO!! IN THE FIRST MATCH KURAMA DEFEATED KARASU, WHO NEVERTHELESS WON THE MATCH ON A TECHNICALITY. IN THE SECOND MATCH, HIEI'S BLACK DRAGON CRUSHED BUI. WE'RE NOW AT THE THIRD MATCH, WITH KUWABARA UP AGAINST THE ELDER TOGURO...WHAT WILL HAPPEN THIS TIME?!

YUYU HAKUSHO VOLUME 12 THE Championship Match Begins!!

CONTENTS

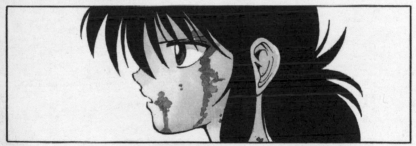

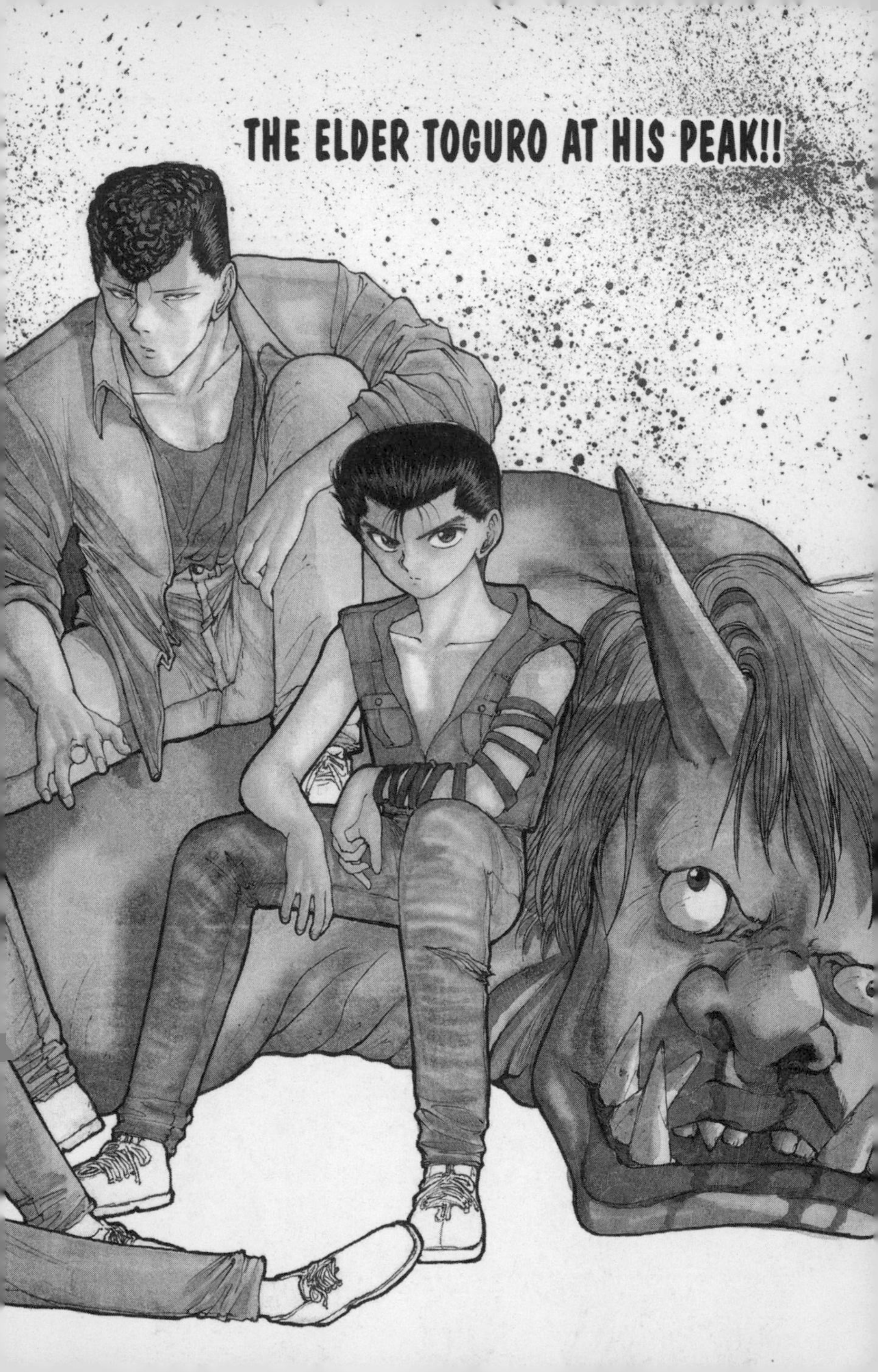
THE ELDER TOGURO AT HIS PEAK!!

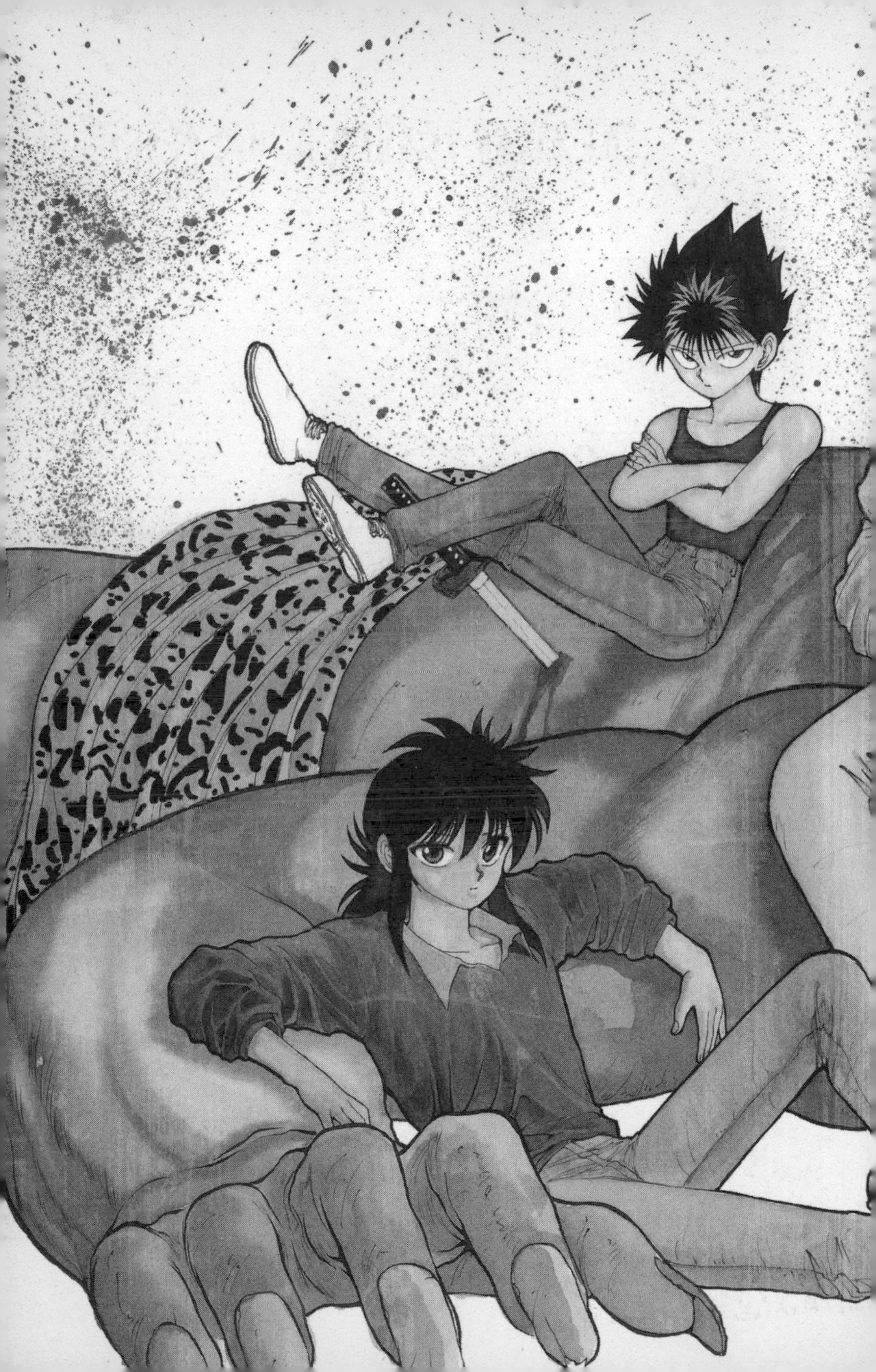

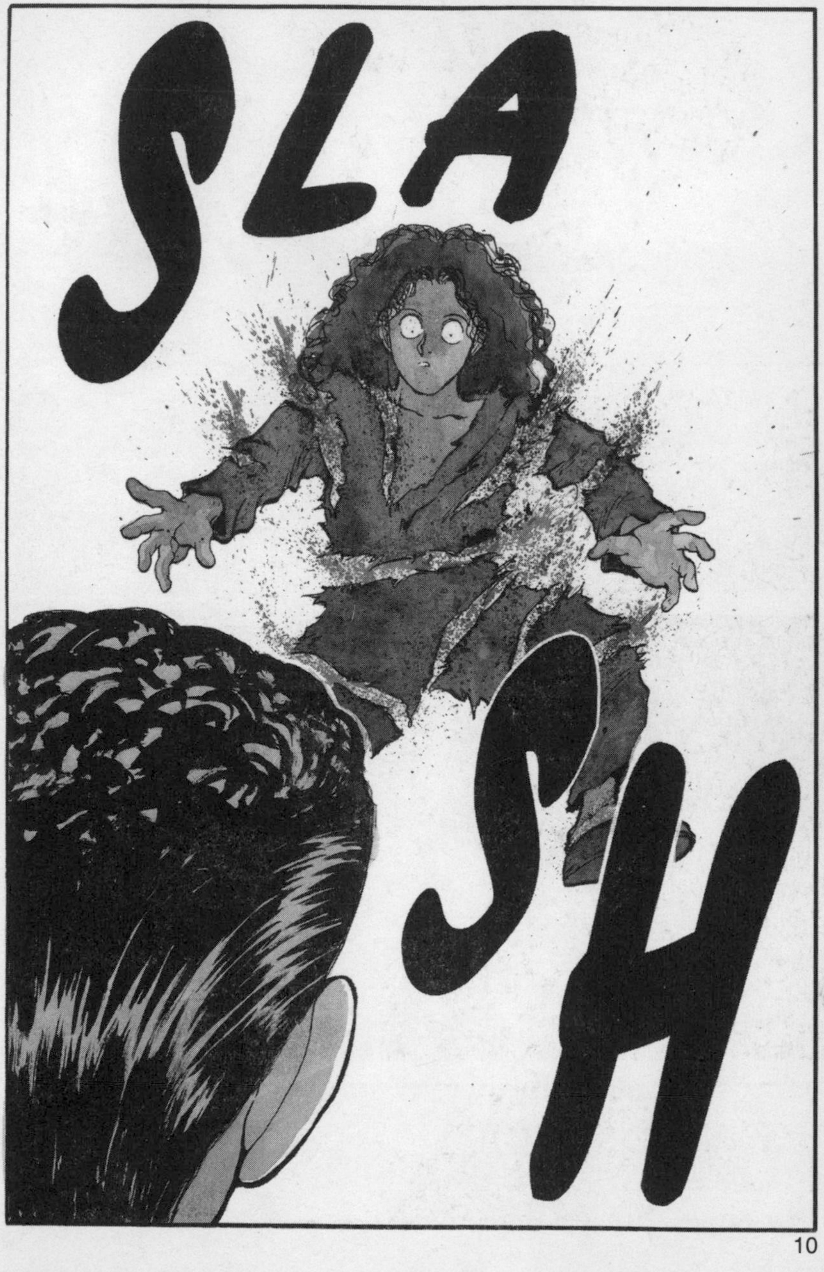
SLASH

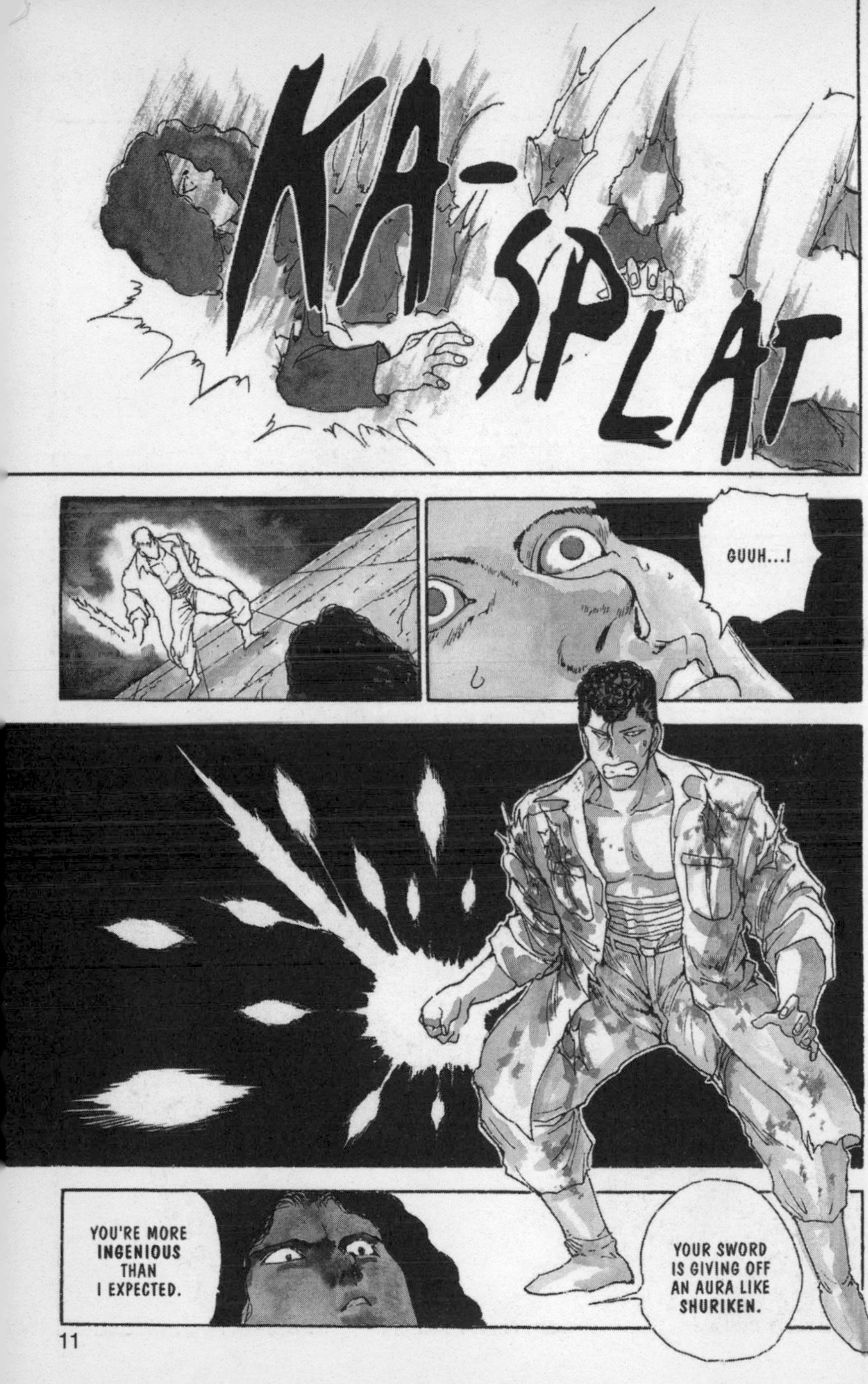
KA-SPLAT
GUUH...!
YOUR SWORD IS GIVING OFF AN AURA LIKE SHURIKEN.
YOU'RE MORE INGENIOUS THAN I EXPECTED.

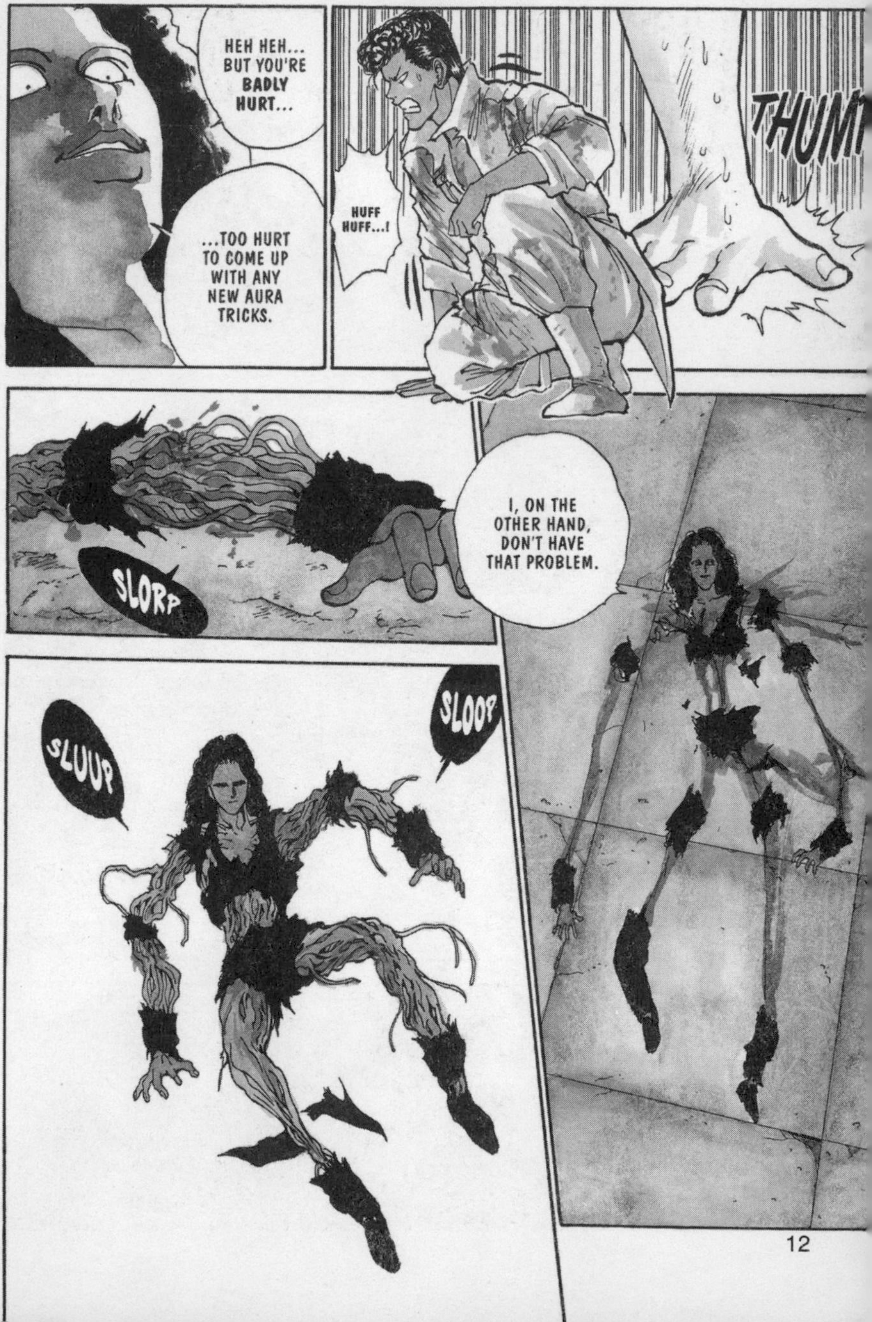
THUM
HUFF HUFF...!
HEH HEH... BUT YOU'RE BADLY HURT...
...TOO HURT TO COME UP WITH ANY NEW AURA TRICKS.
I, ON THE OTHER HAND, DON'T HAVE THAT PROBLEM.
SLORP
SLOOP
SLUUP

READ THIS WAY

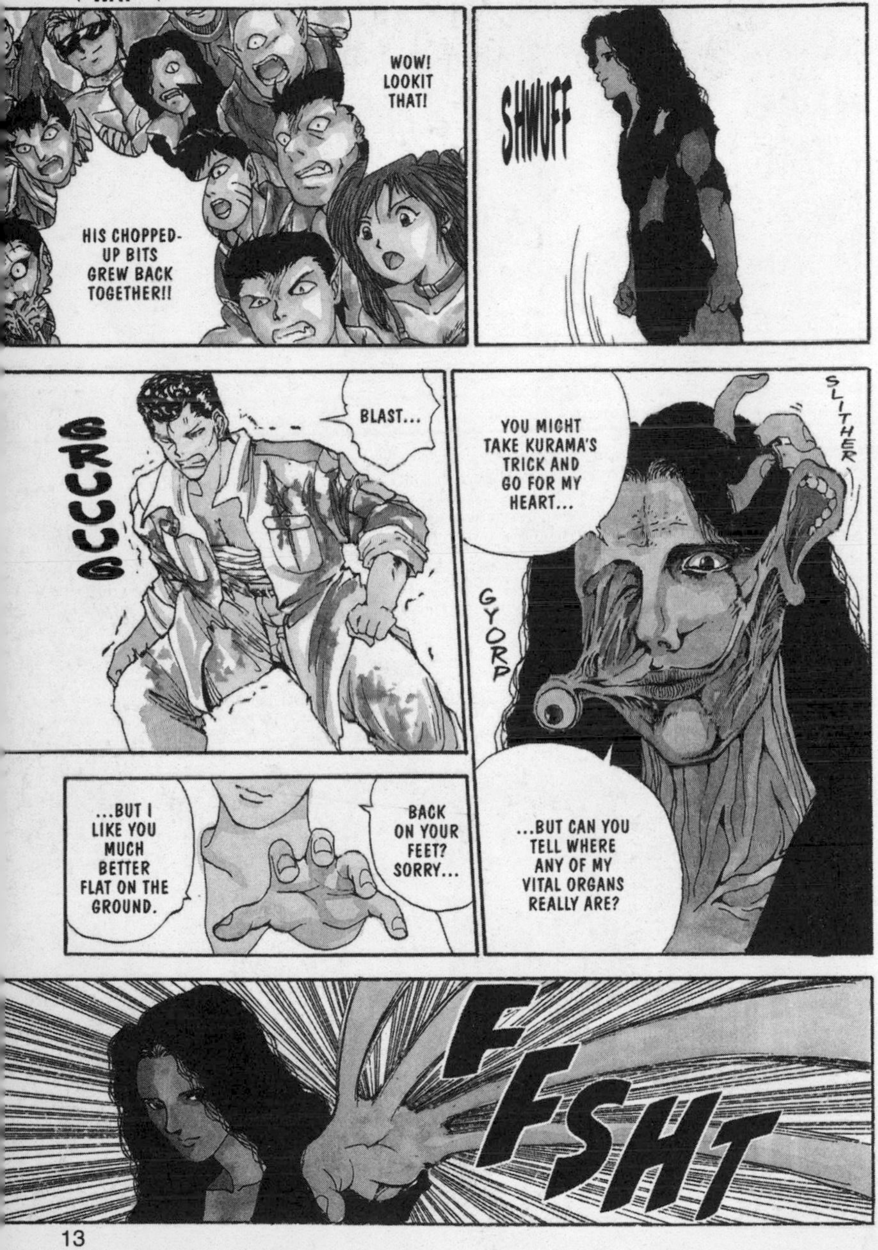
SHWUFF
WOW! LOOKIT THAT!
HIS CHOPPED-UP BITS GREW BACK TOGETHER!!
SLITHER
YOU MIGHT TAKE KURAMA'S TRICK AND GO FOR MY HEART...
GYORP
...BUT CAN YOU TELL WHERE ANY OF MY VITAL ORGANS REALLY ARE?
BLAST...
GRUUUG
BACK ON YOUR FEET? SORRY...
...BUT I LIKE YOU MUCH BETTER FLAT ON THE GROUND.
FFSHT

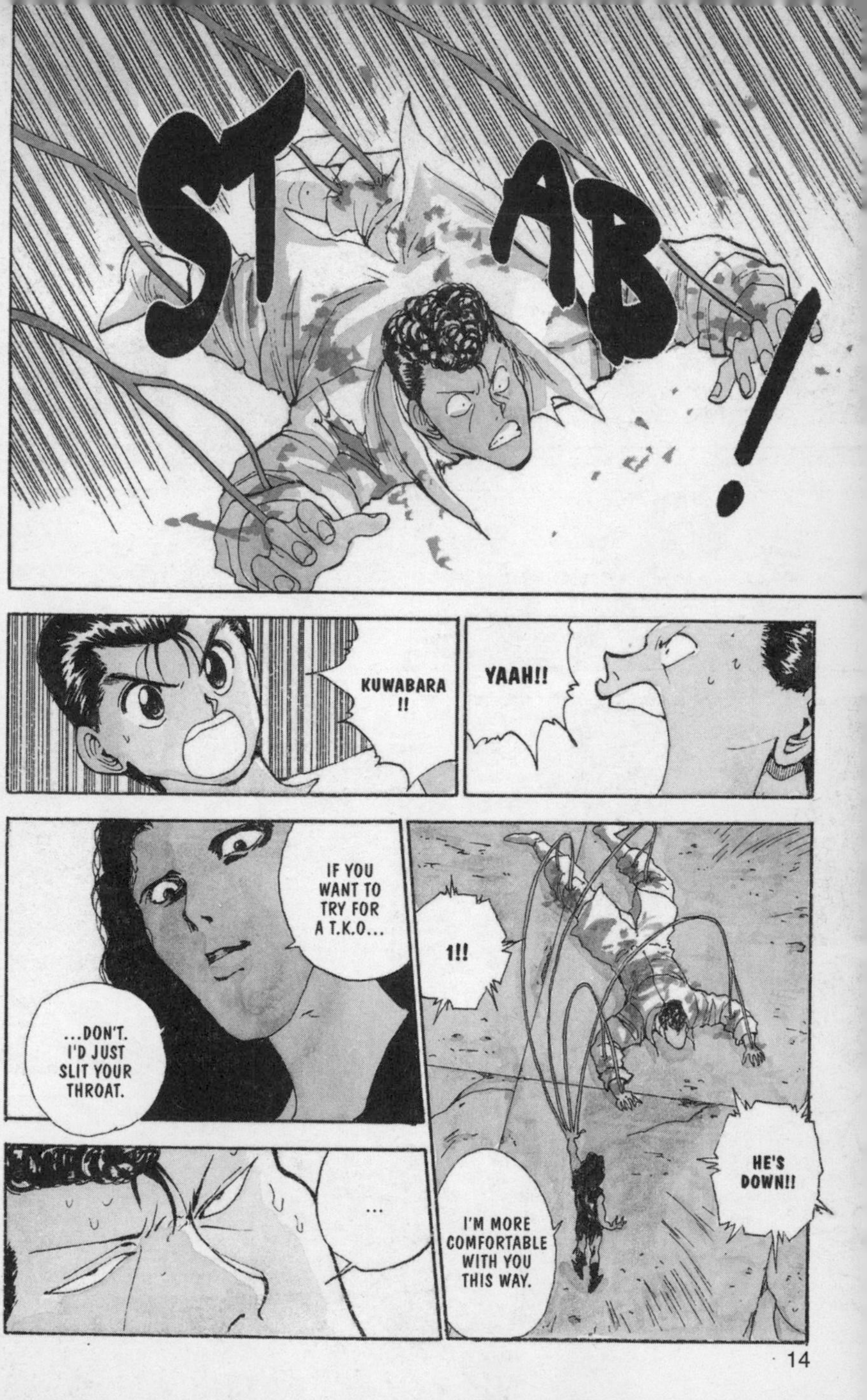
STAB!
YAAH!!
KUWABARA !!
1!!
HE'S DOWN!!
I'M MORE COMFORTABLE WITH YOU THIS WAY.
IF YOU WANT TO TRY FOR A T.K.O...
...DON'T. I'D JUST SLIT YOUR THROAT.
...

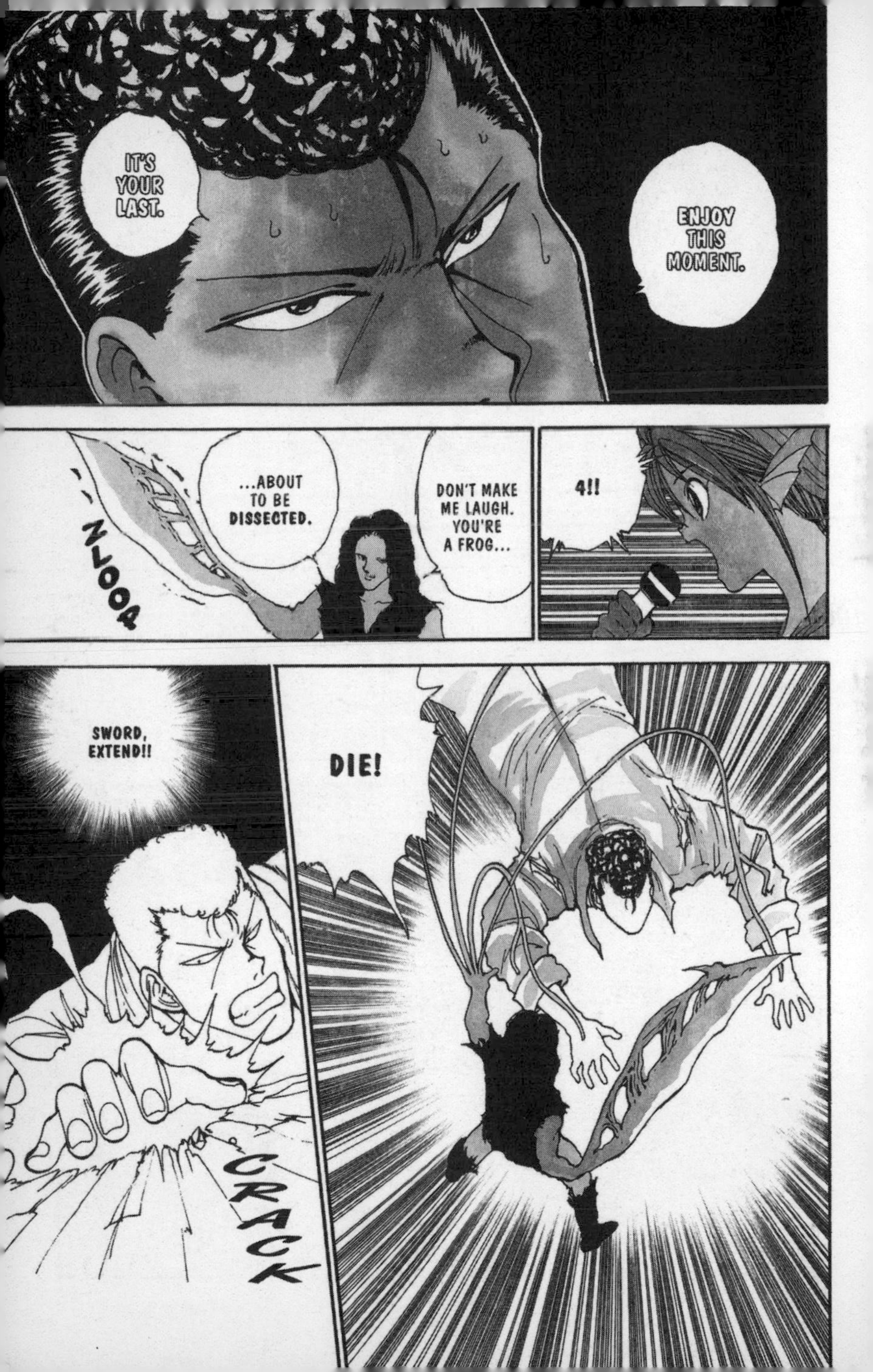
ENJOY THIS MOMENT.
IT'S YOUR LAST.
4!!
DON'T MAKE ME LAUGH. YOU'RE A FROG...
...ABOUT TO BE DISSECTED.
DIE!
SWORD, EXTEND!!
CRACK

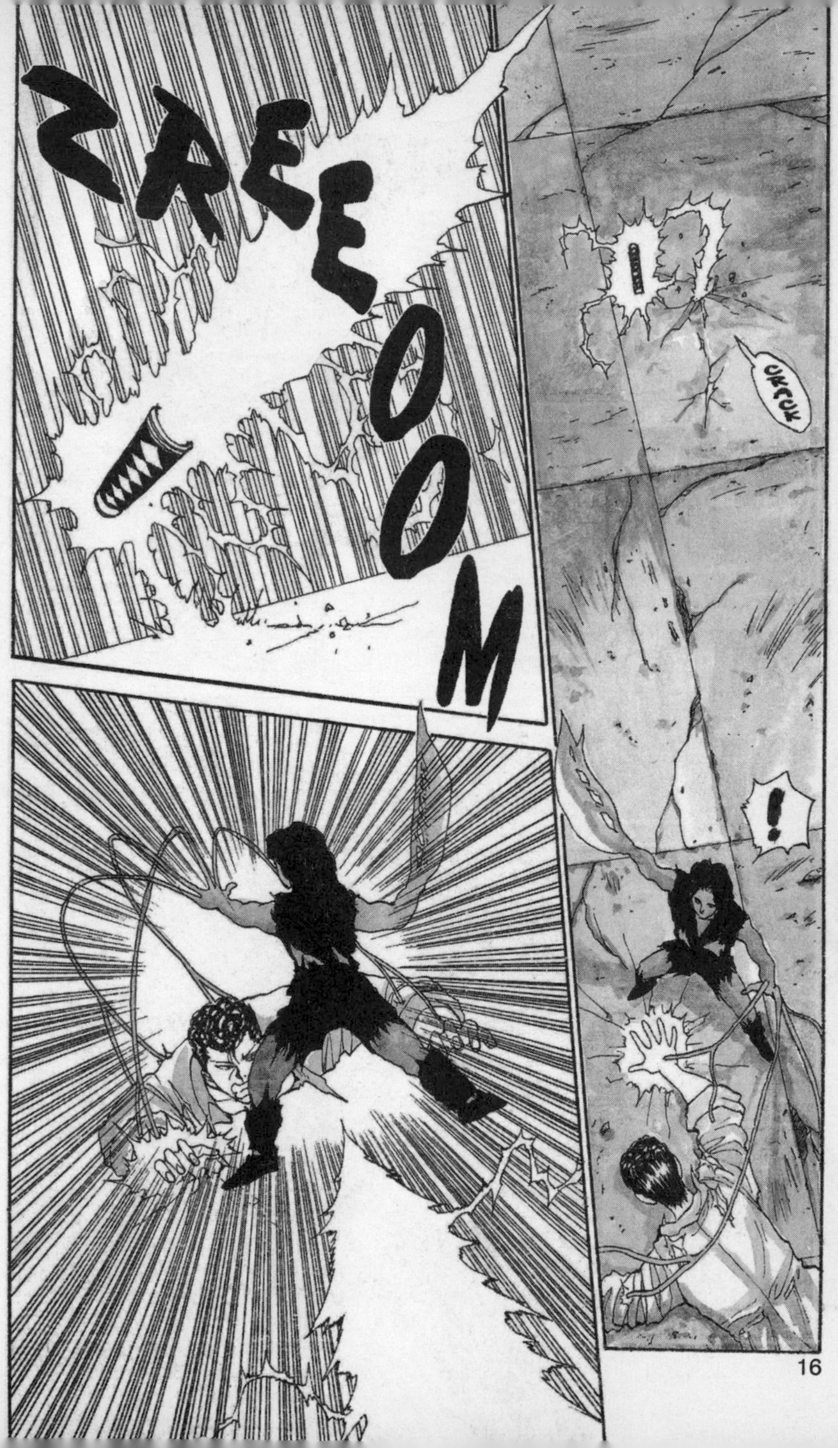
CRACK
!
ZREEOOM

READ THIS WAY

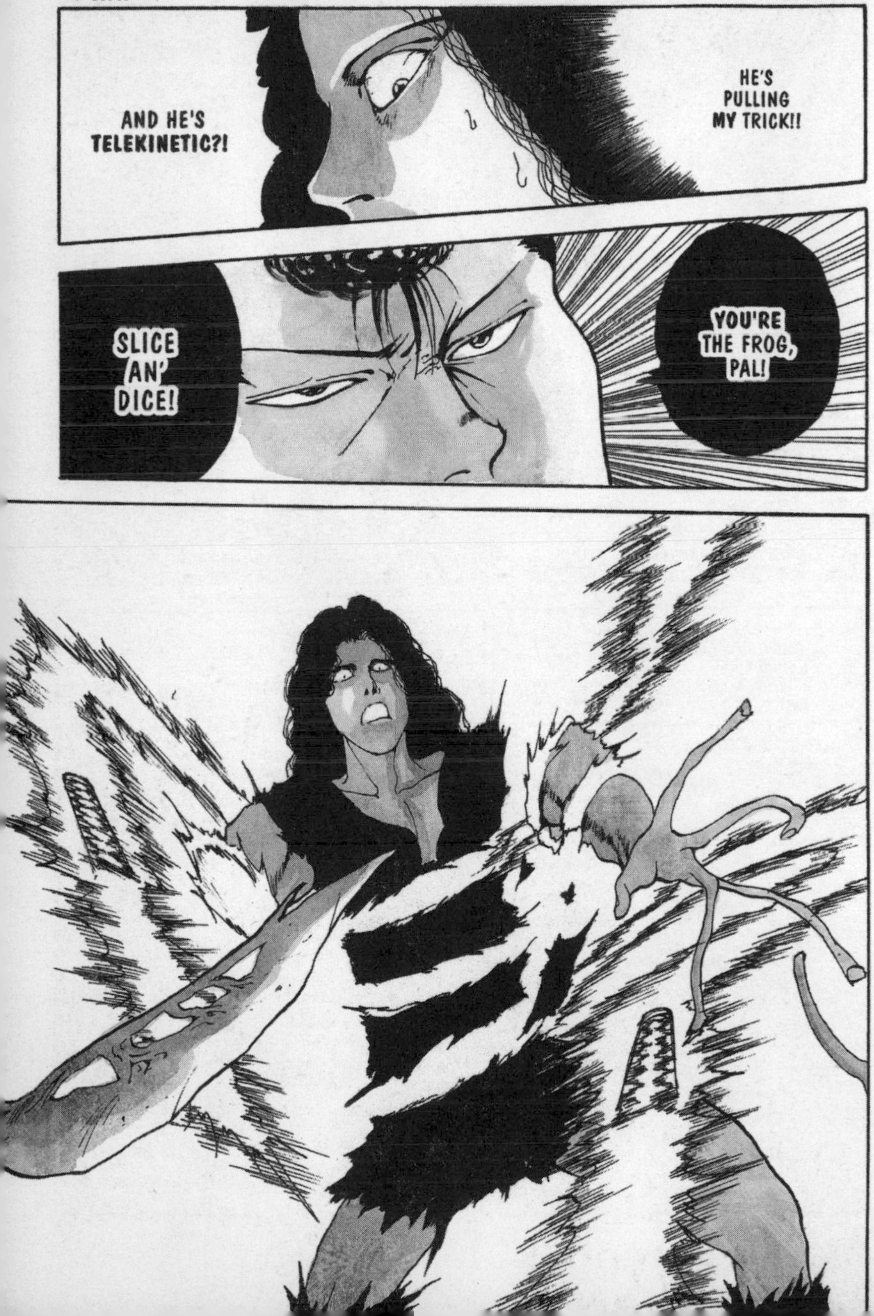
HE'S PULLING MY TRICK!!
AND HE'S TELEKINETIC?!
YOU'RE THE FROG, PAL!
SLICE AN' DICE!

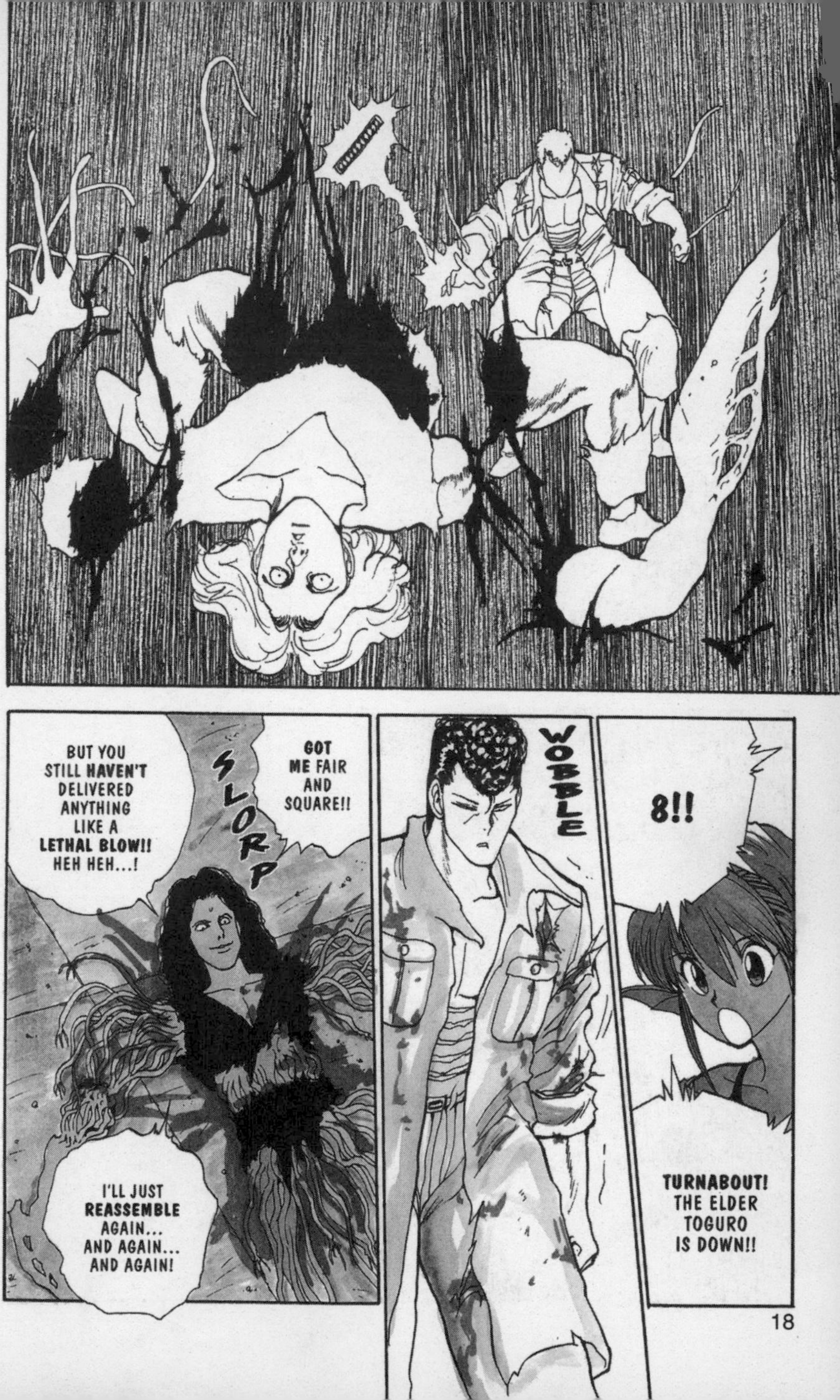
8!!
TURNABOUT! THE ELDER TOGURO IS DOWN!!
WOBBLE
GOT ME FAIR AND SQUARE!!
SLORP
BUT YOU STILL HAVEN'T DELIVERED ANYTHING LIKE A LETHAL BLOW!! HEH HEH...!
I'LL JUST REASSEMBLE AGAIN... AND AGAIN... AND AGAIN!

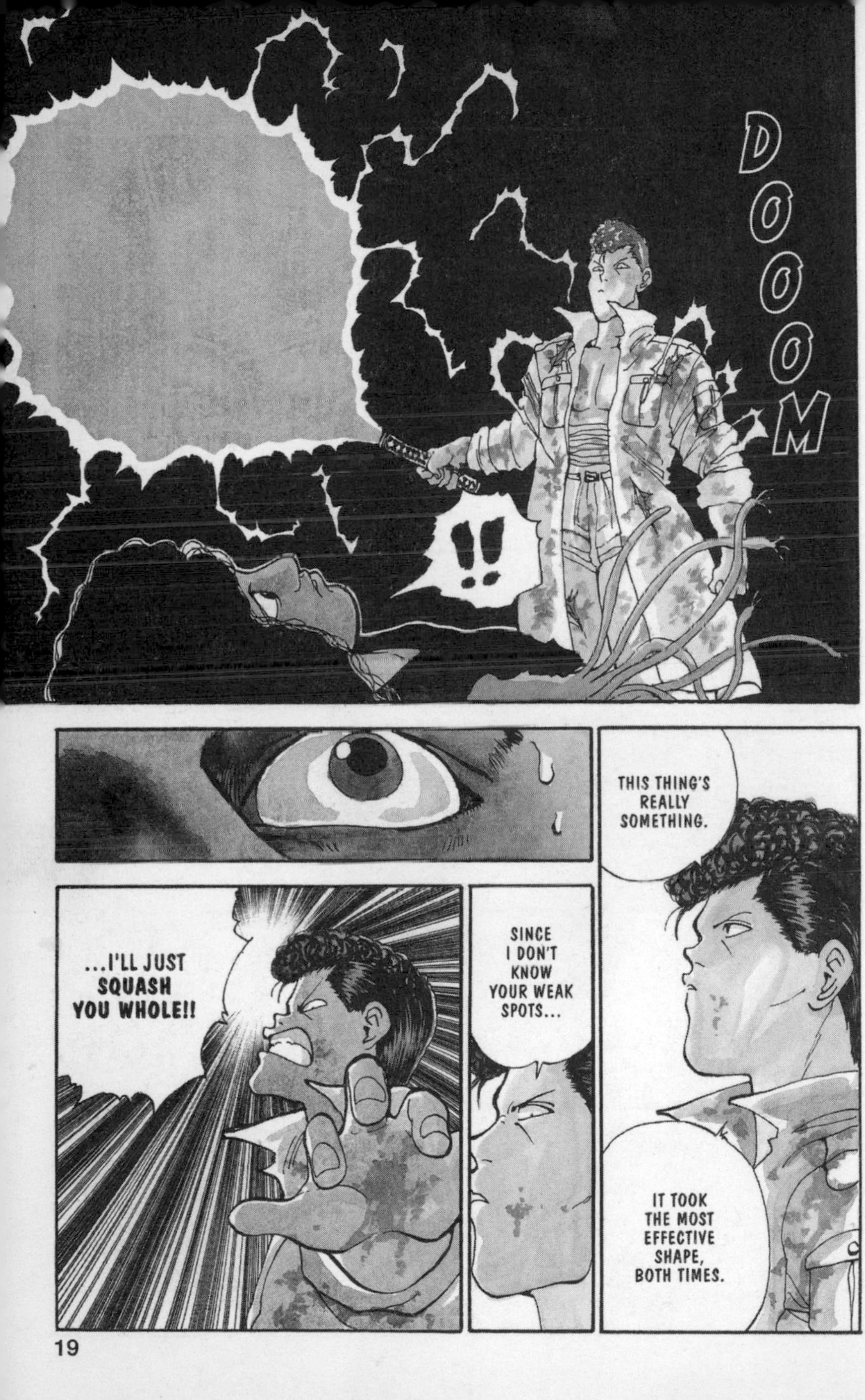
DOOOOM
!!
THIS THING'S REALLY SOMETHING.
IT TOOK THE MOST EFFECTIVE SHAPE, BOTH TIMES.
SINCE I DON'T KNOW YOUR WEAK SPOTS...
...I'LL JUST SQUASH YOU WHOLE!!

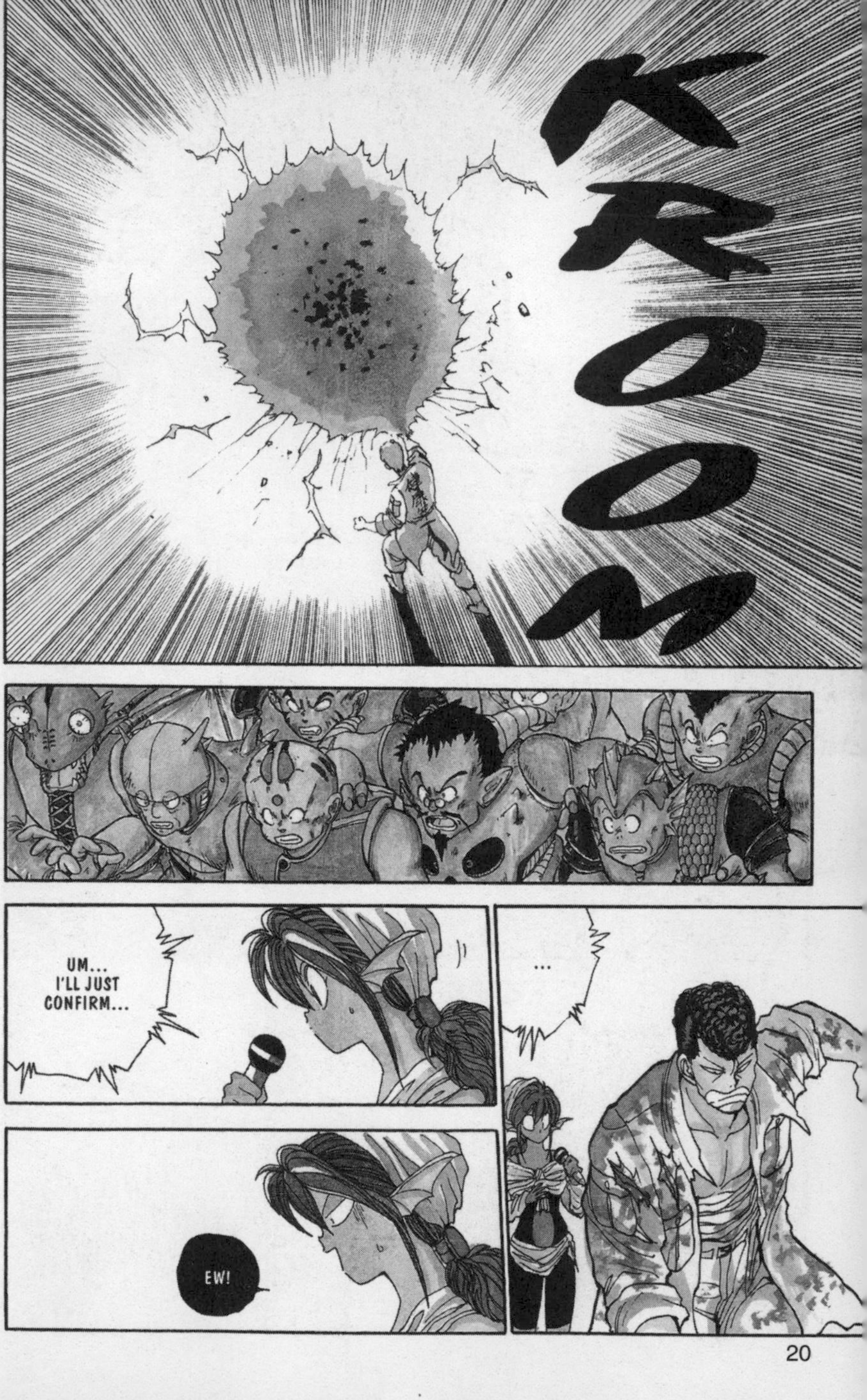
KROOM
...
UM... I'LL JUST CONFIRM...
EW!

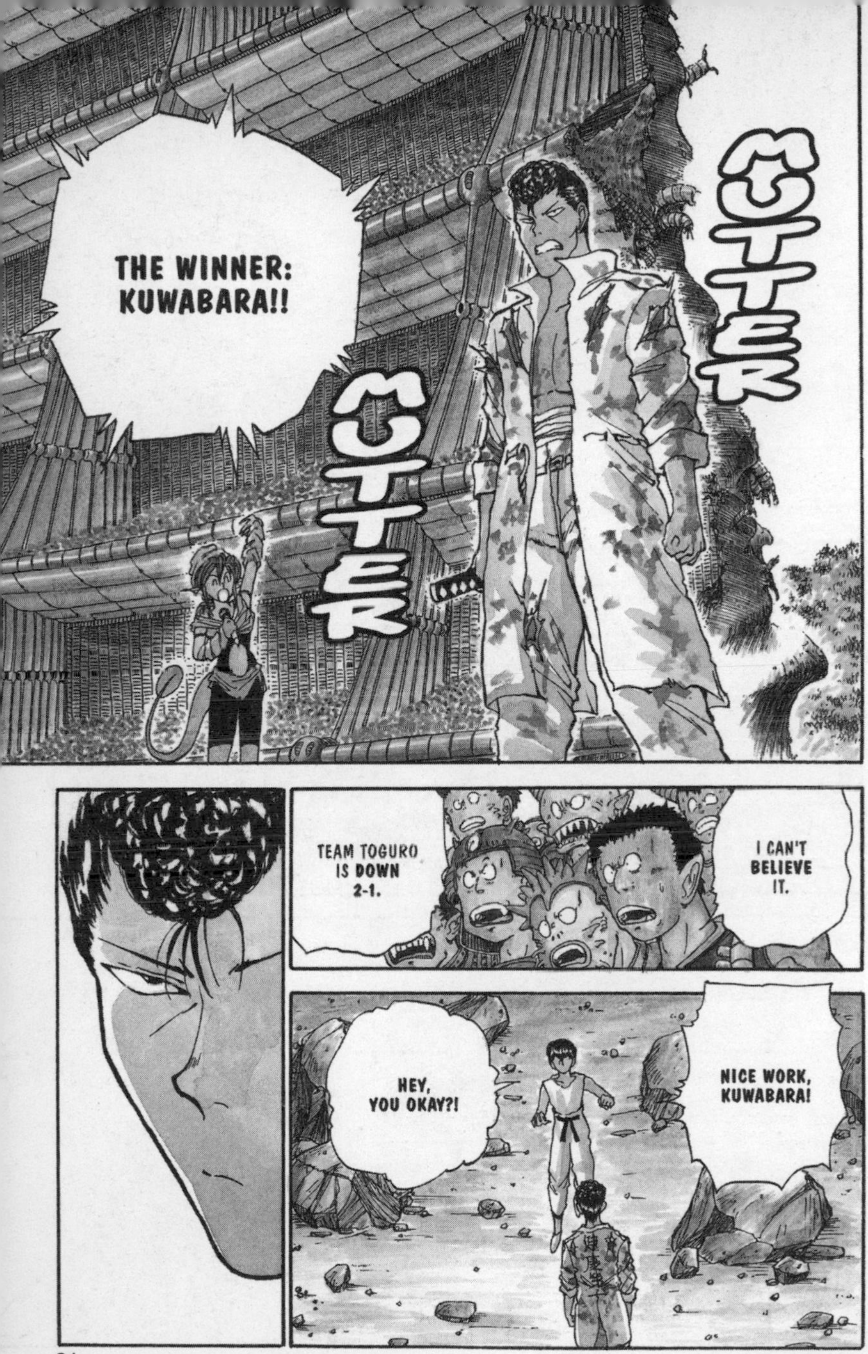
MUTTER
THE WINNER: KUWABARA!!
MUTTER
I CAN'T BELIEVE IT.
TEAM TOGURO IS DOWN 2-1.
NICE WORK, KUWABARA!
HEY, YOU OKAY?!

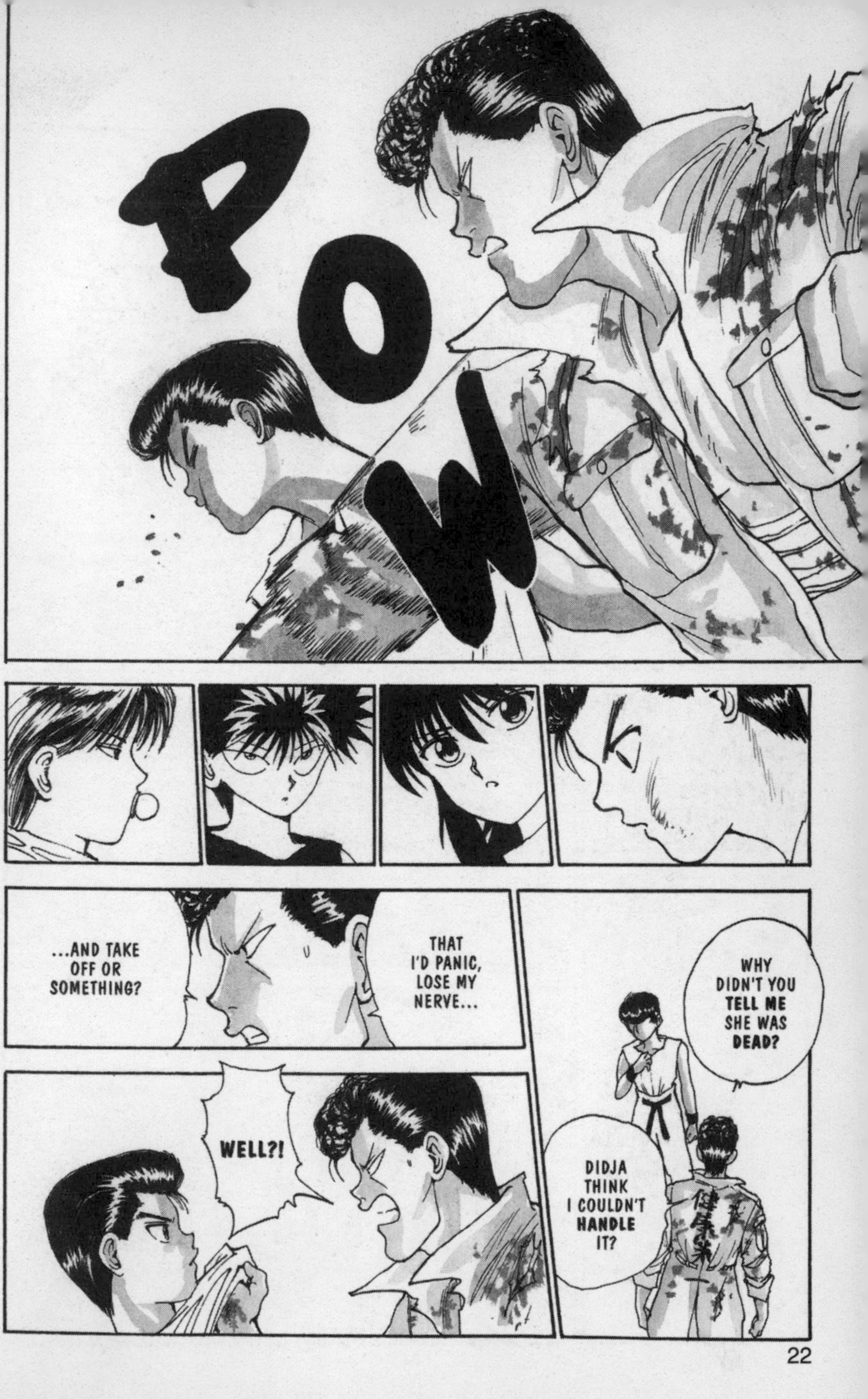
POW
WHY DIDN'T YOU TELL ME SHE WAS DEAD?
DIDJA THINK I COULDN'T HANDLE IT?
THAT I'D PANIC, LOSE MY NERVE...
...AND TAKE OFF OR SOMETHING?
WELL?!

READ THIS WAY

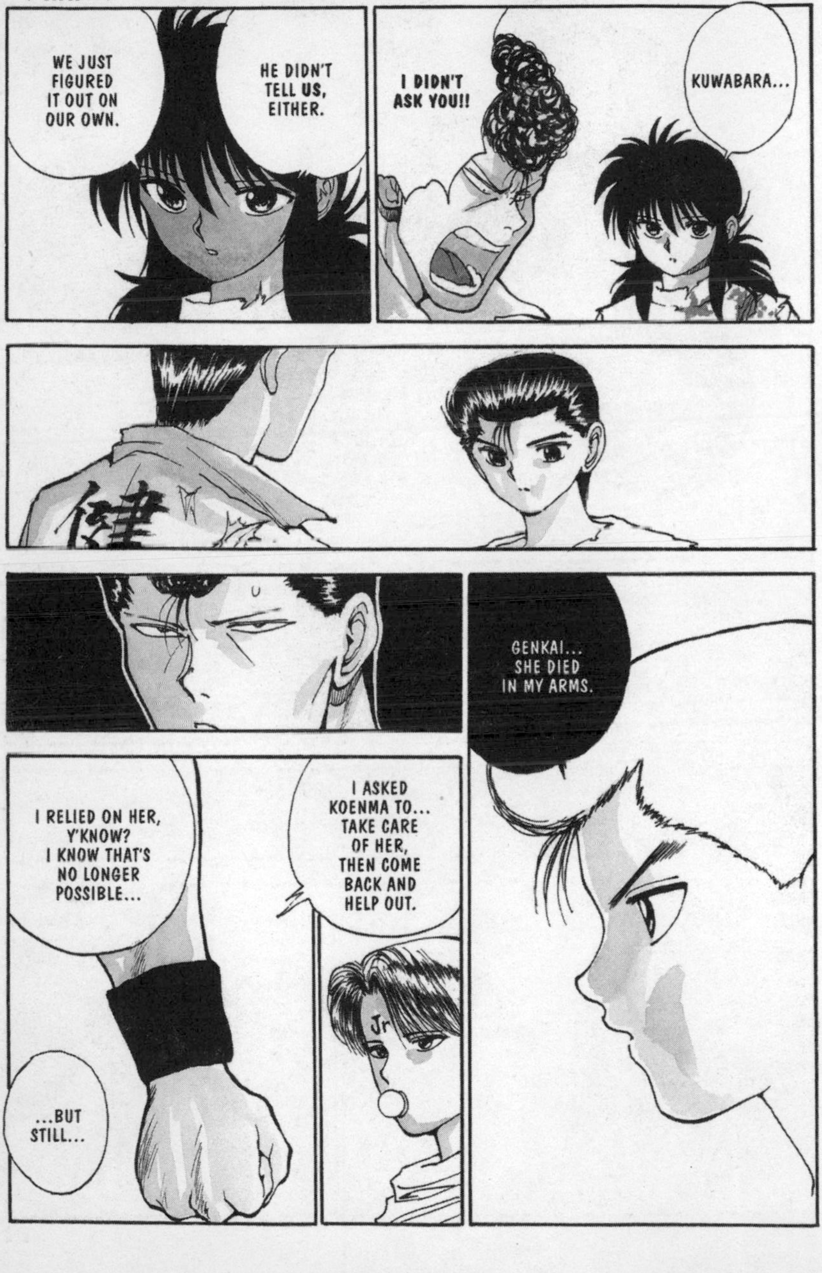
KUWABARA...
I DIDN'T ASK YOU!!
HE DIDN'T TELL US, EITHER.
WE JUST FIGURED IT OUT ON OUR OWN.
GENKAI... SHE DIED IN MY ARMS.
I ASKED KOENMA TO... TAKE CARE OF HER, THEN COME BACK AND HELP OUT.
I RELIED ON HER, Y'KNOW? I KNOW THAT'S NO LONGER POSSIBLE...
...BUT STILL...
Jr

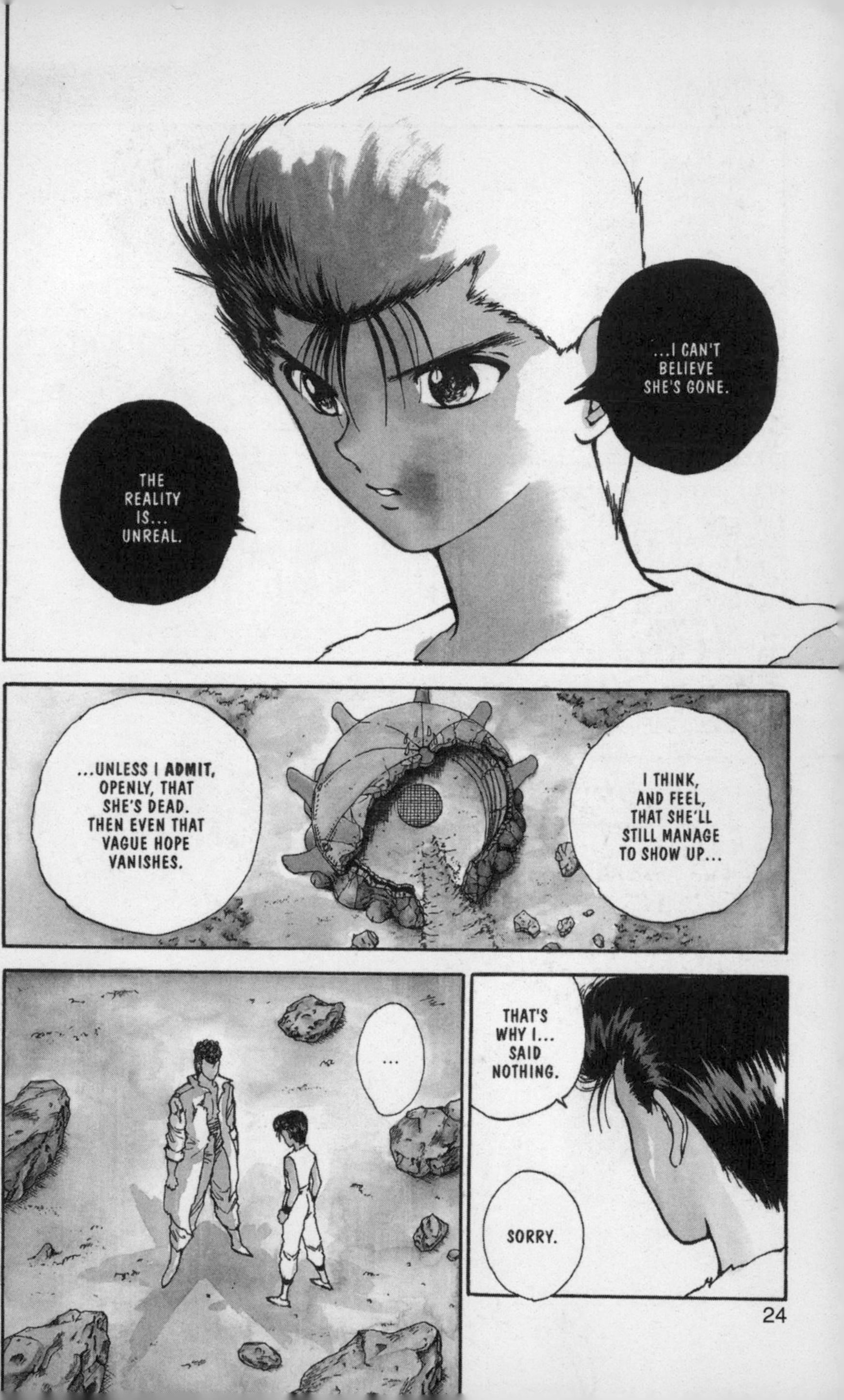
...I CAN'T BELIEVE SHE'S GONE.
THE REALITY IS... UNREAL.
I THINK, AND FEEL, THAT SHE'LL STILL MANAGE TO SHOW UP...
...UNLESS I **ADMIT**, OPENLY, THAT SHE'S DEAD. THEN EVEN THAT VAGUE HOPE VANISHES.
THAT'S WHY I... SAID NOTHING.
SORRY.
...

READ THIS WAY

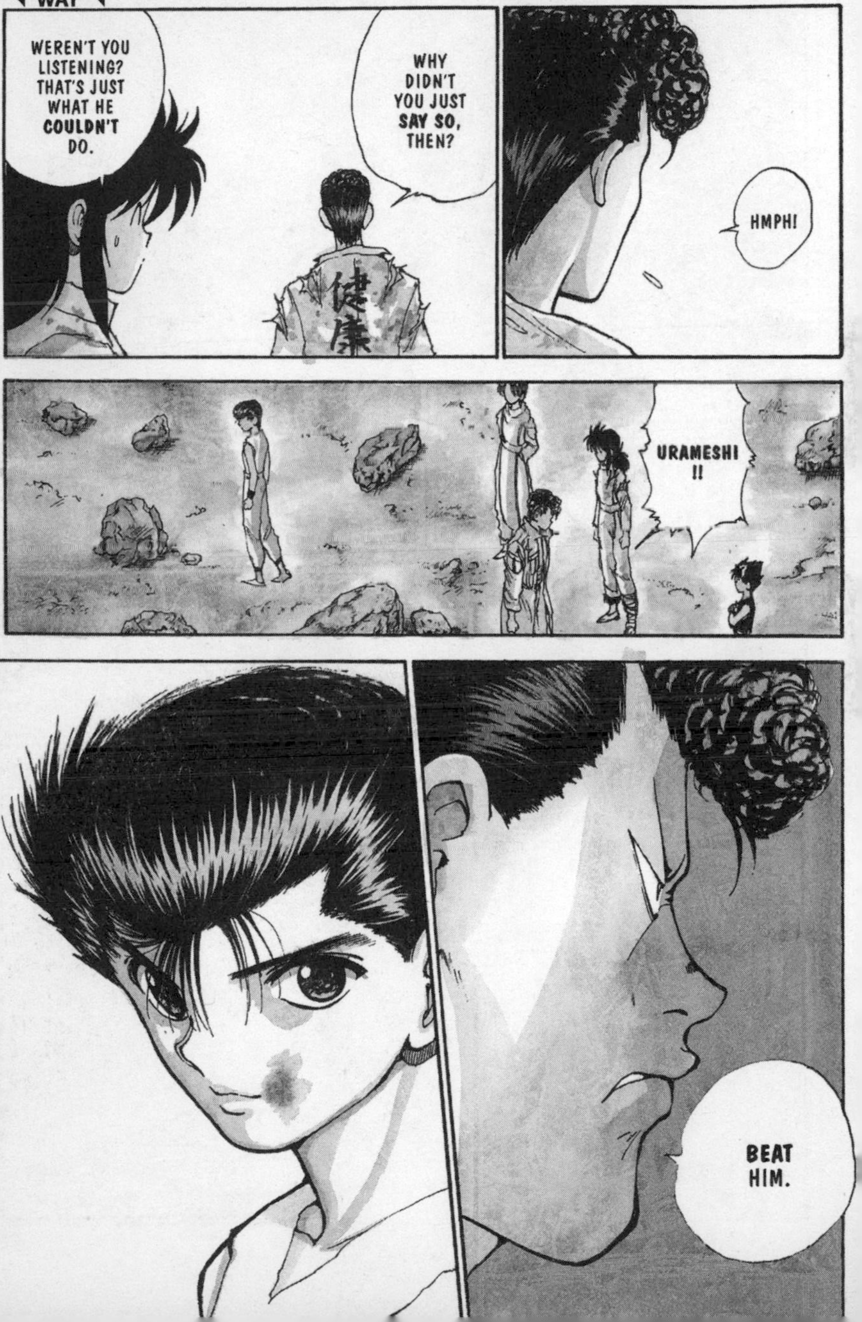
HMPH!
WHY DIDN'T YOU JUST SAY SO, THEN?
WEREN'T YOU LISTENING? THAT'S JUST WHAT HE COULDN'T DO.
URAMESHI !!
BEAT HIM.

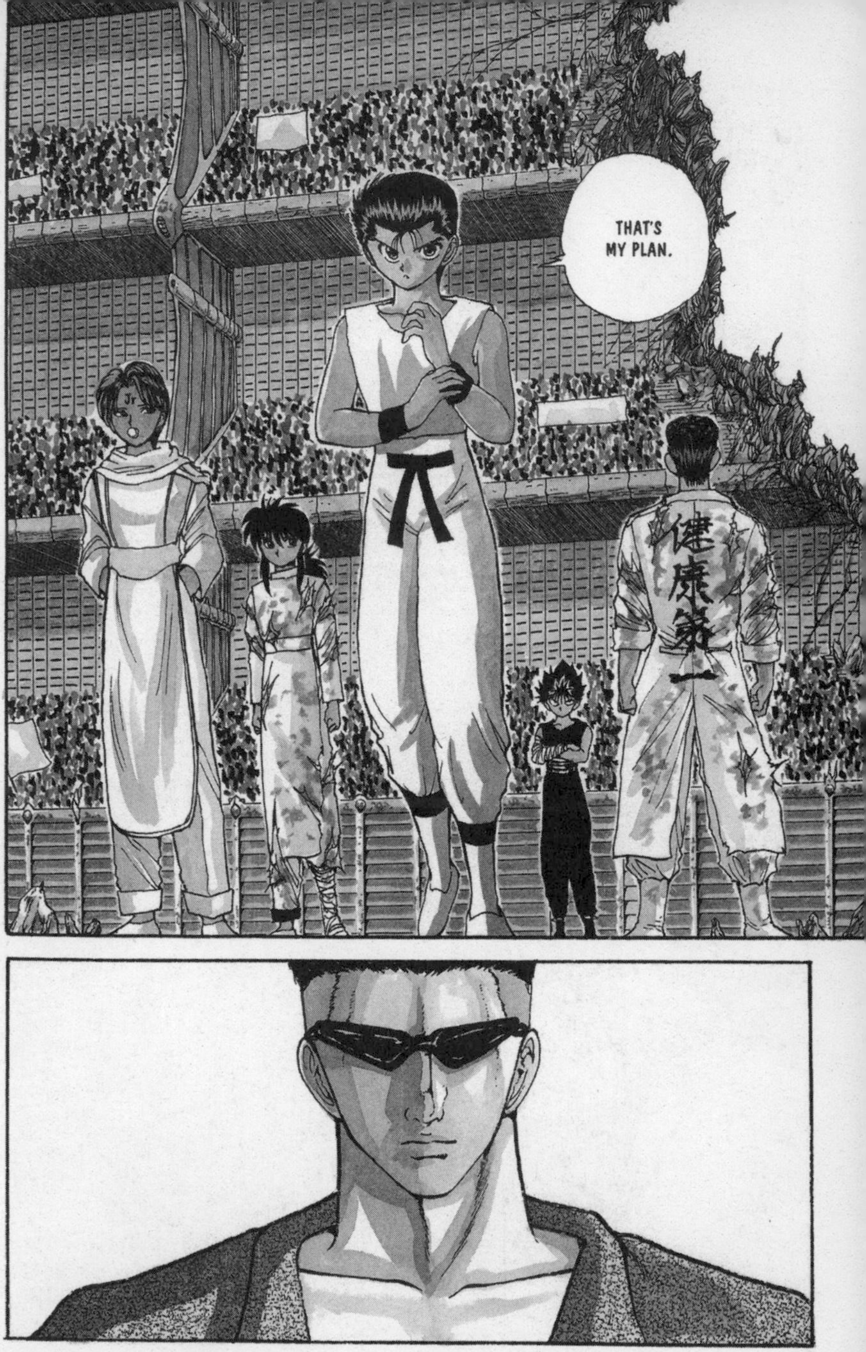
THAT'S MY PLAN.
健康第一

SAKYO'S PROPOSAL!!

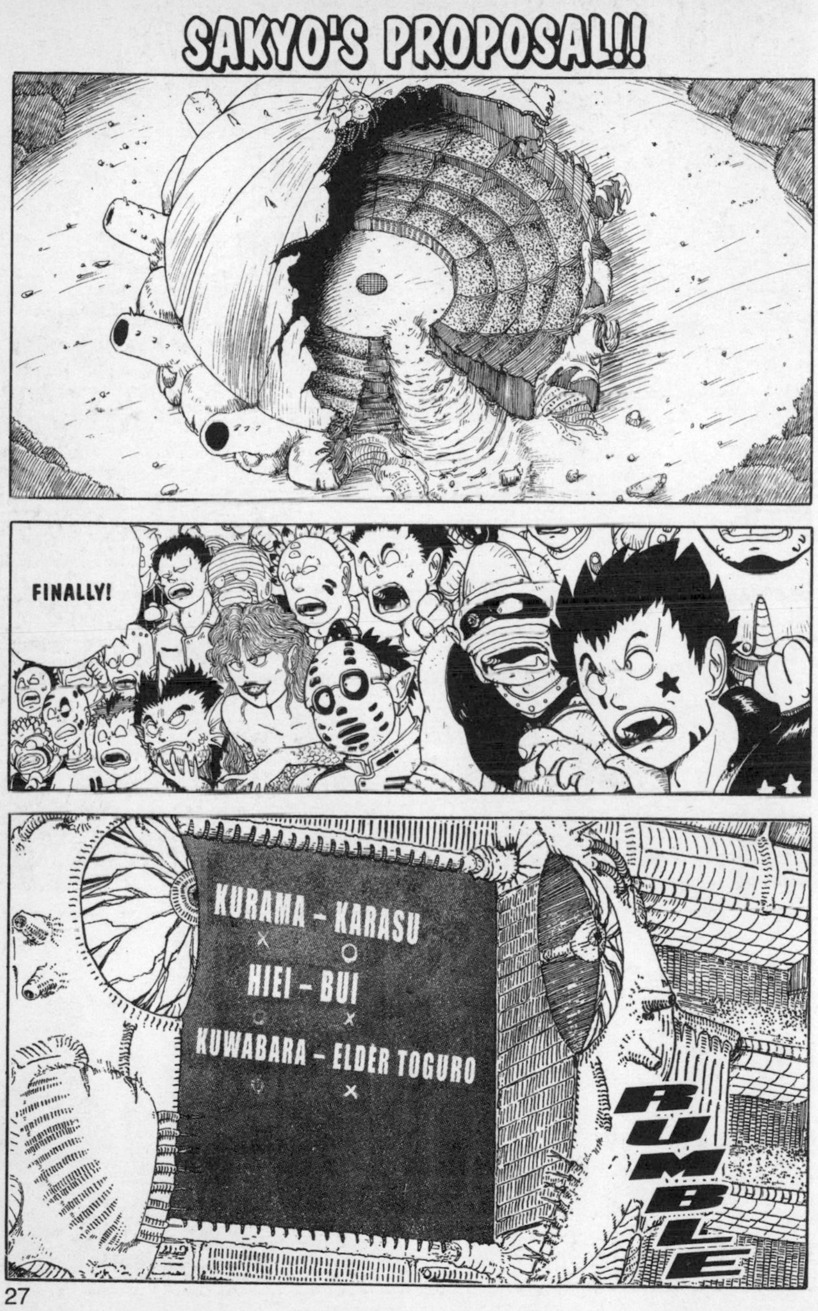
FINALLY!
KURAMA – KARASU
× ○
HIEI – BUI
○ ×
KUWABARA – ELDER TOGURO
○ ×
RUMBLE

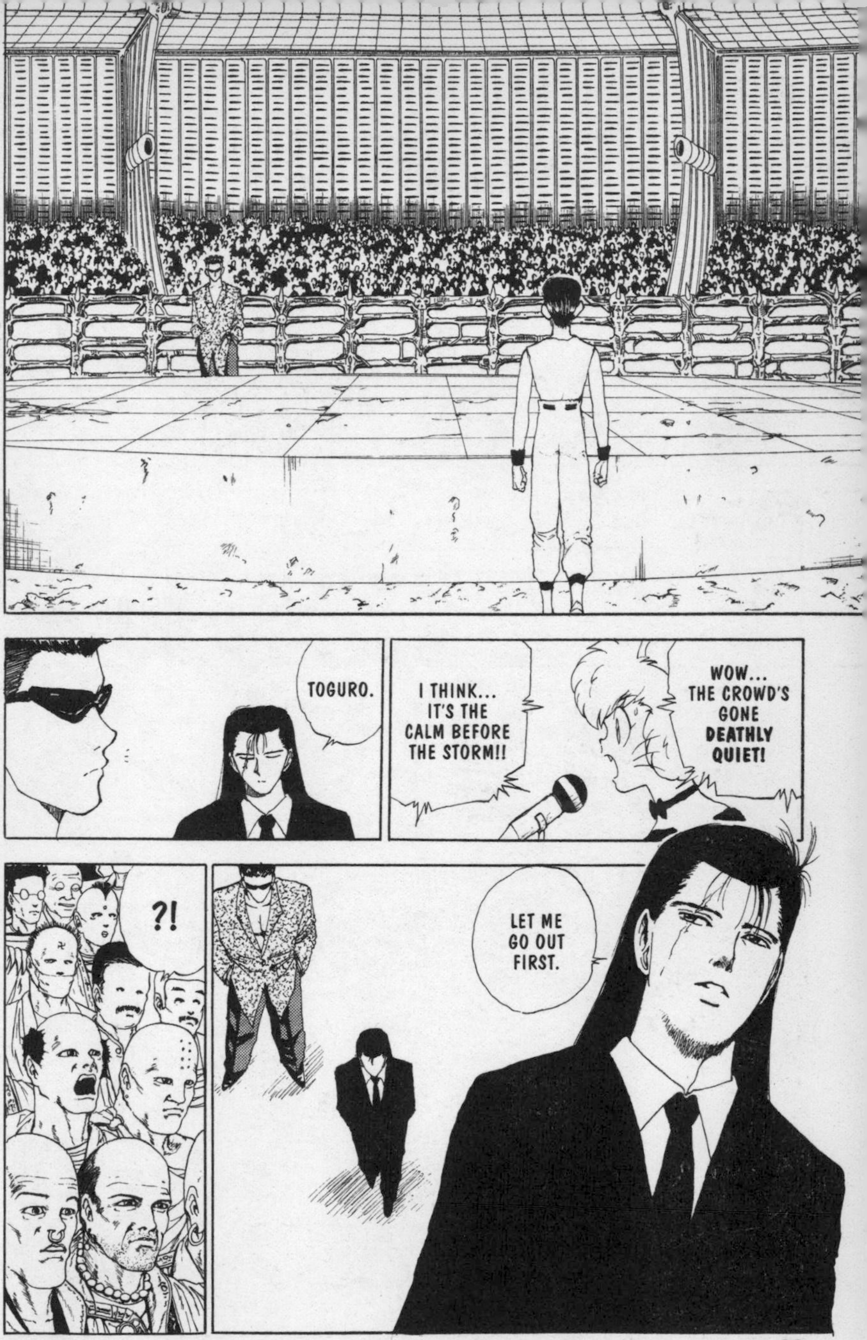
WOW... THE CROWD'S GONE DEATHLY QUIET!
I THINK... IT'S THE CALM BEFORE THE STORM!!
TOGURO.
LET ME GO OUT FIRST.
?!

READ THIS WAY

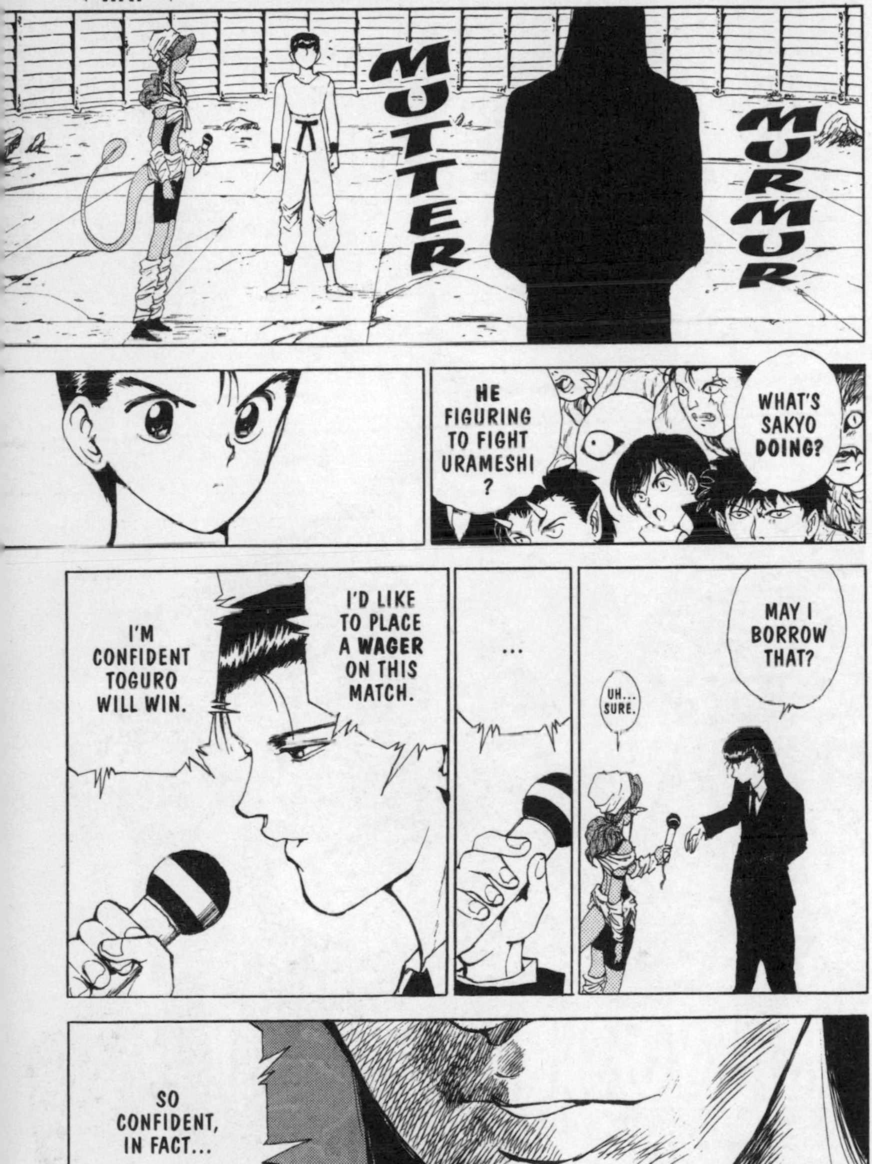
MUTTER
MURMUR
WHAT'S SAKYO DOING?
HE FIGURING TO FIGHT URAMESHI?
MAY I BORROW THAT?
UH... SURE.
...
I'D LIKE TO PLACE A WAGER ON THIS MATCH.
I'M CONFIDENT TOGURO WILL WIN.
SO CONFIDENT, IN FACT...

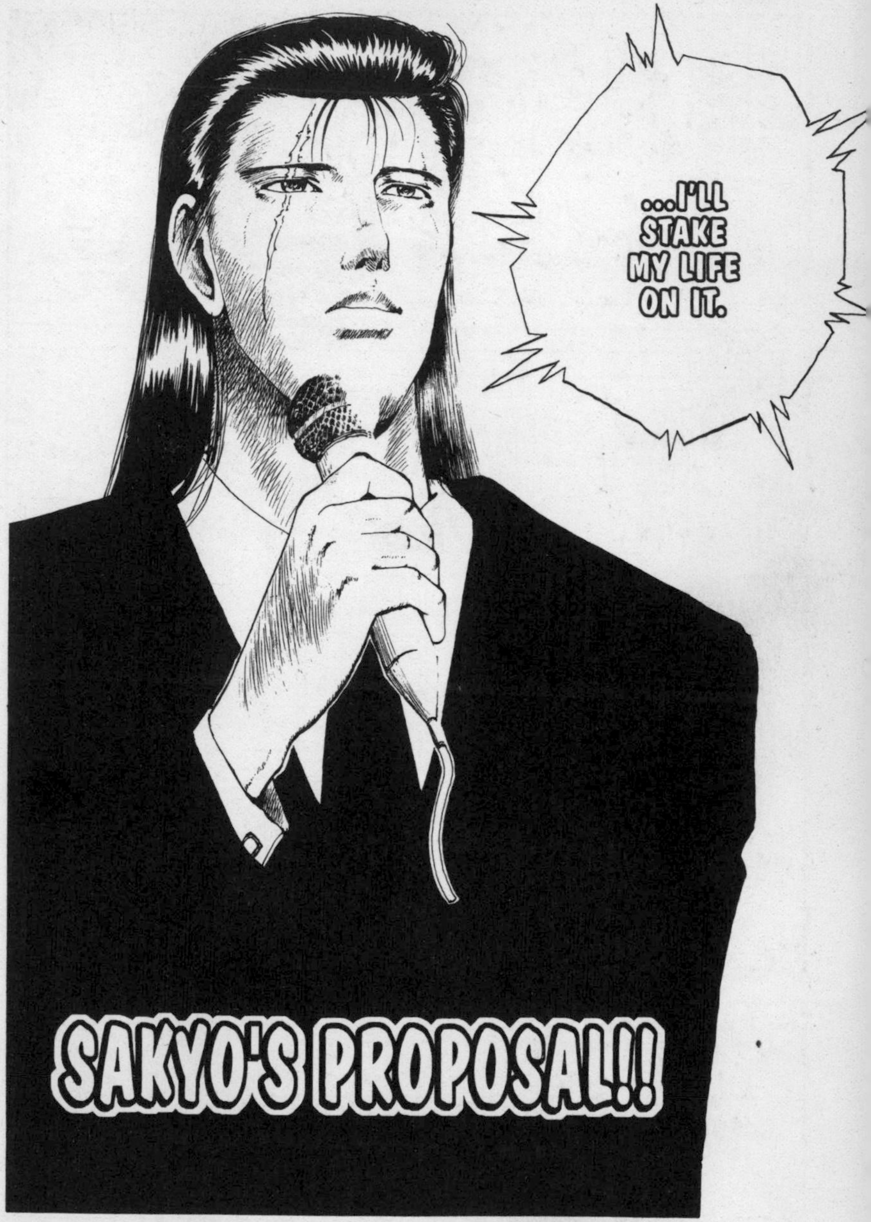
...I'LL STAKE MY LIFE ON IT.
SAKYO'S PROPOSAL!!

READ THIS WAY

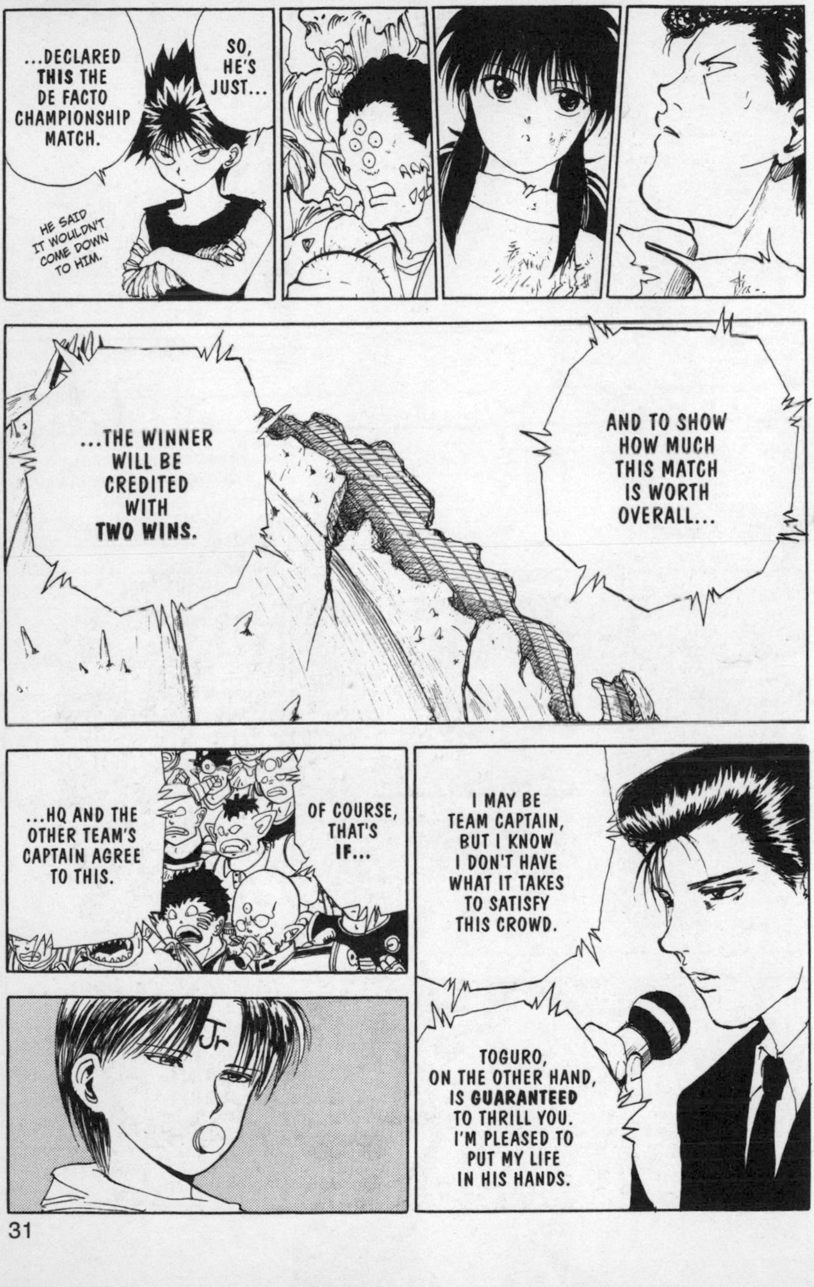

SO, HE'S JUST...
...DECLARED THIS THE DE FACTO CHAMPIONSHIP MATCH.
HE SAID IT WOULDN'T COME DOWN TO HIM.
AND TO SHOW HOW MUCH THIS MATCH IS WORTH OVERALL...
...THE WINNER WILL BE CREDITED WITH TWO WINS.
I MAY BE TEAM CAPTAIN, BUT I KNOW I DON'T HAVE WHAT IT TAKES TO SATISFY THIS CROWD.
TOGURO, ON THE OTHER HAND, IS GUARANTEED TO THRILL YOU. I'M PLEASED TO PUT MY LIFE IN HIS HANDS.
OF COURSE, THAT'S IF...
...HQ AND THE OTHER TEAM'S CAPTAIN AGREE TO THIS.

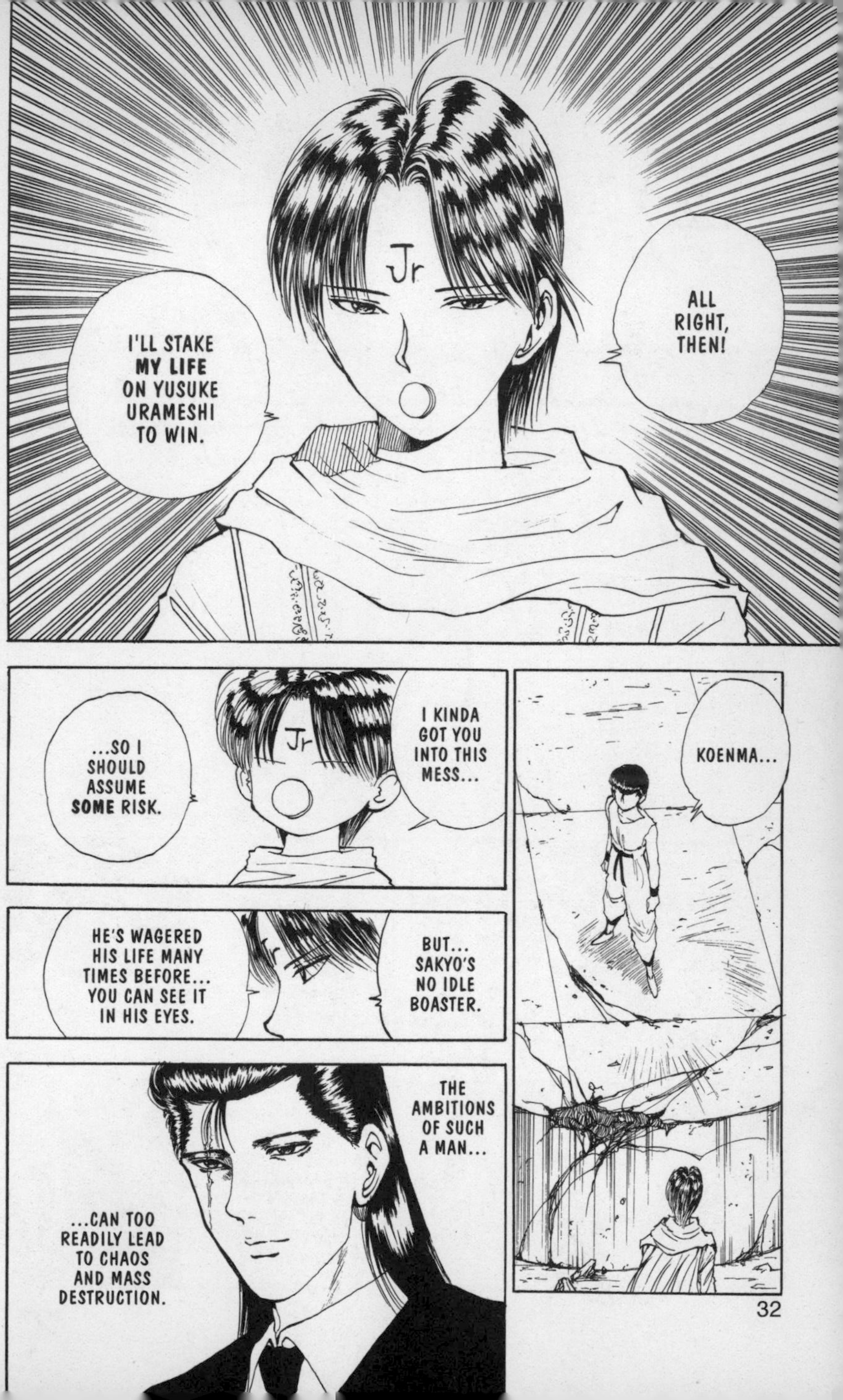
ALL RIGHT, THEN!
I'LL STAKE MY LIFE ON YUSUKE URAMESHI TO WIN.
KOENMA...
I KINDA GOT YOU INTO THIS MESS...
...SO I SHOULD ASSUME SOME RISK.
BUT... SAKYO'S NO IDLE BOASTER.
HE'S WAGERED HIS LIFE MANY TIMES BEFORE... YOU CAN SEE IT IN HIS EYES.
THE AMBITIONS OF SUCH A MAN...
...CAN TOO READILY LEAD TO CHAOS AND MASS DESTRUCTION.

READ THIS WAY

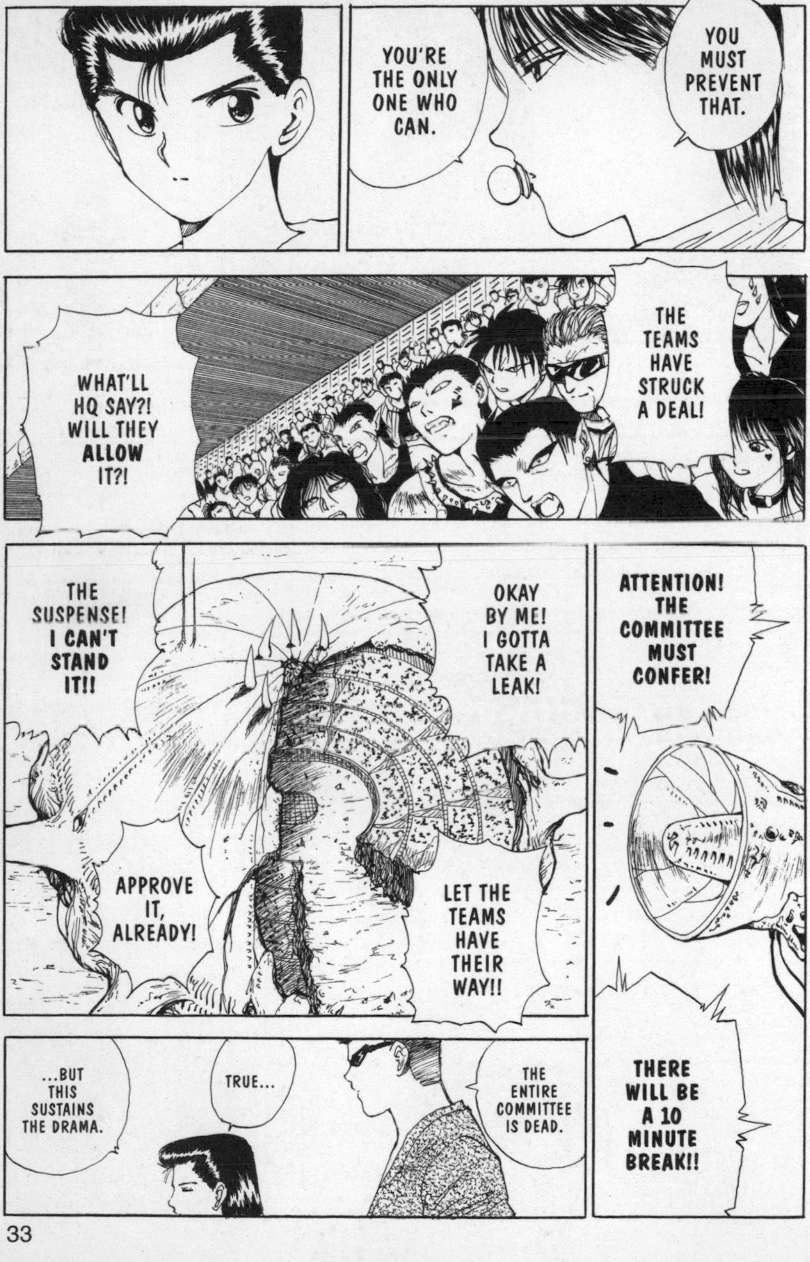
YOU MUST PREVENT THAT.
YOU'RE THE ONLY ONE WHO CAN.
THE TEAMS HAVE STRUCK A DEAL!
WHAT'LL HQ SAY?! WILL THEY ALLOW IT?!
ATTENTION! THE COMMITTEE MUST CONFER!
THERE WILL BE A 10 MINUTE BREAK!!
OKAY BY ME! I GOTTA TAKE A LEAK!
THE SUSPENSE! I CAN'T STAND IT!!
LET THE TEAMS HAVE THEIR WAY!!
APPROVE IT, ALREADY!
THE ENTIRE COMMITTEE IS DEAD.
TRUE...
...BUT THIS SUSTAINS THE DRAMA.

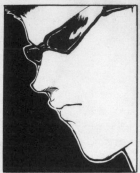

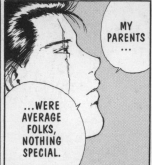

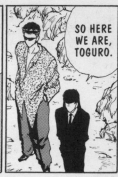

SO HERE WE ARE, TOGURO.
MY PARENTS...
...WERE AVERAGE FOLKS, NOTHING SPECIAL.
MY UPBRINGING WAS NO DIFFERENT. I WAS ONE OF FIVE SIBLINGS, AND WE WERE ALL RAISED WITHOUT FAVORITISM. OBJECTIVELY SPEAKING, IT WAS ALL QUITE IDEAL IN ITS WAY. THE OTHER FOUR ALL BECAME CIVIL SERVANTS.
I ALONE VEERED... FROM THE NORM.
THE DEPRAVITY BEGAN UP HERE...
...THROUGH NO ONE'S FAULT BUT MY OWN.
I WENT THROUGH A PHASE WHERE I CRAVED THE SIGHT OF BLOOD AND GUTS, WANTONLY DISSECTING FROGS, FISH, THEN CATS AND DOGS.
IN LESS THAN THREE YEARS I MOVED ON TO PEOPLE, BUT EVEN THAT GREW UNSATISFYING.
MY SOLE PASSION BECAME **GAMBLING.**
I LIVED FOR IT, WAS GOOD AT IT, AND USED IT TO MAKE MY WAY UP THE UNDERWORLD.

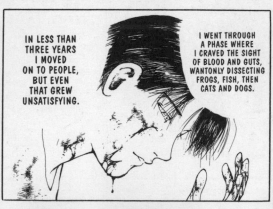

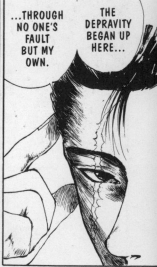

READ THIS WAY

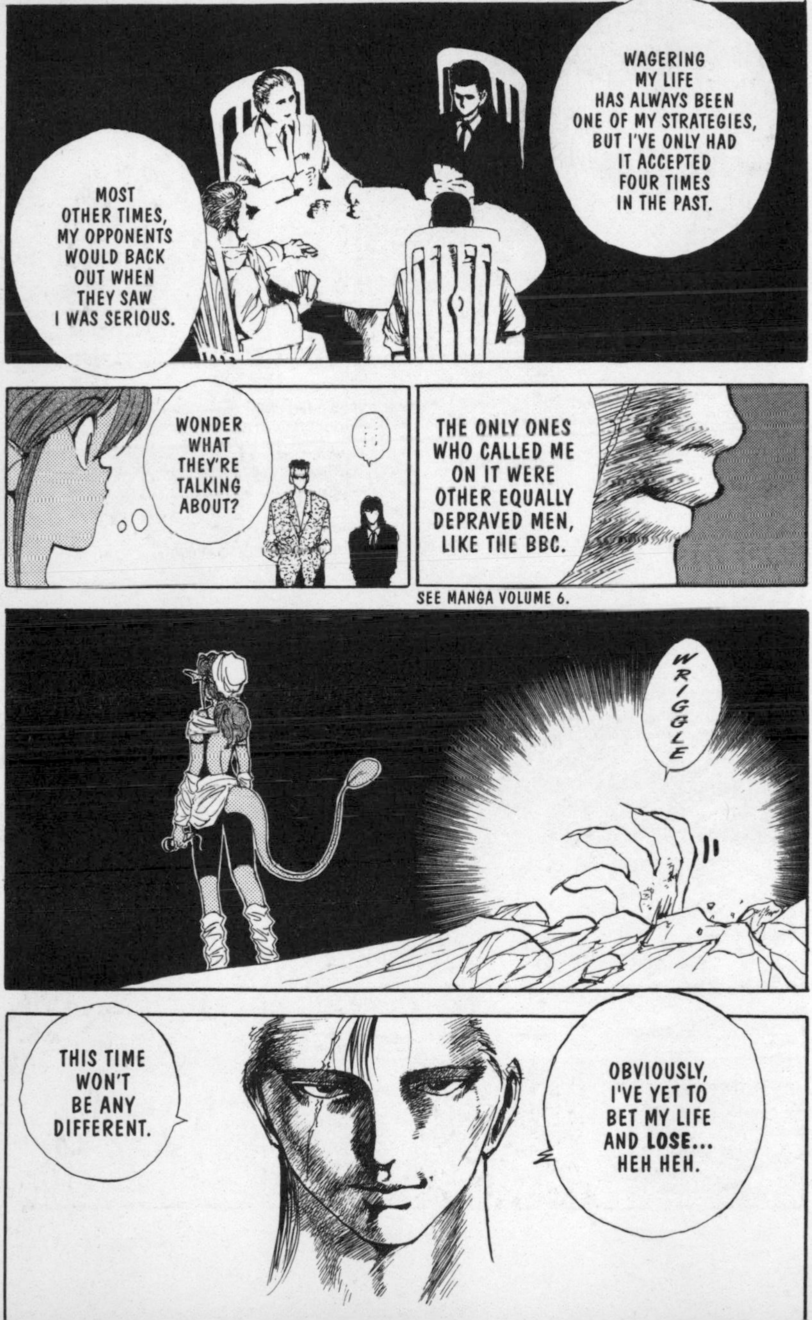
WAGERING MY LIFE HAS ALWAYS BEEN ONE OF MY STRATEGIES, BUT I'VE ONLY HAD IT ACCEPTED FOUR TIMES IN THE PAST.
MOST OTHER TIMES, MY OPPONENTS WOULD BACK OUT WHEN THEY SAW I WAS SERIOUS.
THE ONLY ONES WHO CALLED ME ON IT WERE OTHER EQUALLY DEPRAVED MEN, LIKE THE BBC.
SEE MANGA VOLUME 6.
...
WONDER WHAT THEY'RE TALKING ABOUT?
WRIGGLE
OBVIOUSLY, I'VE YET TO BET MY LIFE AND LOSE... HEH HEH.
THIS TIME WON'T BE ANY DIFFERENT.

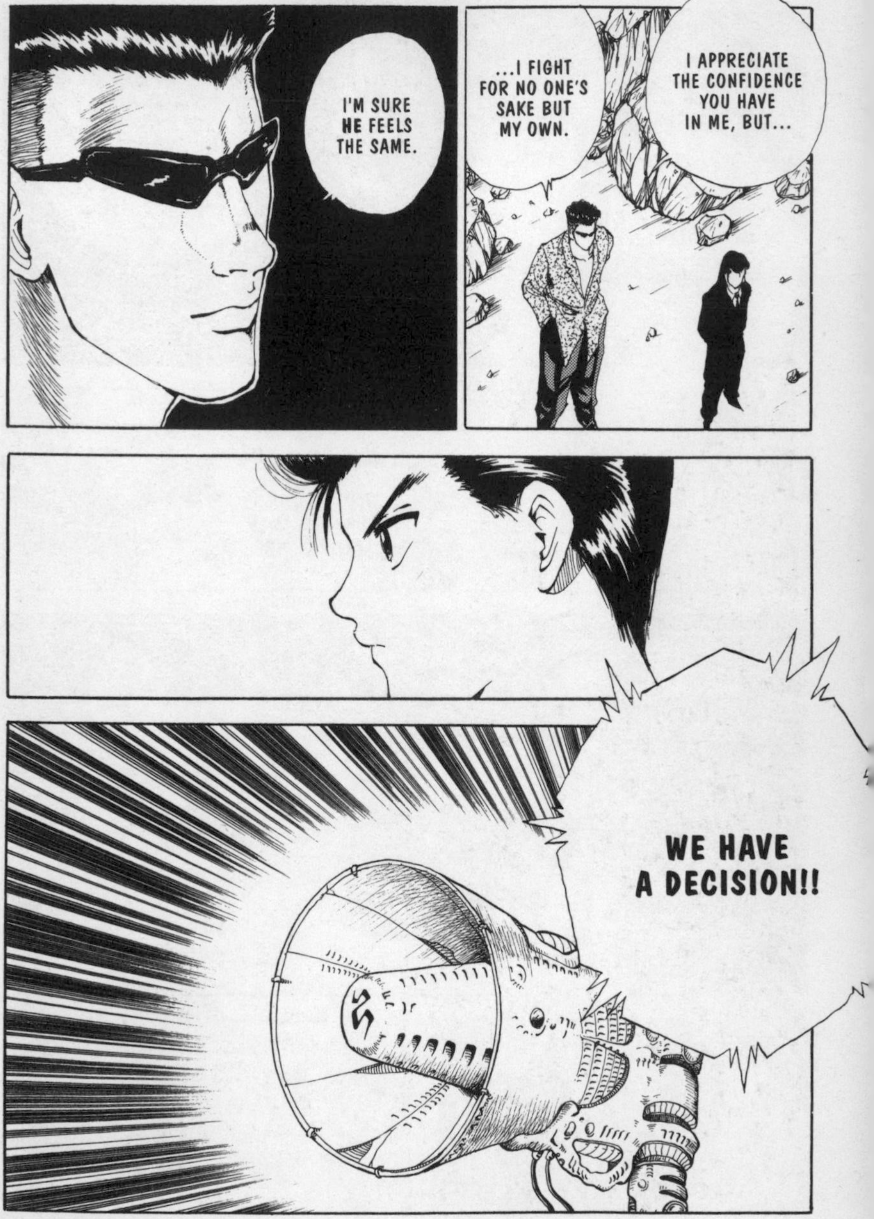
I APPRECIATE THE CONFIDENCE YOU HAVE IN ME, BUT...
...I FIGHT FOR NO ONE'S SAKE BUT MY OWN.
I'M SURE HE FEELS THE SAME.
WE HAVE A DECISION!!

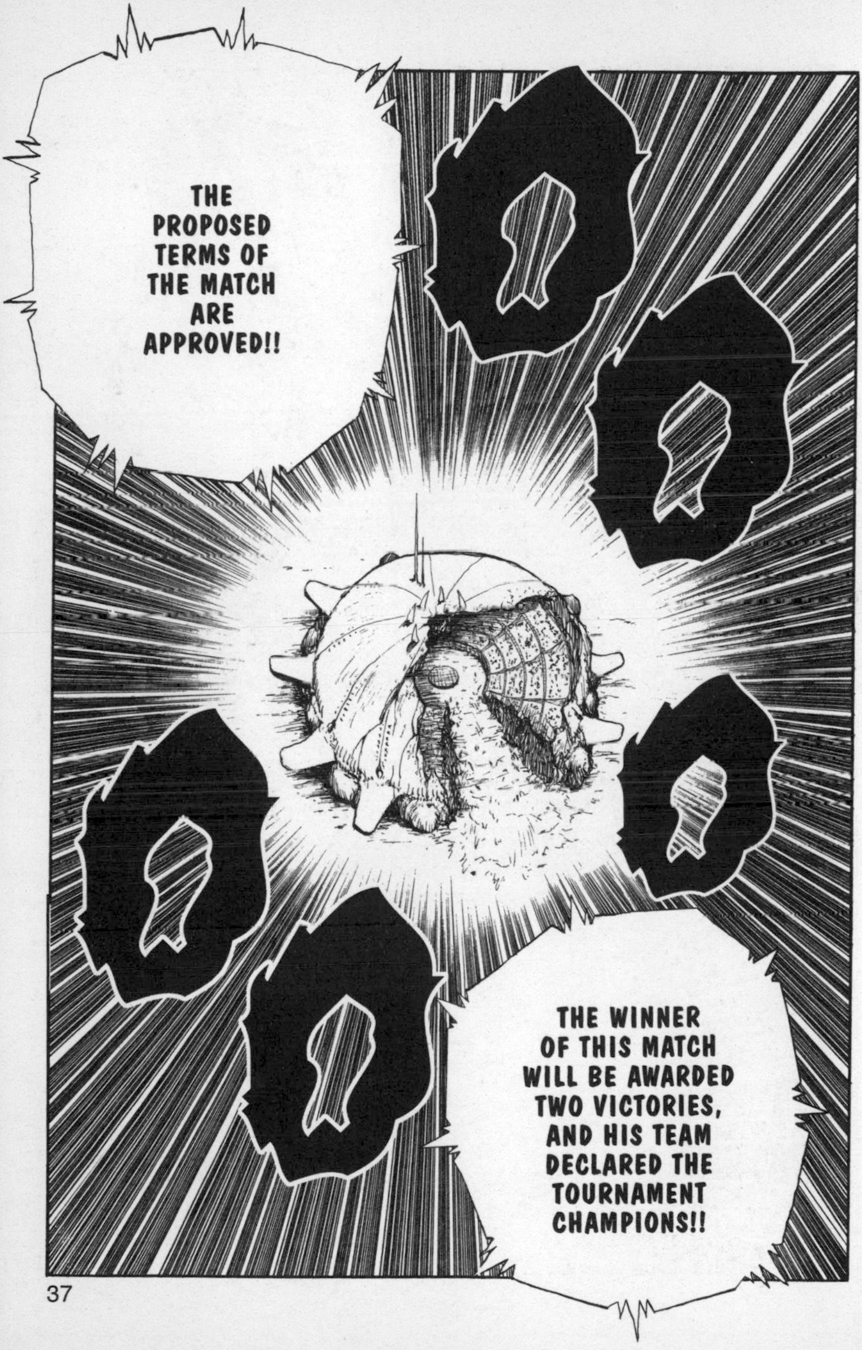
THE PROPOSED TERMS OF THE MATCH ARE APPROVED!!
THE WINNER OF THIS MATCH WILL BE AWARDED TWO VICTORIES, AND HIS TEAM DECLARED THE TOURNAMENT CHAMPIONS!!

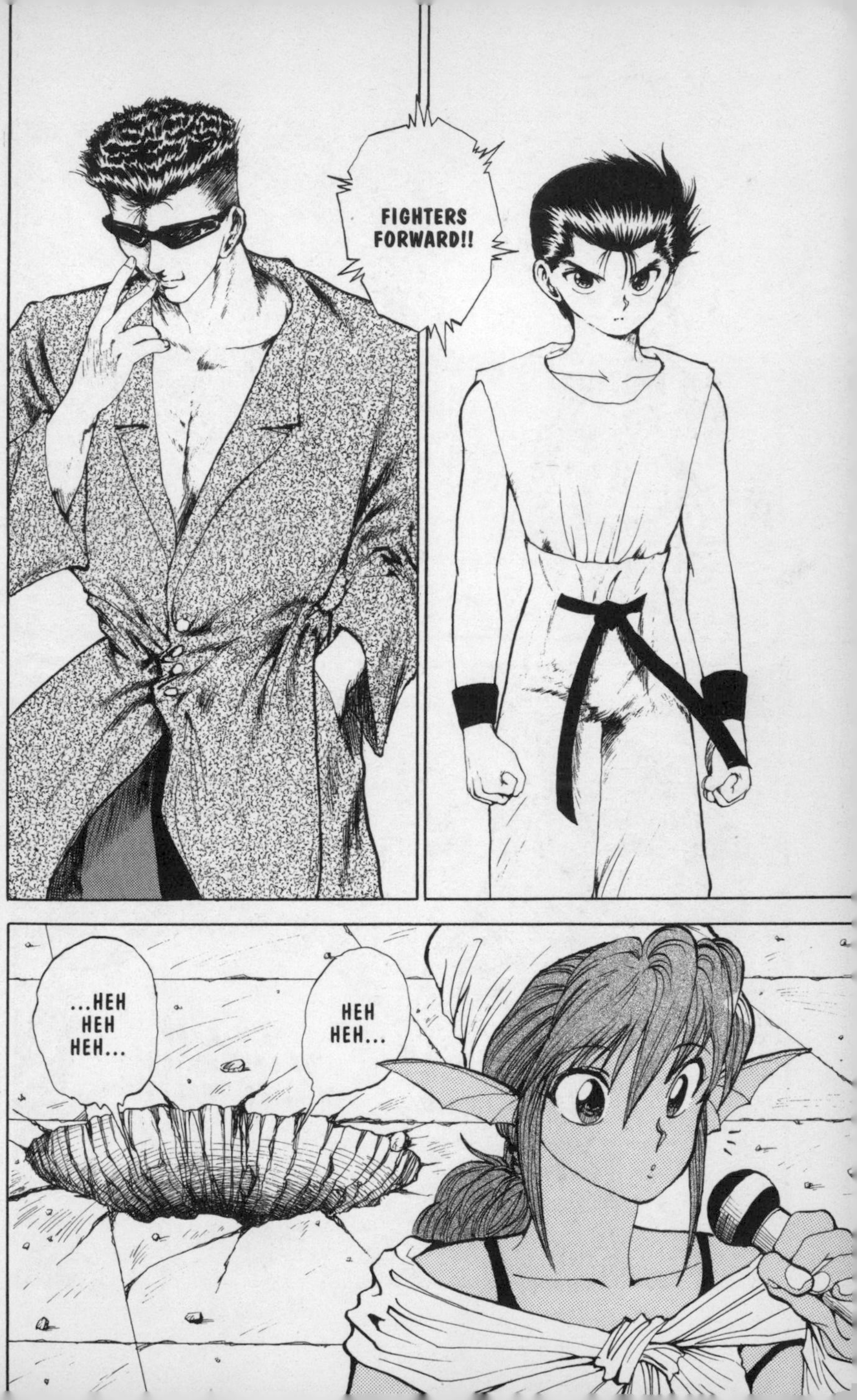
FIGHTERS FORWARD!!
HEH HEH...
...HEH HEH HEH...

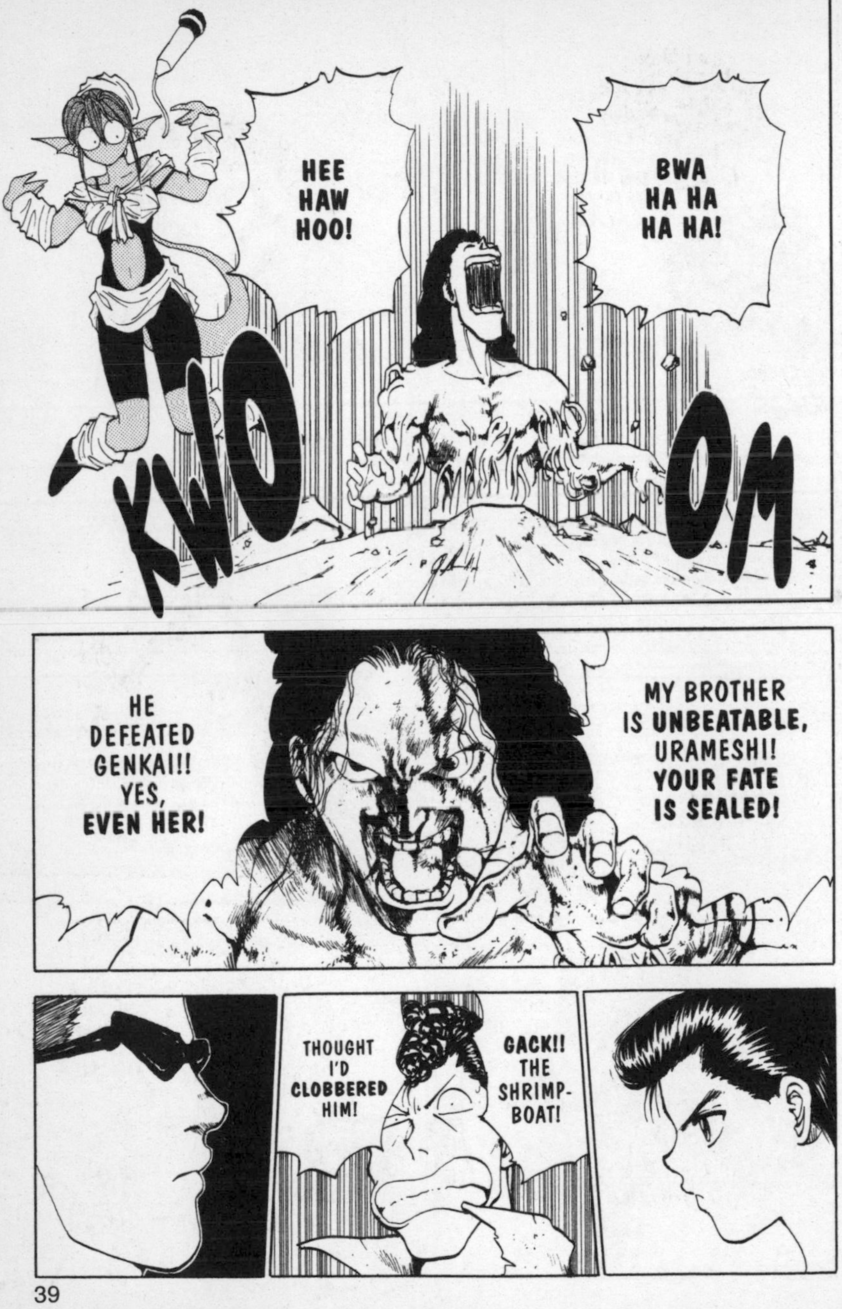

BWA HA HA HA HA!
HEE HAW HOO!
KWO OM
MY BROTHER IS UNBEATABLE, URAMESHI! YOUR FATE IS SEALED!
HE DEFEATED GENKAI!! YES, EVEN HER!
GACK!! THE SHRIMP-BOAT!
THOUGHT I'D CLOBBERED HIM!

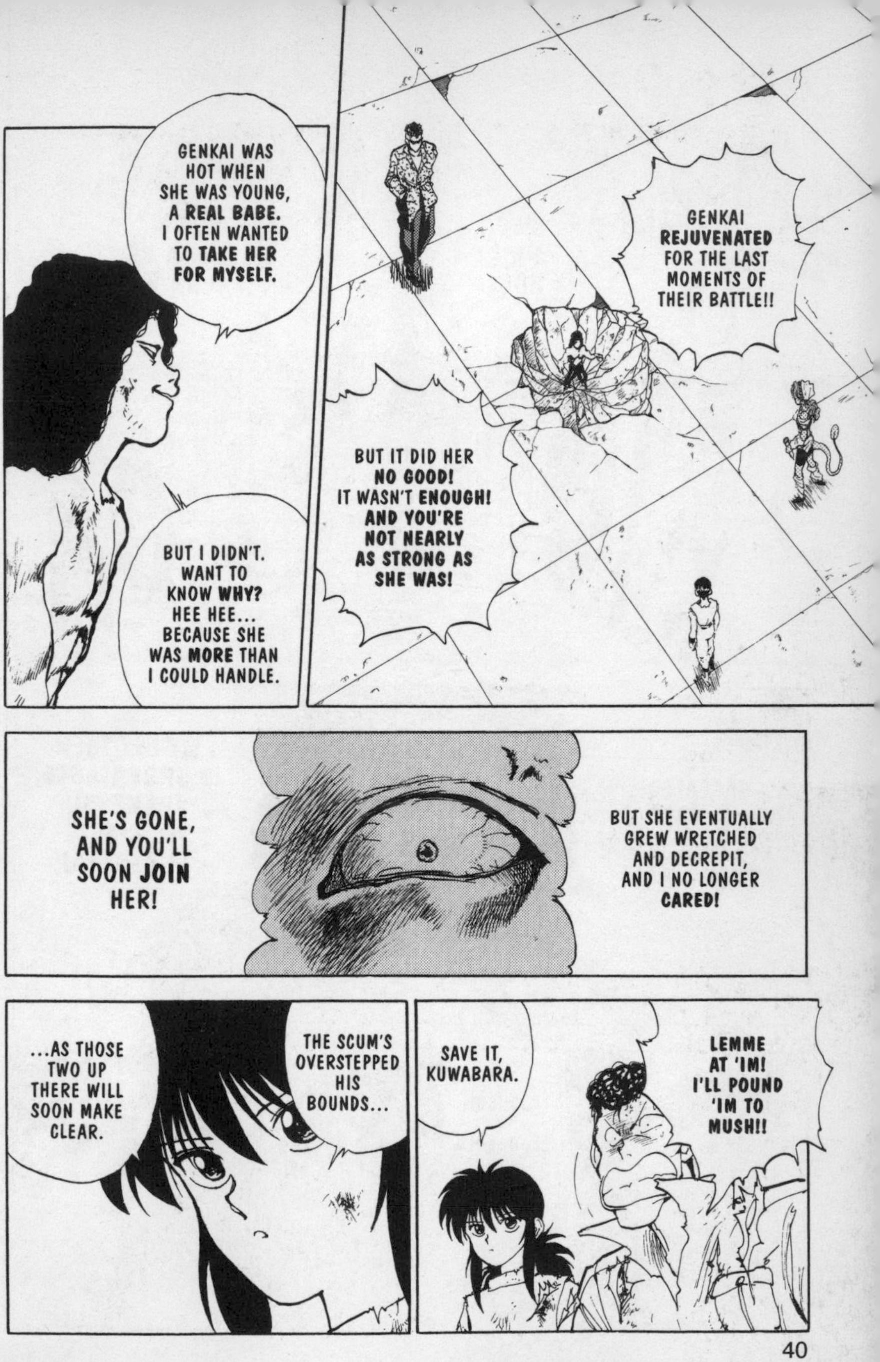
GENKAI REJUVENATED FOR THE LAST MOMENTS OF THEIR BATTLE!!
BUT IT DID HER NO GOOD! IT WASN'T ENOUGH! AND YOU'RE NOT NEARLY AS STRONG AS SHE WAS!
GENKAI WAS HOT WHEN SHE WAS YOUNG, A REAL BABE. I OFTEN WANTED TO TAKE HER FOR MYSELF.
BUT I DIDN'T. WANT TO KNOW WHY? HEE HEE... BECAUSE SHE WAS MORE THAN I COULD HANDLE.
BUT SHE EVENTUALLY GREW WRETCHED AND DECREPIT, AND I NO LONGER CARED!
SHE'S GONE, AND YOU'LL SOON JOIN HER!
LEMME AT 'IM! I'LL POUND 'IM TO MUSH!!
SAVE IT, KUWABARA.
THE SCUM'S OVERSTEPPED HIS BOUNDS...
...AS THOSE TWO UP THERE WILL SOON MAKE CLEAR.

READ THIS WAY

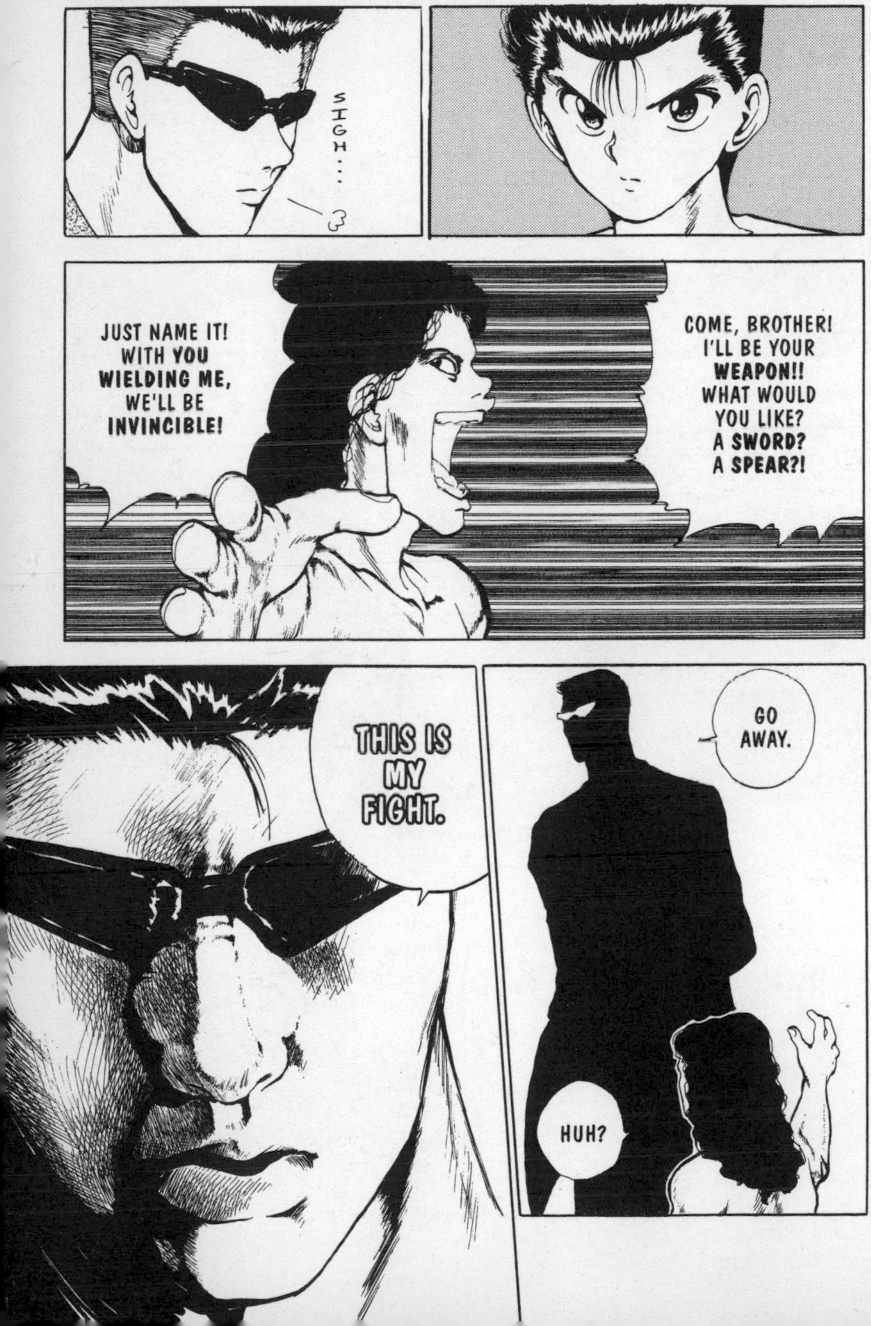
SIGH...
COME, BROTHER! I'LL BE YOUR WEAPON!! WHAT WOULD YOU LIKE? A SWORD? A SPEAR?!
JUST NAME IT! WITH YOU WIELDING ME, WE'LL BE INVINCIBLE!
GO AWAY.
HUH?
THIS IS MY FIGHT.

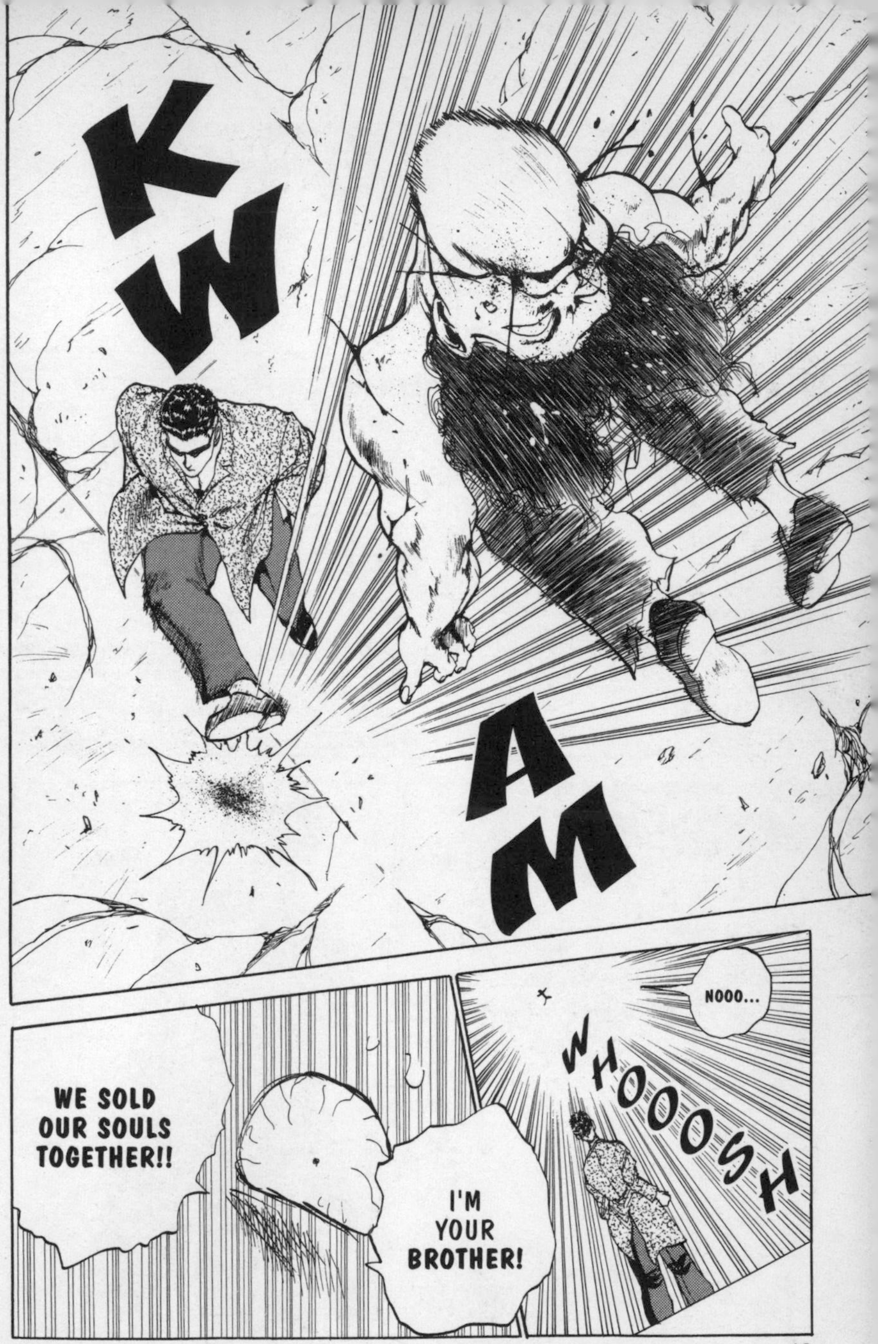
KWAM
NOOO...
WHOOOSH
I'M YOUR BROTHER!
WE SOLD OUR SOULS TOGETHER!!

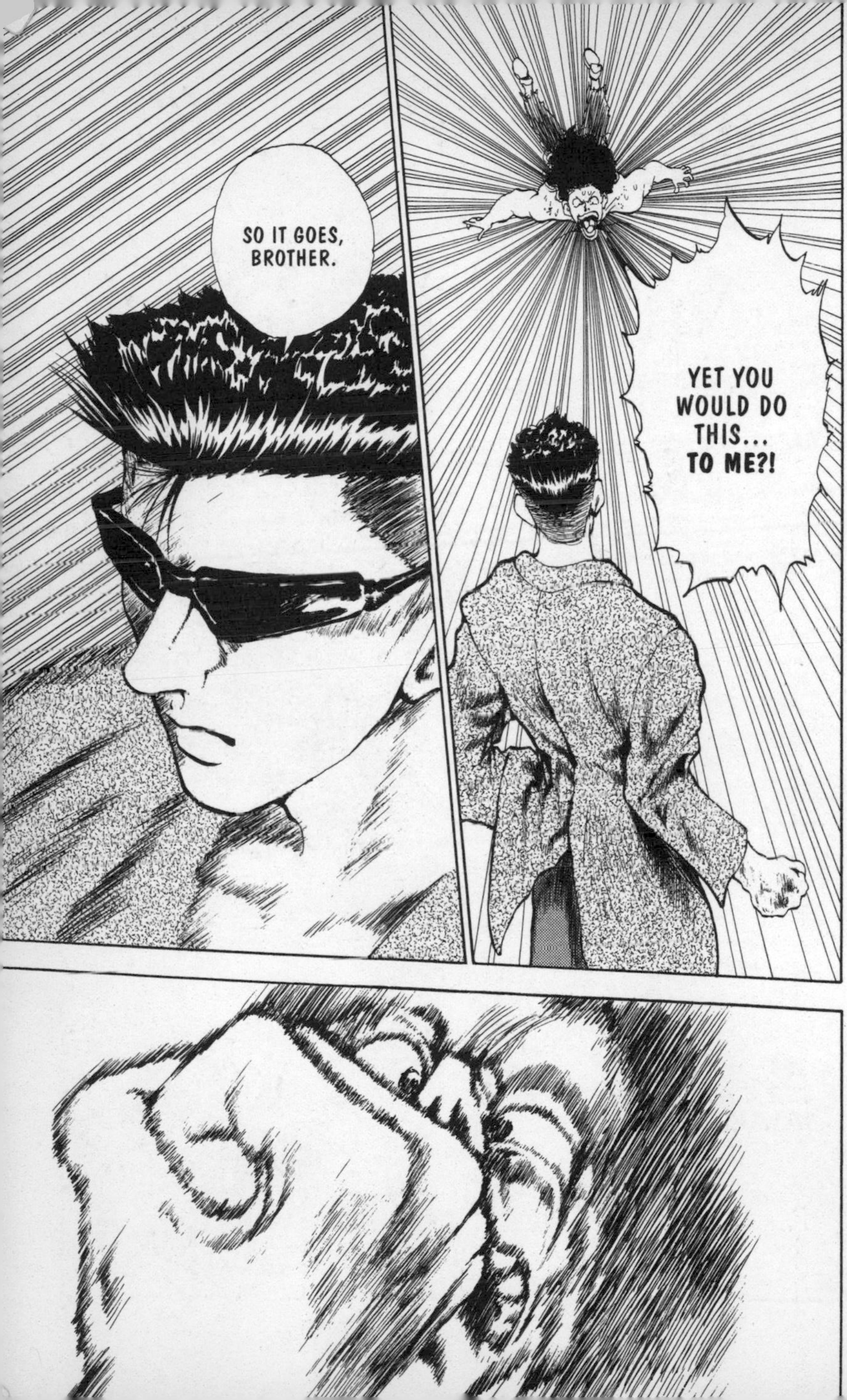
YET YOU WOULD DO THIS... TO ME?!
SO IT GOES, BROTHER.

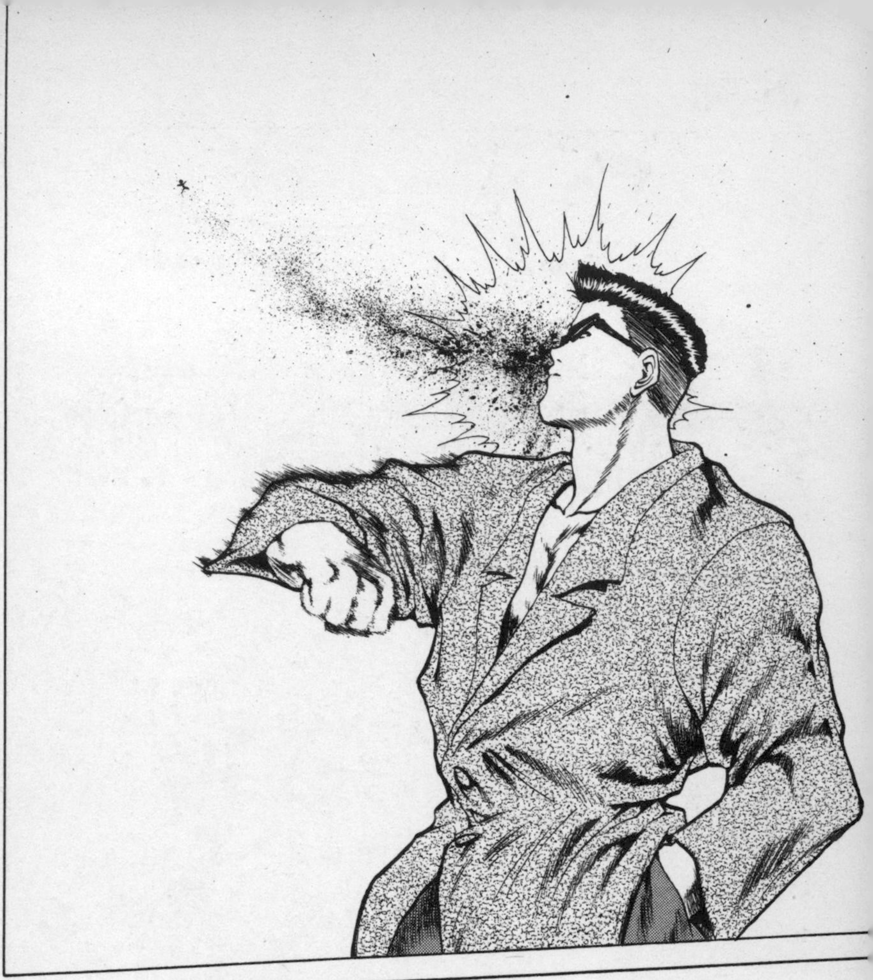
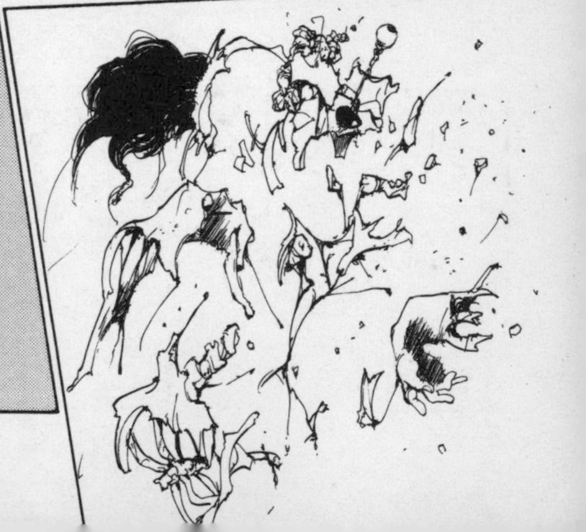
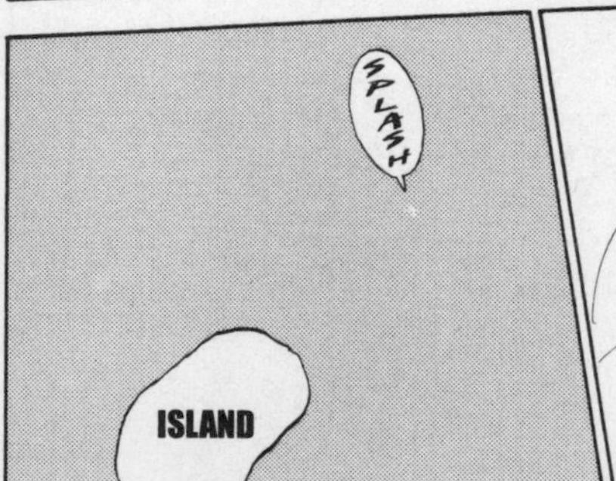
SPLASH
ISLAND

READ THIS WAY

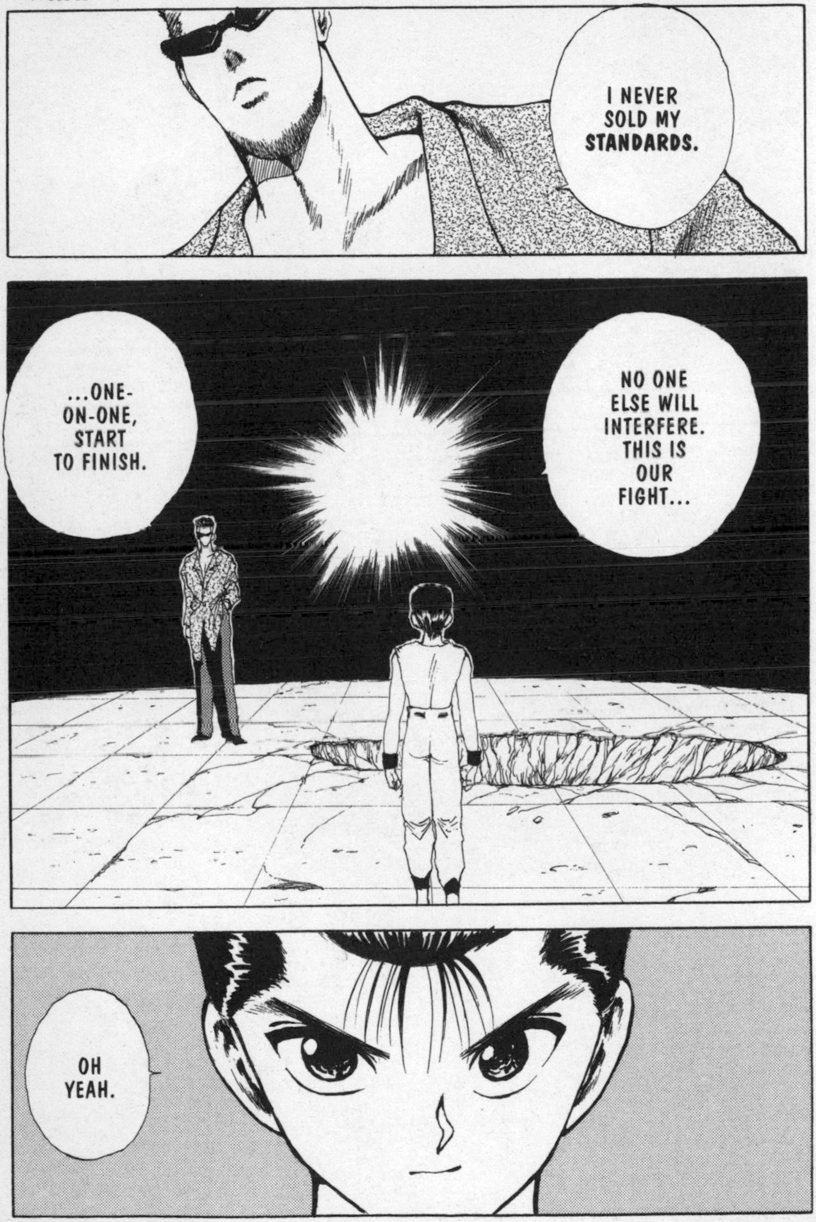
I NEVER SOLD MY **STANDARDS.**
NO ONE ELSE WILL INTERFERE. THIS IS OUR FIGHT...
...ONE-ON-ONE, START TO FINISH.
OH YEAH.

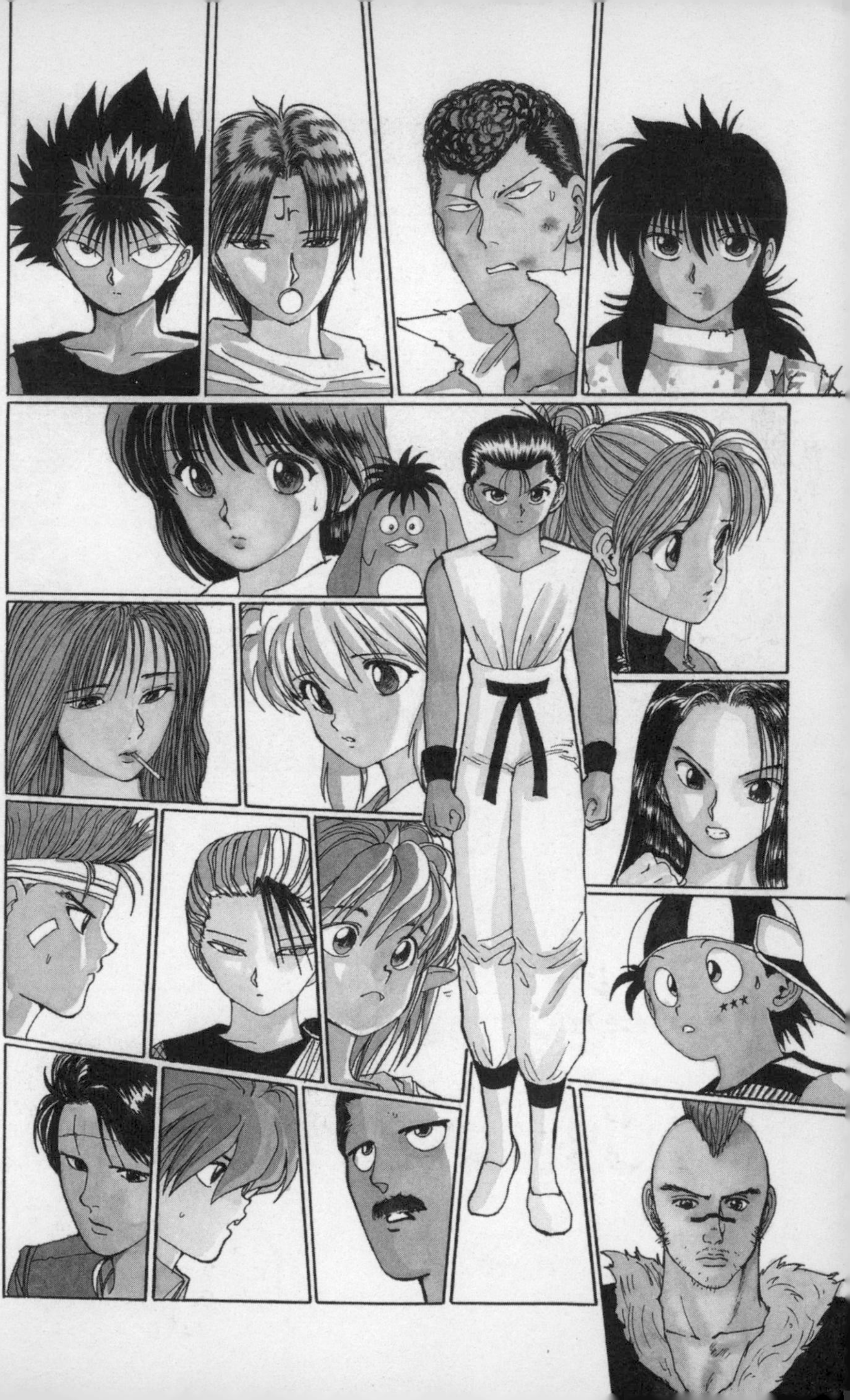
Jr

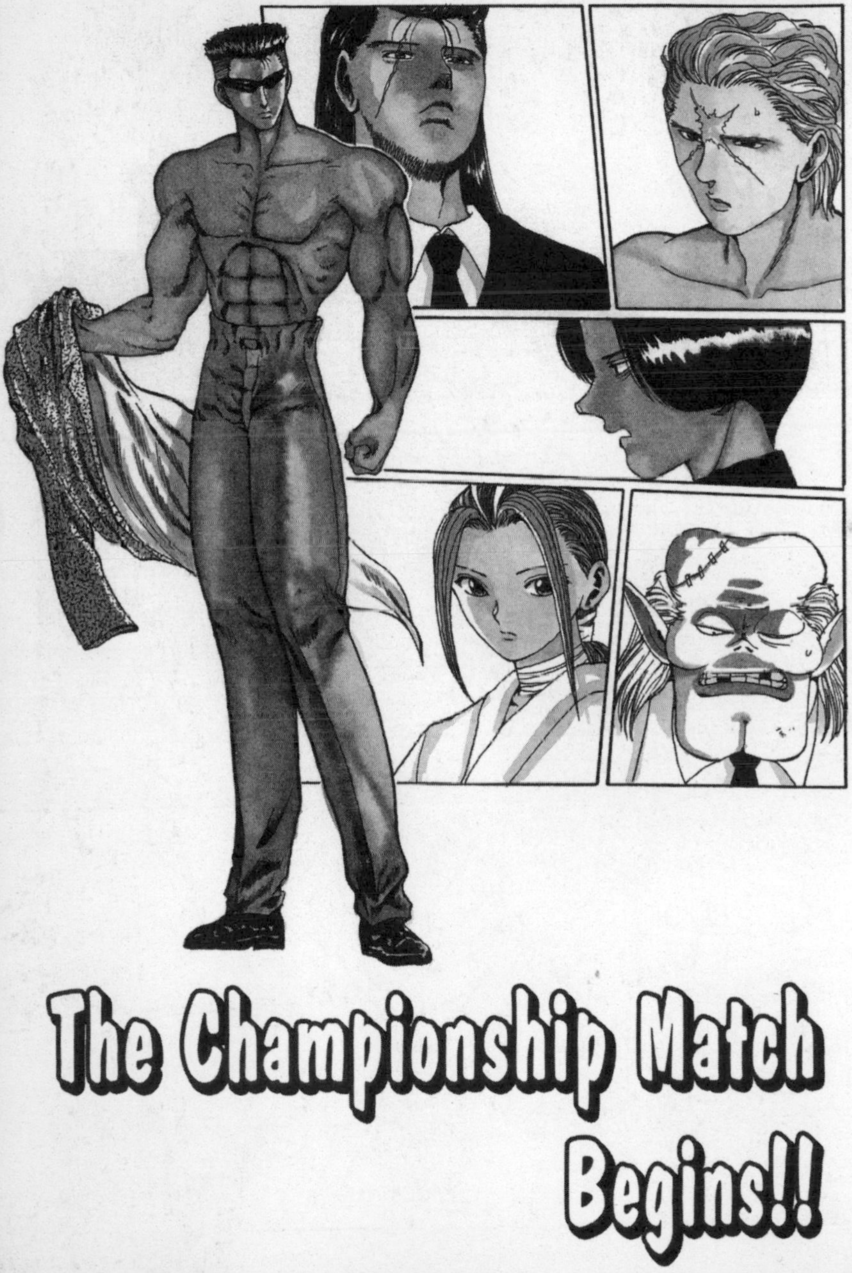

The Championship Match Begins!!

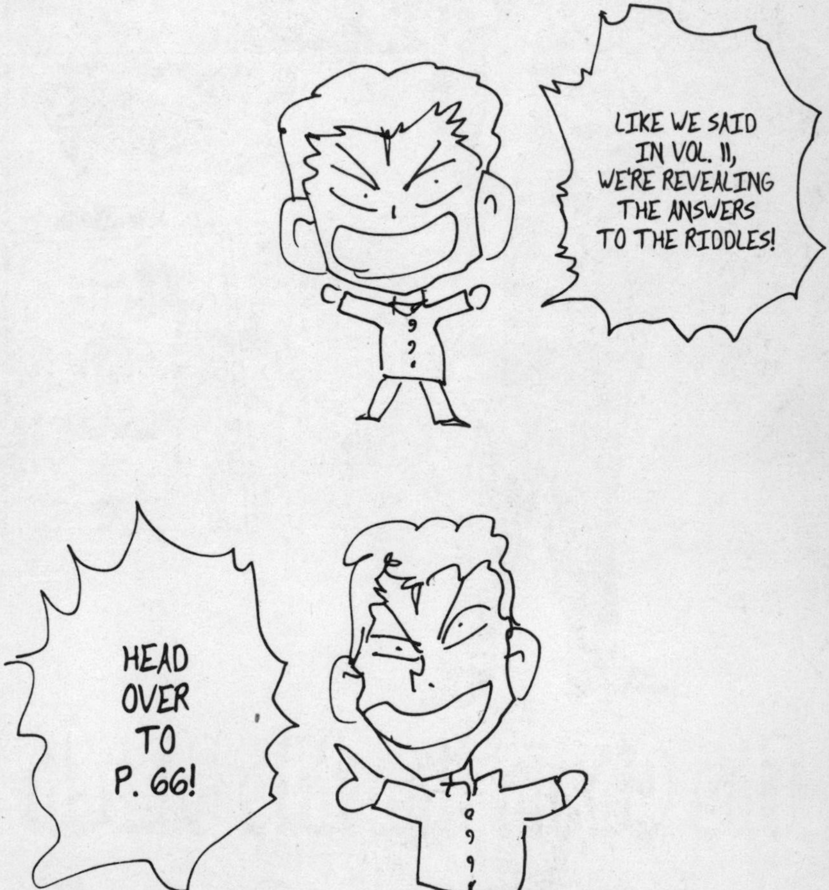
LIKE WE SAID IN VOL. 11, WE'RE REVEALING THE ANSWERS TO THE RIDDLES!
HEAD OVER TO P. 66!

READ THIS WAY

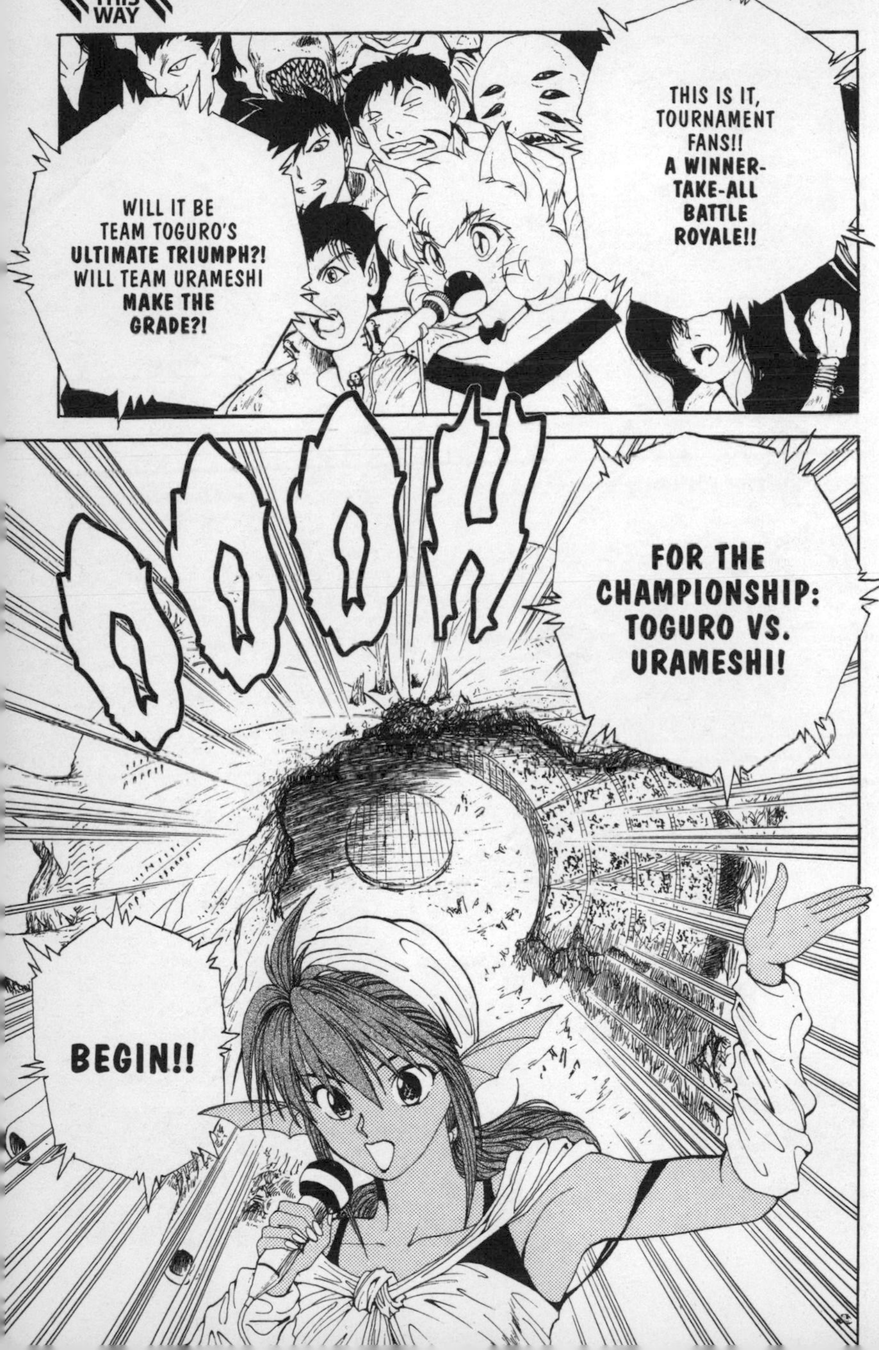
THIS IS IT, TOURNAMENT FANS!! A WINNER-TAKE-ALL BATTLE ROYALE!!
WILL IT BE TEAM TOGURO'S ULTIMATE TRIUMPH?! WILL TEAM URAMESHI MAKE THE GRADE?!
FOR THE CHAMPIONSHIP: TOGURO VS. URAMESHI!
OOOH
BEGIN!!

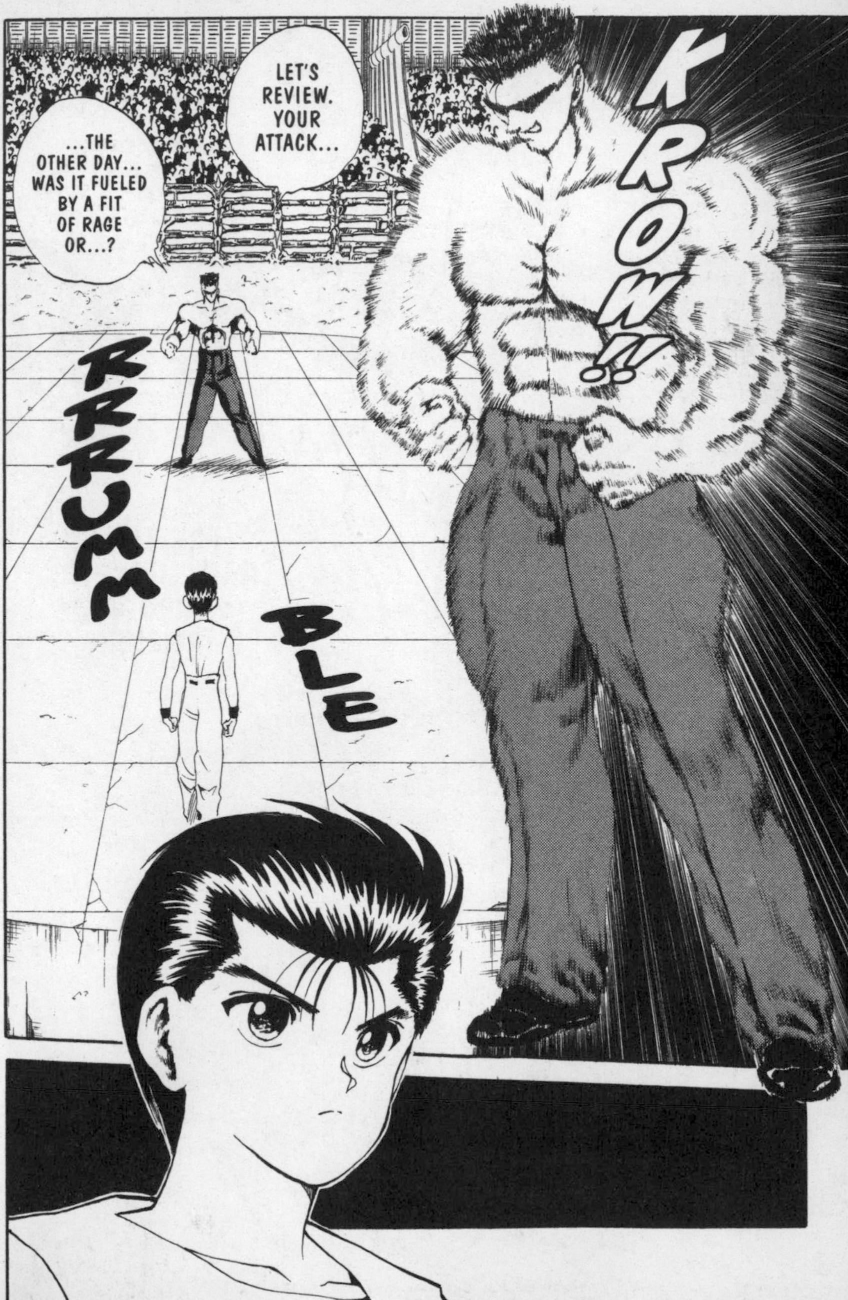
KROW!!
LET'S REVIEW. YOUR ATTACK...
...THE OTHER DAY... WAS IT FUELED BY A FIT OF RAGE OR...?
RRRUMM
BLE

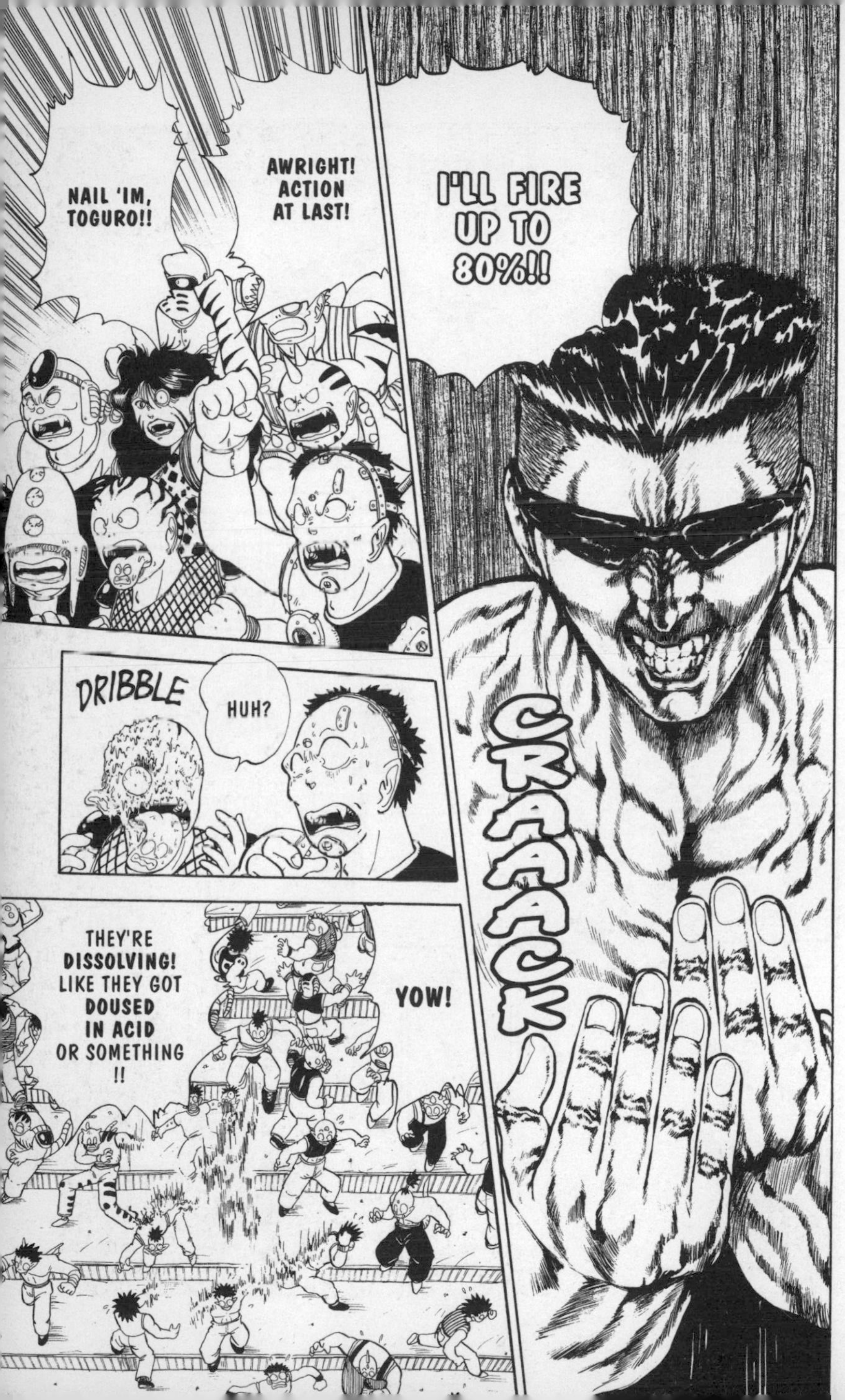
I'LL FIRE UP TO 80%!!
CRAAACK
AWRIGHT! ACTION AT LAST!
NAIL 'IM, TOGURO!!
DRIBBLE
HUH?
YOW!
THEY'RE **DISSOLVING!** LIKE THEY GOT **DOUSED** **IN ACID** OR SOMETHING !!

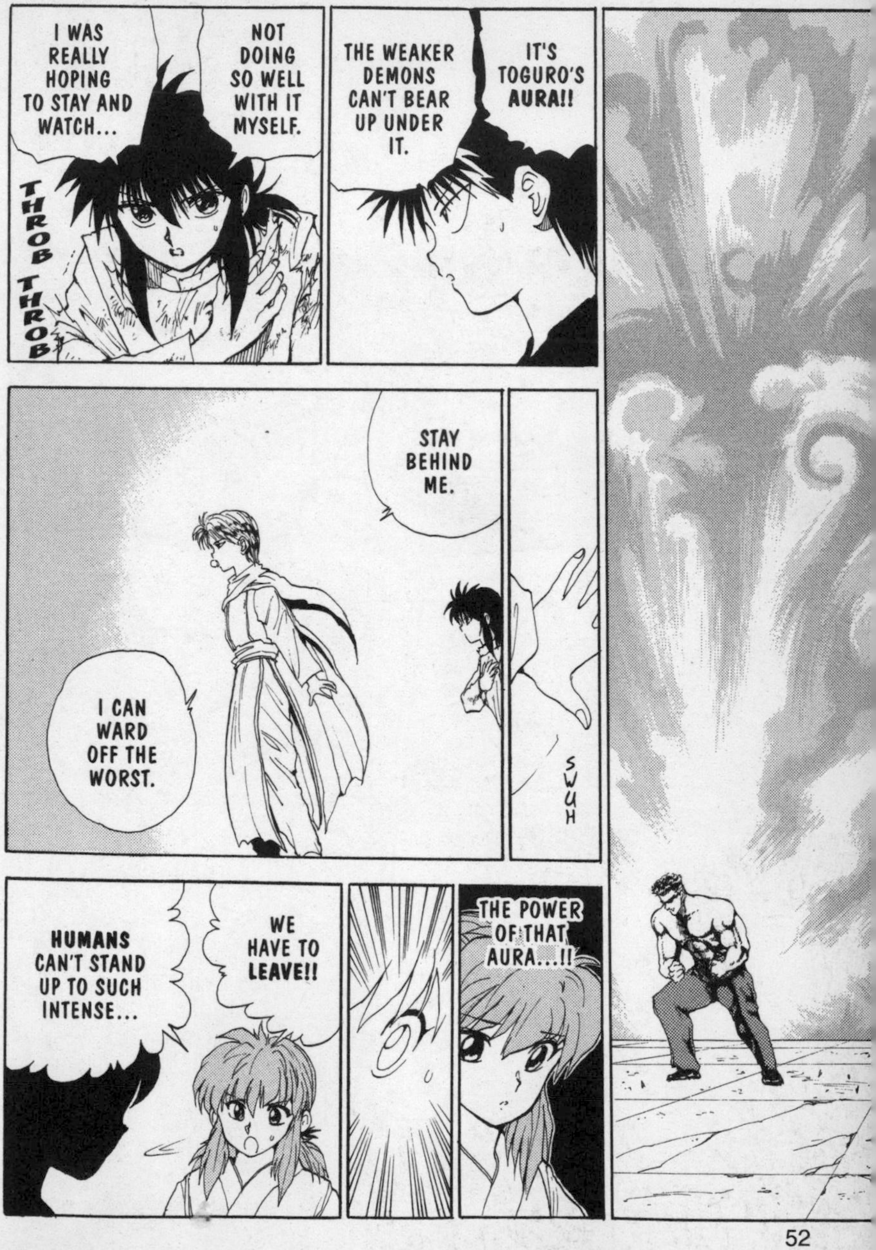
IT'S TOGURO'S AURA!!
THE WEAKER DEMONS CAN'T BEAR UP UNDER IT.
NOT DOING SO WELL WITH IT MYSELF.
I WAS REALLY HOPING TO STAY AND WATCH...
THROB THROB
SWUH
STAY BEHIND ME.
I CAN WARD OFF THE WORST.
THE POWER OF THAT AURA...!!
WE HAVE TO LEAVE!!
HUMANS CAN'T STAND UP TO SUCH INTENSE...

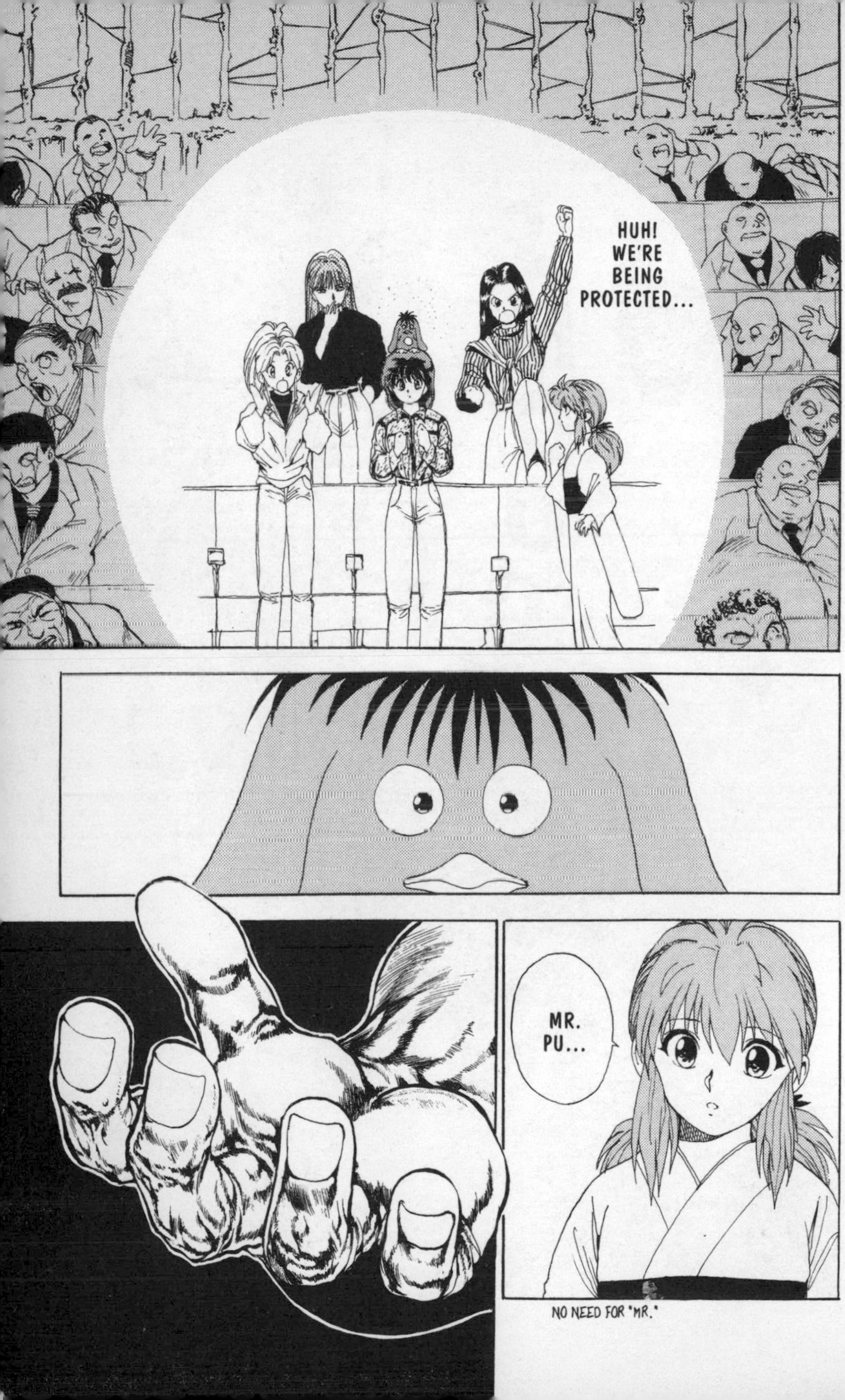
HUH! WE'RE BEING PROTECTED...
MR. PU...
NO NEED FOR "MR."

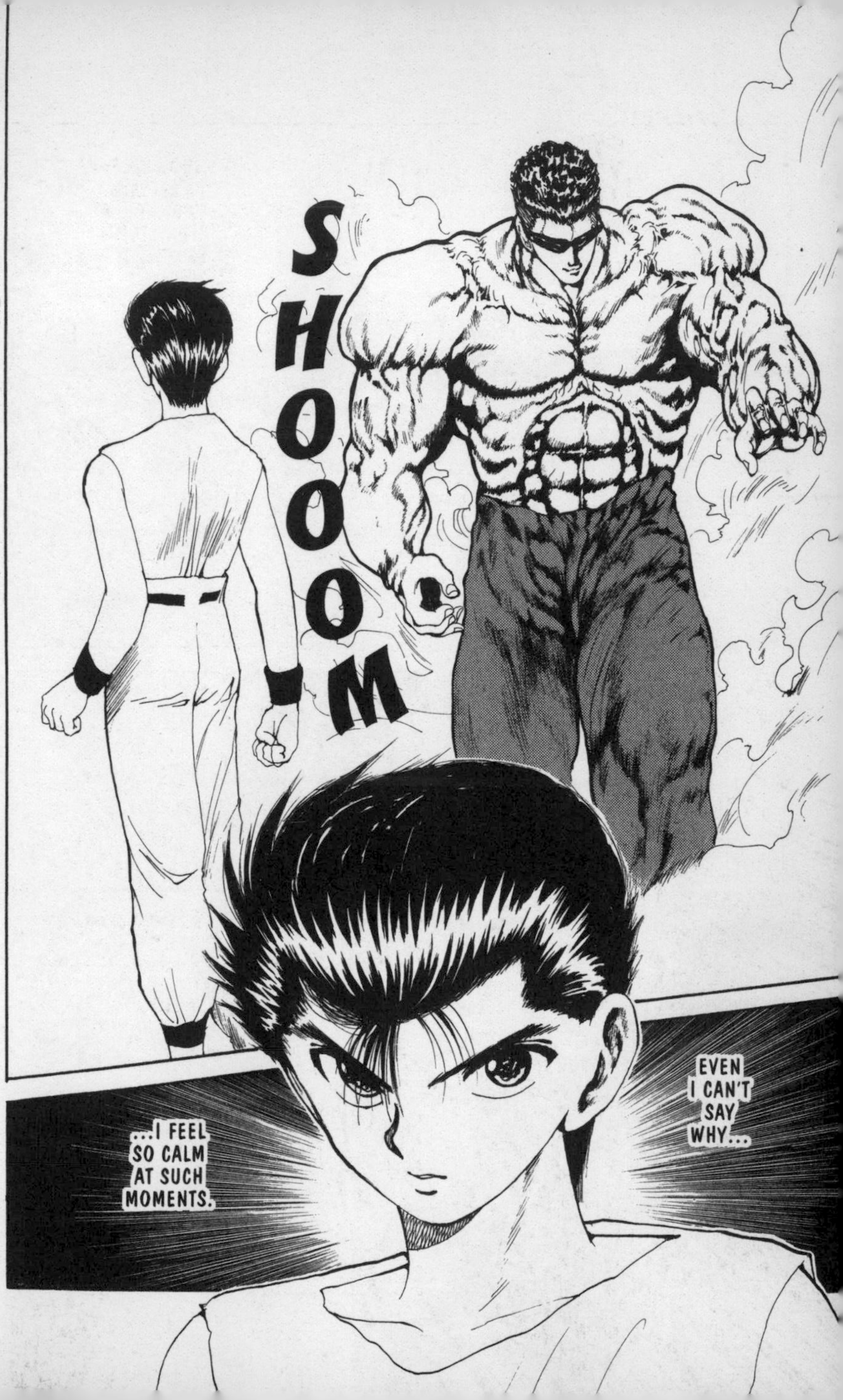
SHOOM
EVEN I CAN'T SAY WHY...
...I FEEL SO CALM AT SUCH MOMENTS.

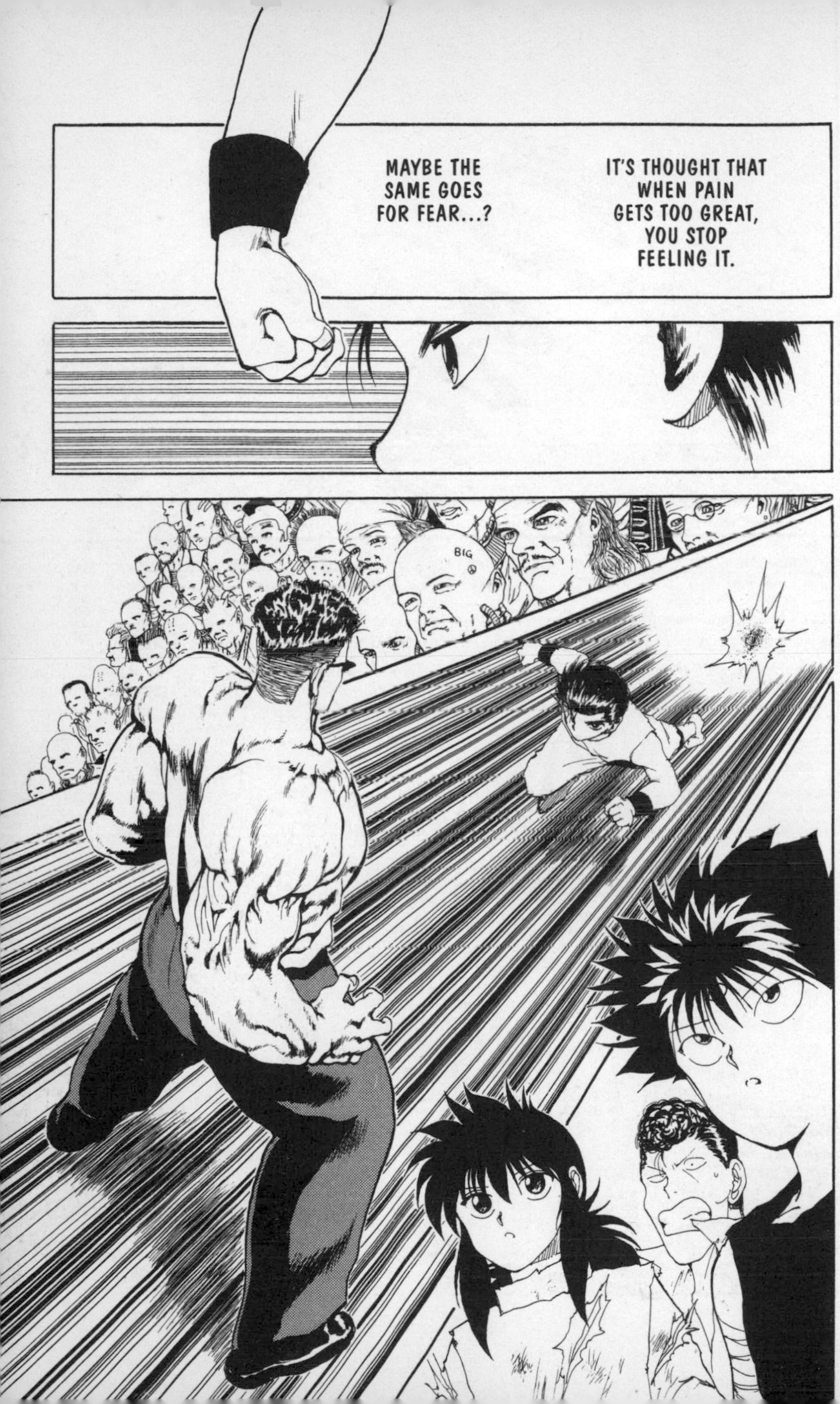
IT'S THOUGHT THAT WHEN PAIN GETS TOO GREAT, YOU STOP FEELING IT.
MAYBE THE SAME GOES FOR FEAR...?
BIG

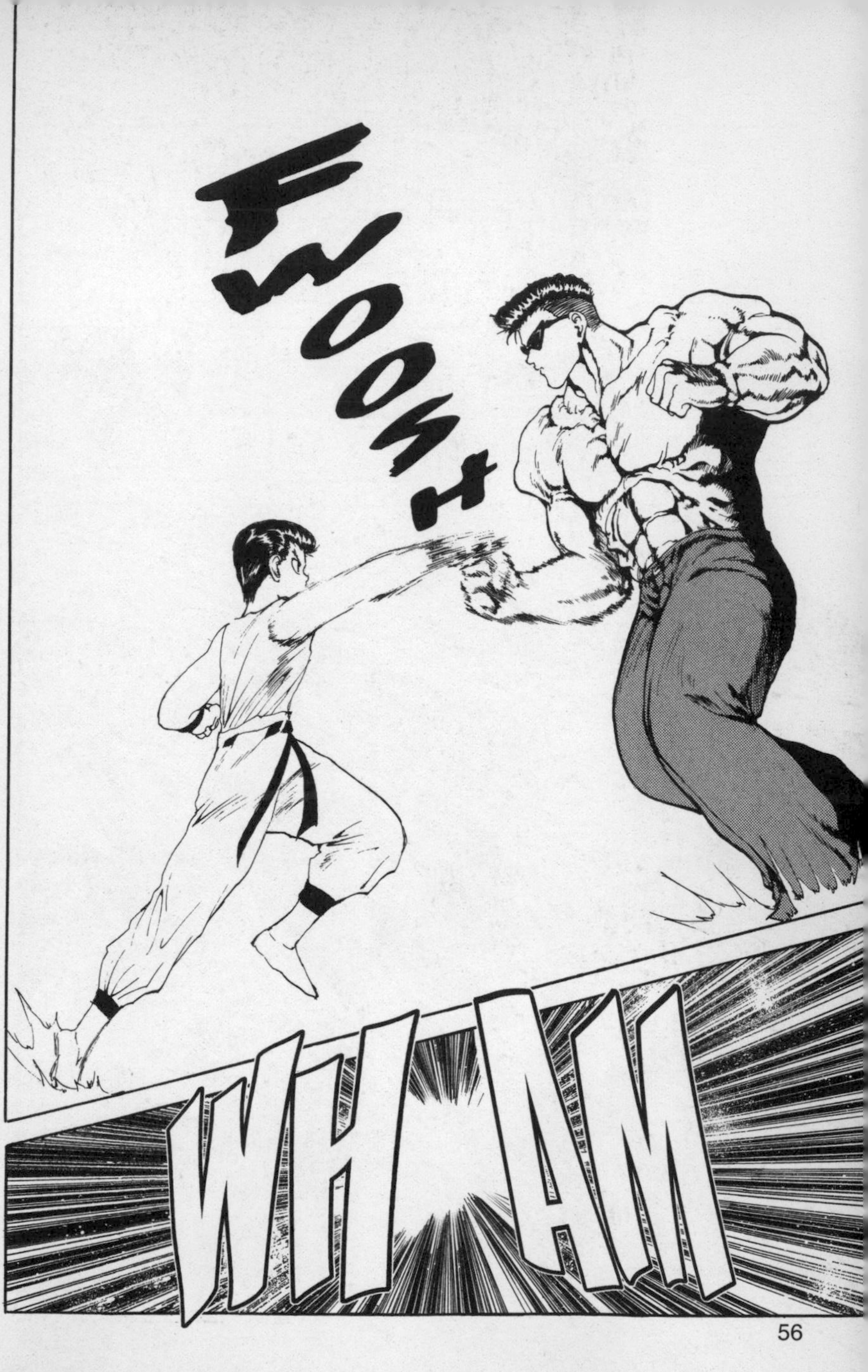
FWOOM!
WHAM

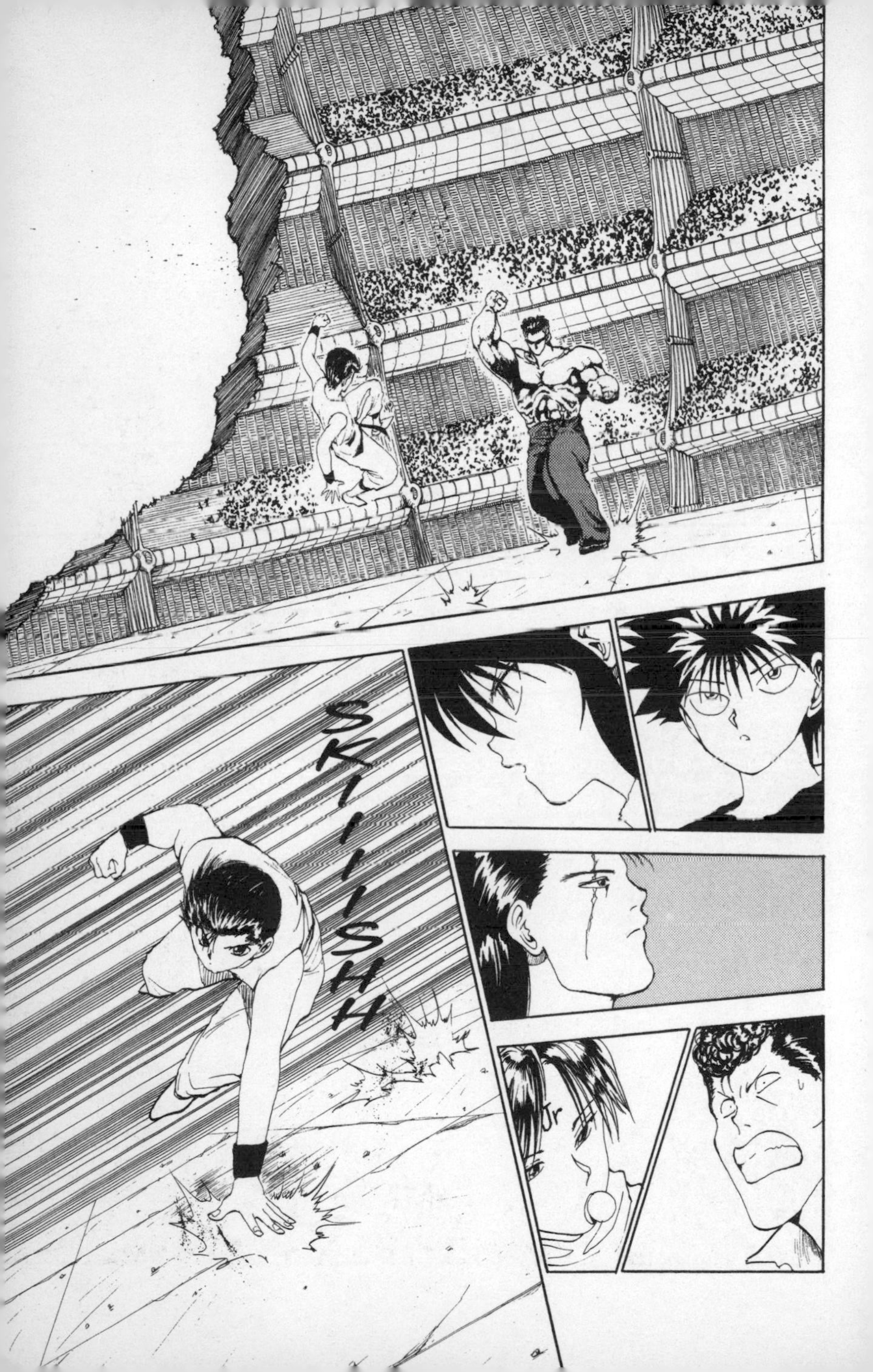
SKIIIISHH

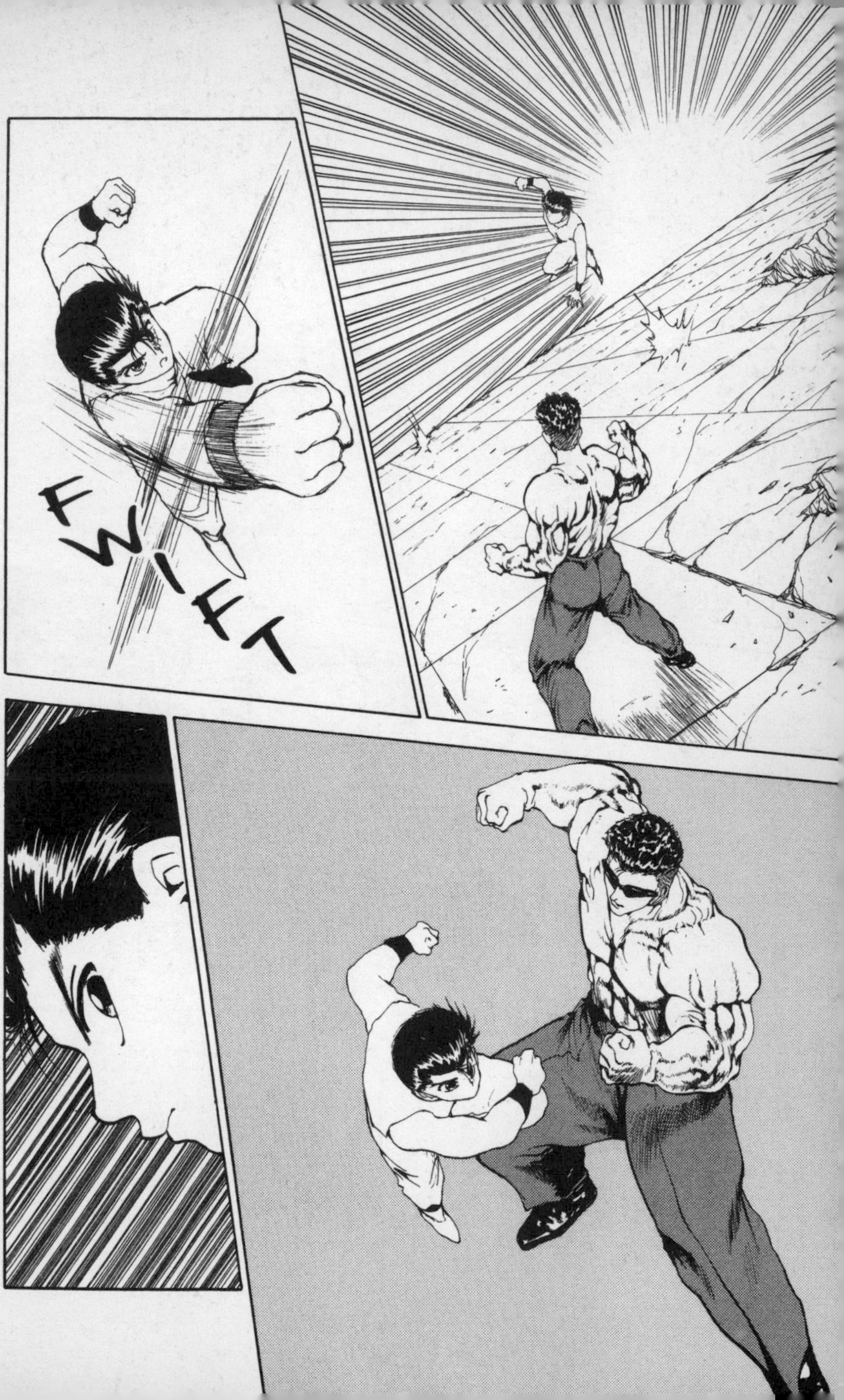
FWIFT

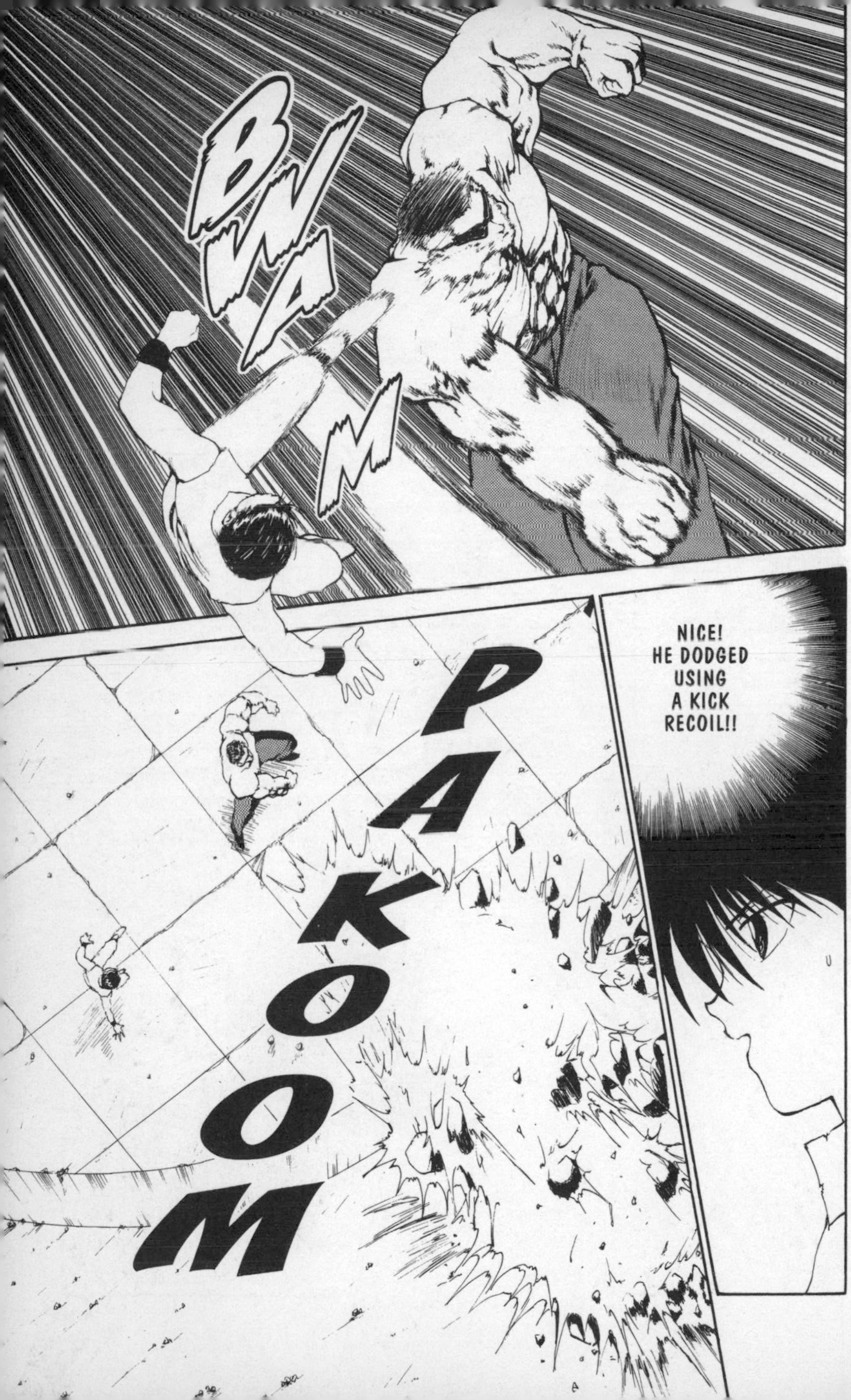
BWAM
NICE! HE DODGED USING A KICK RECOIL!!
PAKOOM

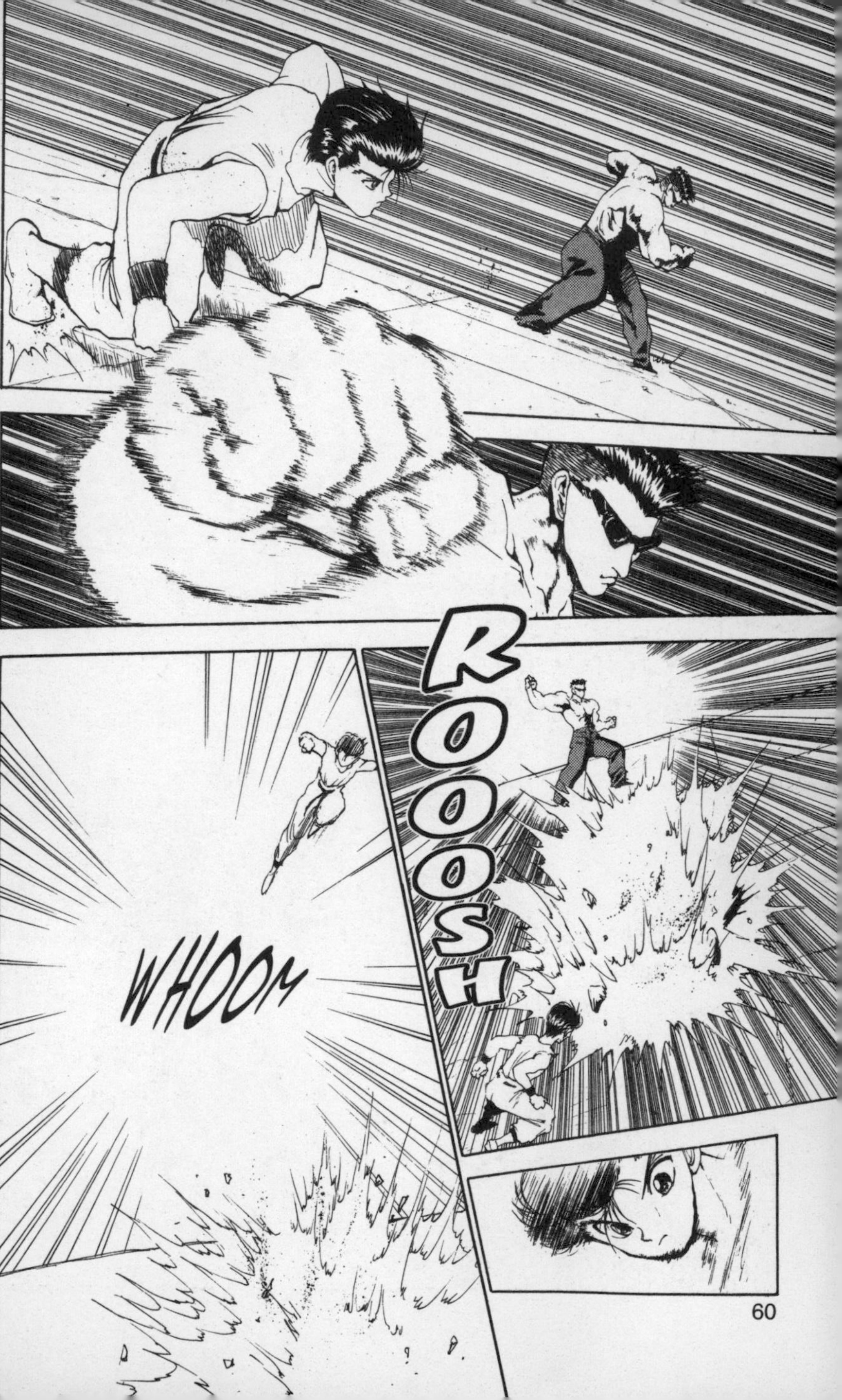
ROOOOSH
WHOOM

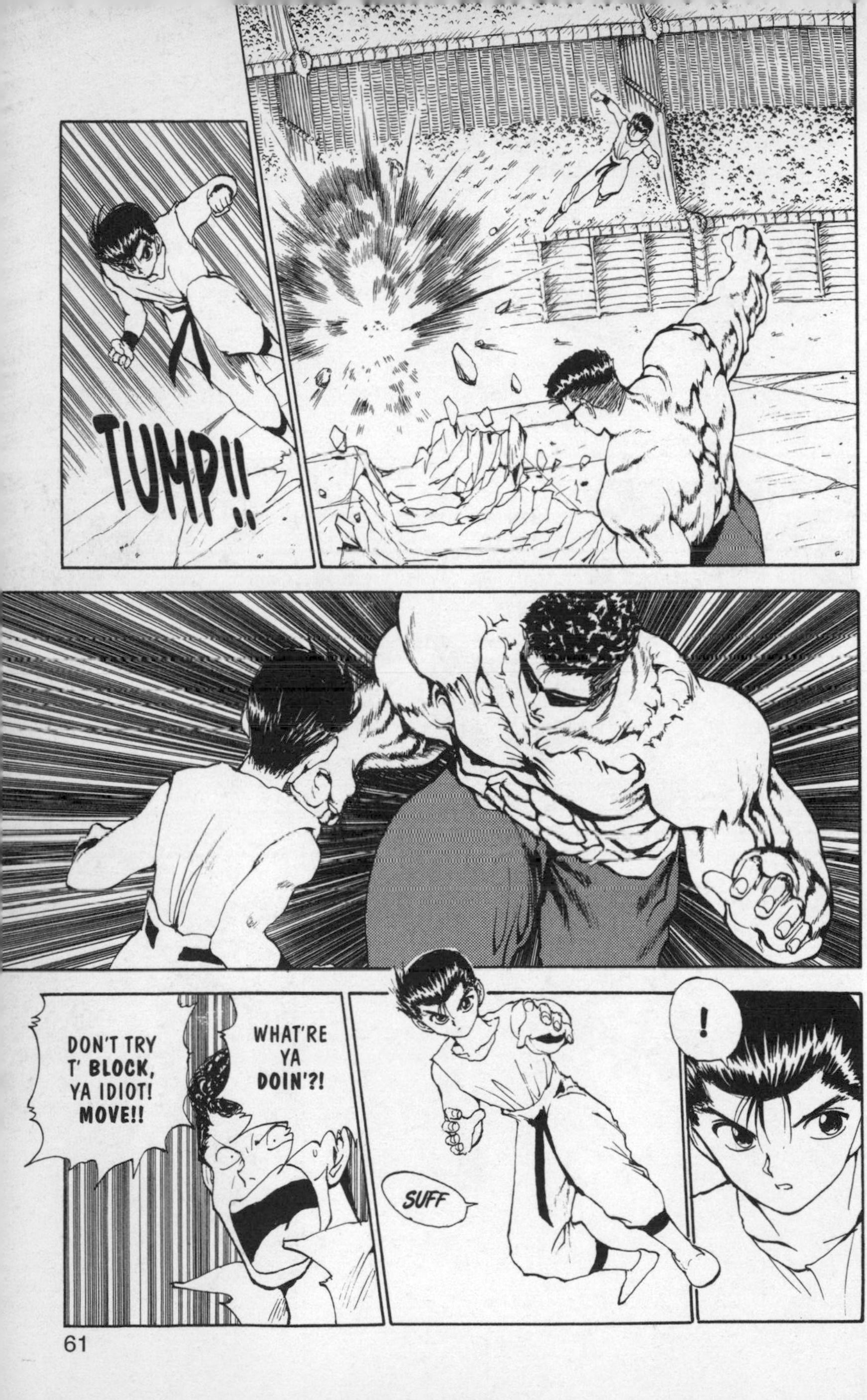
TUMP!!
!
SUFF
WHAT'RE YA DOIN'?!
DON'T TRY T' BLOCK, YA IDIOT! MOVE!!

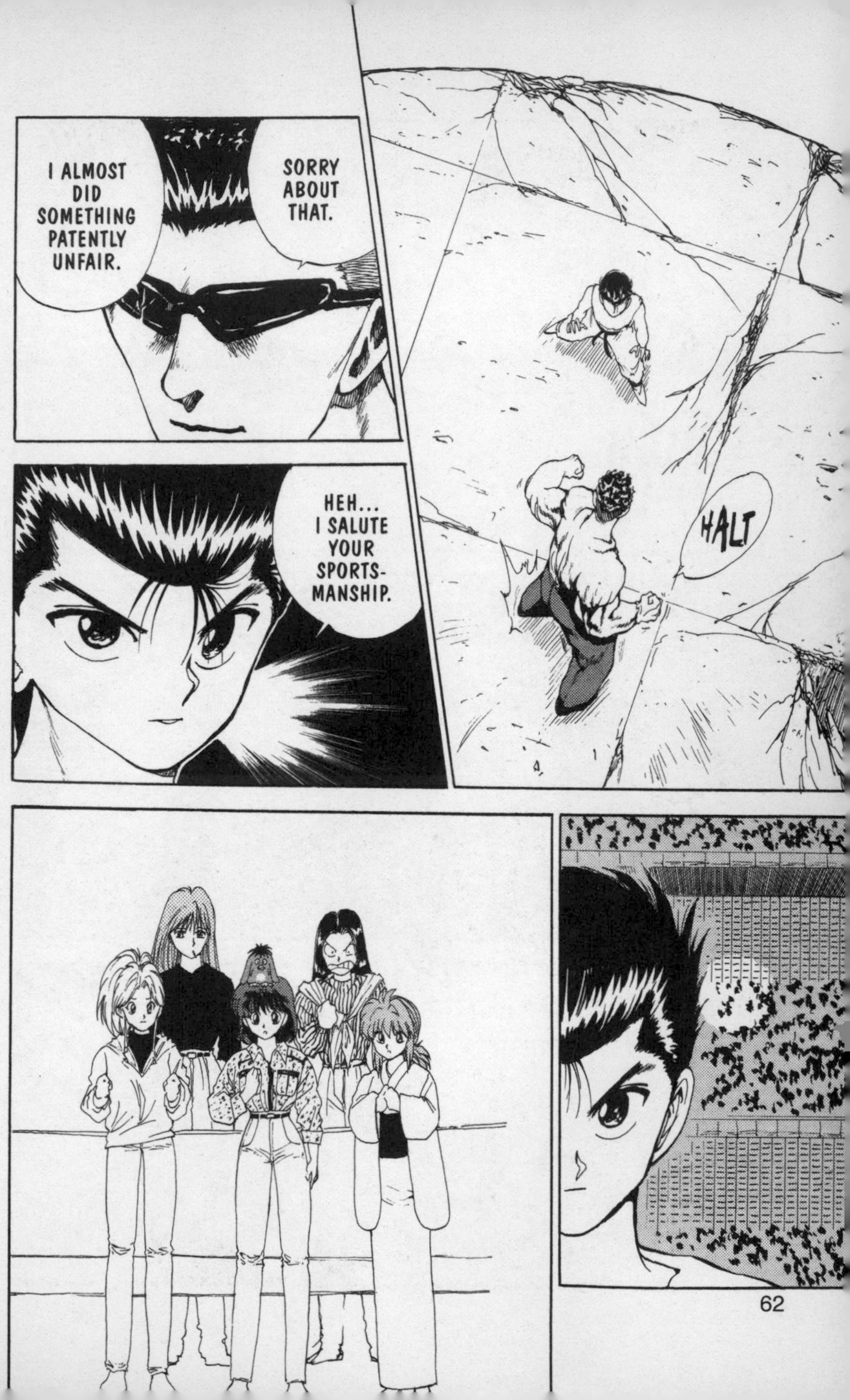
HALT
SORRY ABOUT THAT.
I ALMOST DID SOMETHING PATENTLY UNFAIR.
HEH... I SALUTE YOUR SPORTS-MANSHIP.

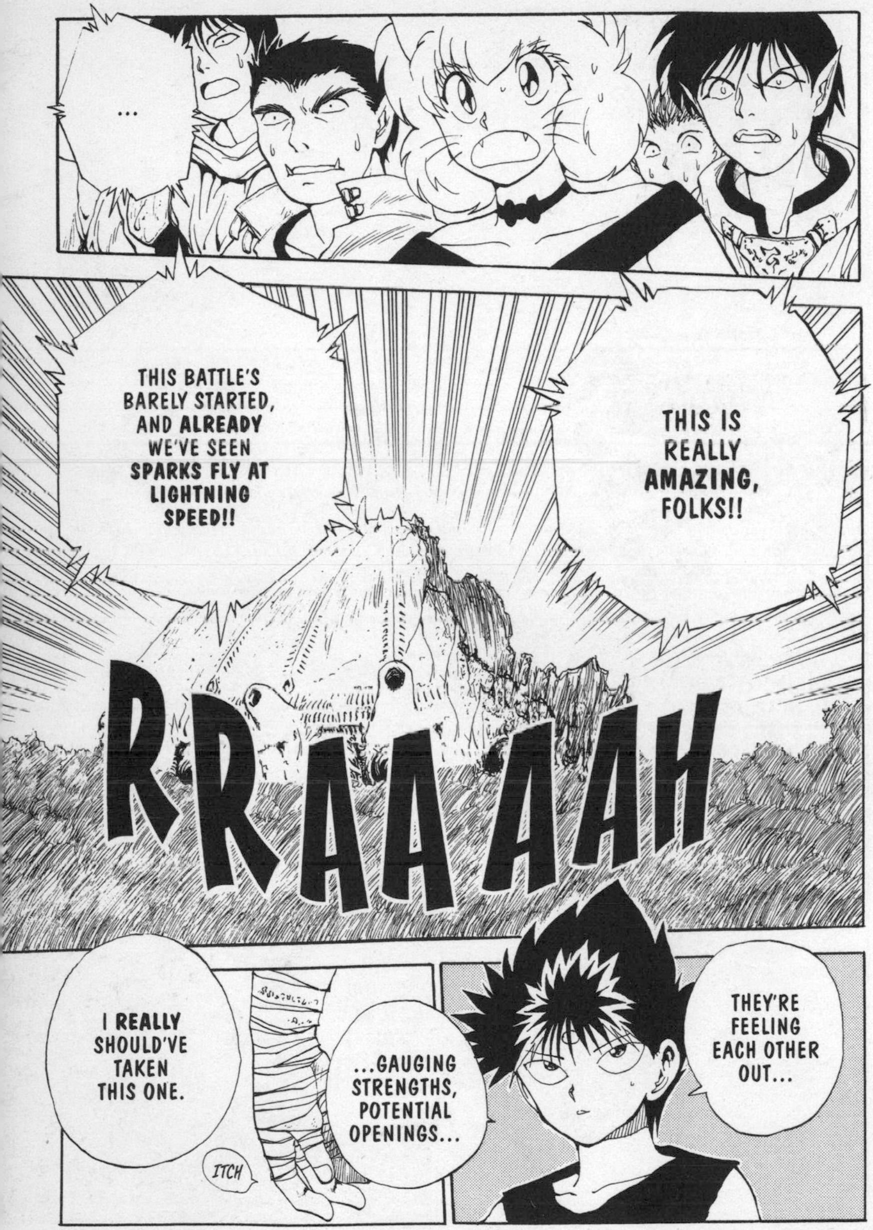
...
THIS IS REALLY AMAZING, FOLKS!!
THIS BATTLE'S BARELY STARTED, AND ALREADY WE'VE SEEN SPARKS FLY AT LIGHTNING SPEED!!
RRAAAAH
THEY'RE FEELING EACH OTHER OUT...
...GAUGING STRENGTHS, POTENTIAL OPENINGS...
I REALLY SHOULD'VE TAKEN THIS ONE.
ITCH

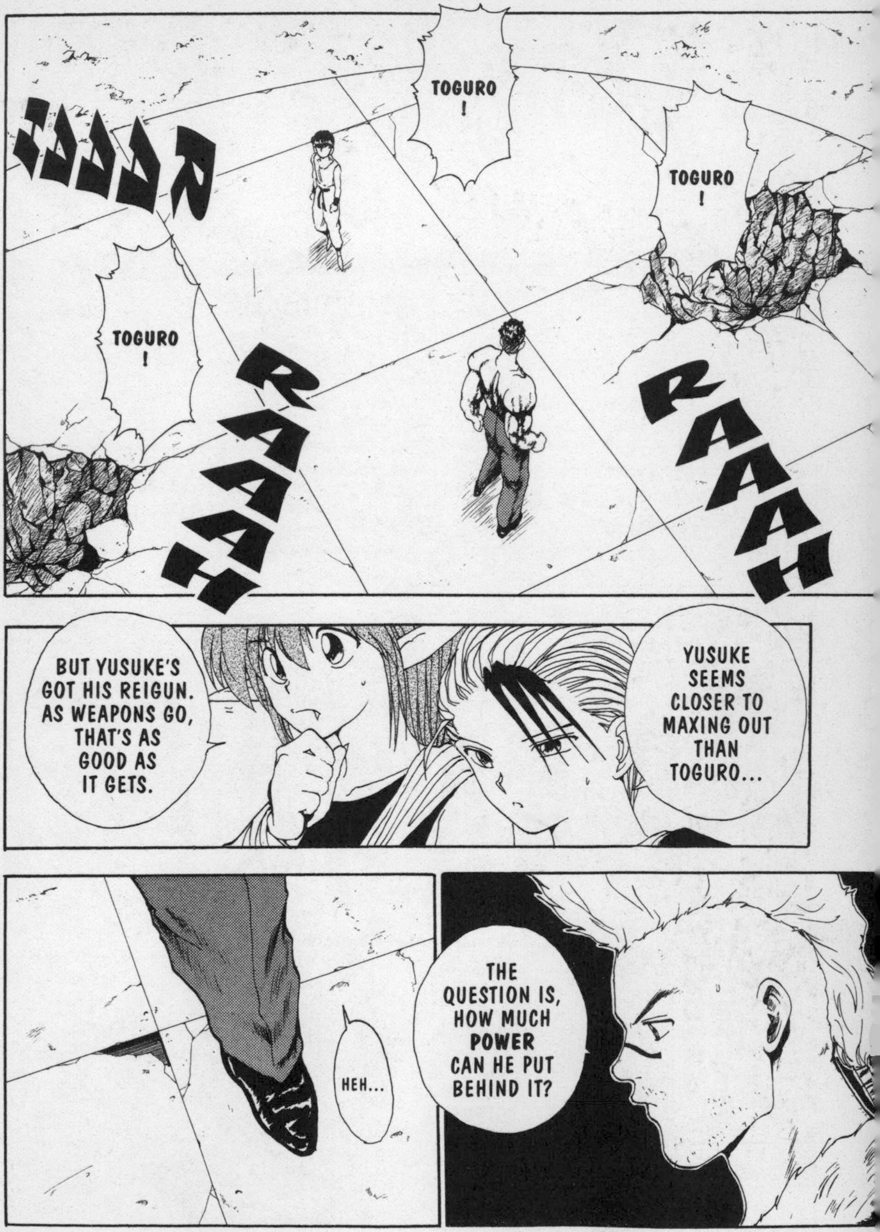
TOGURO !
TOGURO !
TOGURO !
RAAAH
RAAAH
DDDR
YUSUKE SEEMS CLOSER TO MAXING OUT THAN TOGURO...
BUT YUSUKE'S GOT HIS REIGUN. AS WEAPONS GO, THAT'S AS GOOD AS IT GETS.
THE QUESTION IS, HOW MUCH **POWER** CAN HE PUT BEHIND IT?
HEH...

HE SHAVED OFF HIS SIDEBURNS.

READ THIS WAY

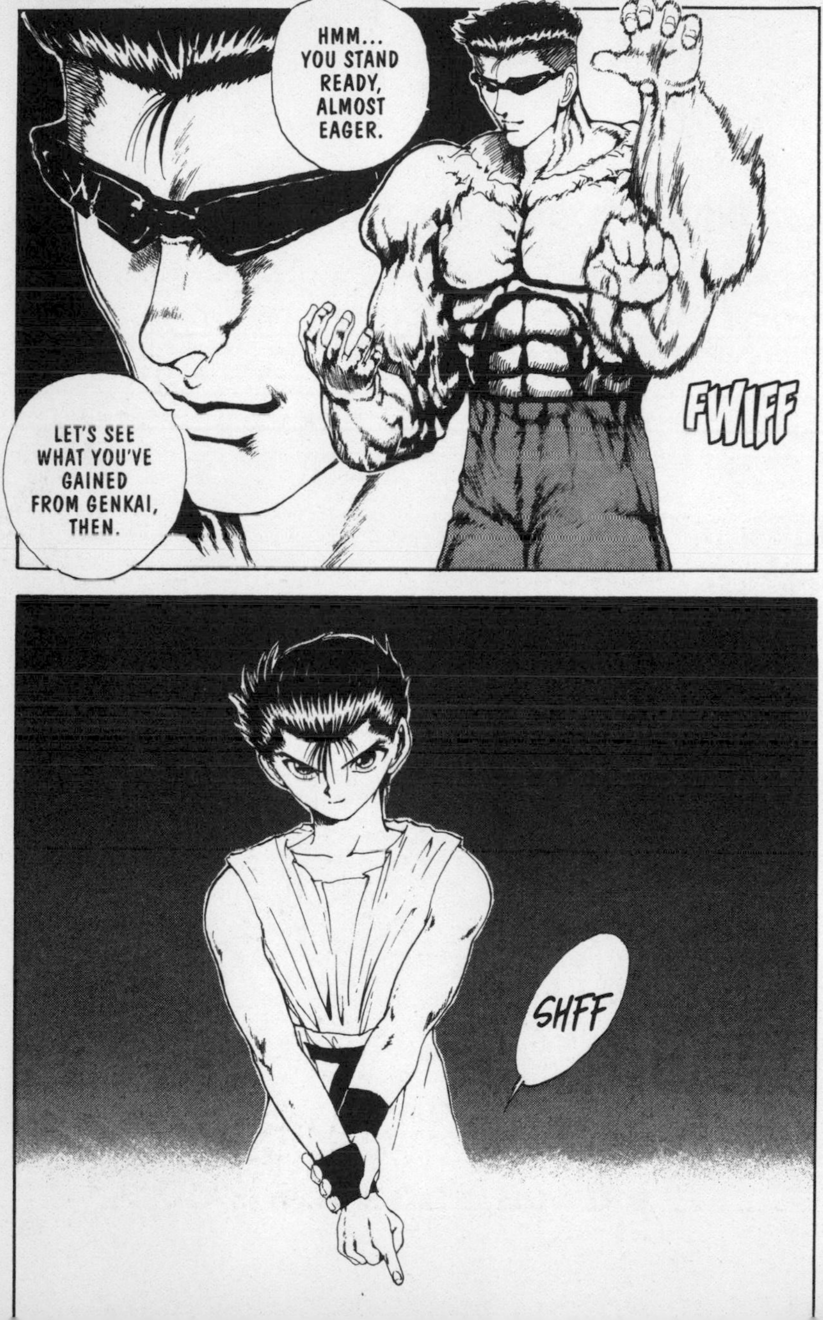
HMM... YOU STAND READY, ALMOST EAGER.
FWIFF
LET'S SEE WHAT YOU'VE GAINED FROM GENKAI, THEN.
SHFF

ANSWER TO YUYU HAKUSHO PUZZLES: 1

HINT: BUY THE FIRST CD OF THE ANIME, OR
                    LEARN IT FROM WATCHING IT ON TV.

ANSWER: KUWABARA

"NU"
IS THE
LAST
LETTER
LEFT.

● THE PUZZLE APPEARS IN GN VOL. 11, P.68.

NO EFFECT?!

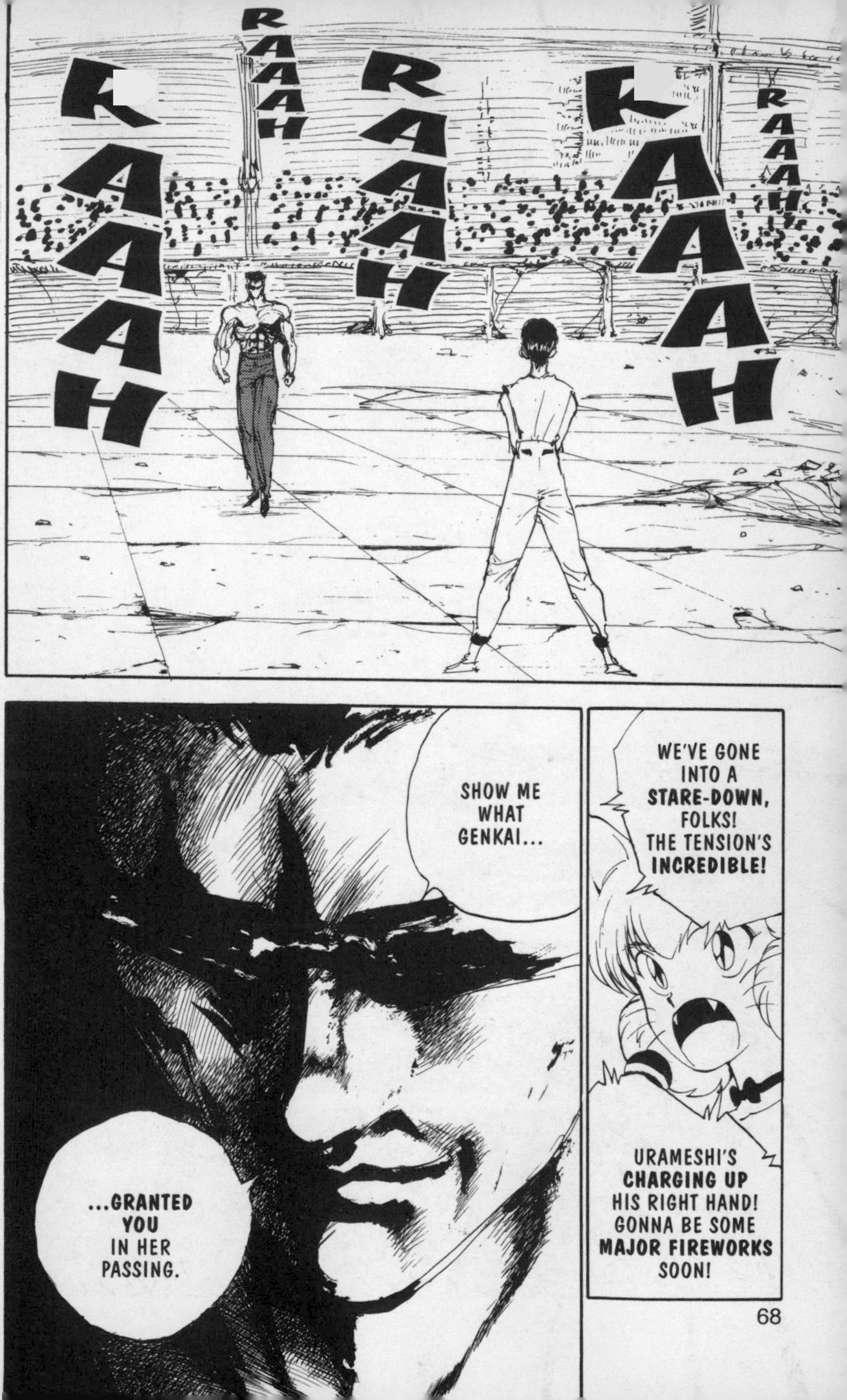
RAAAH
RAAAH
RAAAH
RAAAH
RAAAH
WE'VE GONE INTO A STARE-DOWN, FOLKS! THE TENSION'S INCREDIBLE!
URAMESHI'S CHARGING UP HIS RIGHT HAND! GONNA BE SOME MAJOR FIREWORKS SOON!
SHOW ME WHAT GENKAI...
...GRANTED YOU IN HER PASSING.

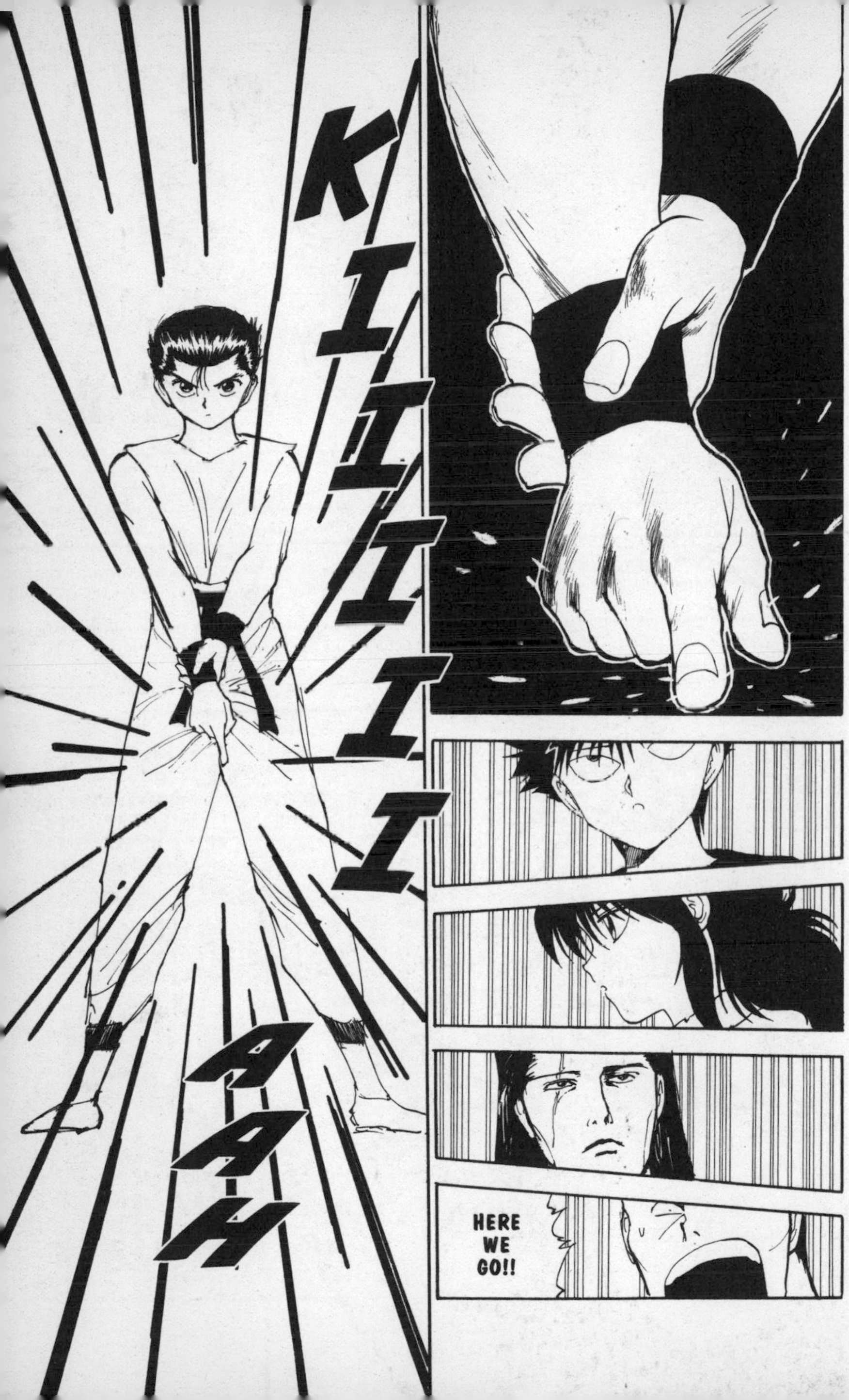
HERE WE GO!!
KIIIII
AAH

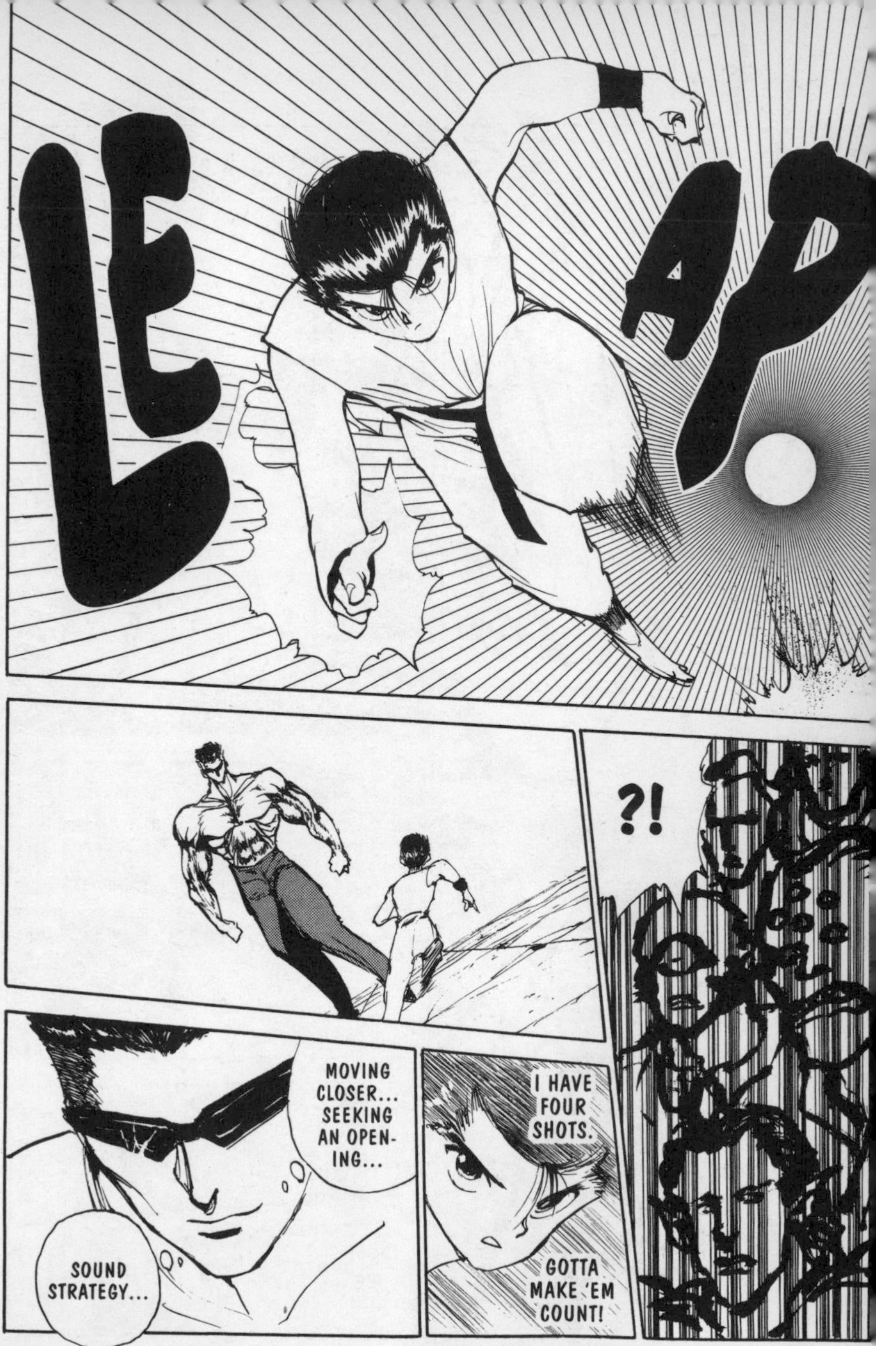
LEAP
?!
I HAVE FOUR SHOTS.
GOTTA MAKE 'EM COUNT!
MOVING CLOSER... SEEKING AN OPEN-ING...
SOUND STRATEGY...

READ THIS WAY

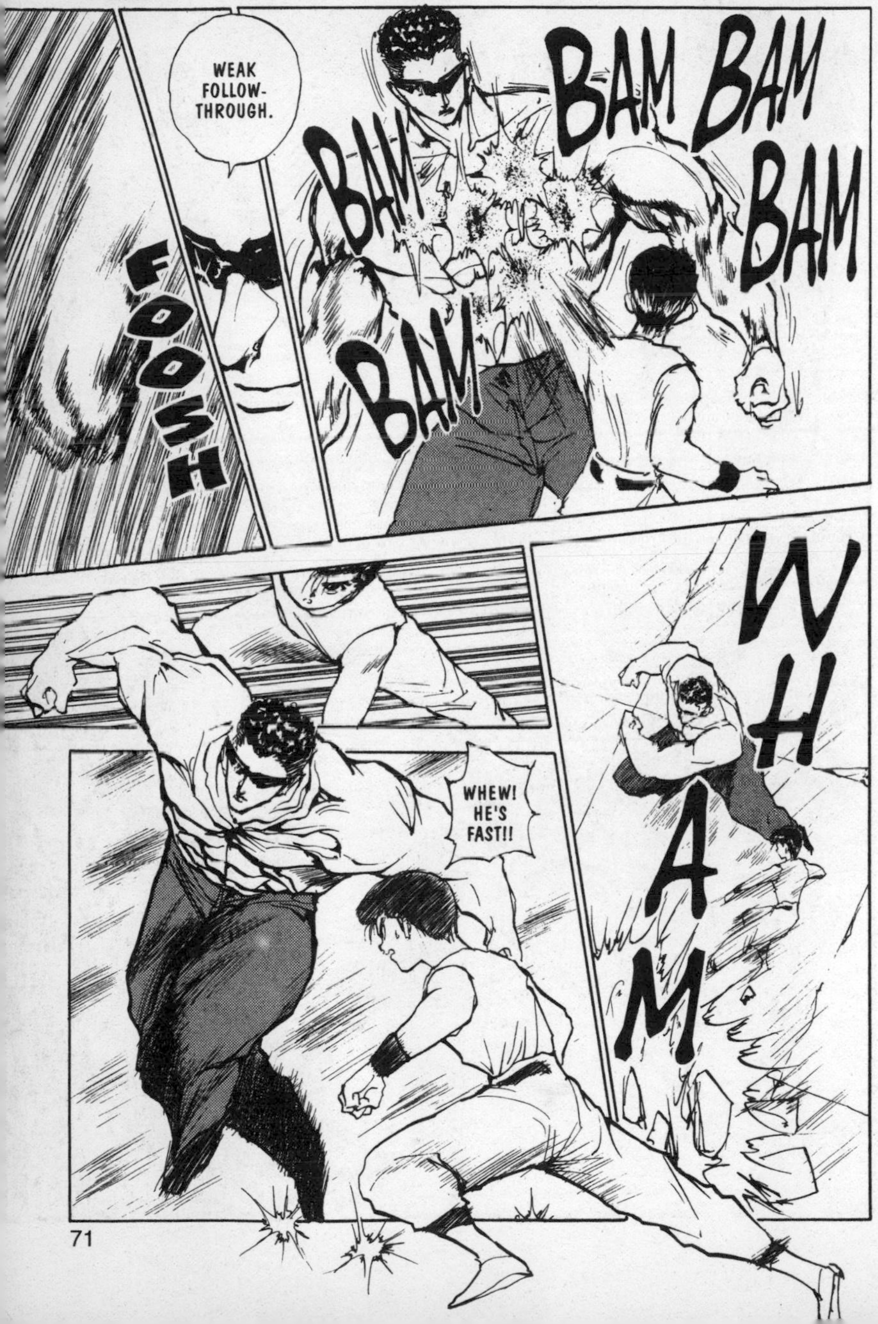
BAM BAM BAM BAM BAM BAM
WEAK FOLLOW-THROUGH.
FOOSH
WHAM
WHEW! HE'S FAST!!

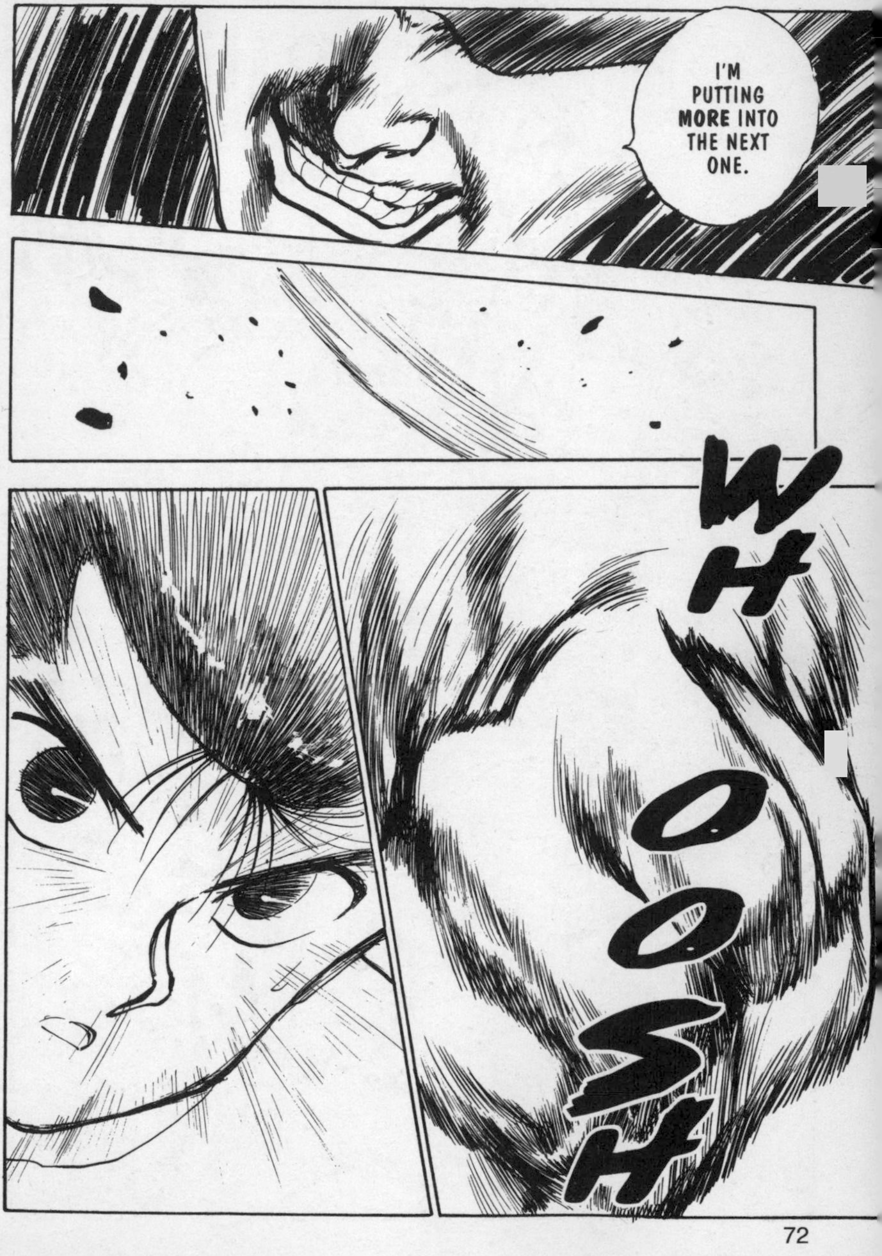
I'M PUTTING MORE INTO THE NEXT ONE.
WHOOSH

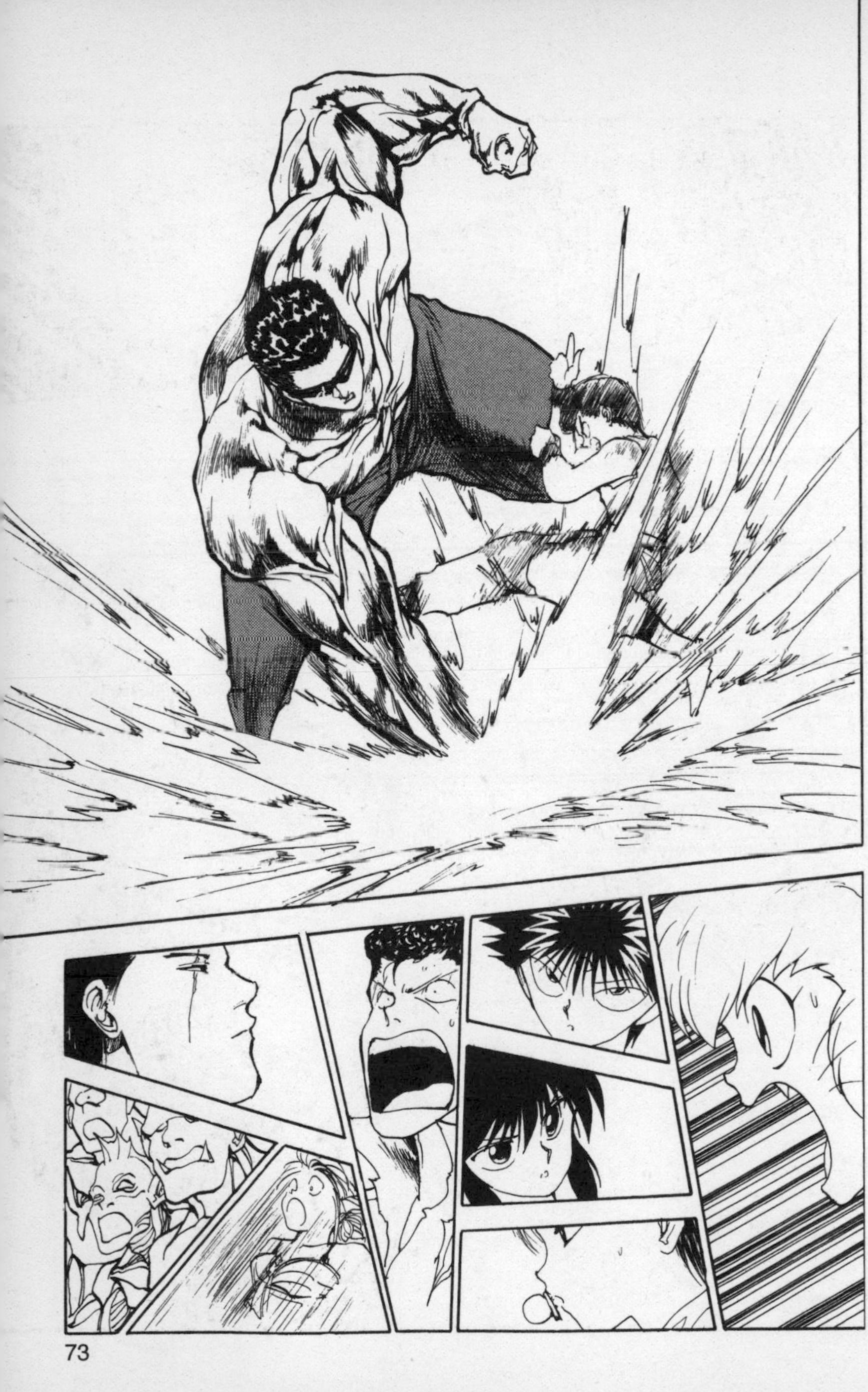

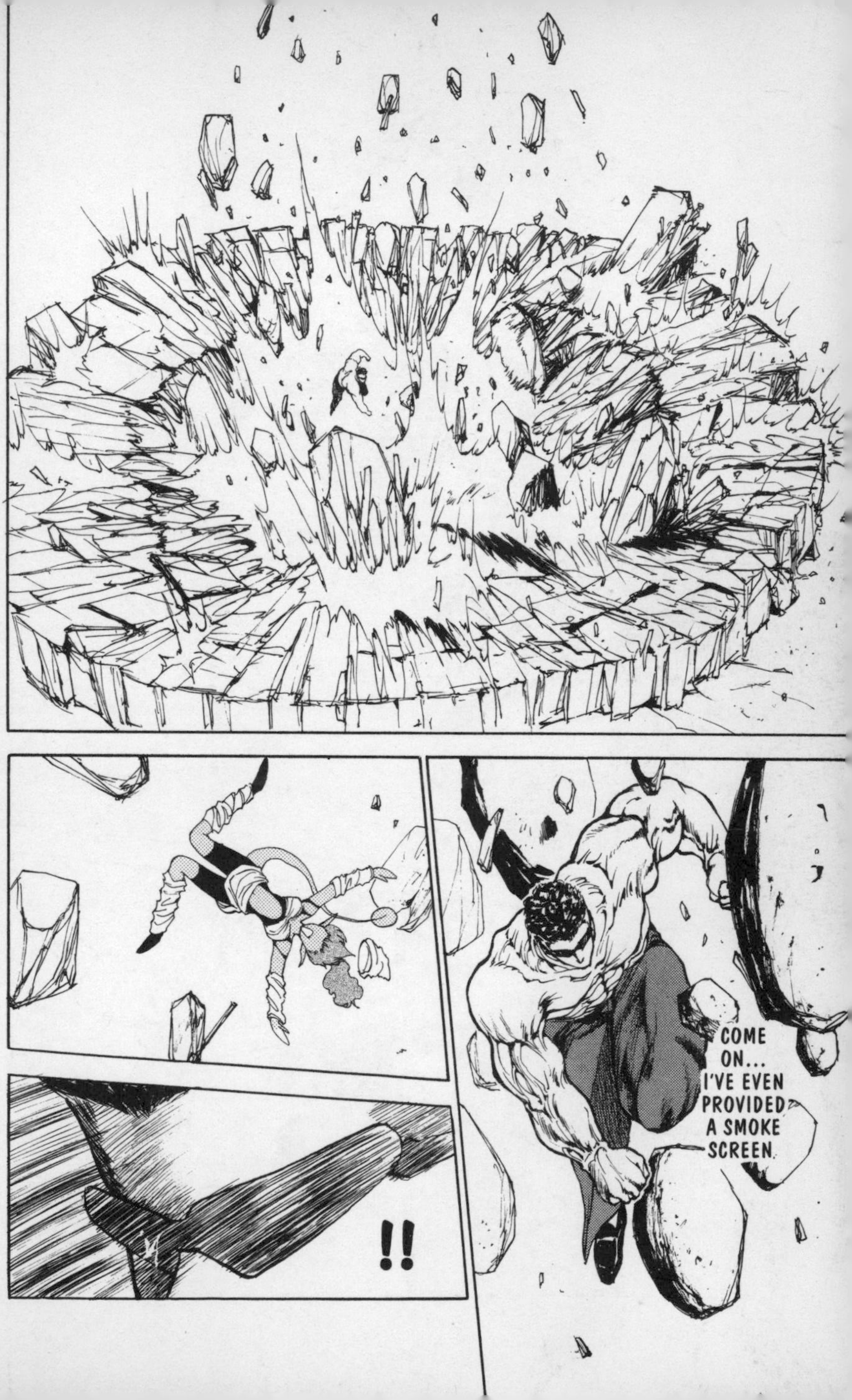
COME ON... I'VE EVEN PROVIDED A SMOKE SCREEN.
!!

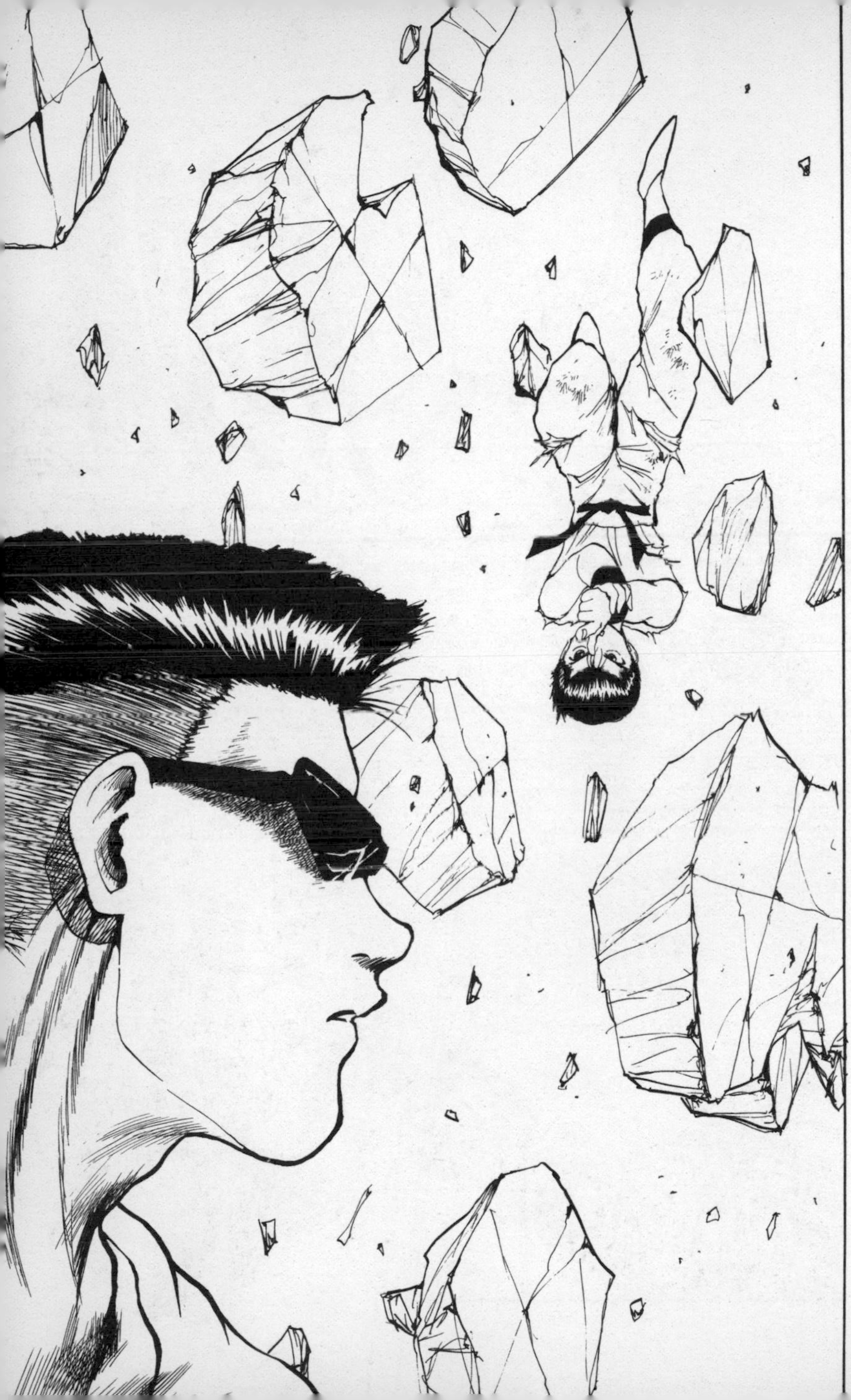

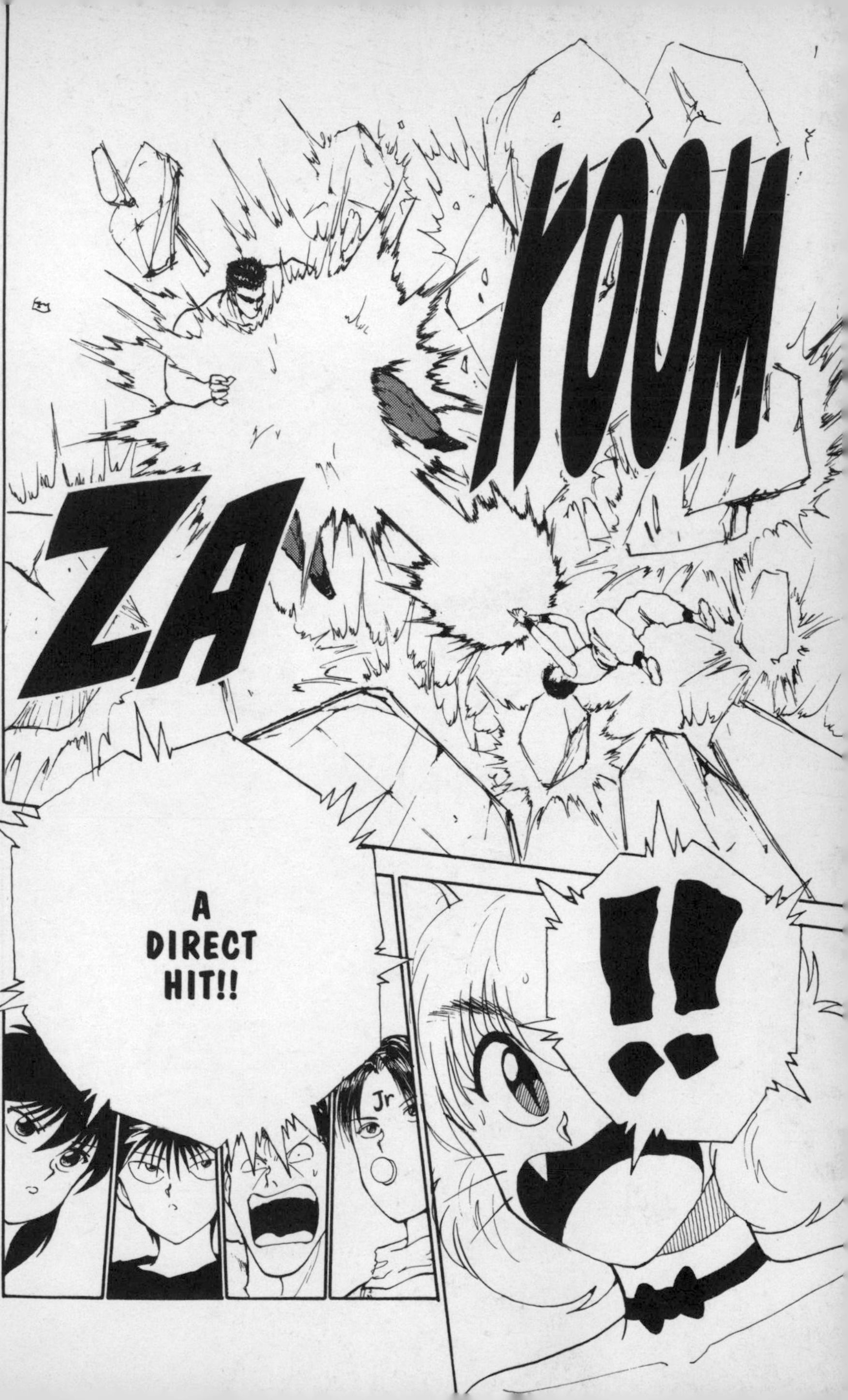
YOOM
ZA
!!
A DIRECT HIT!!
Jr

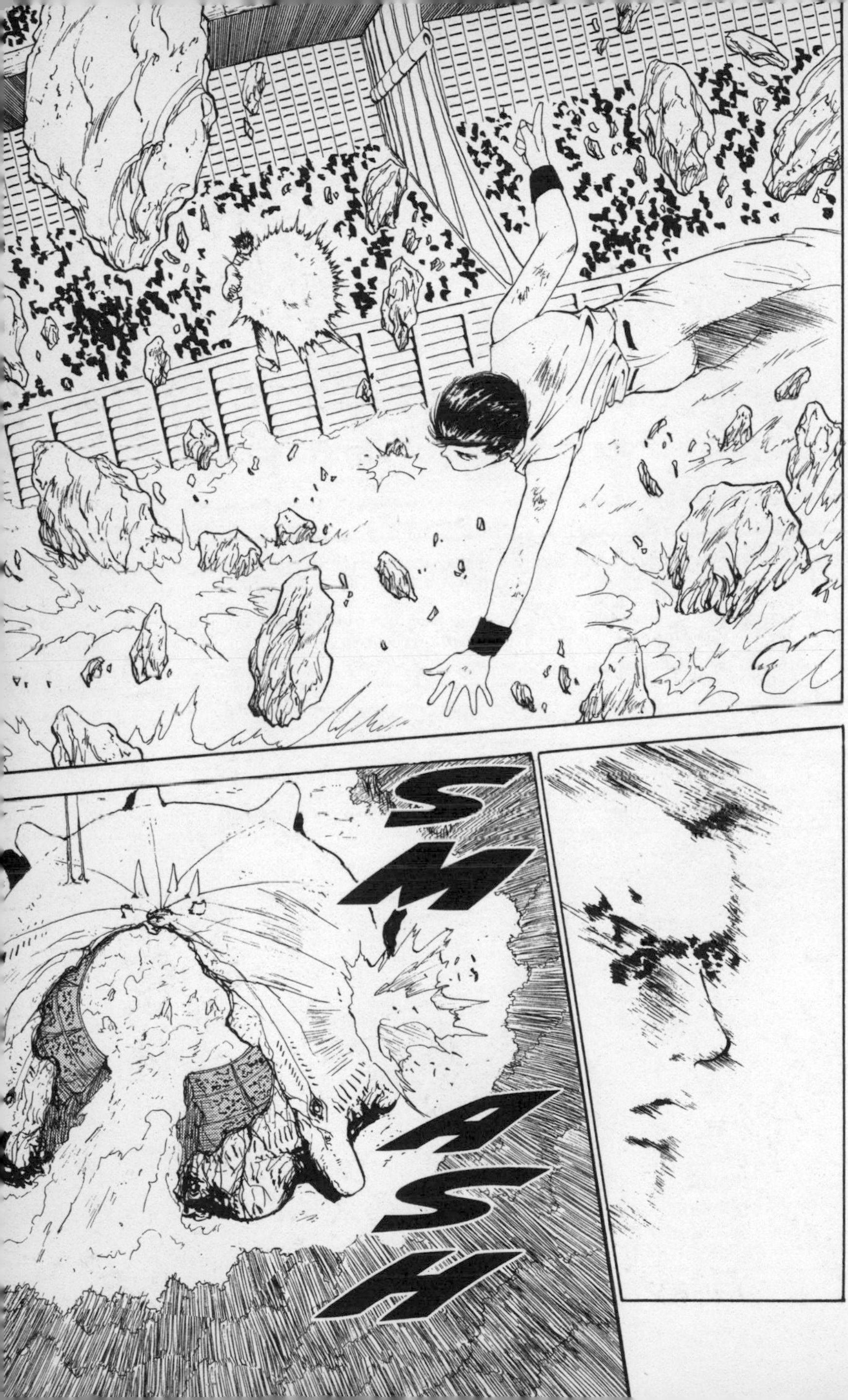
SMASH

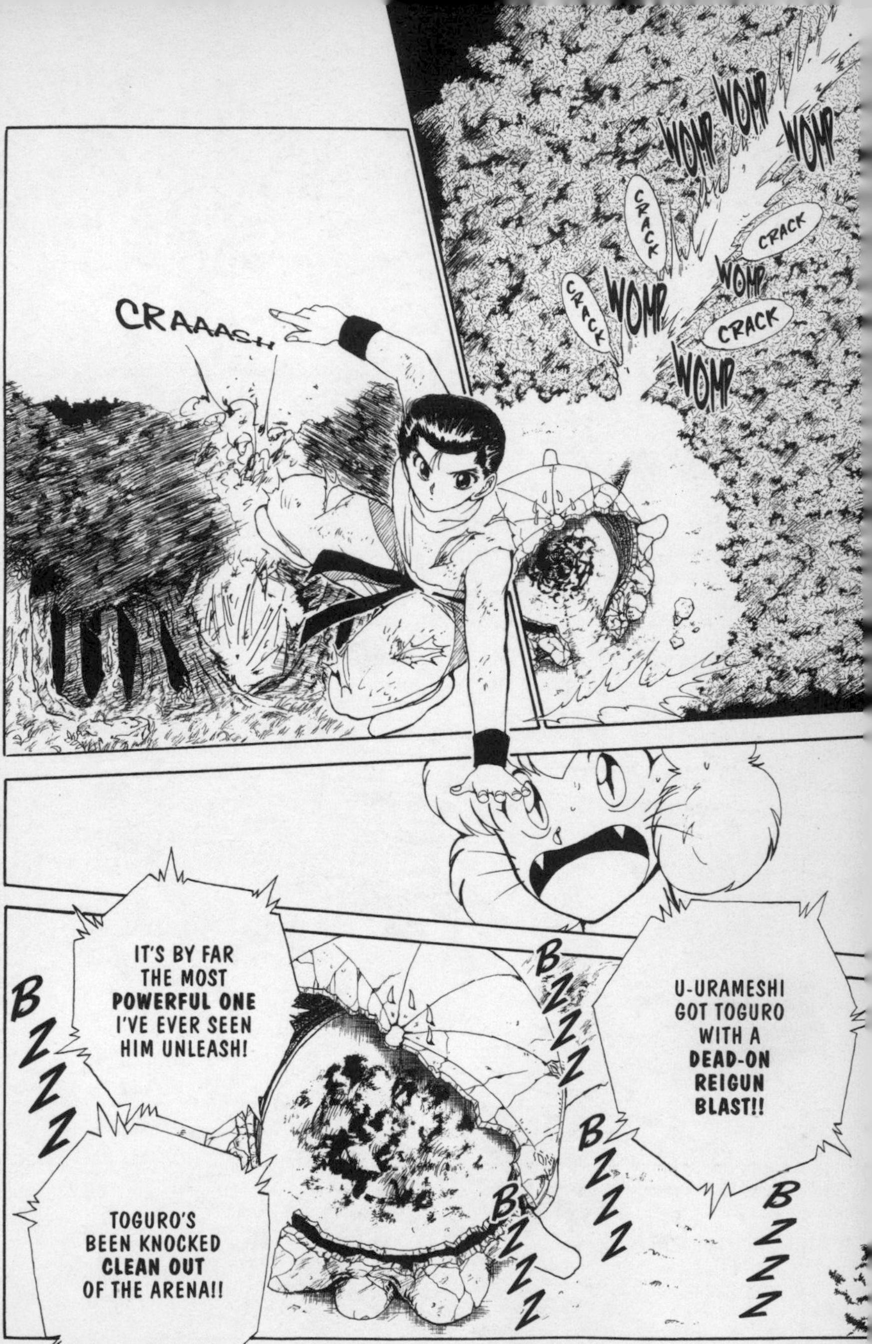
WOMP WOMP
WOMP
CRACK
CRACK
WOMP
CRACK
WOMP
CRACK
WOMP
CRAAASH
U-URAMESHI GOT TOGURO WITH A **DEAD-ON REIGUN BLAST!!**
BZZZ
BZZZ
BZZZ
IT'S BY FAR THE MOST **POWERFUL ONE** I'VE EVER SEEN HIM UNLEASH!
BZZZ
BZZZ
TOGURO'S BEEN KNOCKED **CLEAN OUT** OF THE ARENA!!

READ THIS WAY

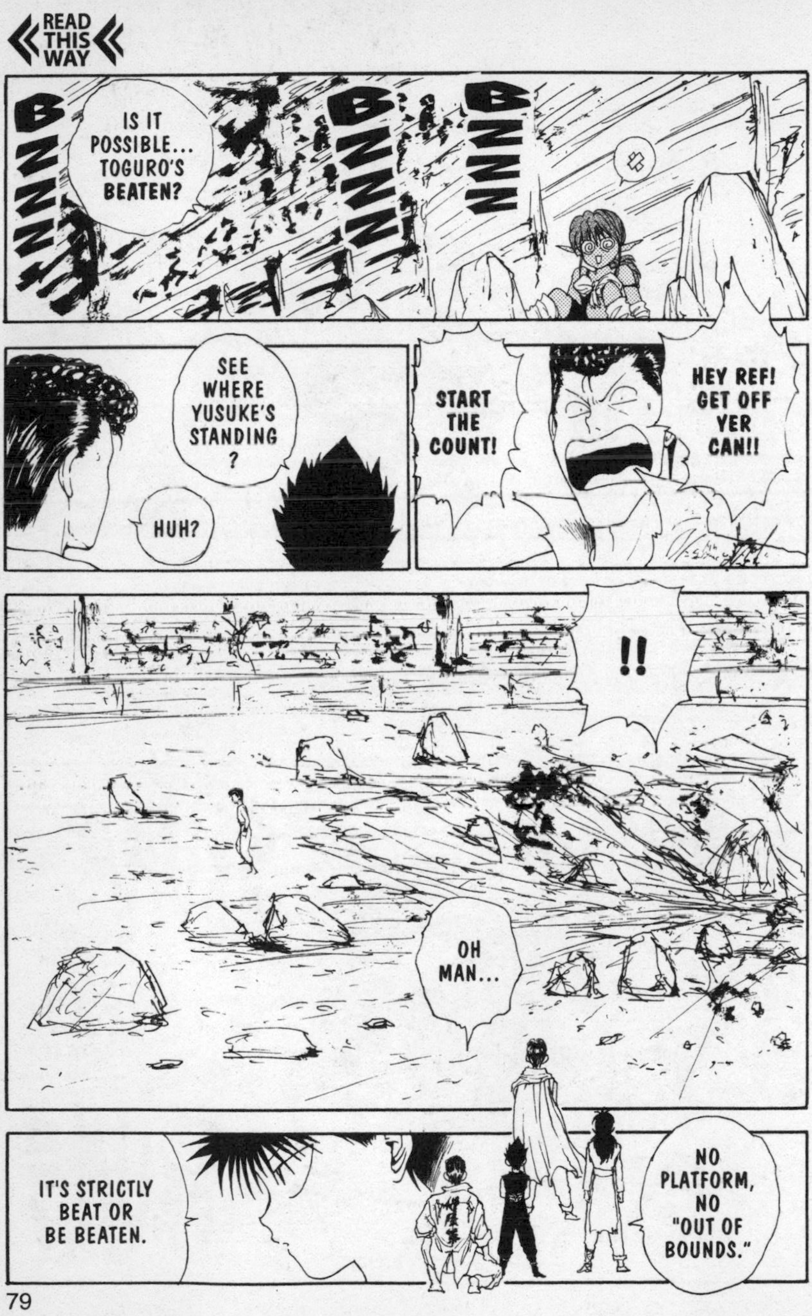

BZZZ
BZZZZ
IS IT POSSIBLE... TOGURO'S BEATEN?
BZZZZ
HEY REF! GET OFF YER CAN!!
START THE COUNT!
SEE WHERE YUSUKE'S STANDING?
HUH?
!!
OH MAN...
NO PLATFORM, NO "OUT OF BOUNDS."
IT'S STRICTLY BEAT OR BE BEATEN.

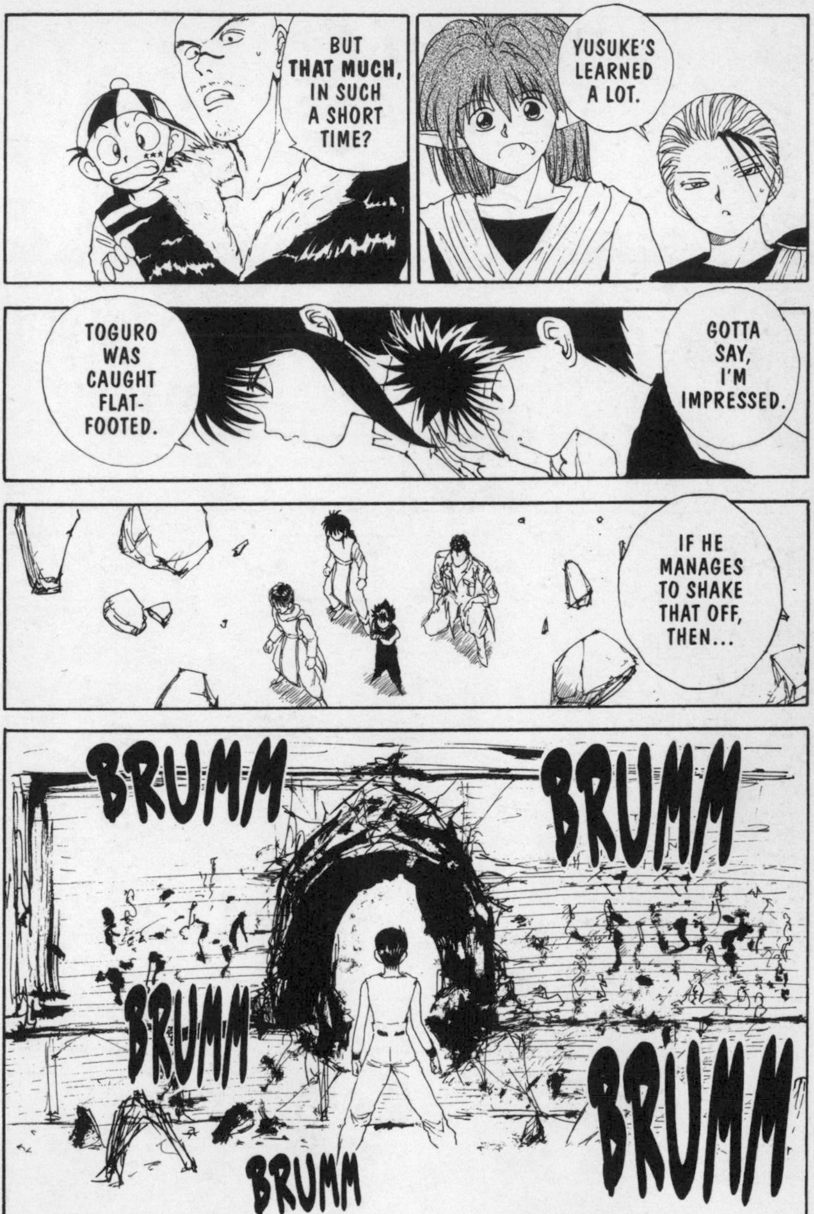
YUSUKE'S LEARNED A LOT.
BUT THAT MUCH, IN SUCH A SHORT TIME?
GOTTA SAY, I'M IMPRESSED.
TOGURO WAS CAUGHT FLAT-FOOTED.
IF HE MANAGES TO SHAKE THAT OFF, THEN...
BRUMM
BRUMM
BRUMM
BRUMM
BRUMM

READ THIS WAY

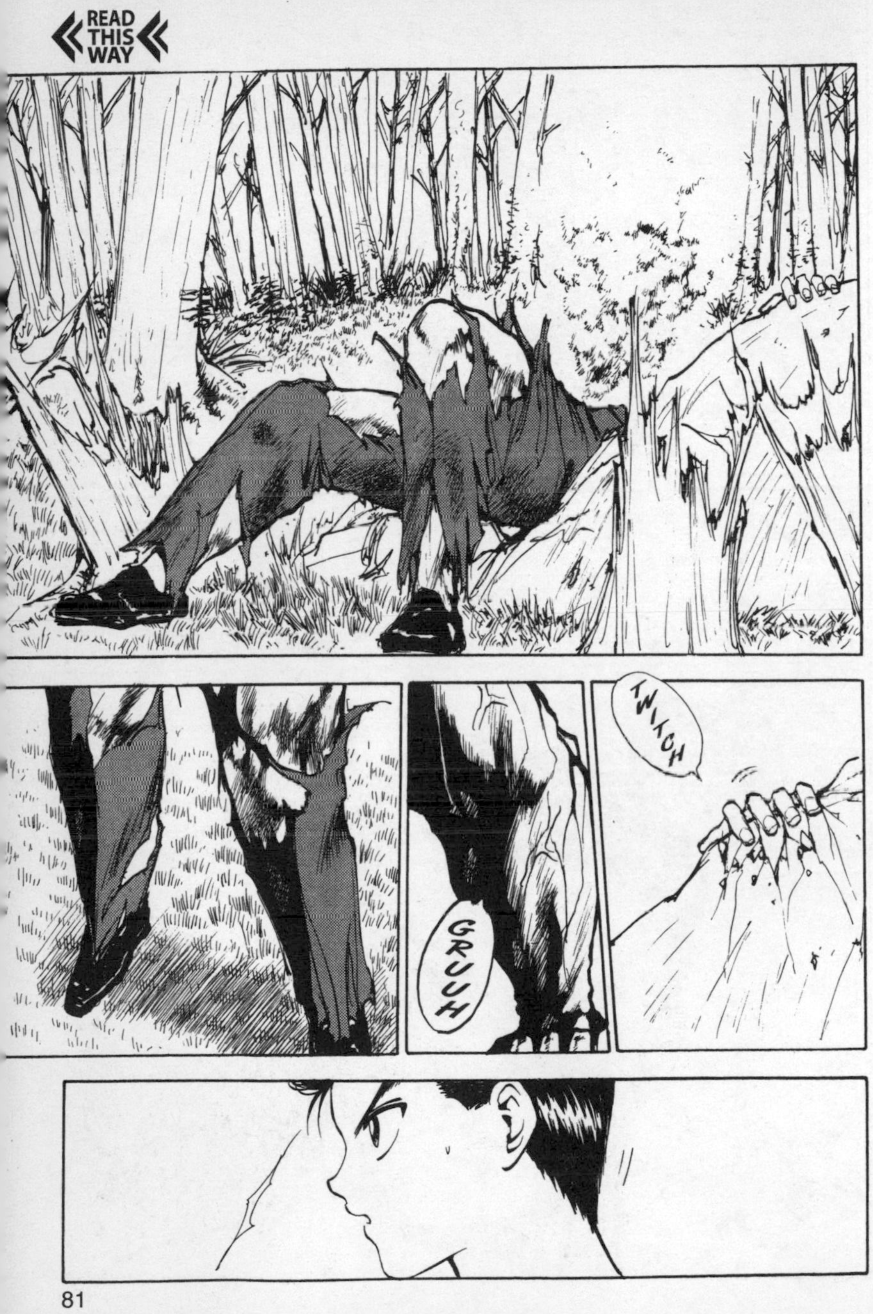
TWITCH
GRUUH

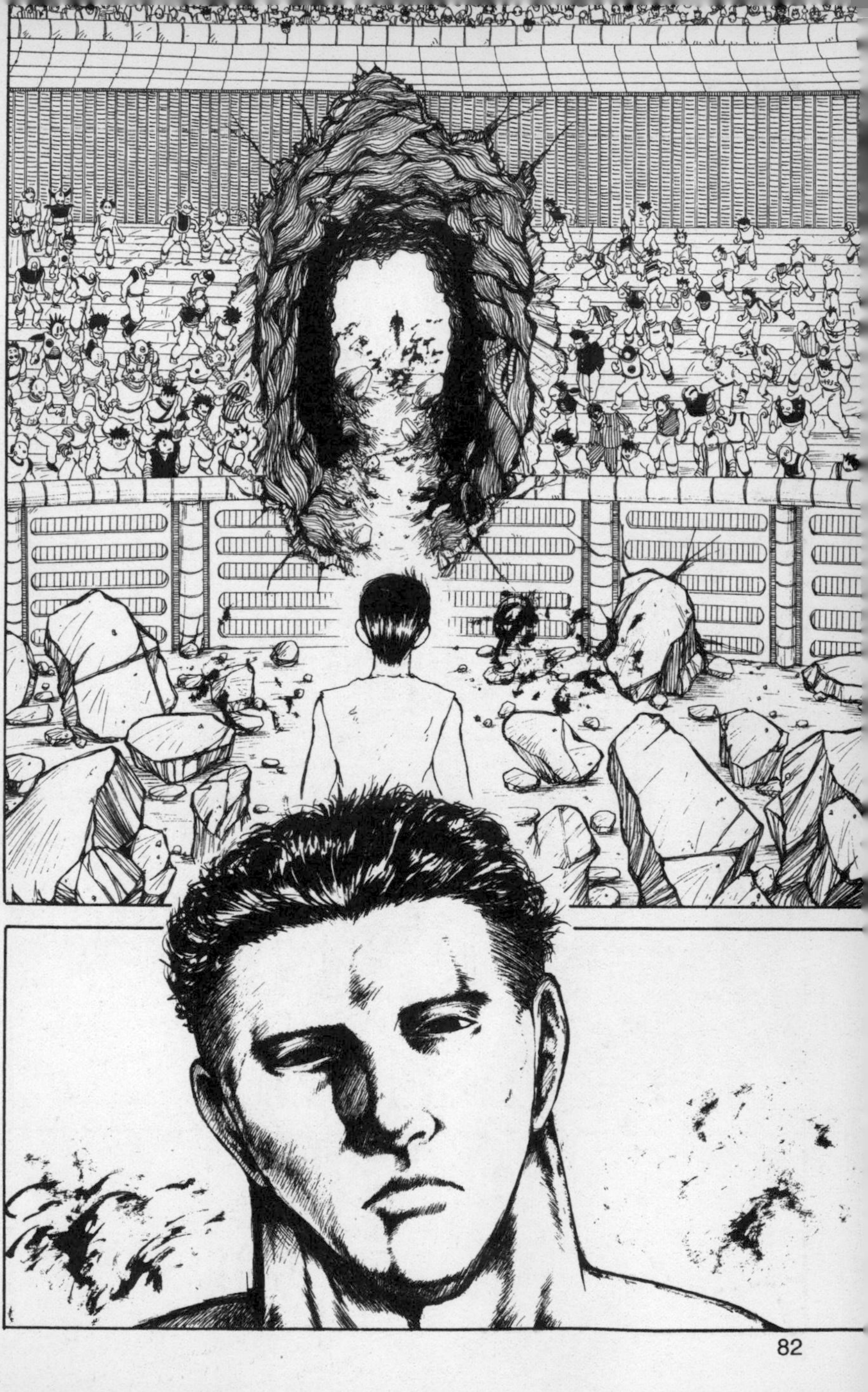

READ THIS WAY

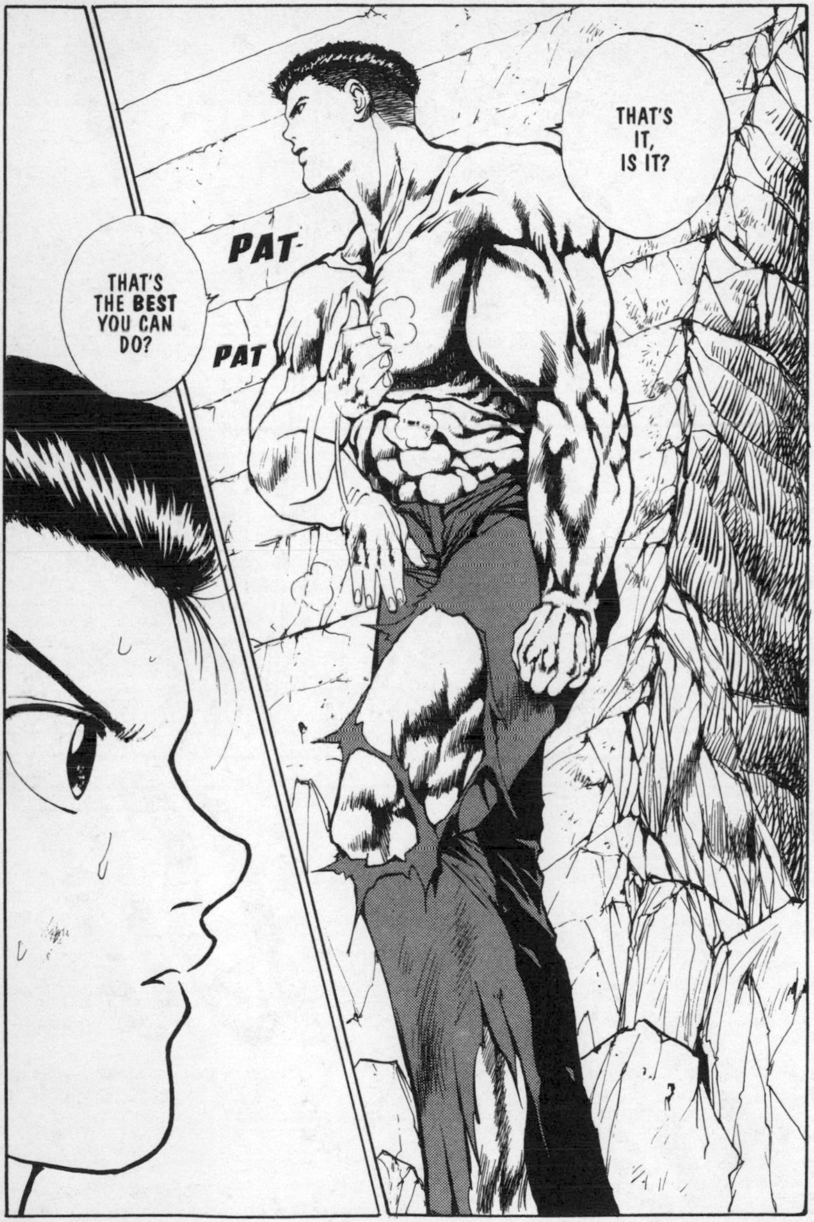
THAT'S IT, IS IT?
PAT
PAT
THAT'S THE BEST YOU CAN DO?

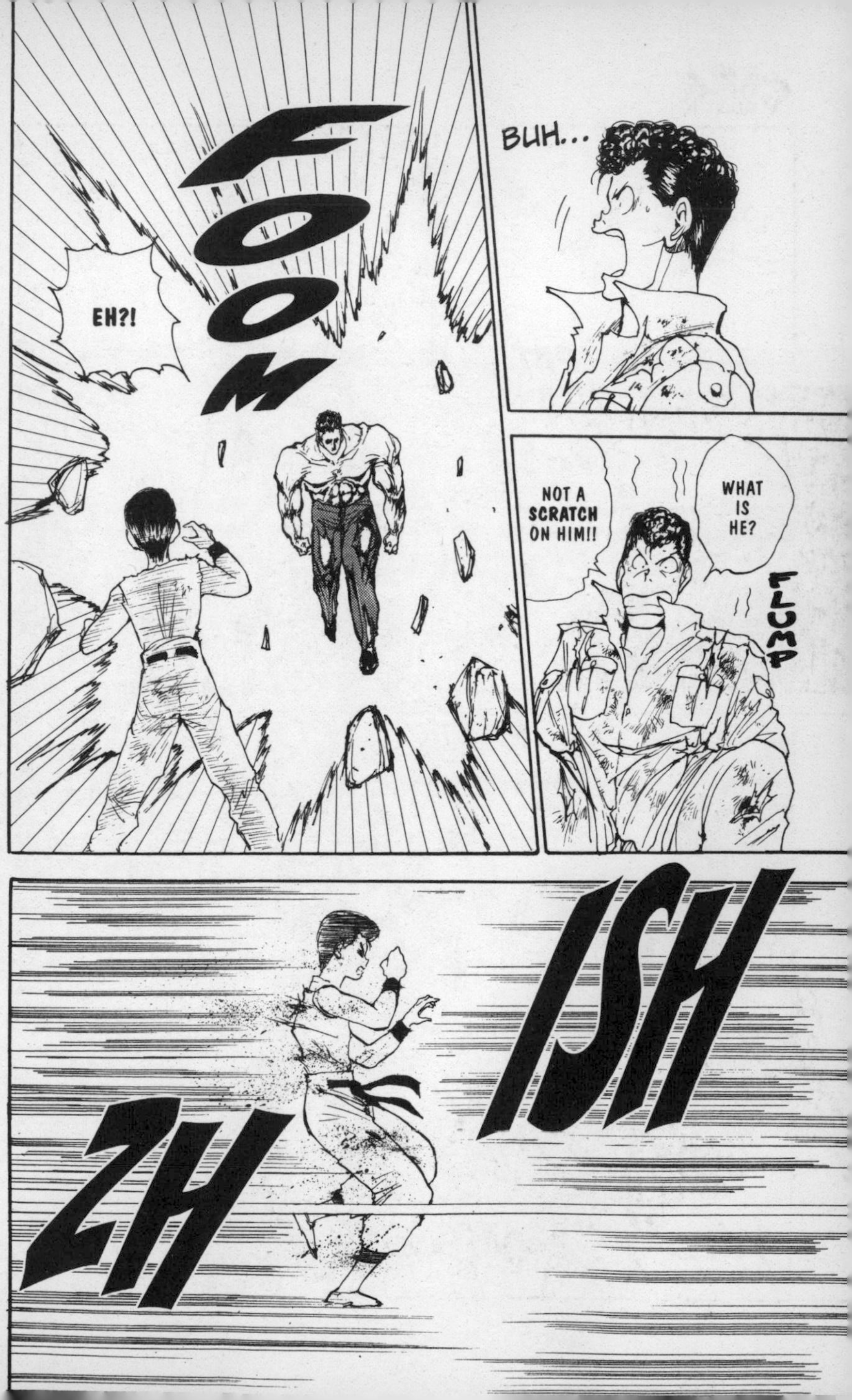
BUH...
WHAT IS HE?
NOT A SCRATCH ON HIM!!
FLUMP
FOOM
EH?!
ZH
ISH

READ THIS WAY

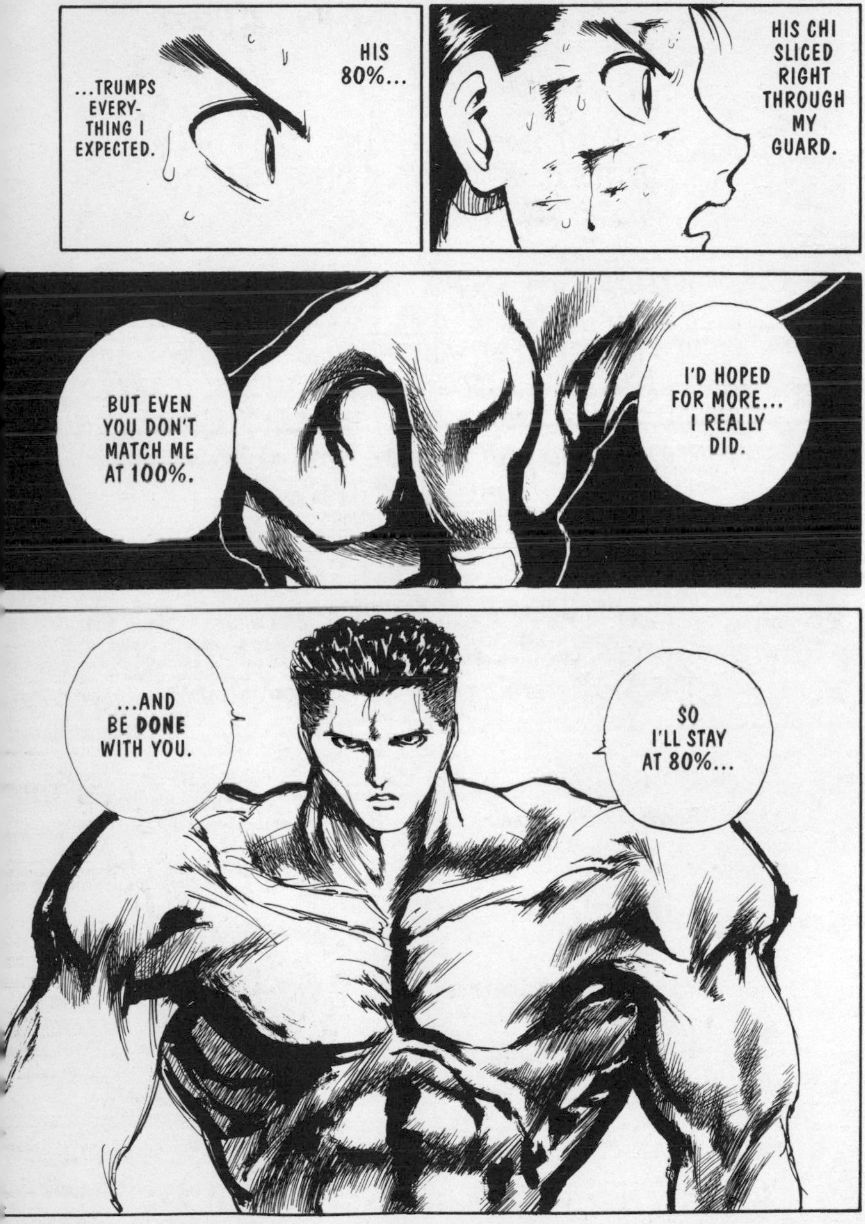

HIS CHI SLICED RIGHT THROUGH MY GUARD.
HIS 80%...
...TRUMPS EVERY-THING I EXPECTED.
I'D HOPED FOR MORE... I REALLY DID.
BUT EVEN YOU DON'T MATCH ME AT 100%.
SO I'LL STAY AT 80%...
...AND BE **DONE** WITH YOU.

ANSWER TO YUYU HAKUSHO PUZZLES: 2

HINT: ONLY ONE PERSON IS LYING. FIND HIM AND YOU'LL FIGURE OUT THE ANSWER TO THE SECOND QUESTION.

HOW TO SOLVE IT: SUPPOSE THAT KURAMA IS LYING. THEN HE MUST'VE WON. KUWABARA WOULD BE TELLING THE TRUTH, SO HE'S THIRD. HIEI WOULD ALSO BE TELLING THE TRUTH, SO HE'S SECOND. BUT THEN YUSUKE WOULD HAVE TO BE FOURTH, AND IT DOESN'T ADD UP BECAUSE THAT WOULD MAKE HIM A SECOND LIAR. THEREFORE, KURAMA IS NOT LYING.

ANSWER: REPEAT THE PROCESS AND KEEP ELIMINATING THE CHOICES, UNTIL YUSUKE IS THE ONLY ONE LEFT. THEREFORE, THEY PLACE IN THE ORDER OF:

1ST:	2ND:	3RD:	4TH:
YUSUKE	KUWABARA	HIEI	KURAMA

I BEAT **THREE** PEOPLE, NOT TWO.

● THE PUZZLE APPEARS IN MANGA VOLUME 11, P.88.

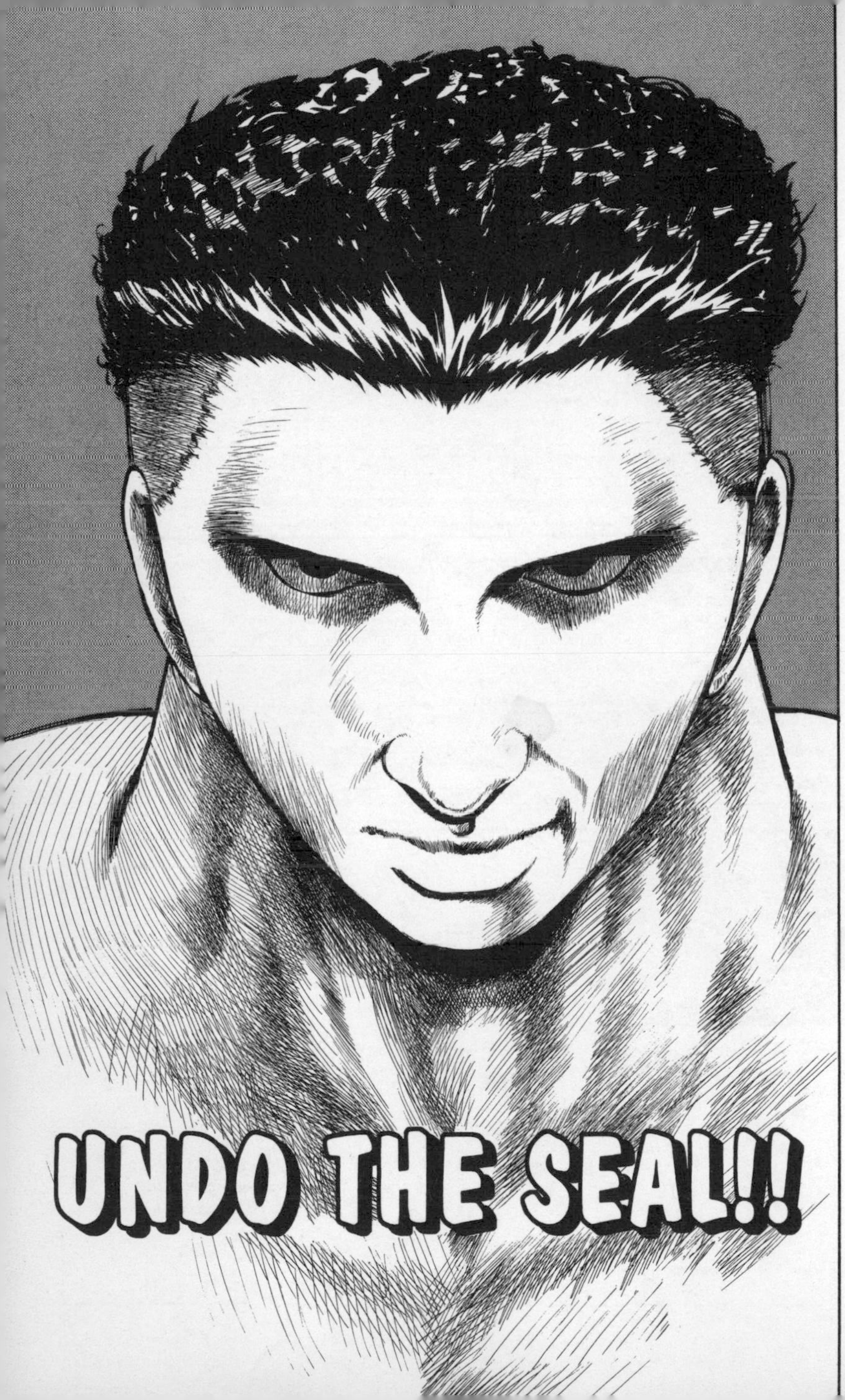
UNDO THE SEAL!!

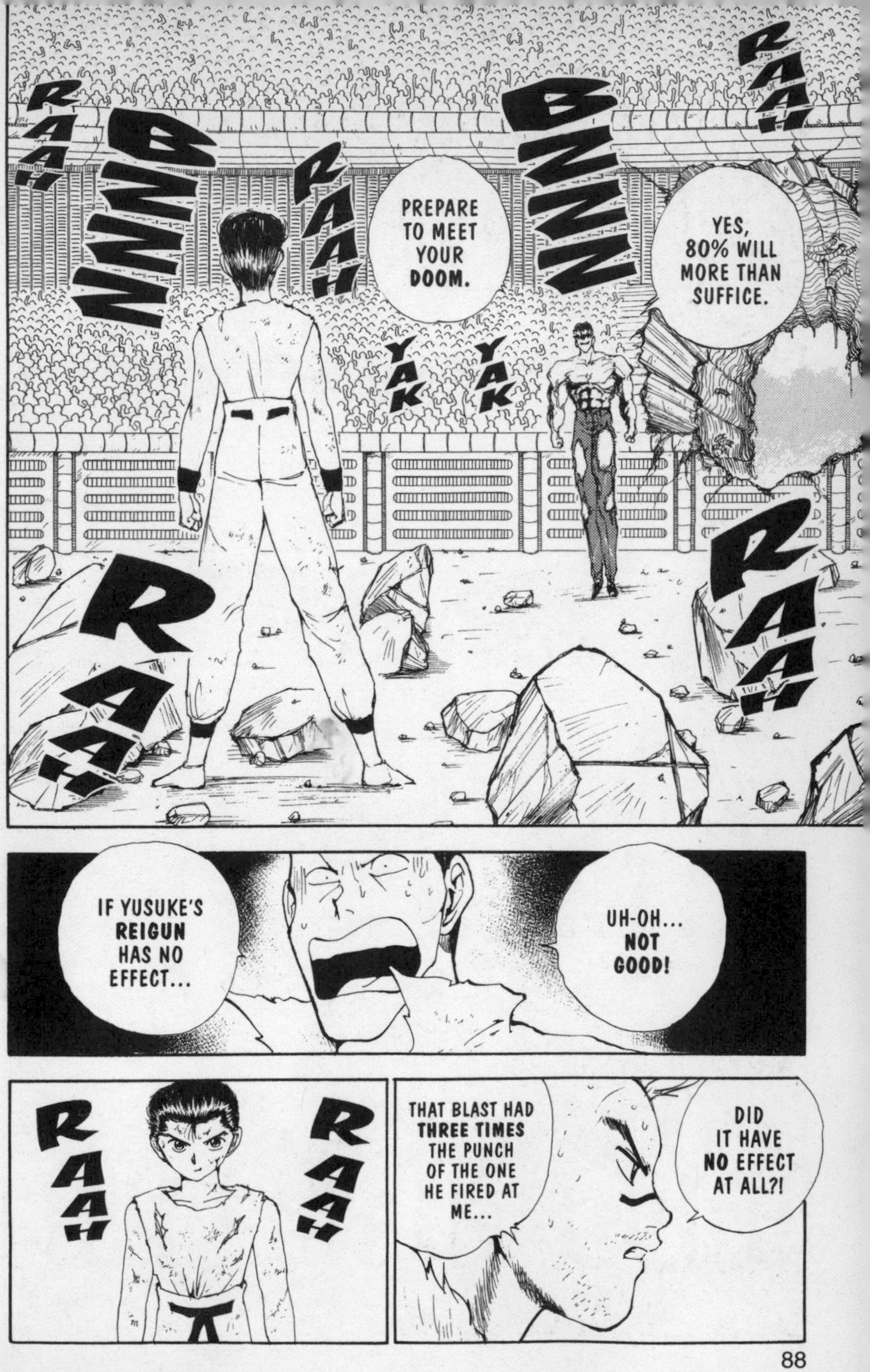
RAAH
YES, 80% WILL MORE THAN SUFFICE.
PREPARE TO MEET YOUR DOOM.
RAAH
RAAH!
YAK YAK
RAAH
RAAH
UH-OH... NOT GOOD!
IF YUSUKE'S REIGUN HAS NO EFFECT...
DID IT HAVE NO EFFECT AT ALL?!
THAT BLAST HAD THREE TIMES THE PUNCH OF THE ONE HE FIRED AT ME...
RAAH
RAAH

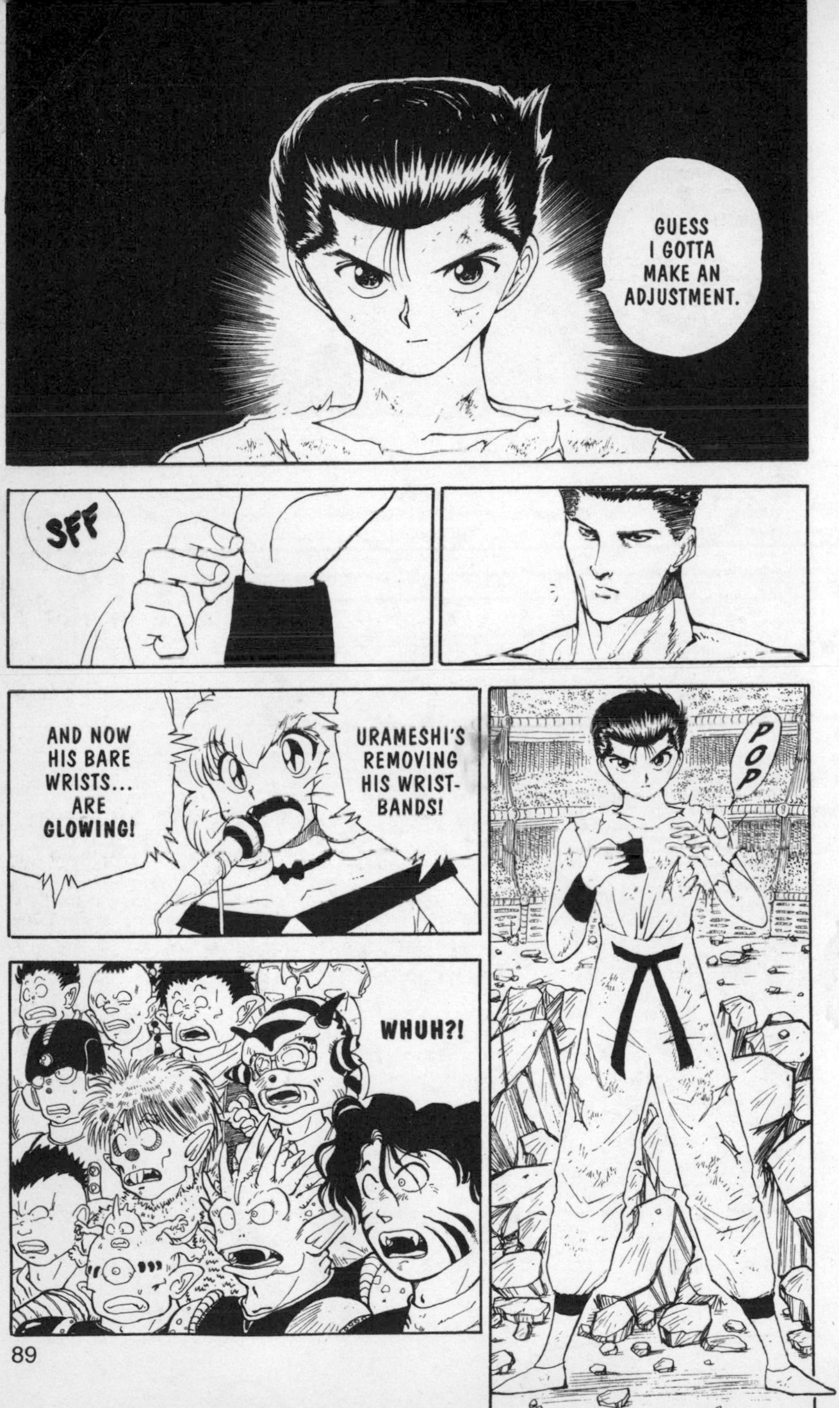
GUESS I GOTTA MAKE AN ADJUSTMENT.
SFF
POP
URAMESHI'S REMOVING HIS WRIST-BANDS!
AND NOW HIS BARE WRISTS... ARE GLOWING!
WHUH?!

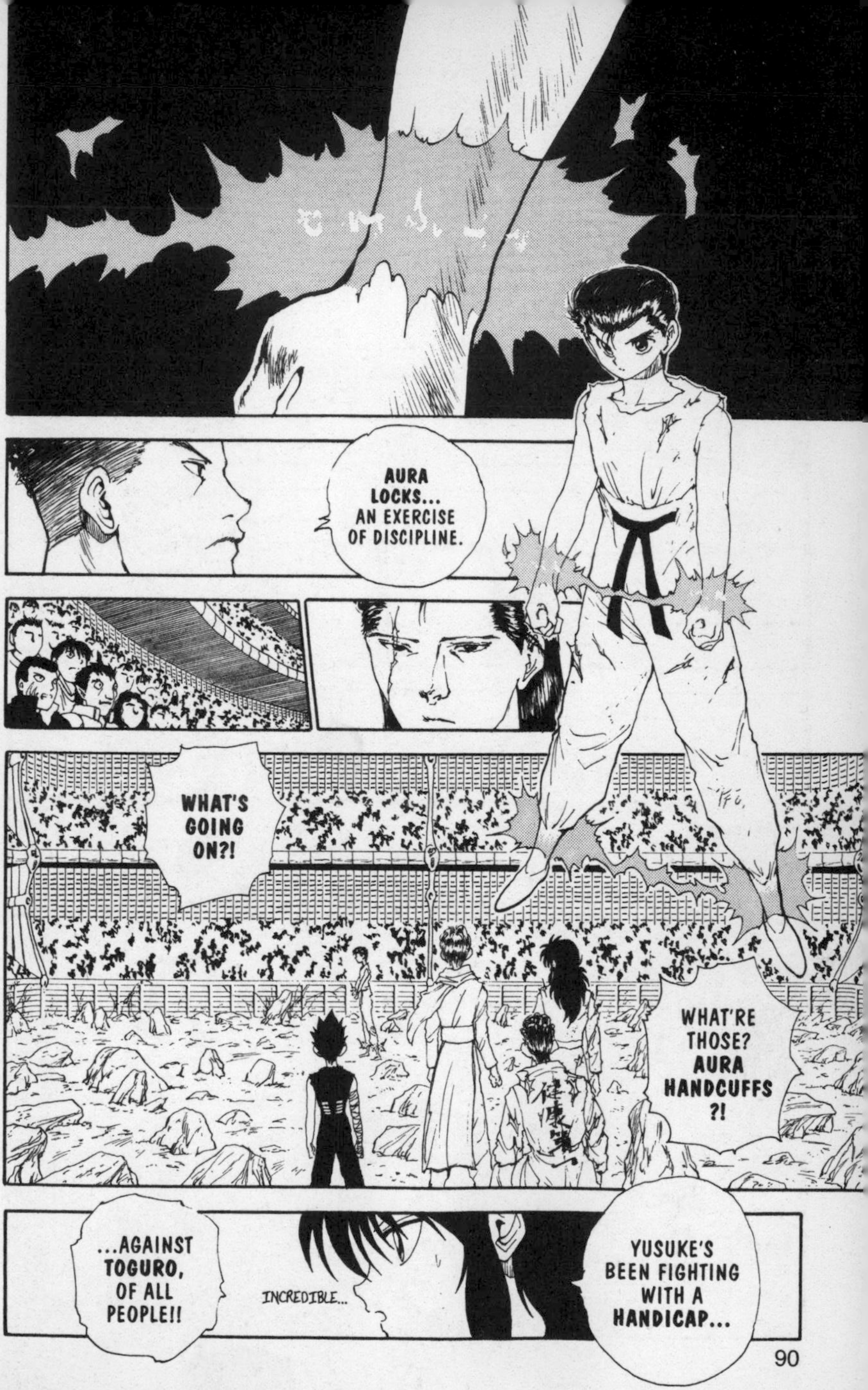
AURA LOCKS... AN EXERCISE OF DISCIPLINE.
WHAT'S GOING ON?!
WHAT'RE THOSE? AURA HANDCUFFS ?!
YUSUKE'S BEEN FIGHTING WITH A HANDICAP...
INCREDIBLE...
...AGAINST TOGURO, OF ALL PEOPLE!!

READ THIS WAY

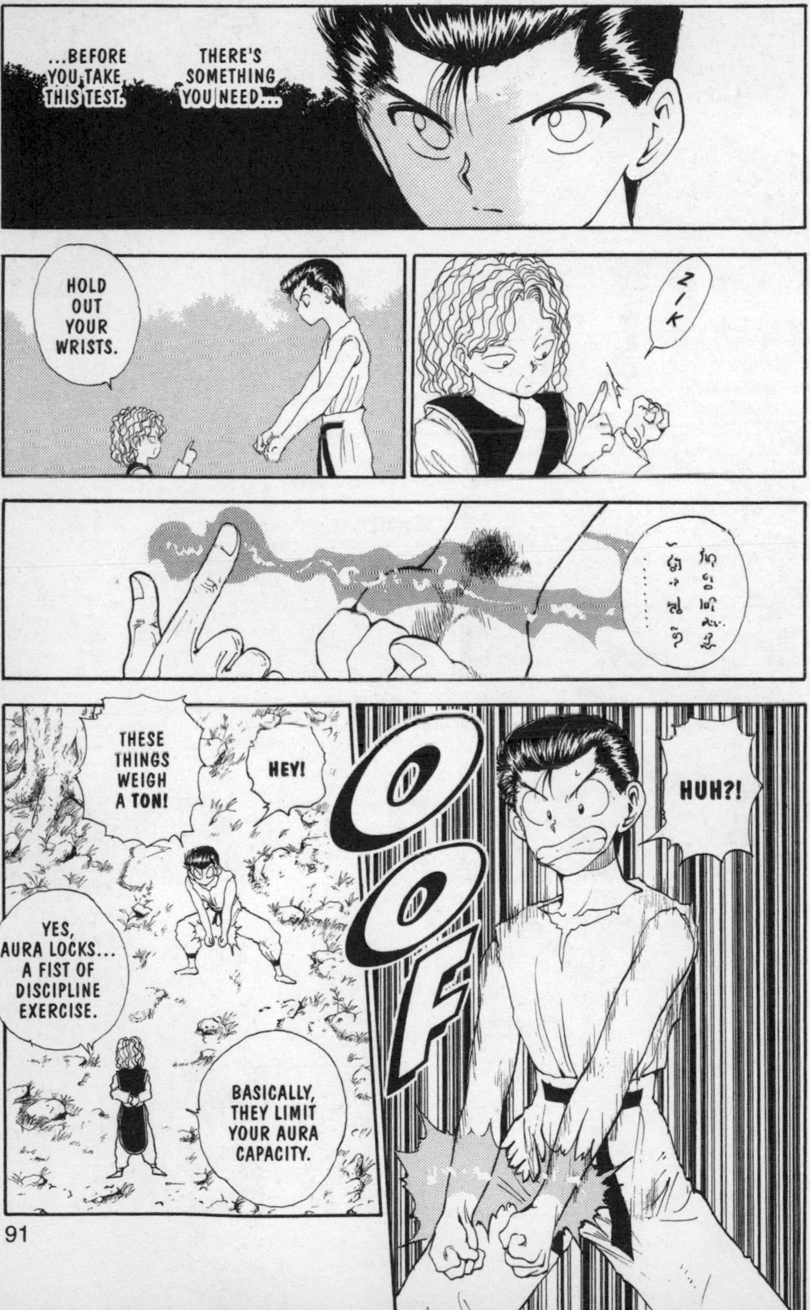
THERE'S SOMETHING YOU NEED...
...BEFORE YOU TAKE THIS TEST.
ZIK
HOLD OUT YOUR WRISTS.
HUH?!
OOF
HEY!
THESE THINGS WEIGH A TON!
YES, AURA LOCKS... A FIST OF DISCIPLINE EXERCISE.
BASICALLY, THEY LIMIT YOUR AURA CAPACITY.

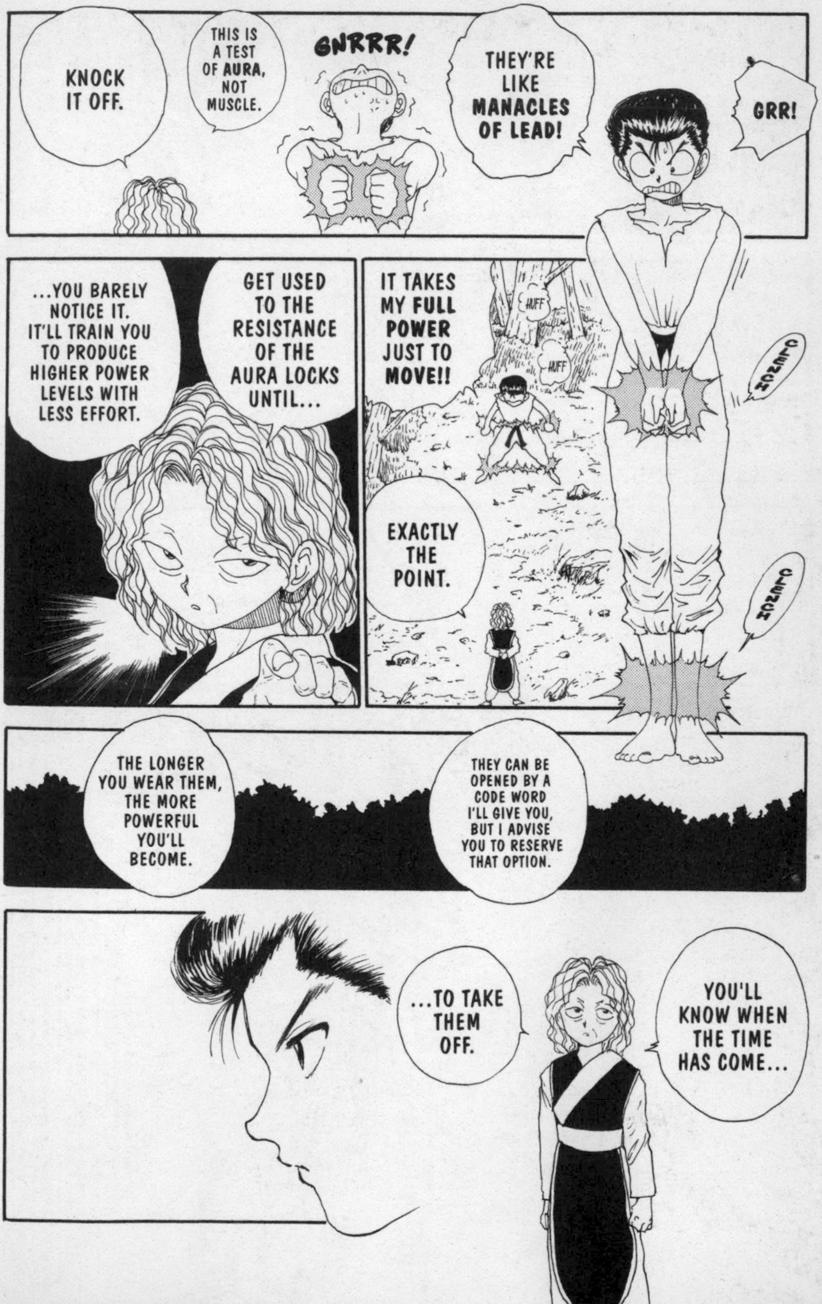
GRR!
THEY'RE LIKE MANACLES OF LEAD!
GNRRR!
THIS IS A TEST OF AURA, NOT MUSCLE.
KNOCK IT OFF.
CLENCH
CLENCH
IT TAKES MY FULL POWER JUST TO MOVE!!
HUFF
HUFF
EXACTLY THE POINT.
GET USED TO THE RESISTANCE OF THE AURA LOCKS UNTIL...
...YOU BARELY NOTICE IT. IT'LL TRAIN YOU TO PRODUCE HIGHER POWER LEVELS WITH LESS EFFORT.
THEY CAN BE OPENED BY A CODE WORD I'LL GIVE YOU, BUT I ADVISE YOU TO RESERVE THAT OPTION.
THE LONGER YOU WEAR THEM, THE MORE POWERFUL YOU'LL BECOME.
YOU'LL KNOW WHEN THE TIME HAS COME...
...TO TAKE THEM OFF.

READ THIS WAY

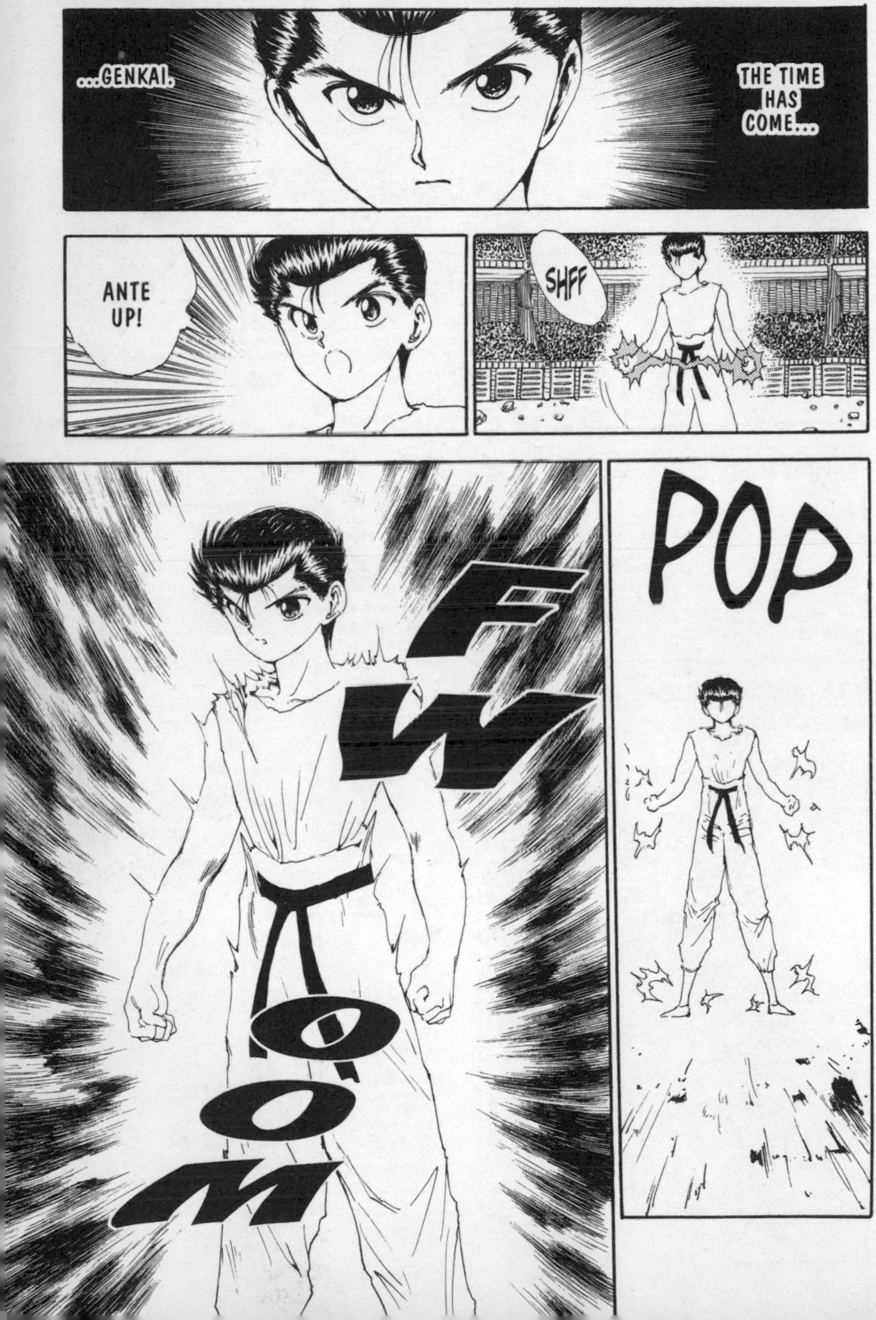
THE TIME HAS COME...
...GENKAI.
SHFF
ANTE UP!
POP
FWOOM

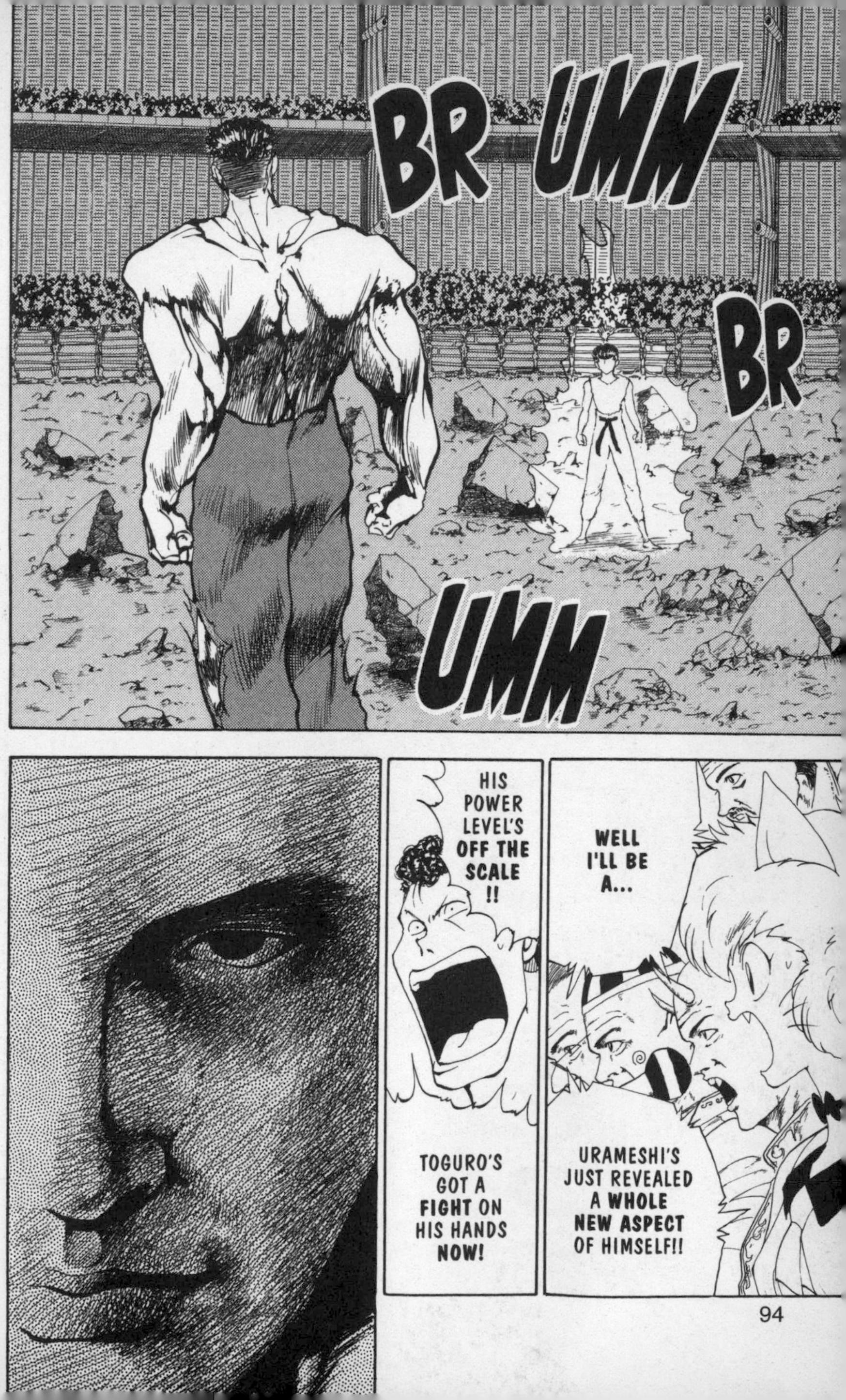
BRUMM
BRUMM
WELL I'LL BE A...
URAMESHI'S JUST REVEALED A WHOLE NEW ASPECT OF HIMSELF!!
HIS POWER LEVEL'S OFF THE SCALE!!
TOGURO'S GOT A FIGHT ON HIS HANDS NOW!

READ THIS WAY

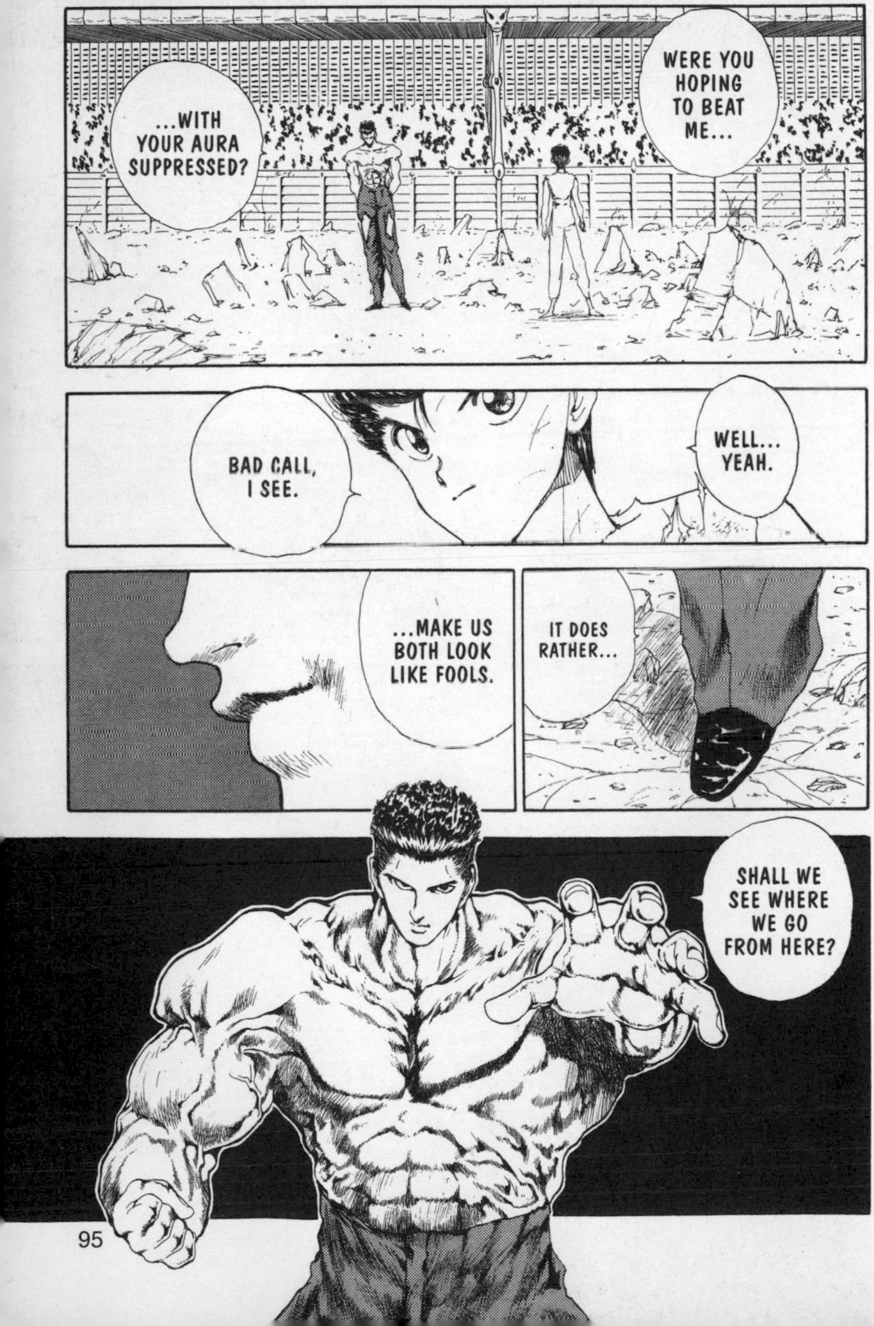
WERE YOU HOPING TO BEAT ME...
...WITH YOUR AURA SUPPRESSED?
WELL... YEAH.
BAD CALL, I SEE.
IT DOES RATHER...
...MAKE US BOTH LOOK LIKE FOOLS.
SHALL WE SEE WHERE WE GO FROM HERE?

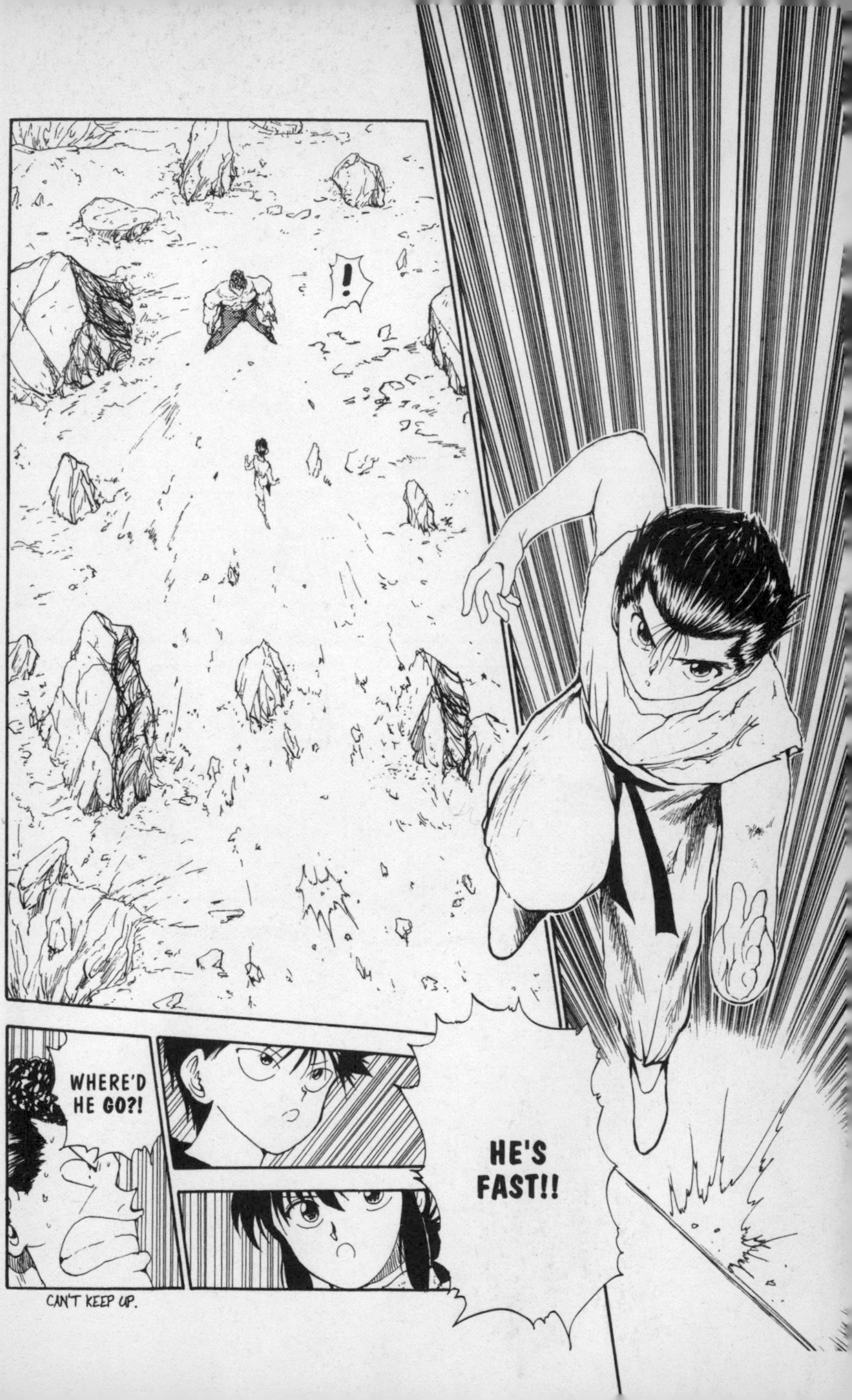
HE'S FAST!!
!
WHERE'D HE GO?!
CAN'T KEEP UP.

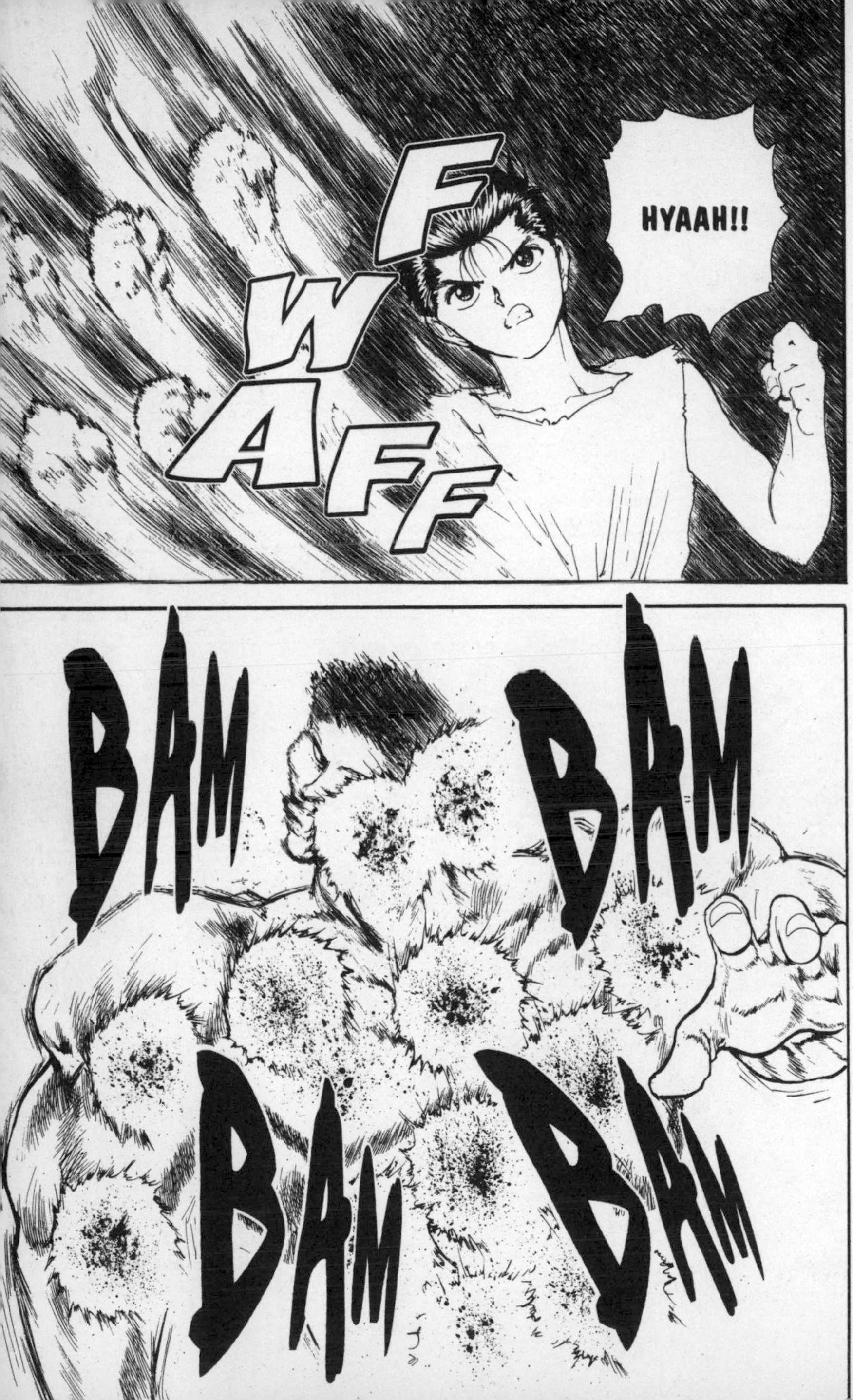
HYAAH!!
FWAFF
BAM
BAM
BAM
BAM

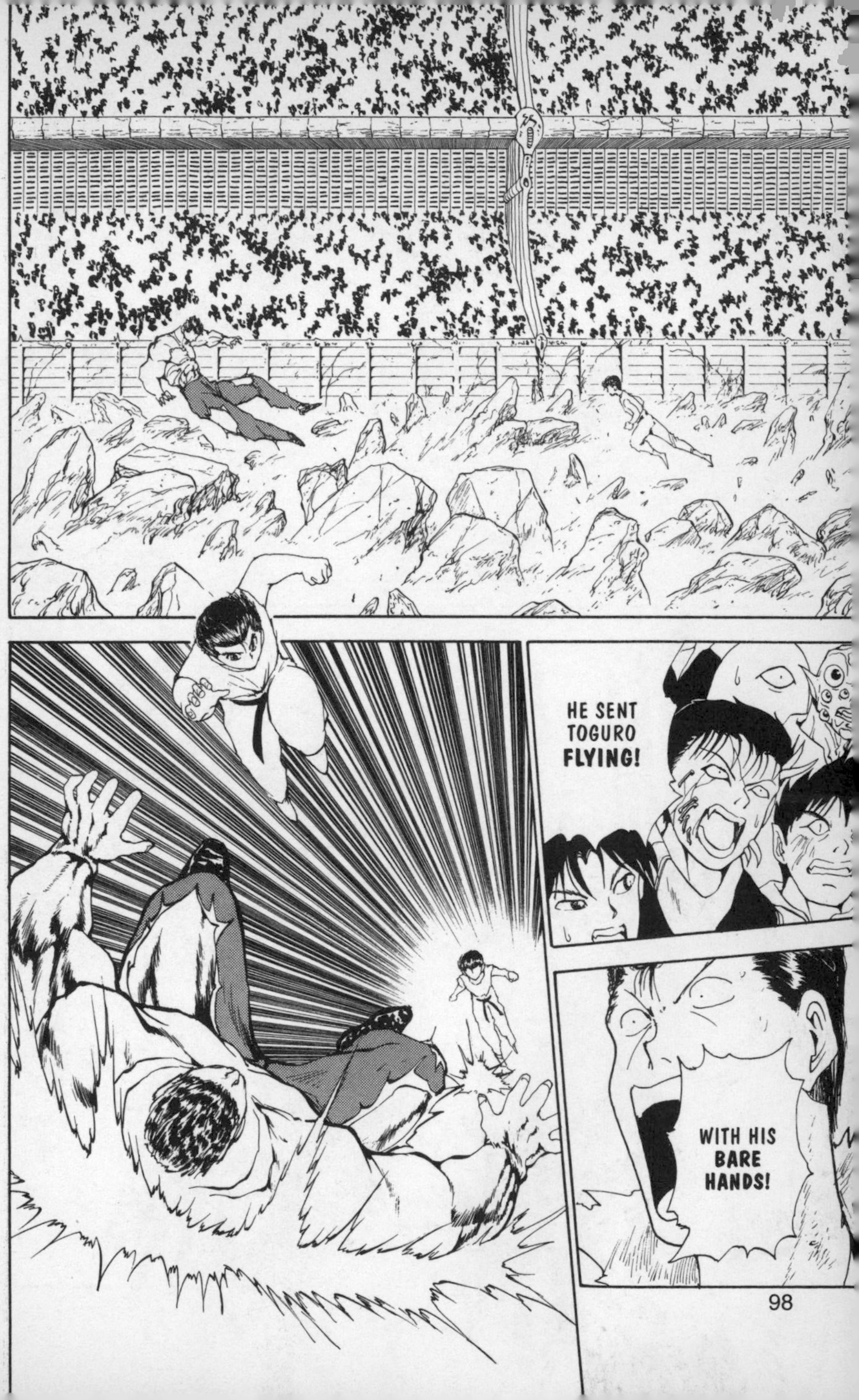
HE SENT TOGURO FLYING!
WITH HIS BARE HANDS!

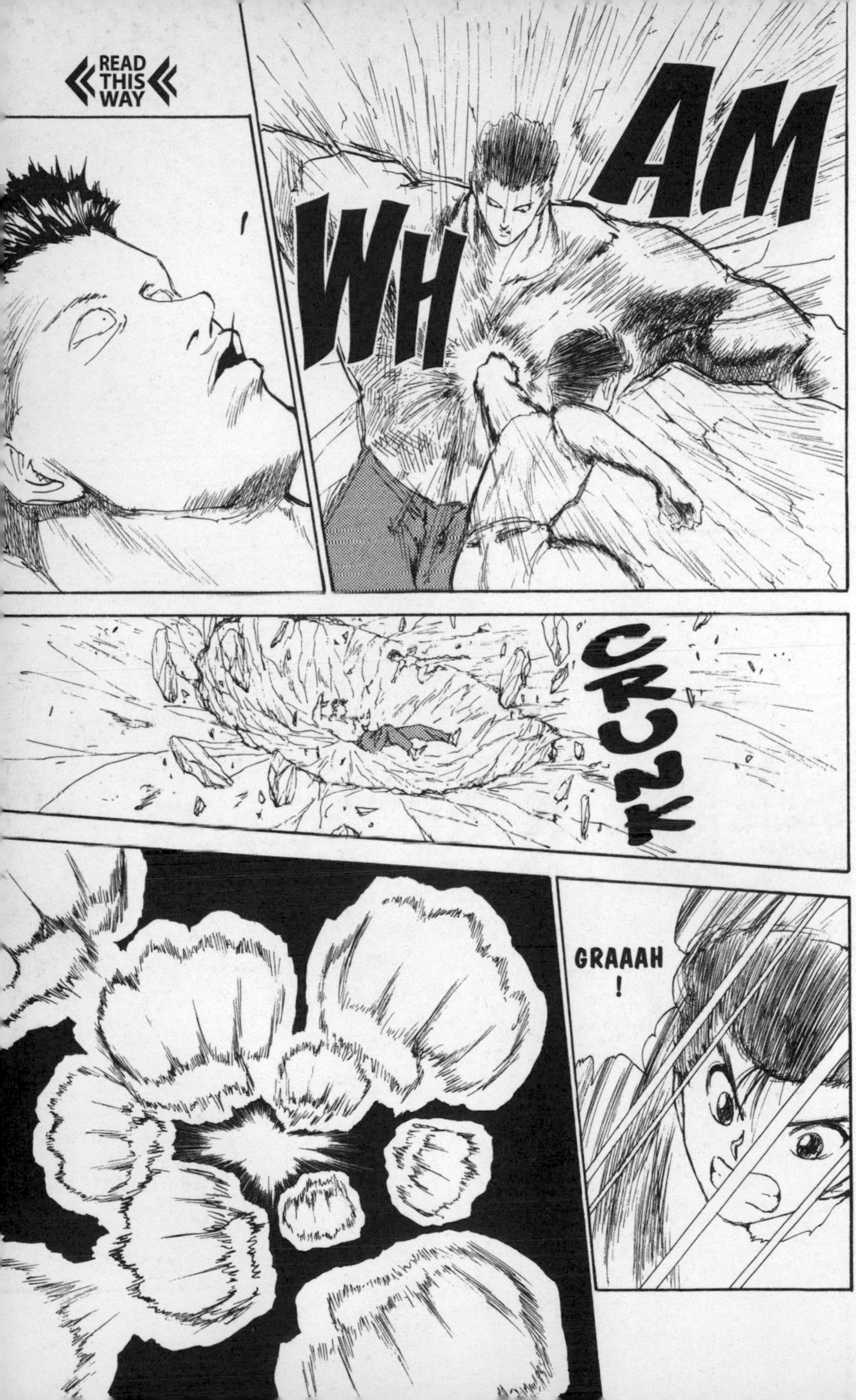
READ THIS WAY
WHAM
CRUNK
GRAAAH!

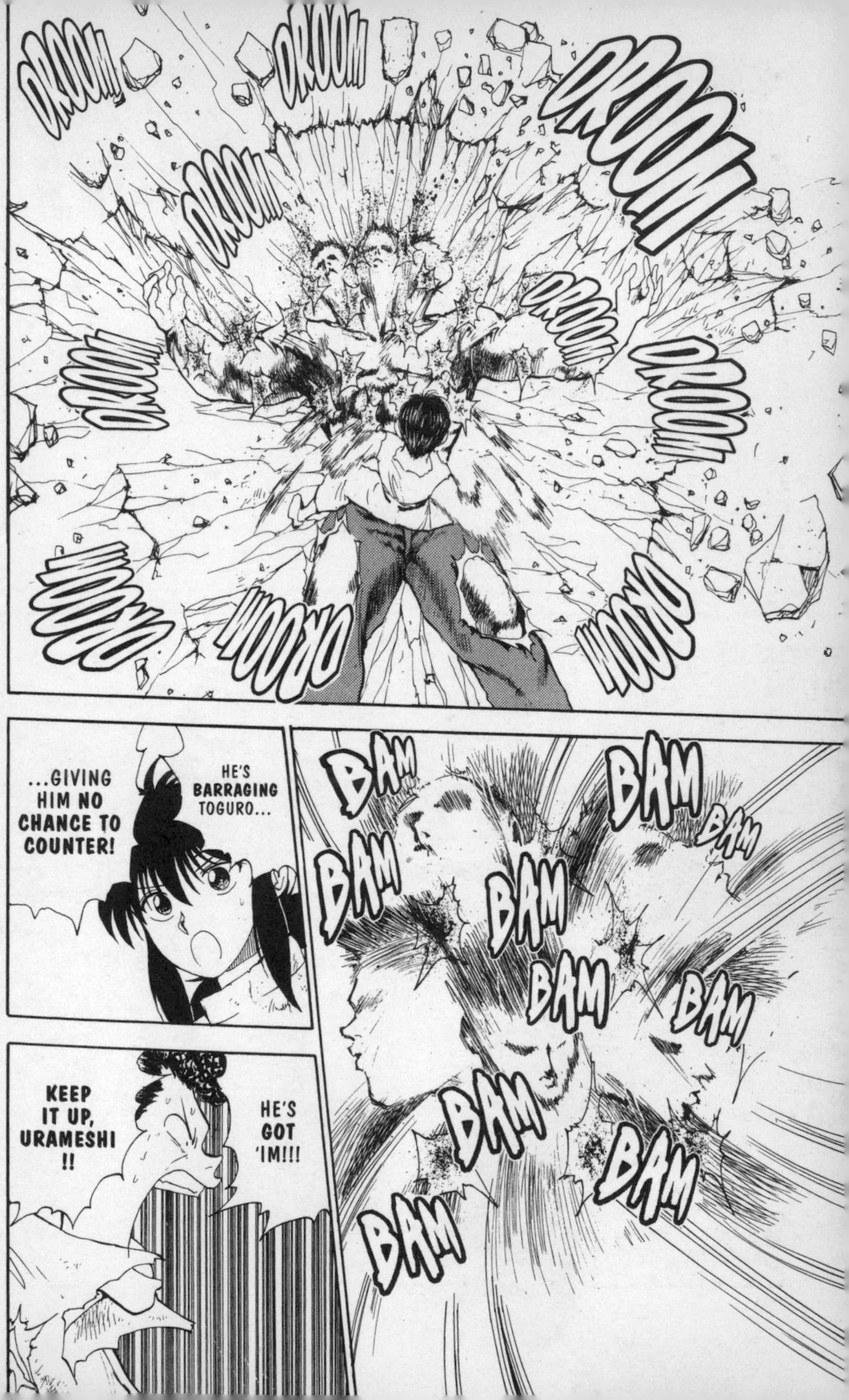
DROOM
DROOM
DROOM
DROOM
DROOM
DROOM
DROOM
DROOM
DROOM
DROOM
BAM
BAM
BAM
BAM
BAM
BAM
BAM
BAM
BAM
BAM
BAM
HE'S BARRAGING TOGURO...
...GIVING HIM NO CHANCE TO COUNTER!
HE'S GOT 'IM!!!
KEEP IT UP, URAMESHI !!

READ THIS WAY

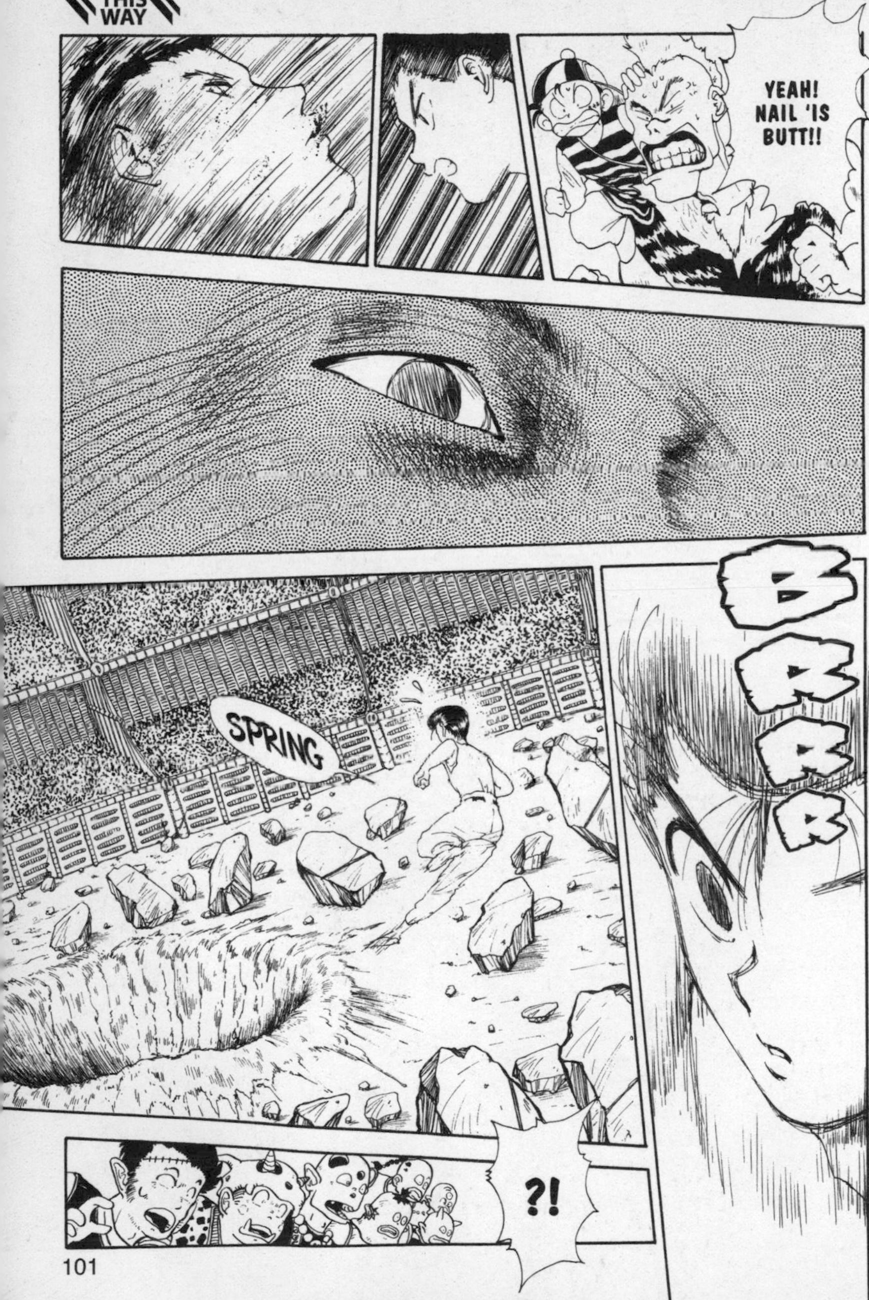
YEAH! NAIL 'IS BUTT!!
BRRR
SPRING
?!

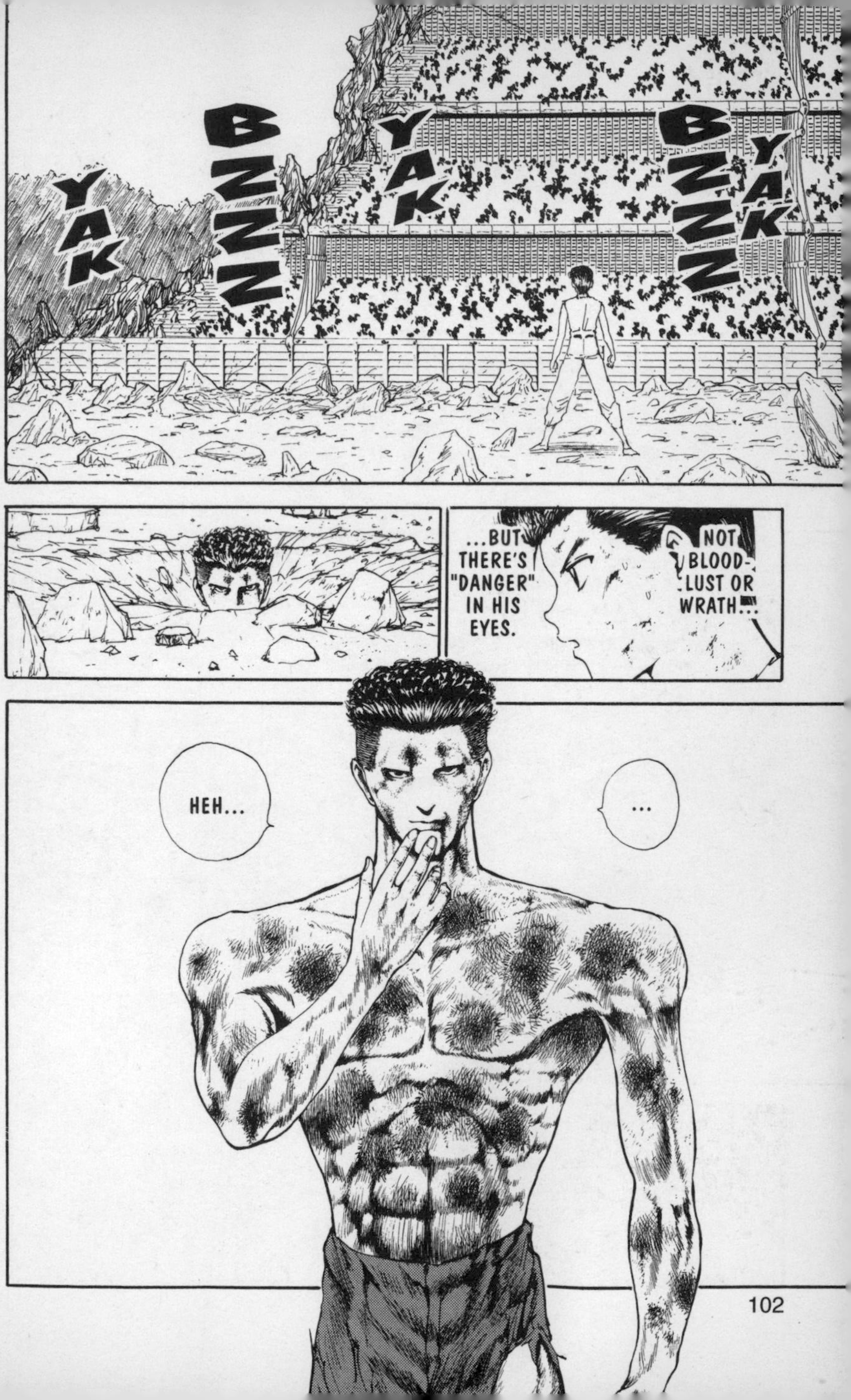

BZZZ
YAK
YAK
BZZZ
YAK
NOT BLOOD-LUST OR WRATH...
...BUT THERE'S "DANGER" IN HIS EYES.
...
HEH...

READ THIS WAY

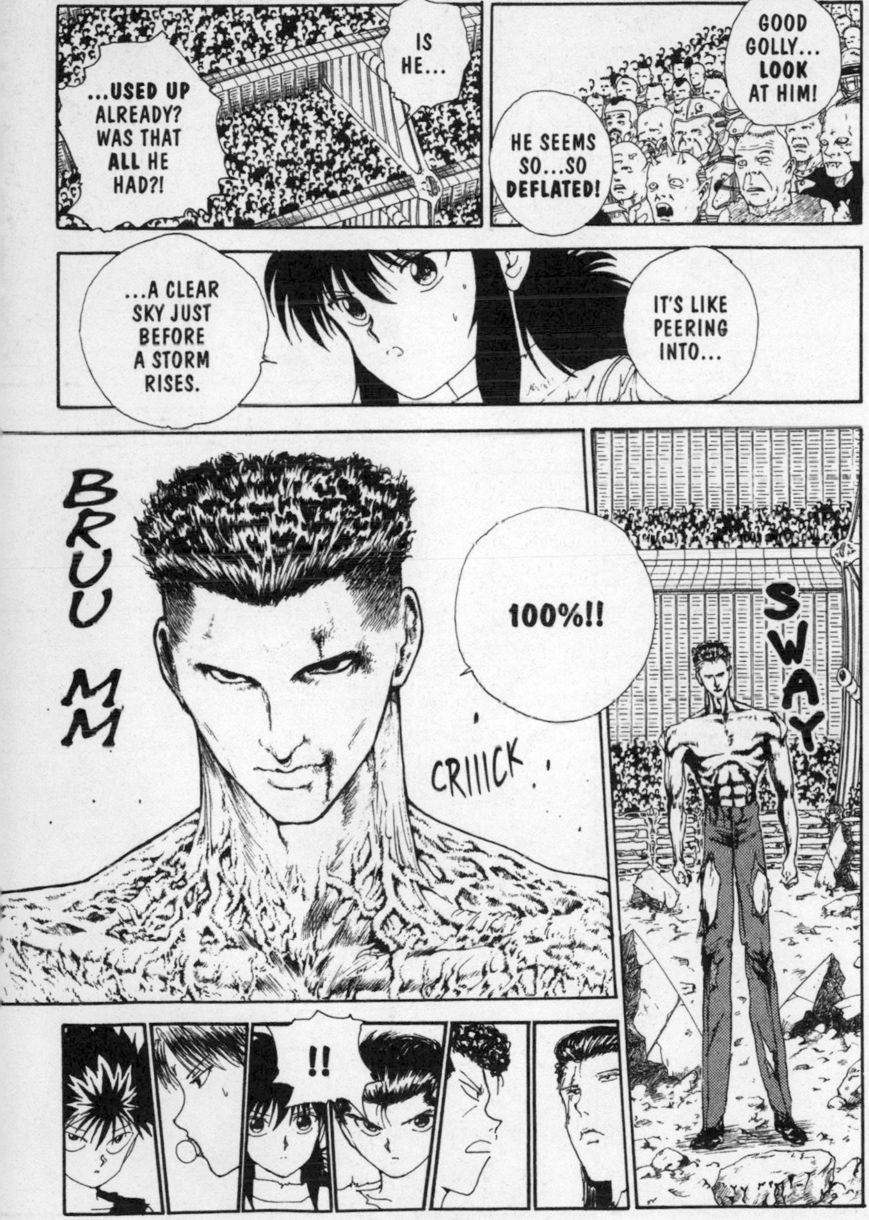
GOOD GOLLY... LOOK AT HIM!
HE SEEMS SO...SO DEFLATED!
IS HE...
...USED UP ALREADY? WAS THAT ALL HE HAD?!
IT'S LIKE PEERING INTO...
...A CLEAR SKY JUST BEFORE A STORM RISES.
SWAY
BRUUMM
100%!!
CRIIICK
!!

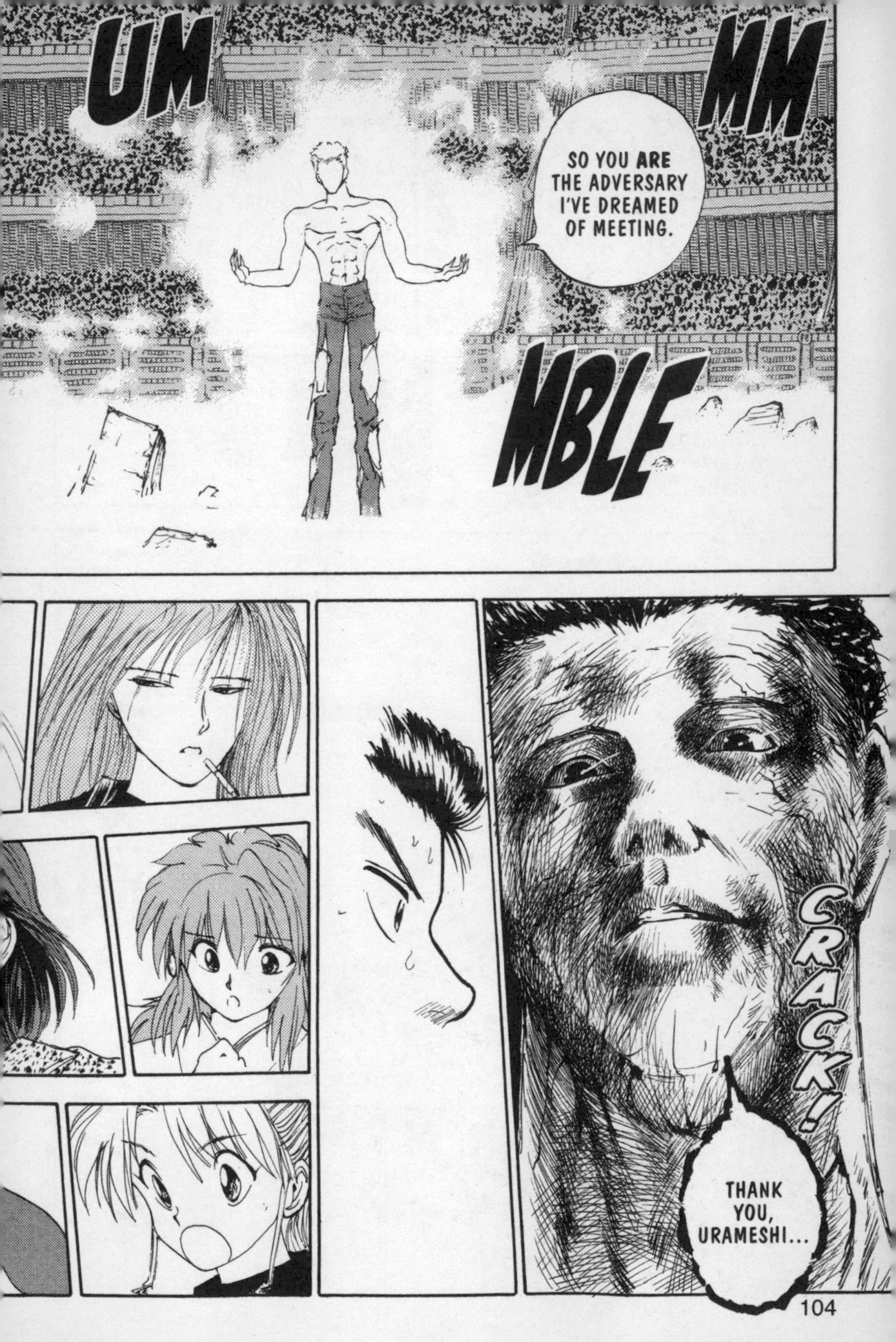
MM
SO YOU ARE THE ADVERSARY I'VE DREAMED OF MEETING.
UM
MBLE
CRACK!
THANK YOU, URAMESHI...

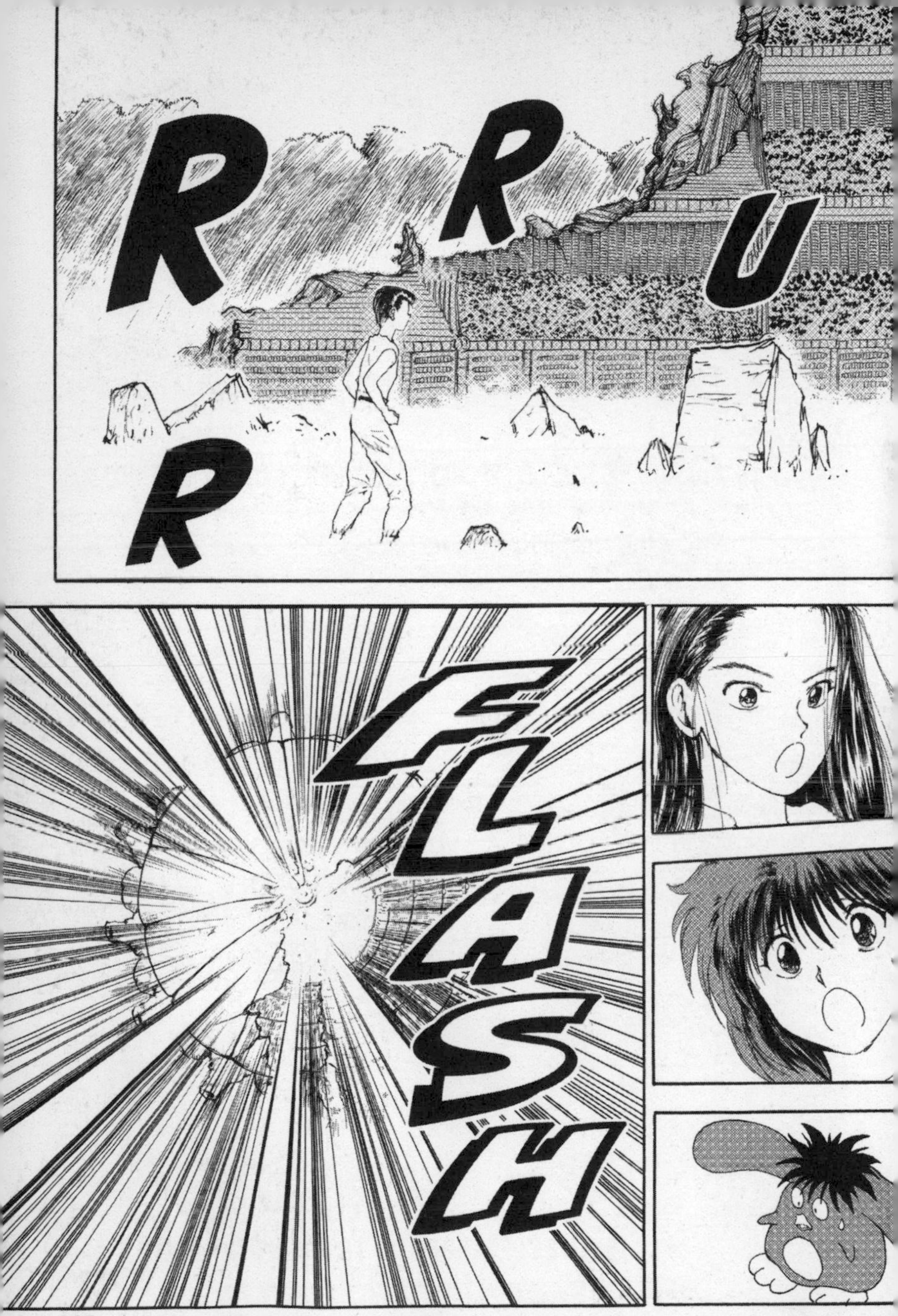
R R U
R
FLASH

ANSWER TO YUYU HAKUSHO PUZZLES: 3

HINT: START ASSIGNING NUMBERS TO THE CARDS ACCORDING TO WHAT THE CHARACTERS SAY.

HOW TO SOLVE IT: THERE ARE FOUR DIFFERENT NUMBERS, AND THEY ARE 2, 3, 6, AND 8. THERE ARE FOUR 3'S LEFT. A, B, AND I ARE THE SAME NUMBER, SO THEY MUST BE 3'S. KEEP FILLING THEM IN...

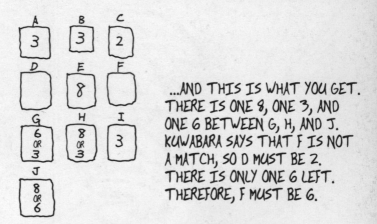

...AND THIS IS WHAT YOU GET. THERE IS ONE 8, ONE 3, AND ONE 6 BETWEEN G, H, AND J. KUWABARA SAYS THAT F IS NOT A MATCH, SO D MUST BE 2. THERE IS ONLY ONE 6 LEFT. THEREFORE, F MUST BE 6.

● THE PUZZLE APPEARS IN MANGA VOLUME 11, P. 106.

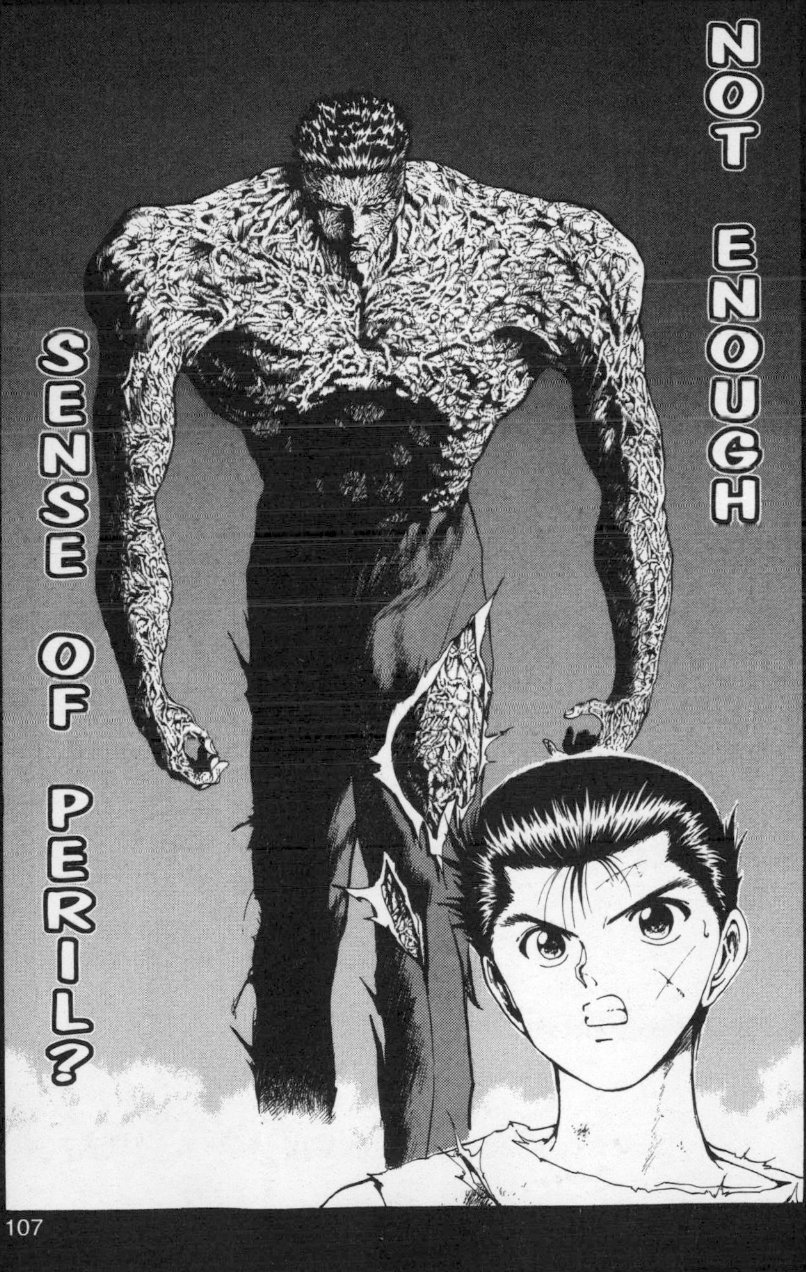
NOT ENOUGH
SENSE OF PERIL?

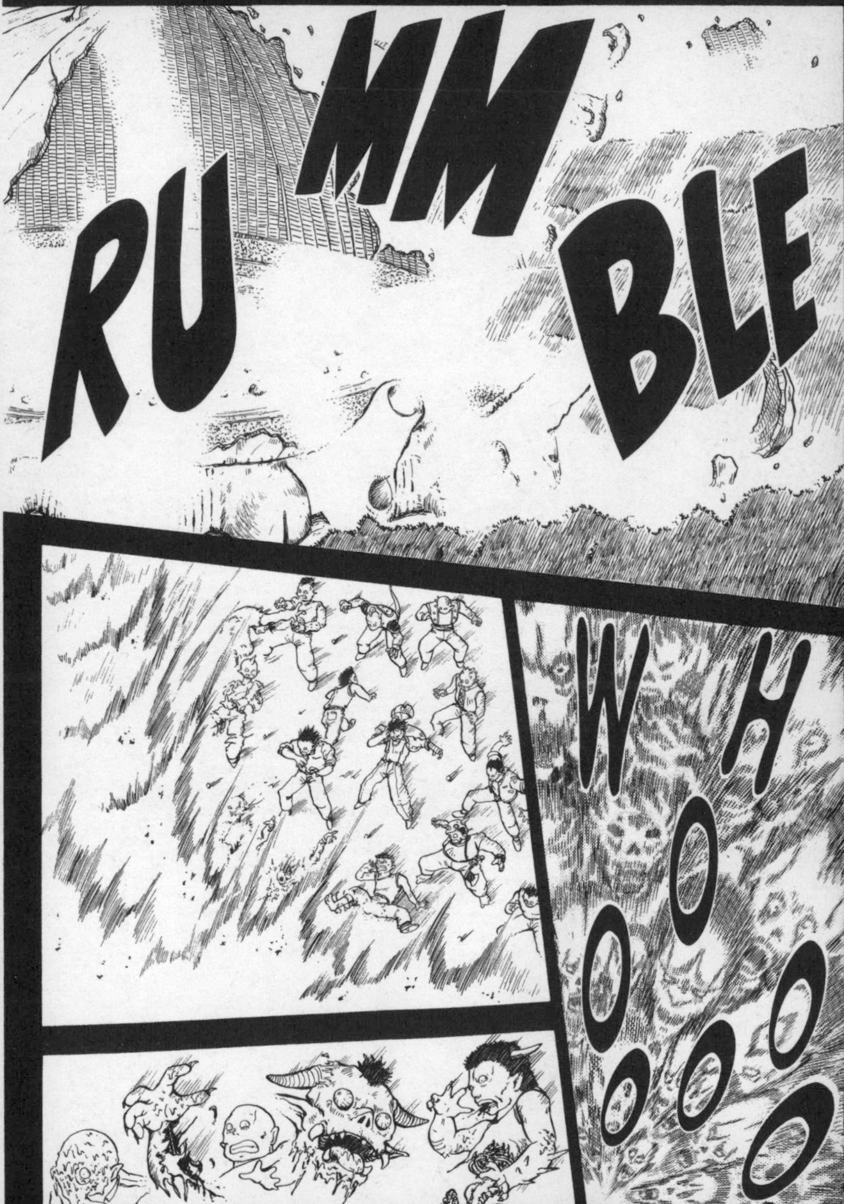
RUMMBLE
WHOOOOOO

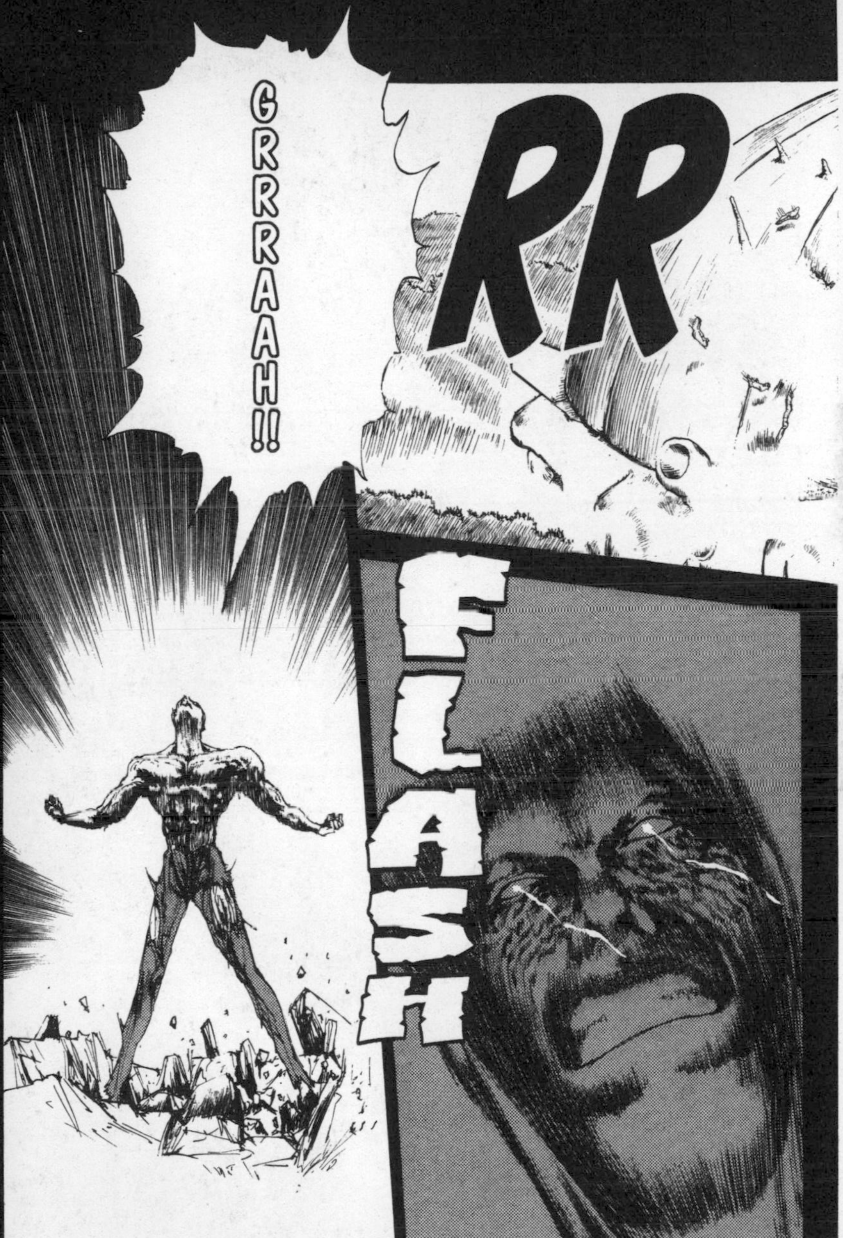
RR
FLASH
GRRRAAH!!

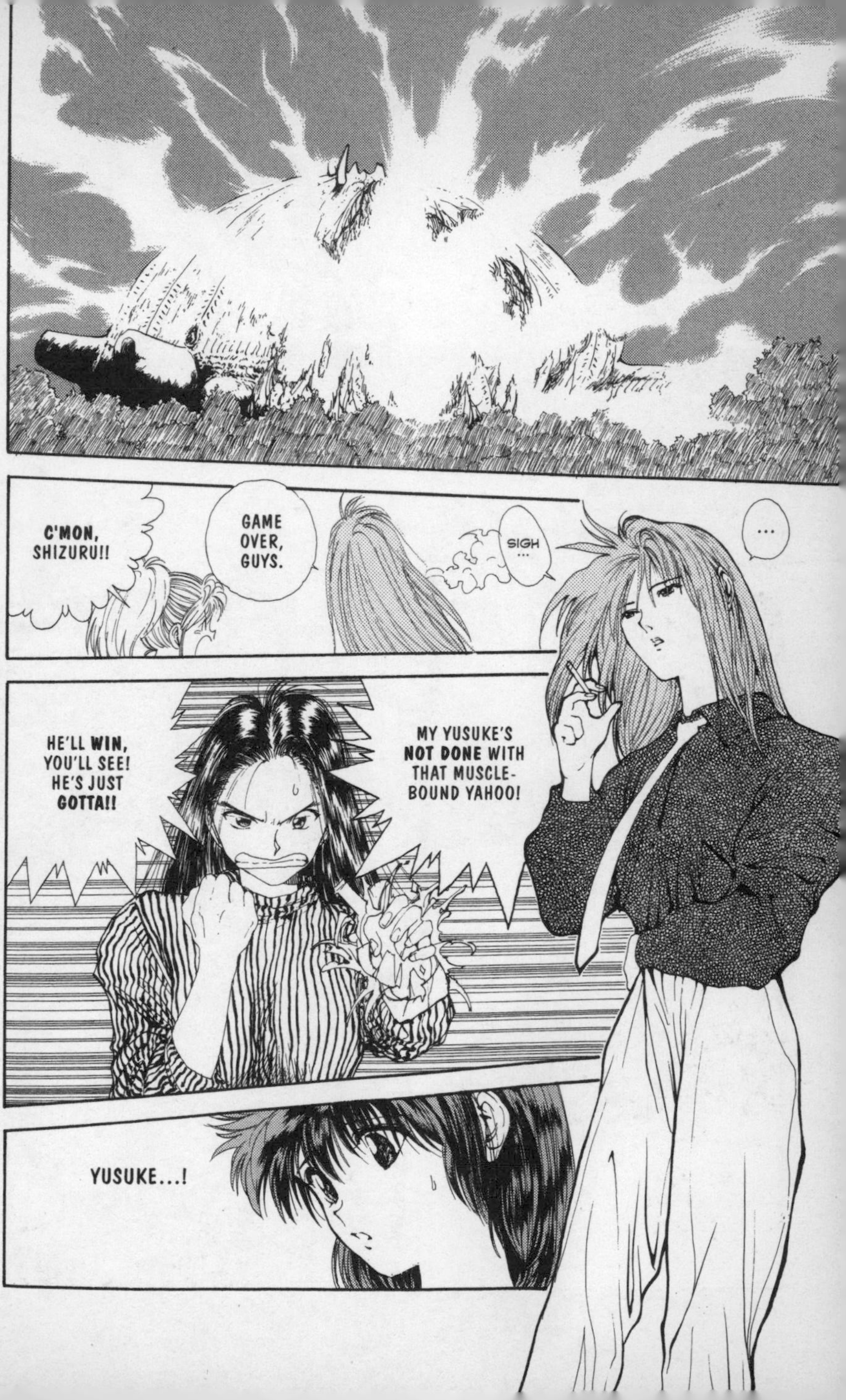
...
SIGH...
GAME OVER, GUYS.
C'MON, SHIZURU!!
MY YUSUKE'S NOT DONE WITH THAT MUSCLE-BOUND YAHOO!
HE'LL WIN, YOU'LL SEE! HE'S JUST GOTTA!!
YUSUKE...!

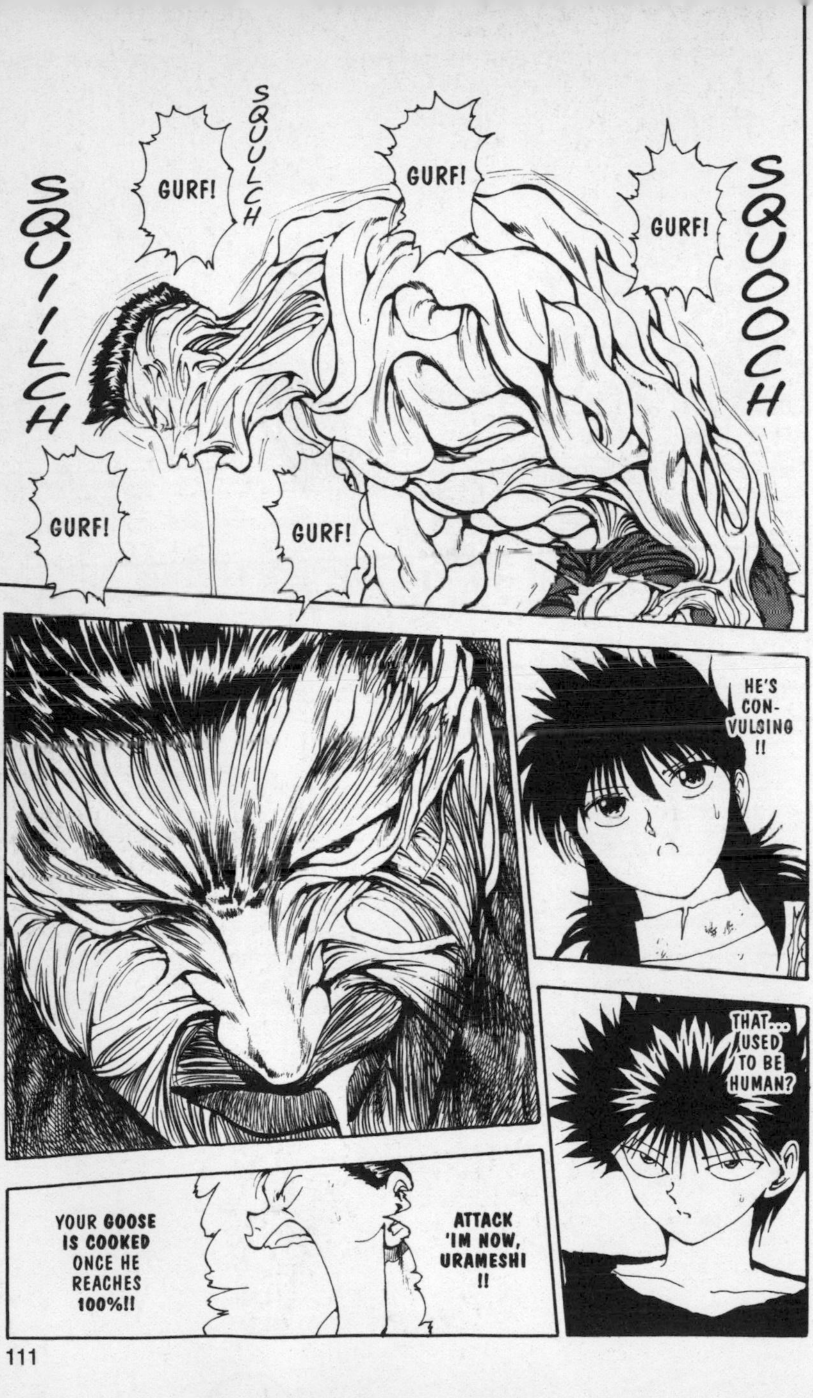
SQUOOOCH
GURF!
GURF!
SQUUULCH
GURF!
SQUIIILCH
GURF!
GURF!
HE'S CONVULSING!!
THAT... USED TO BE HUMAN?
ATTACK 'IM NOW, URAMESHI!!
YOUR GOOSE IS COOKED ONCE HE REACHES 100%!!

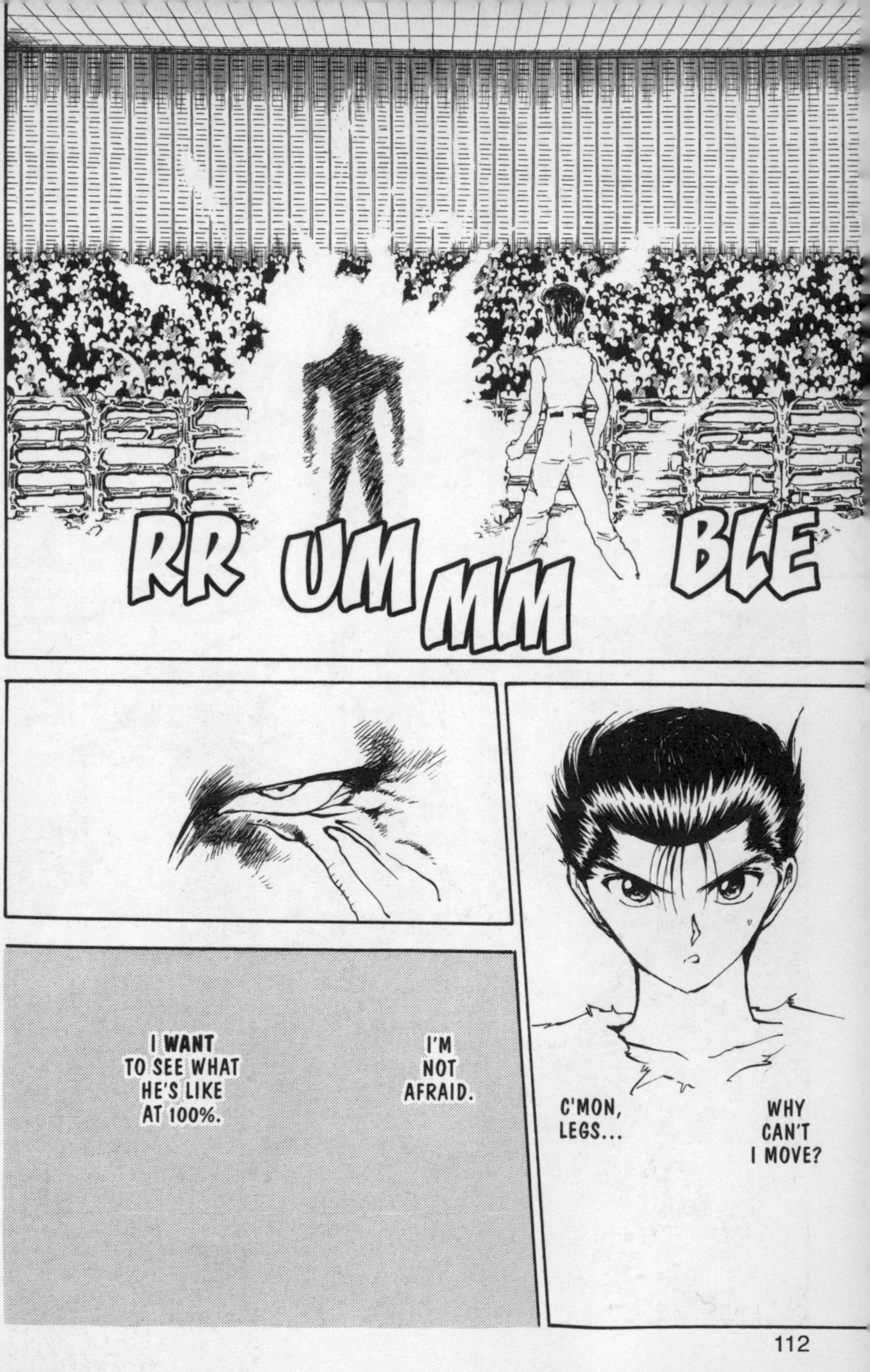
RR UM MM BLE
WHY CAN'T I MOVE?
C'MON, LEGS...
I'M NOT AFRAID.
I WANT TO SEE WHAT HE'S LIKE AT 100%.

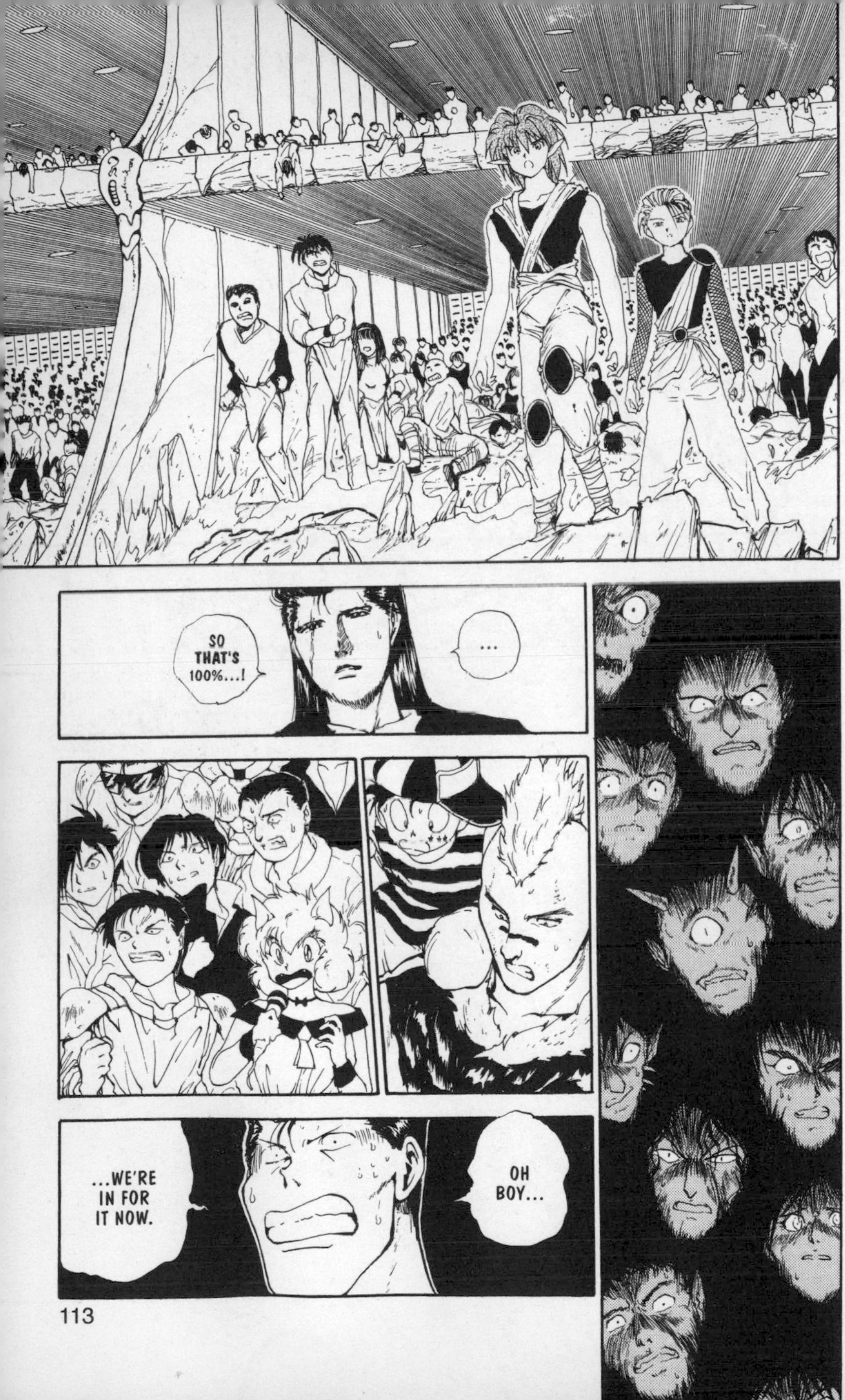
...
SO THAT'S 100%...!
OH BOY...
...WE'RE IN FOR IT NOW.

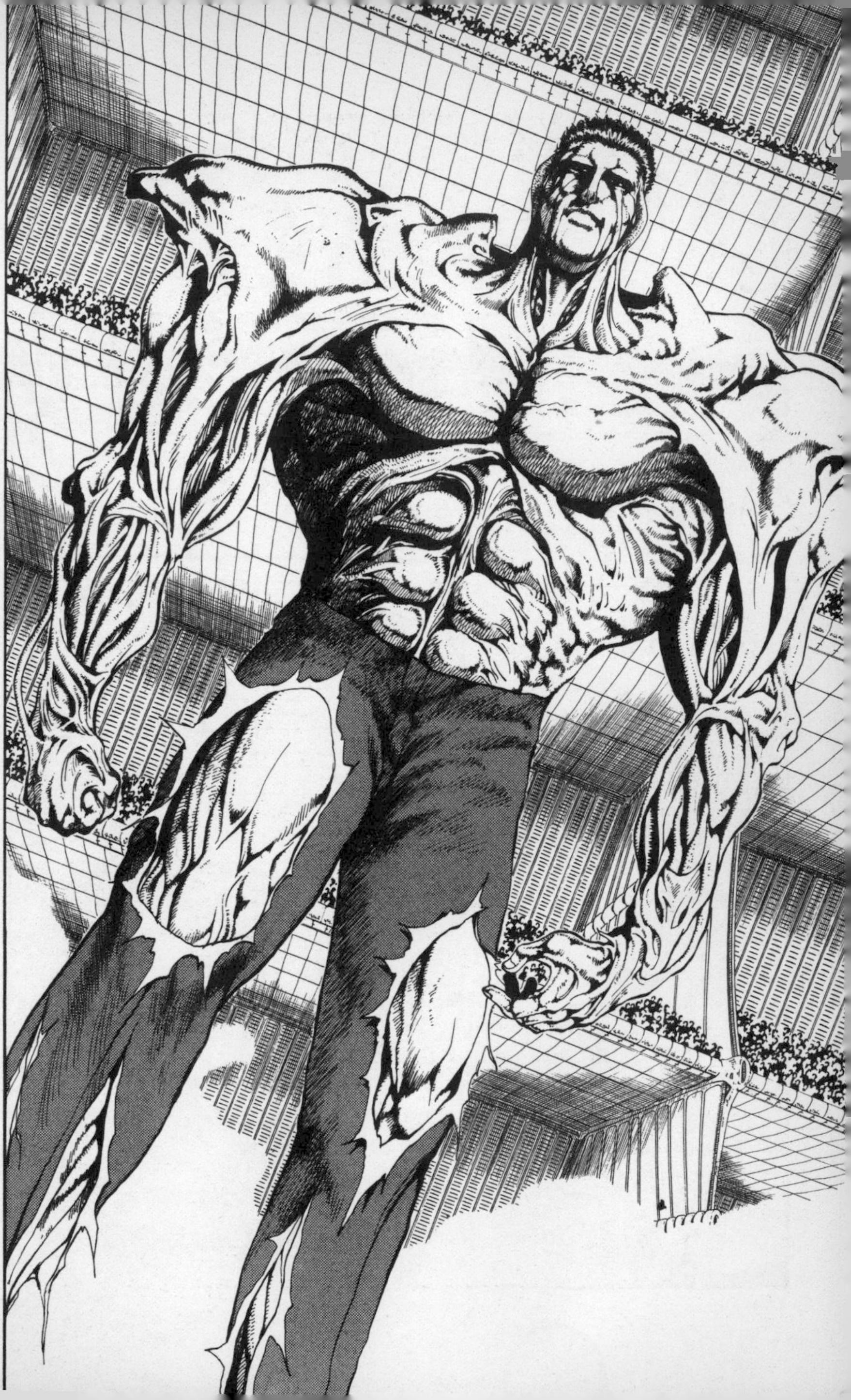

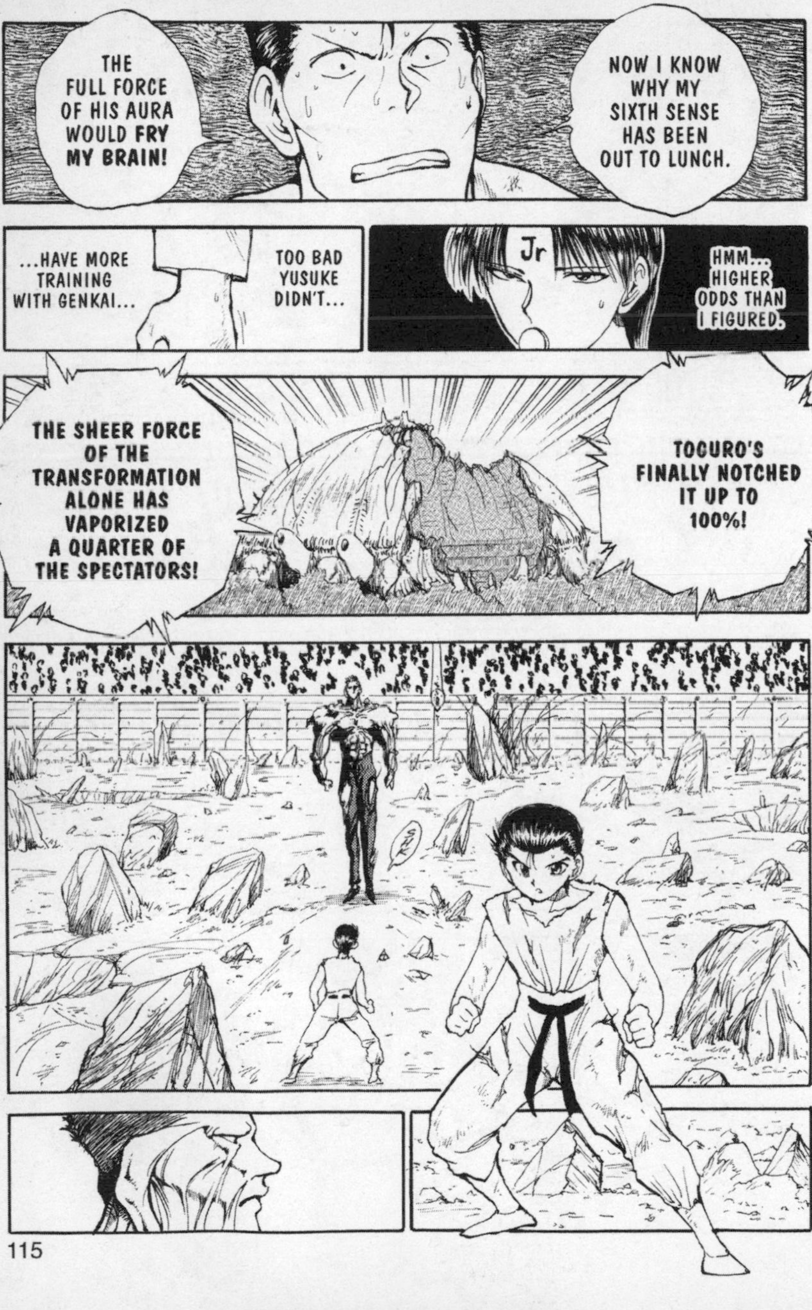
NOW I KNOW WHY MY SIXTH SENSE HAS BEEN OUT TO LUNCH.
THE FULL FORCE OF HIS AURA WOULD FRY MY BRAIN!
Jr
HMM... HIGHER ODDS THAN I FIGURED.
TOO BAD YUSUKE DIDN'T...
...HAVE MORE TRAINING WITH GENKAI...
TOGURO'S FINALLY NOTCHED IT UP TO 100%!
THE SHEER FORCE OF THE TRANSFORMATION ALONE HAS VAPORIZED A QUARTER OF THE SPECTATORS!

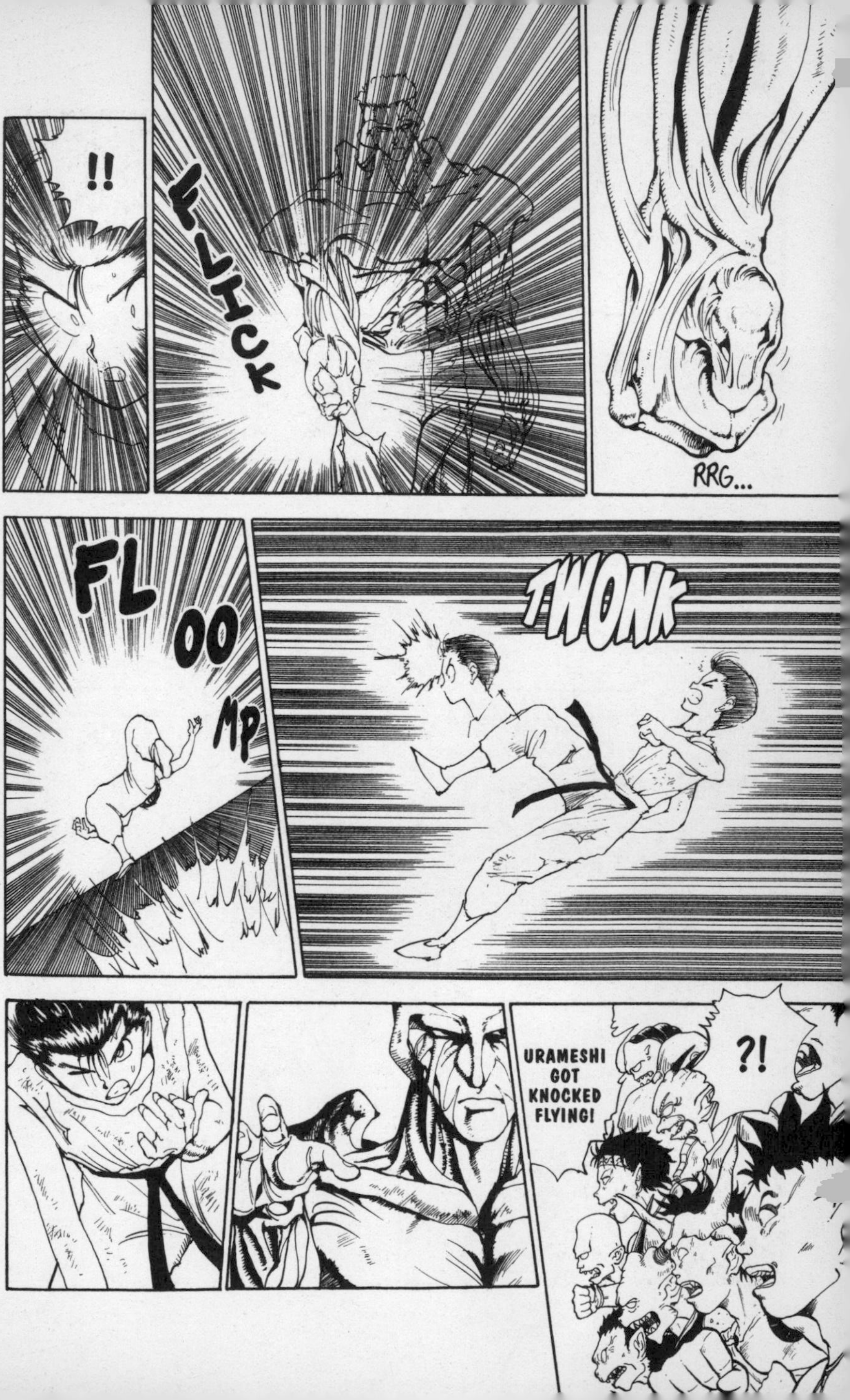
RRG...
FLICK
!!
TWONK
FLOOMP
?!
URAMESHI GOT KNOCKED FLYING!

READ THIS WAY

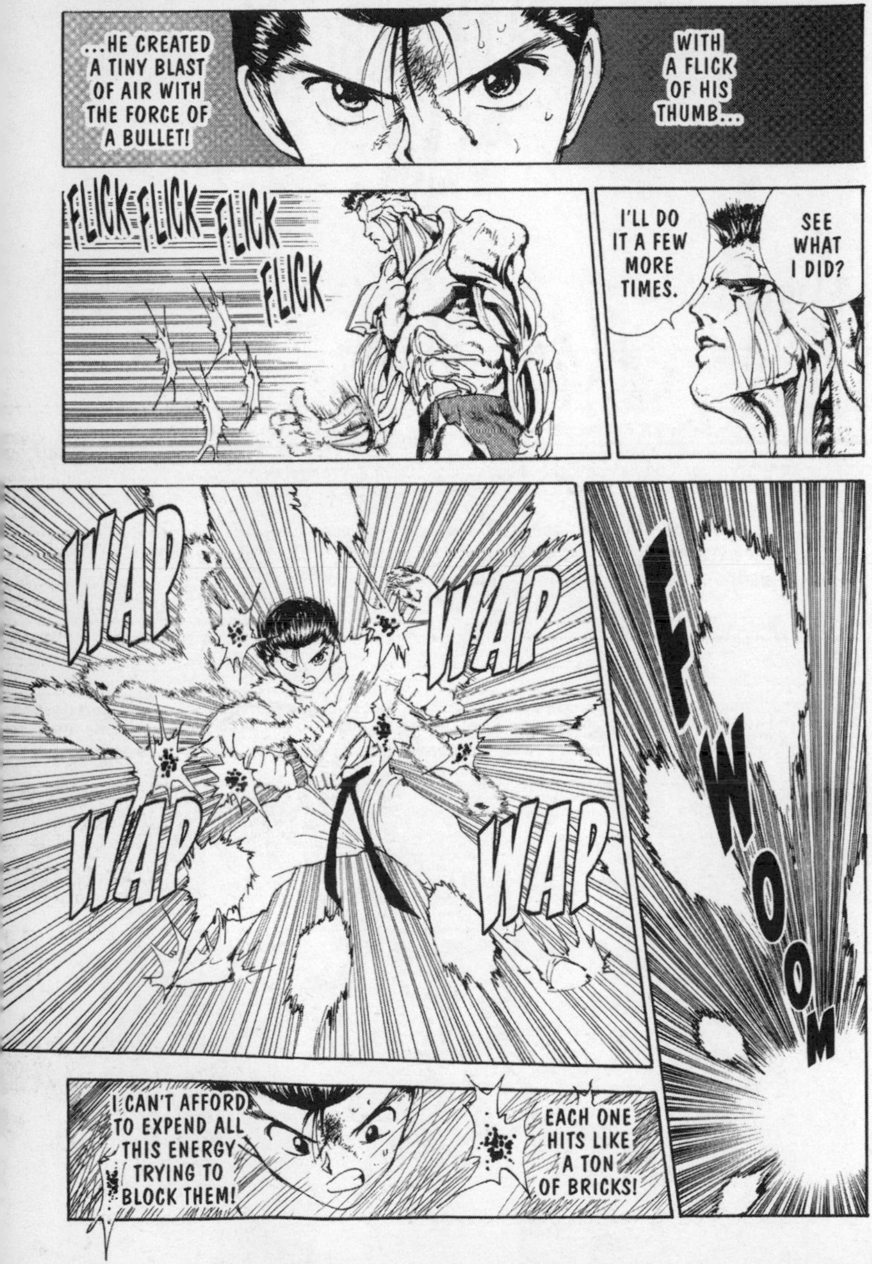
WITH A FLICK OF HIS THUMB...
...HE CREATED A TINY BLAST OF AIR WITH THE FORCE OF A BULLET!
SEE WHAT I DID?
I'LL DO IT A FEW MORE TIMES.
FLICK FLICK FLICK FLICK
FWOOOM
WAP WAP WAP WAP
EACH ONE HITS LIKE A TON OF BRICKS!
I CAN'T AFFORD TO EXPEND ALL THIS ENERGY TRYING TO BLOCK THEM!

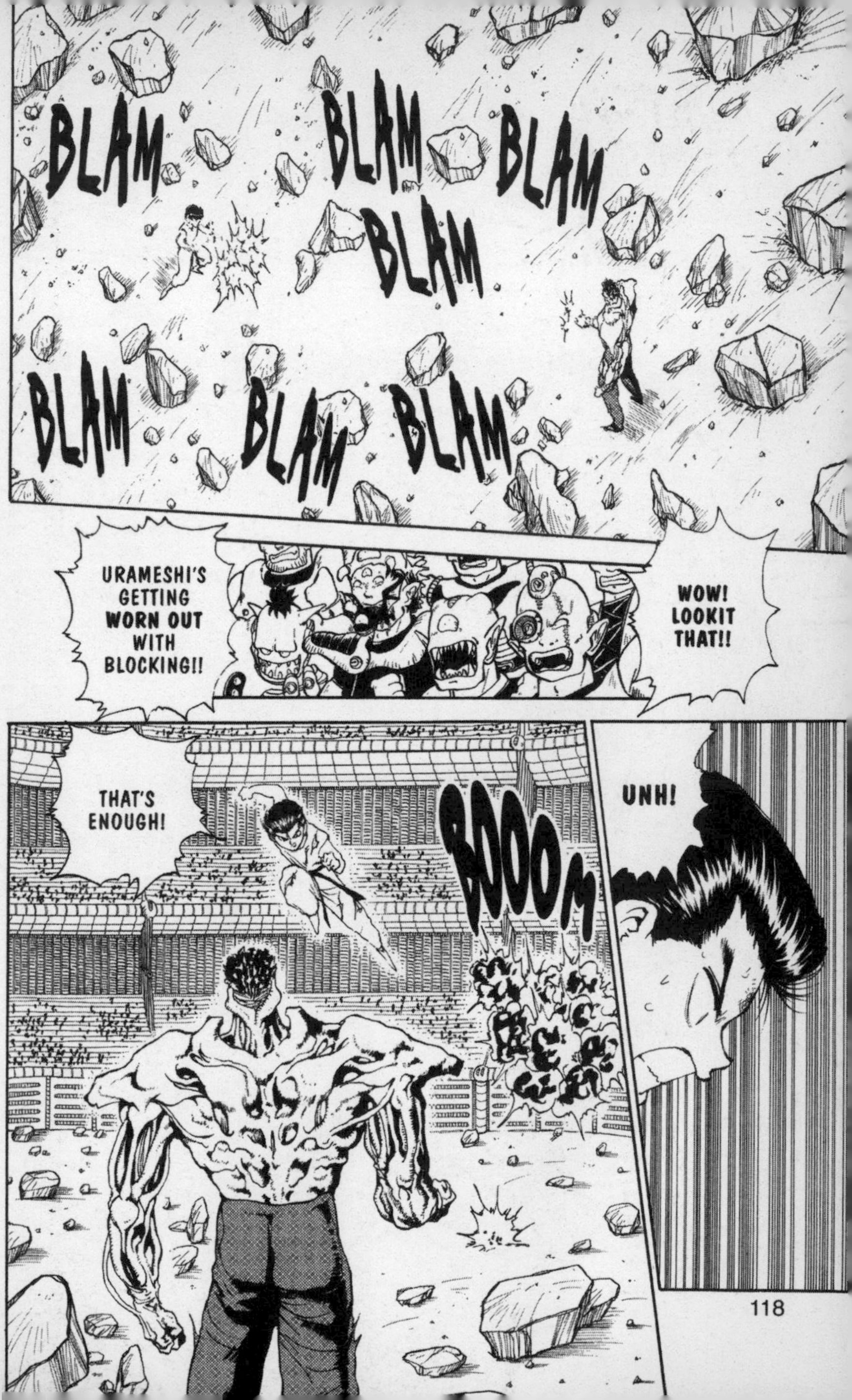
BLAM
BLAM
BLAM
BLAM
BLAM
BLAM
BLAM
WOW! LOOKIT THAT!!
URAMESHI'S GETTING WORN OUT WITH BLOCKING!!
UNH!
THAT'S ENOUGH!
BOOOM

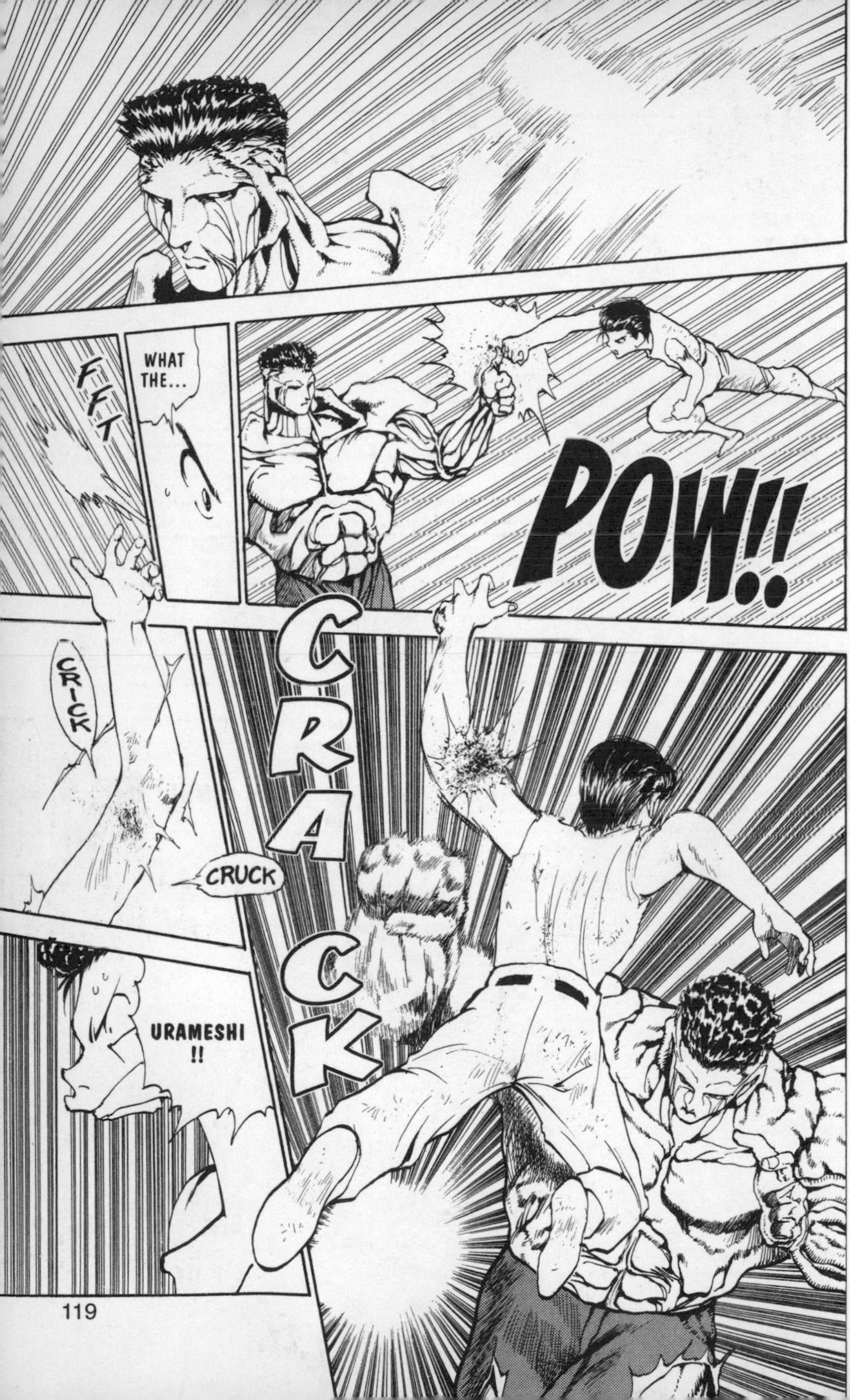
POW!!
WHAT THE...
FFT
CRACK
CRICK
CRUCK
URAMESHI !!

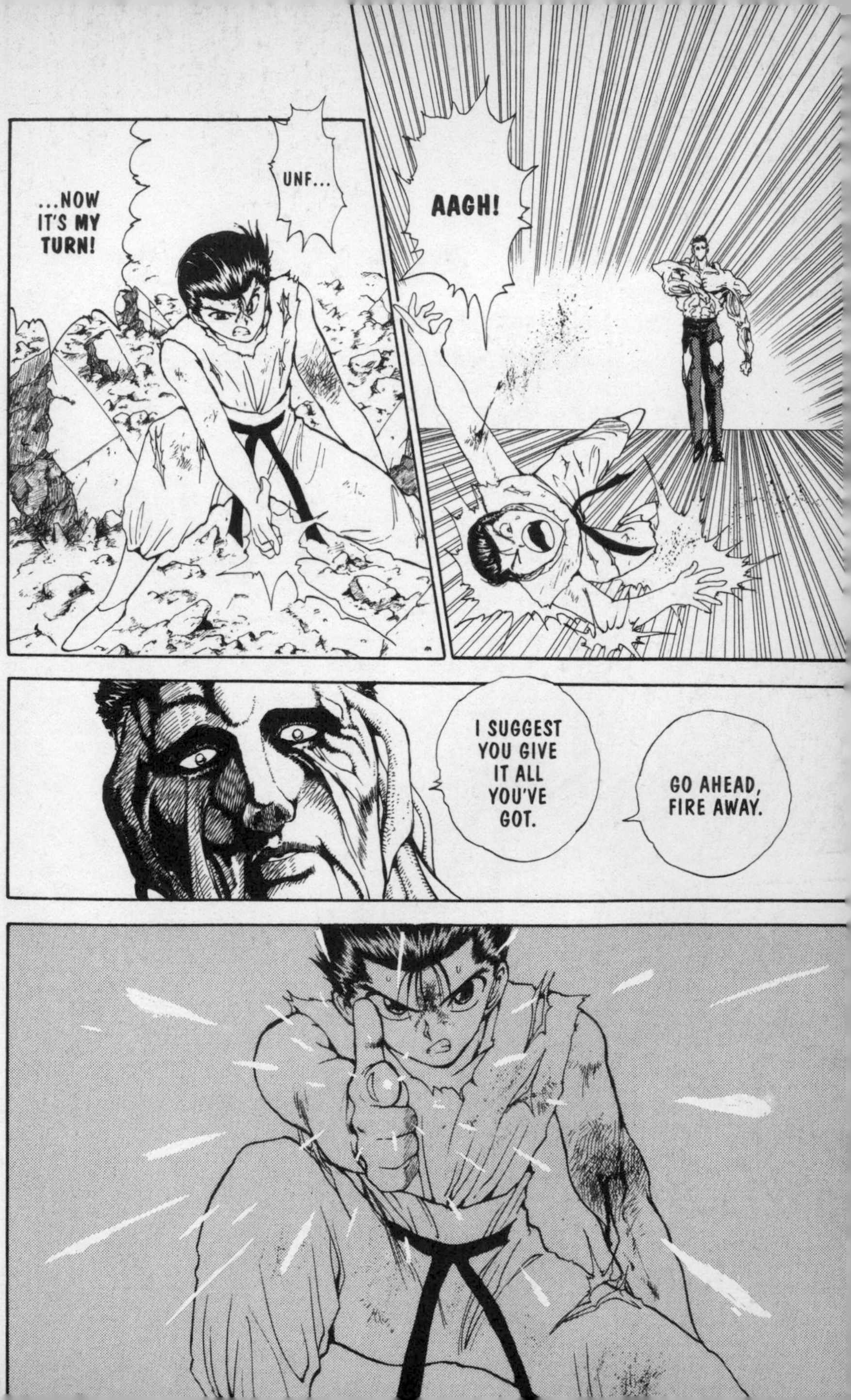
AAGH!
UNF...
...NOW IT'S MY TURN!
GO AHEAD, FIRE AWAY.
I SUGGEST YOU GIVE IT ALL YOU'VE GOT.

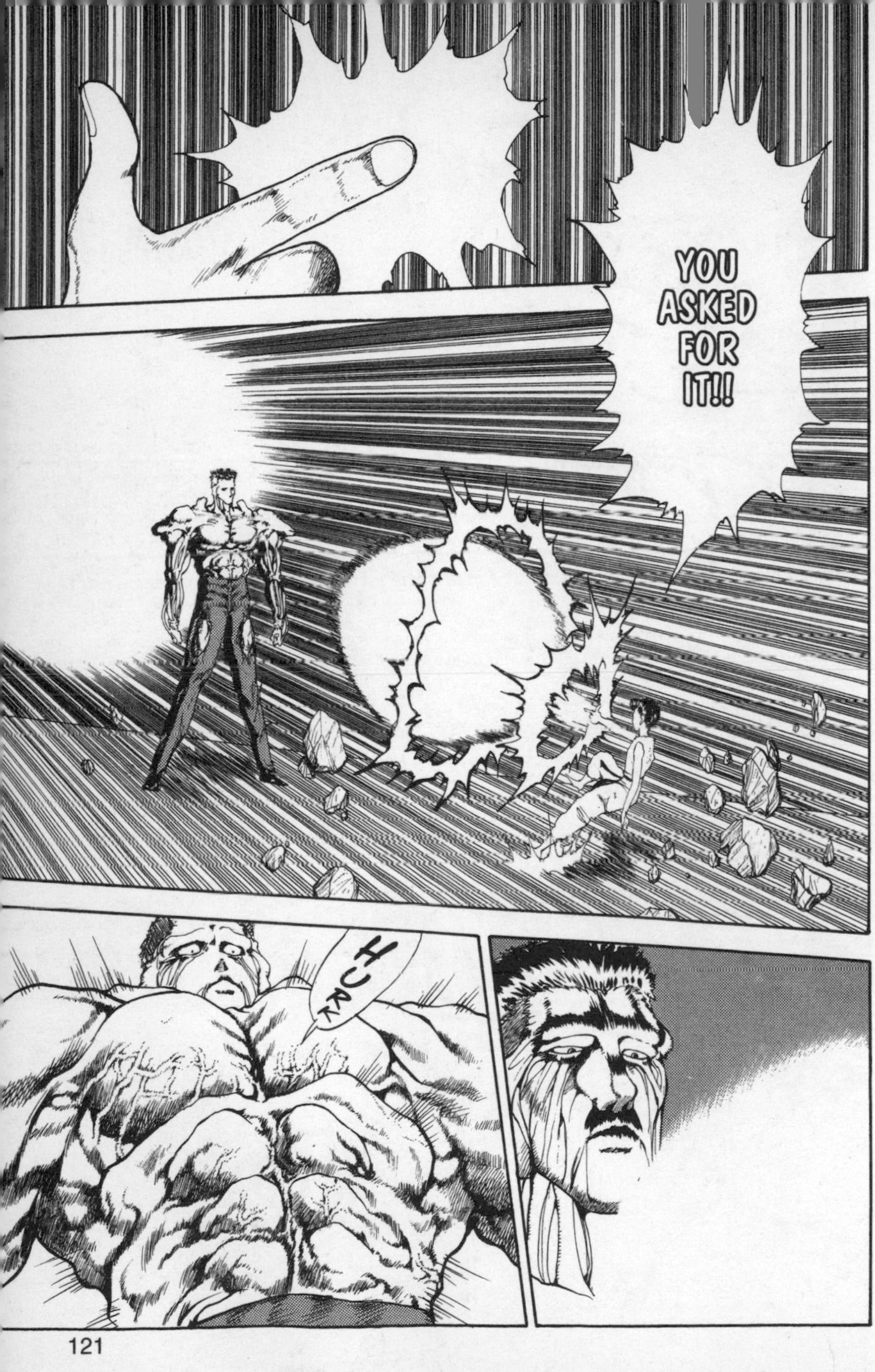
YOU ASKED FOR IT!!
HURK

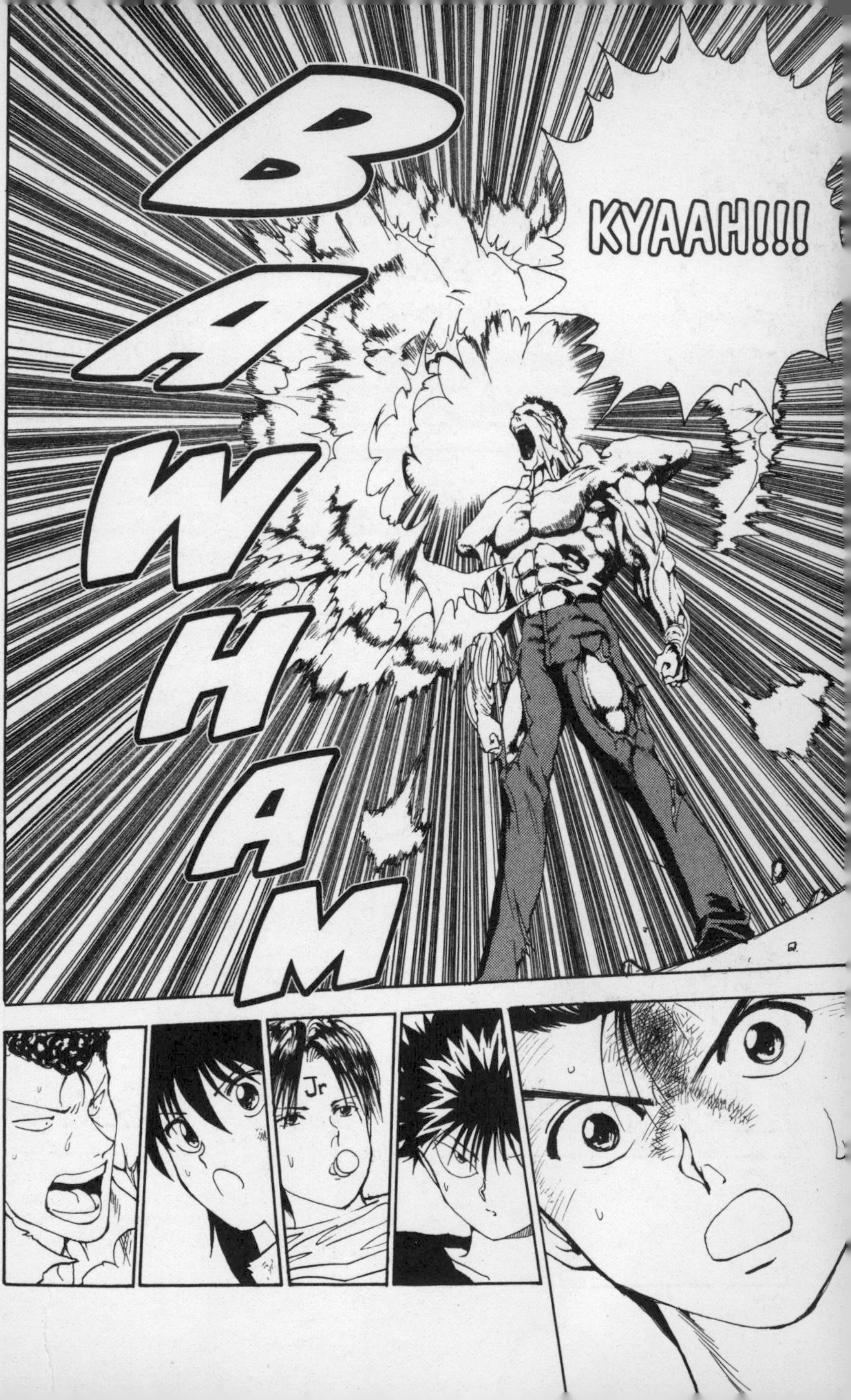
KYAAH!!!
BAWHAM
Jr

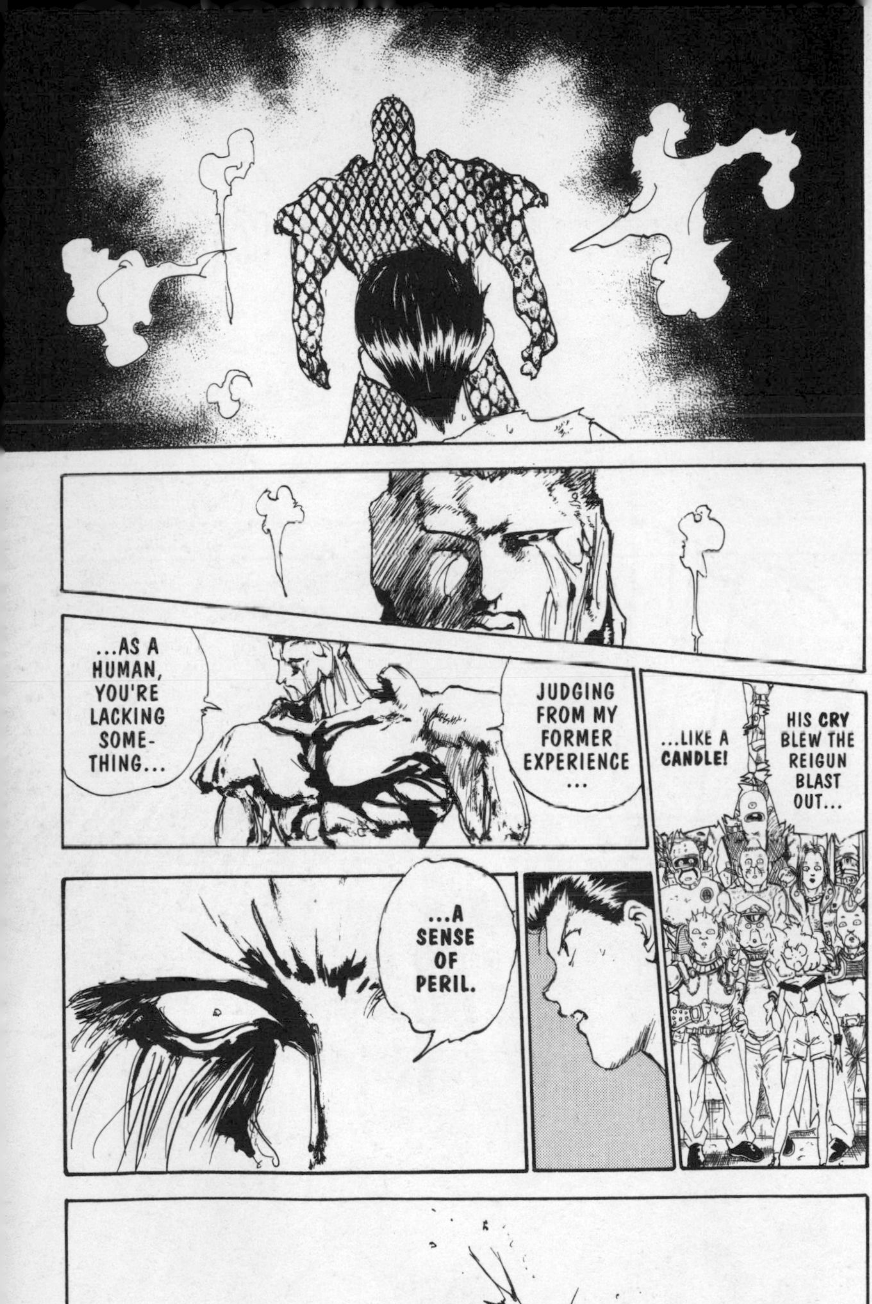
HIS CRY BLEW THE REIGUN BLAST OUT...
...LIKE A CANDLE!
JUDGING FROM MY FORMER EXPERIENCE ...
...AS A HUMAN, YOU'RE LACKING SOME-THING...
...A SENSE OF PERIL.

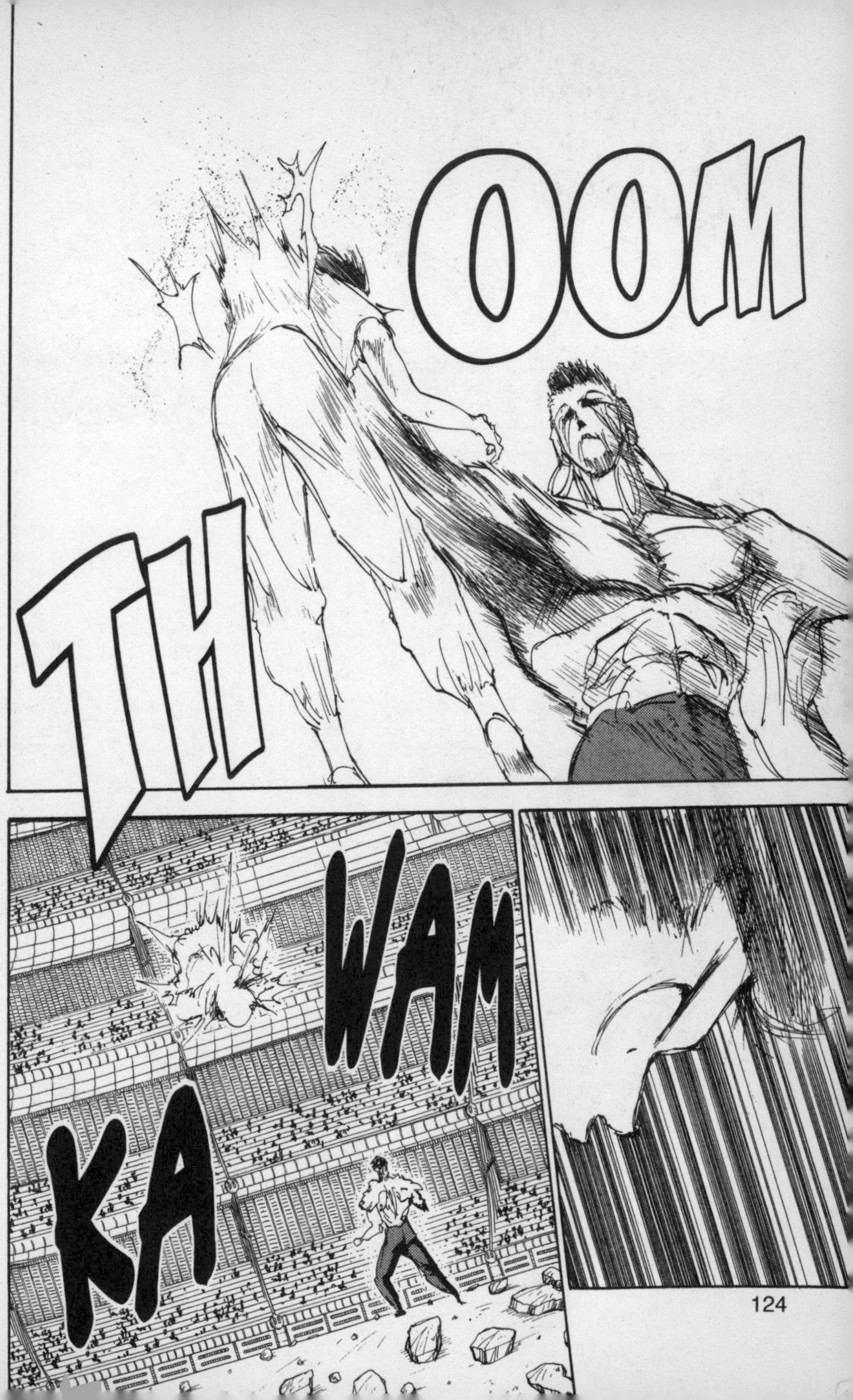
THOOM
KAWAM

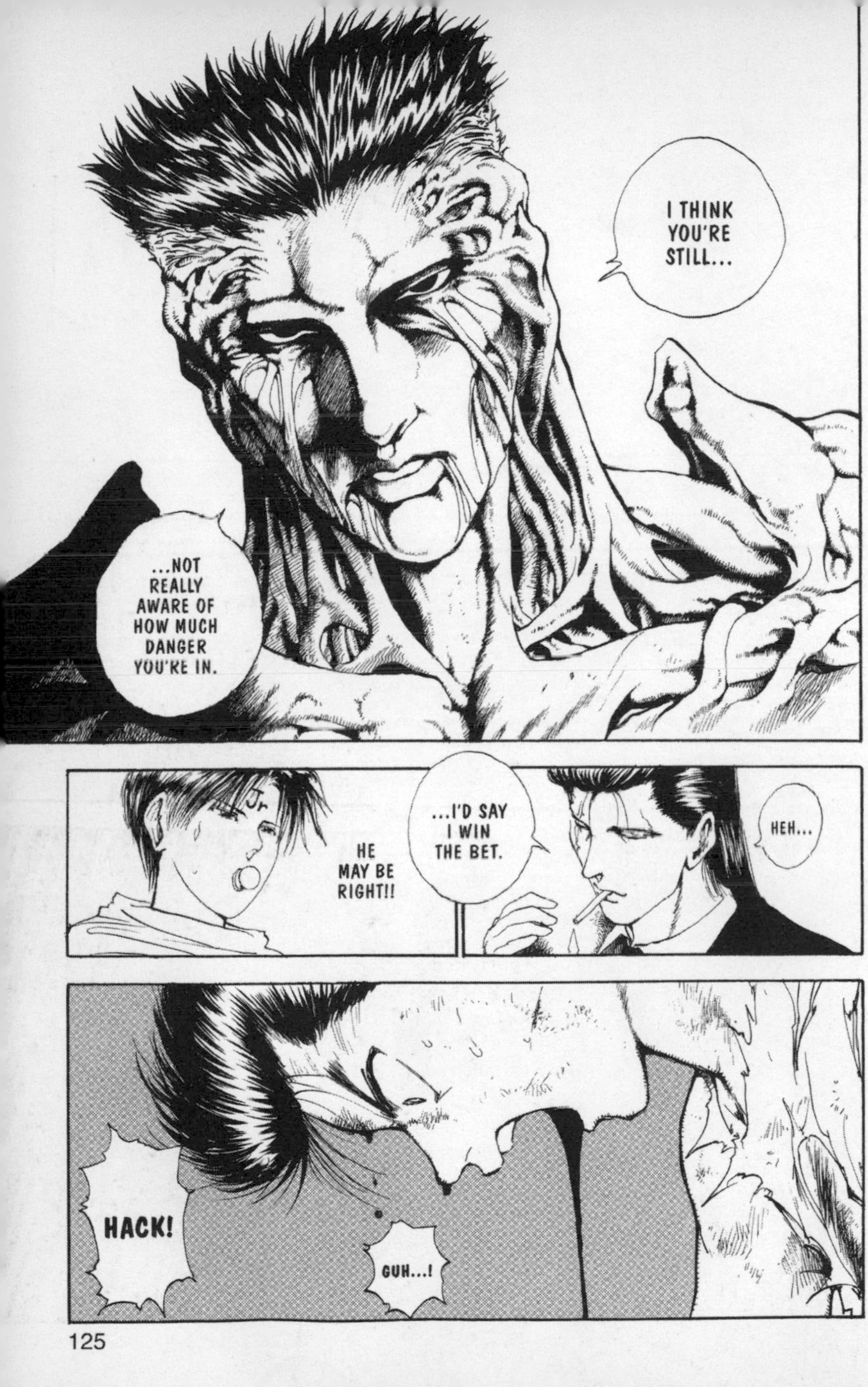
I THINK YOU'RE STILL...
...NOT REALLY AWARE OF HOW MUCH DANGER YOU'RE IN.
HEH...
...I'D SAY I WIN THE BET.
HE MAY BE RIGHT!!
HACK!
GUH...!

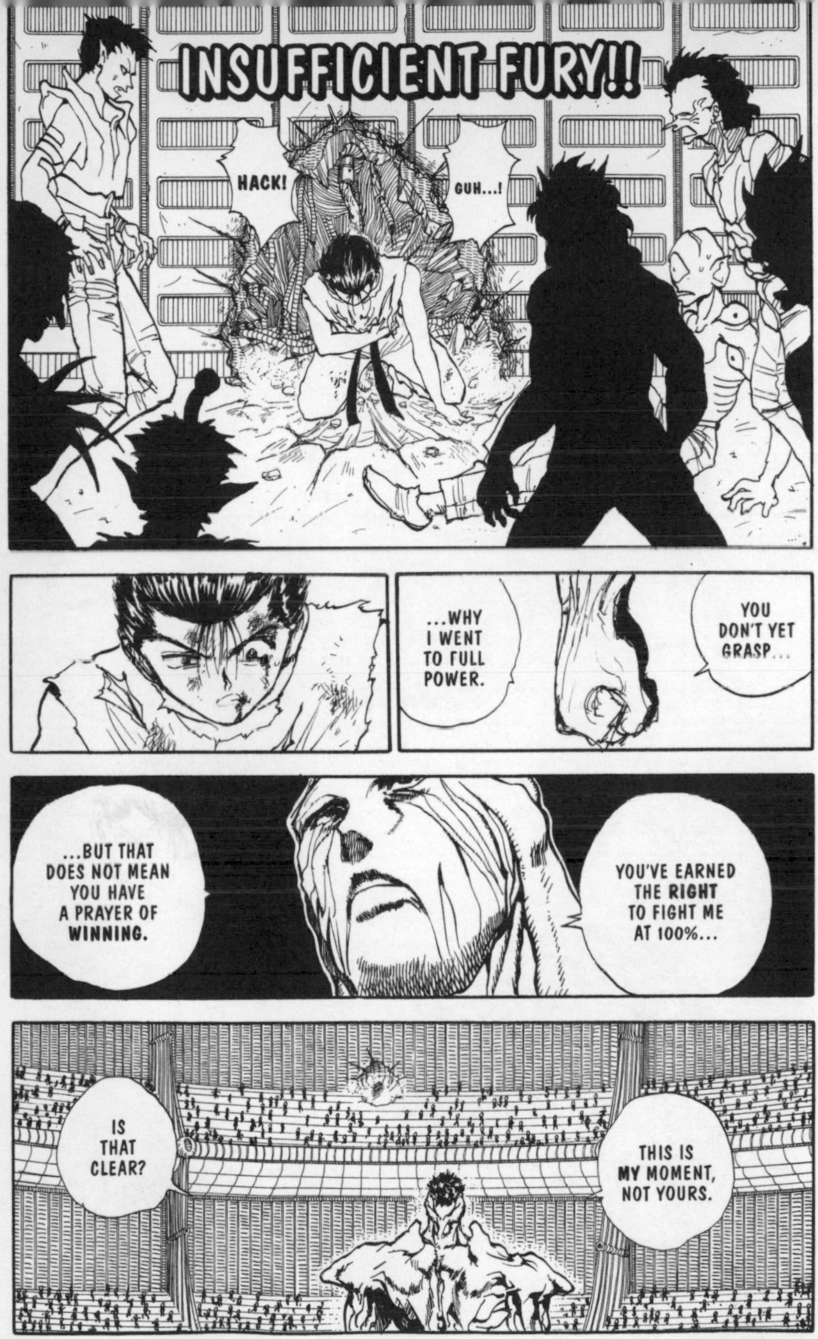
INSUFFICIENT FURY!!
GUH...!
HACK!
YOU DON'T YET GRASP...
...WHY I WENT TO FULL POWER.
YOU'VE EARNED THE RIGHT TO FIGHT ME AT 100%...
...BUT THAT DOES NOT MEAN YOU HAVE A PRAYER OF WINNING.
THIS IS MY MOMENT, NOT YOURS.
IS THAT CLEAR?

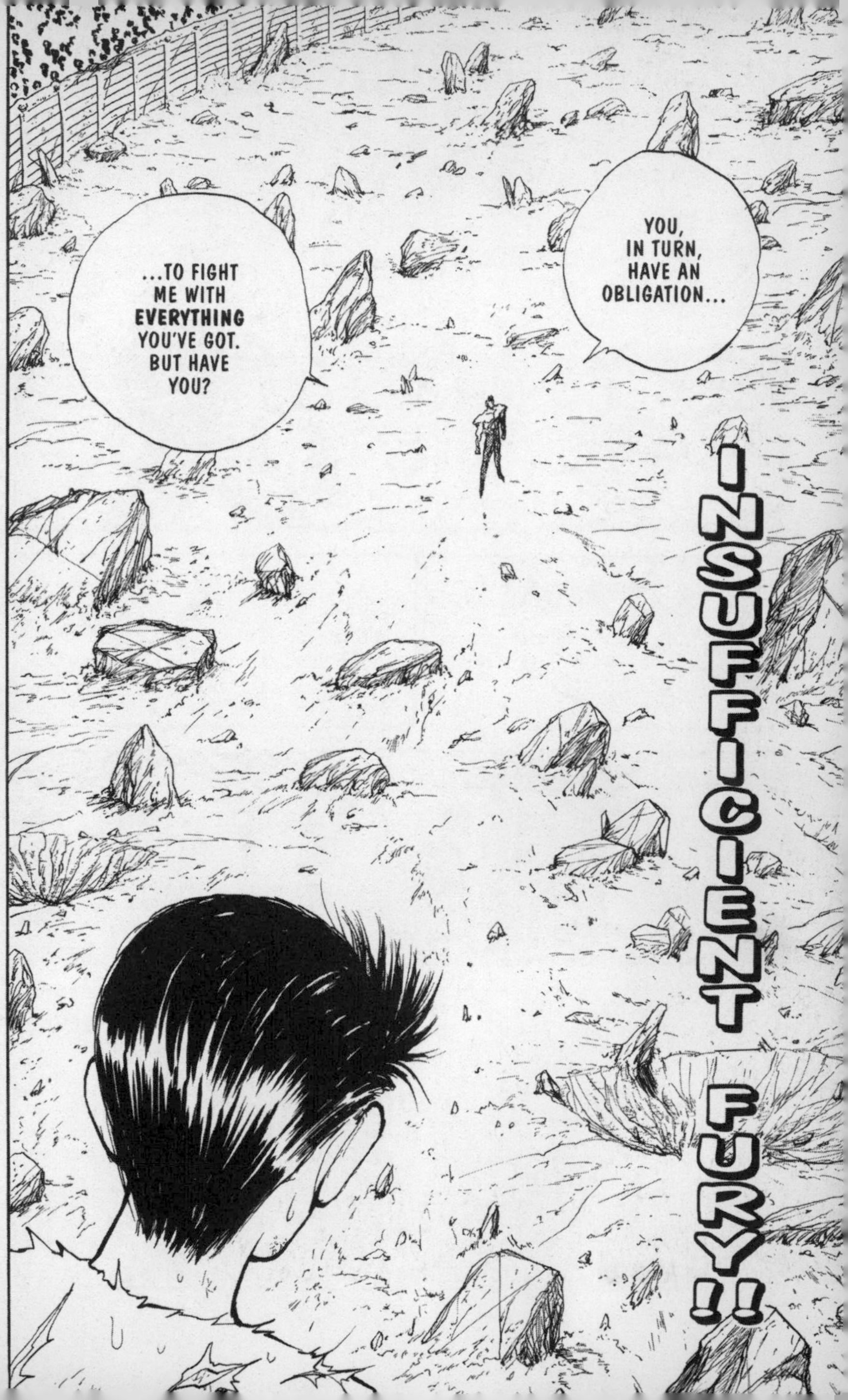
YOU, IN TURN, HAVE AN OBLIGATION...
...TO FIGHT ME WITH **EVERYTHING** YOU'VE GOT. BUT HAVE YOU?
INSUFFICIENT FURY!!

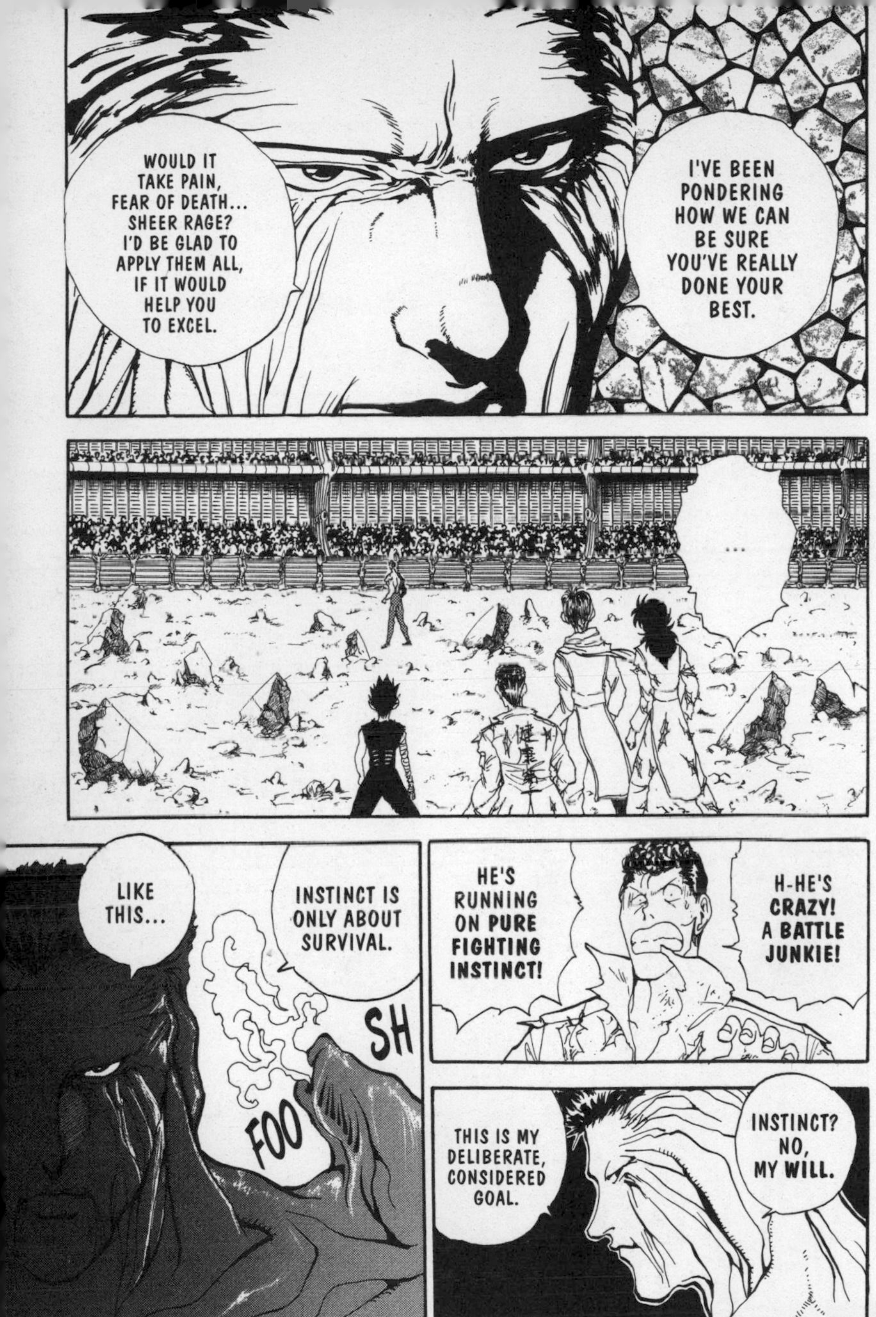
I'VE BEEN PONDERING HOW WE CAN BE SURE YOU'VE REALLY DONE YOUR BEST.
WOULD IT TAKE PAIN, FEAR OF DEATH... SHEER RAGE? I'D BE GLAD TO APPLY THEM ALL, IF IT WOULD HELP YOU TO EXCEL.
...
H-HE'S CRAZY! A BATTLE JUNKIE!
HE'S RUNNING ON PURE FIGHTING INSTINCT!
INSTINCT? NO, MY WILL.
THIS IS MY DELIBERATE, CONSIDERED GOAL.
INSTINCT IS ONLY ABOUT SURVIVAL.
LIKE THIS...
SH
FOO

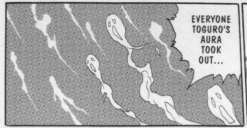

?!!
WHAT?!
EVERYONE TOGURO'S AURA TOOK OUT...
...HE'S SUCKING THEM UP!!
H-HE'S FEEDING ON THEM!
THIS MODE DOES RATHER GIVE ME AN APPETITE.
I CONSUME THEIR CHI, STARTING WITH THE WEAKEST.
IN 20 MINUTES I'LL FINISH OFF EVERYONE IN THIS ARENA.
DON'T YOU HAVE...
FRIENDS HERE CHEERING FOR YOU?
HEH HEH

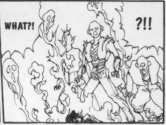

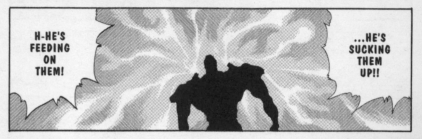

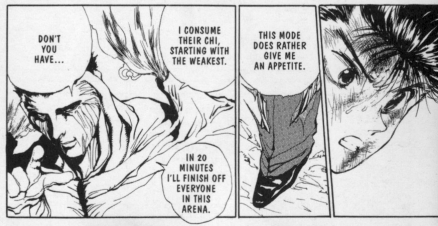

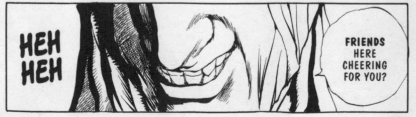

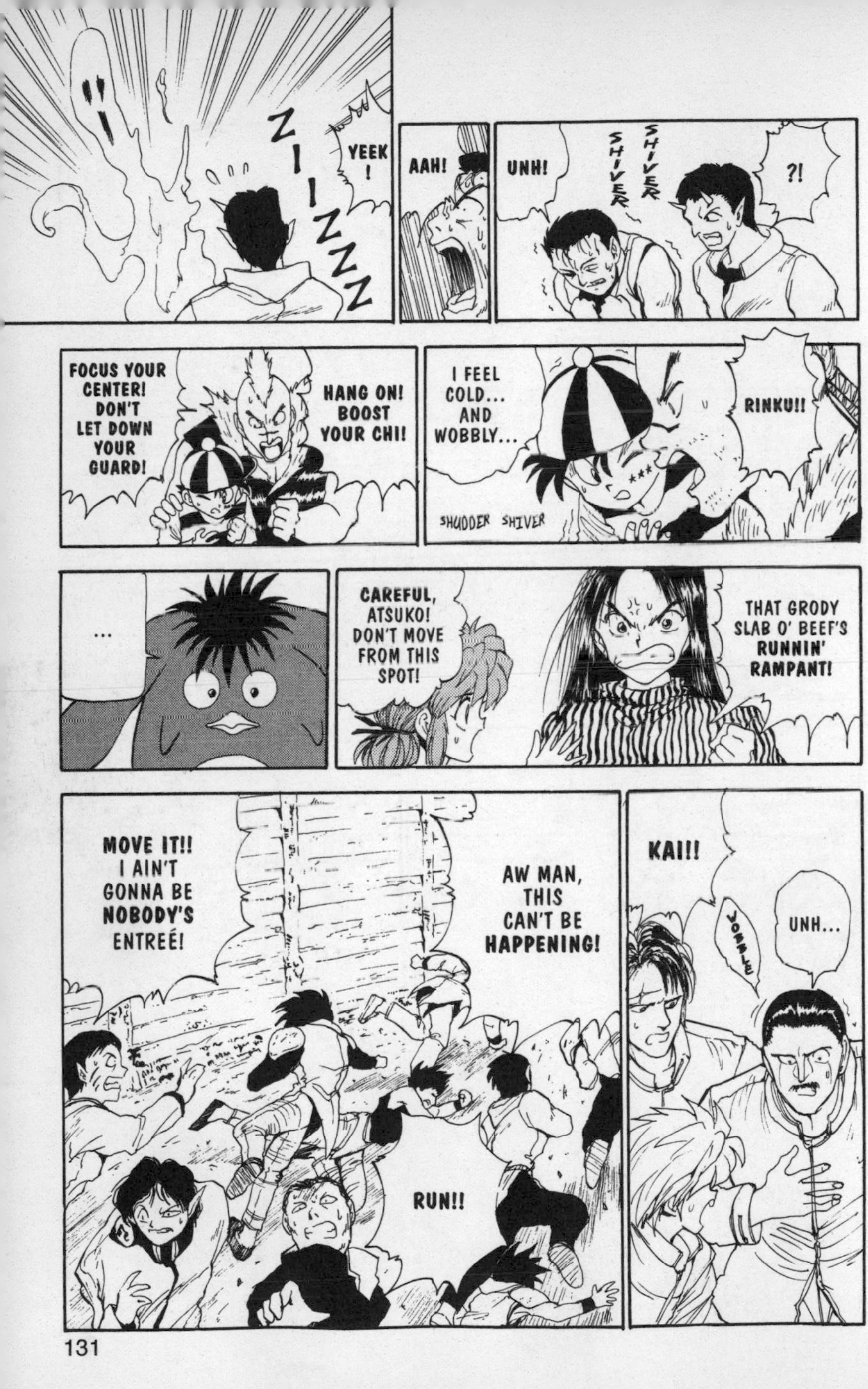
?!
SHIVER SHIVER
UNH!
AAH!
YEEK!
ZIIZZZ
RINKU!!
I FEEL COLD... AND WOBBLY...
SHUDDER SHIVER
HANG ON! BOOST YOUR CHI!
FOCUS YOUR CENTER! DON'T LET DOWN YOUR GUARD!
THAT GRODY SLAB O' BEEF'S RUNNIN' RAMPANT!
CAREFUL, ATSUKO! DON'T MOVE FROM THIS SPOT!
...
UNH...
WOBBLE
KAI!!
AW MAN, THIS CAN'T BE HAPPENING!
MOVE IT!! I AIN'T GONNA BE NOBODY'S ENTREÉ!
RUN!!

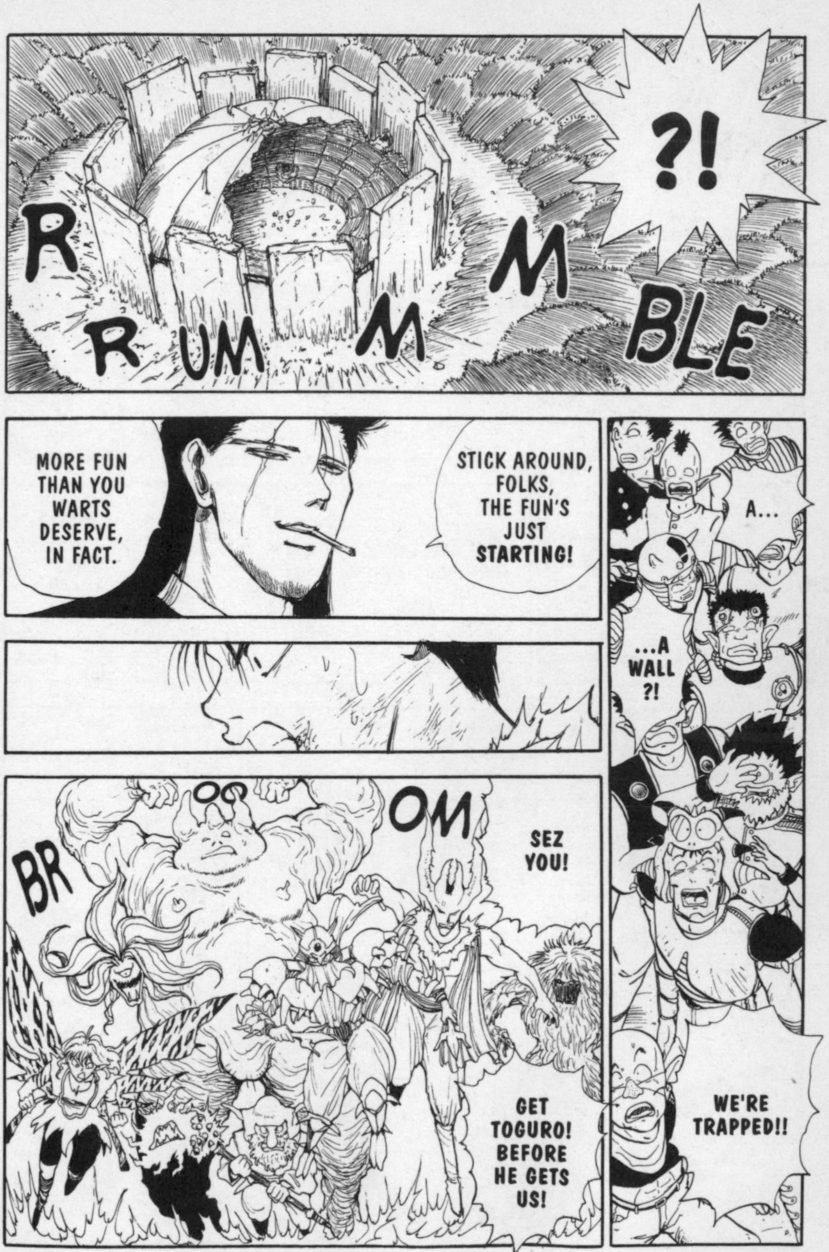
?!
RRUMMMBLE
A...
...A WALL ?!
WE'RE TRAPPED!!
STICK AROUND, FOLKS, THE FUN'S JUST STARTING!
MORE FUN THAN YOU WARTS DESERVE, IN FACT.
SEZ YOU!
BROOOM
GET TOGURO! BEFORE HE GETS US!

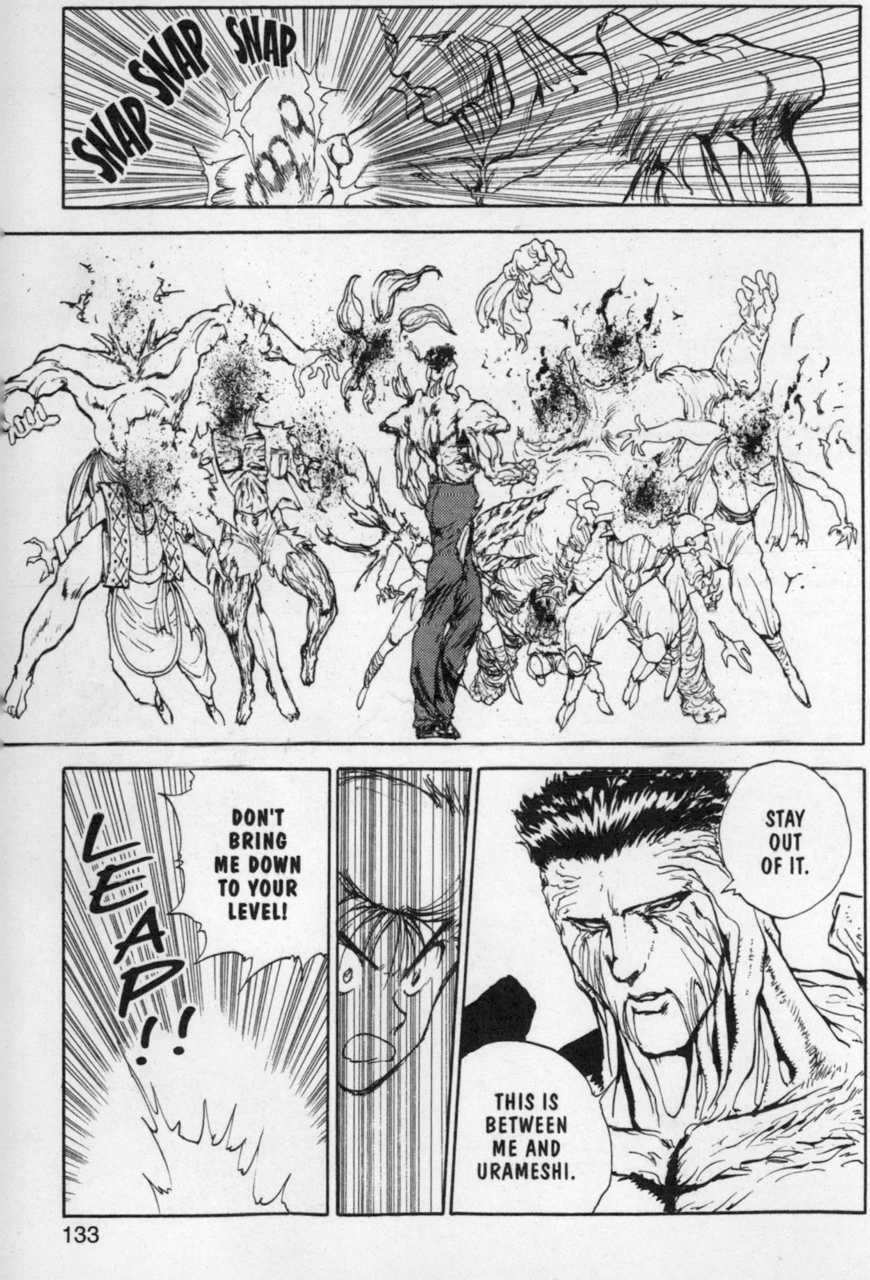
SNAP SNAP SNAP
STAY OUT OF IT.
THIS IS BETWEEN ME AND URAMESHI.
DON'T BRING ME DOWN TO YOUR LEVEL!
LEAP!!

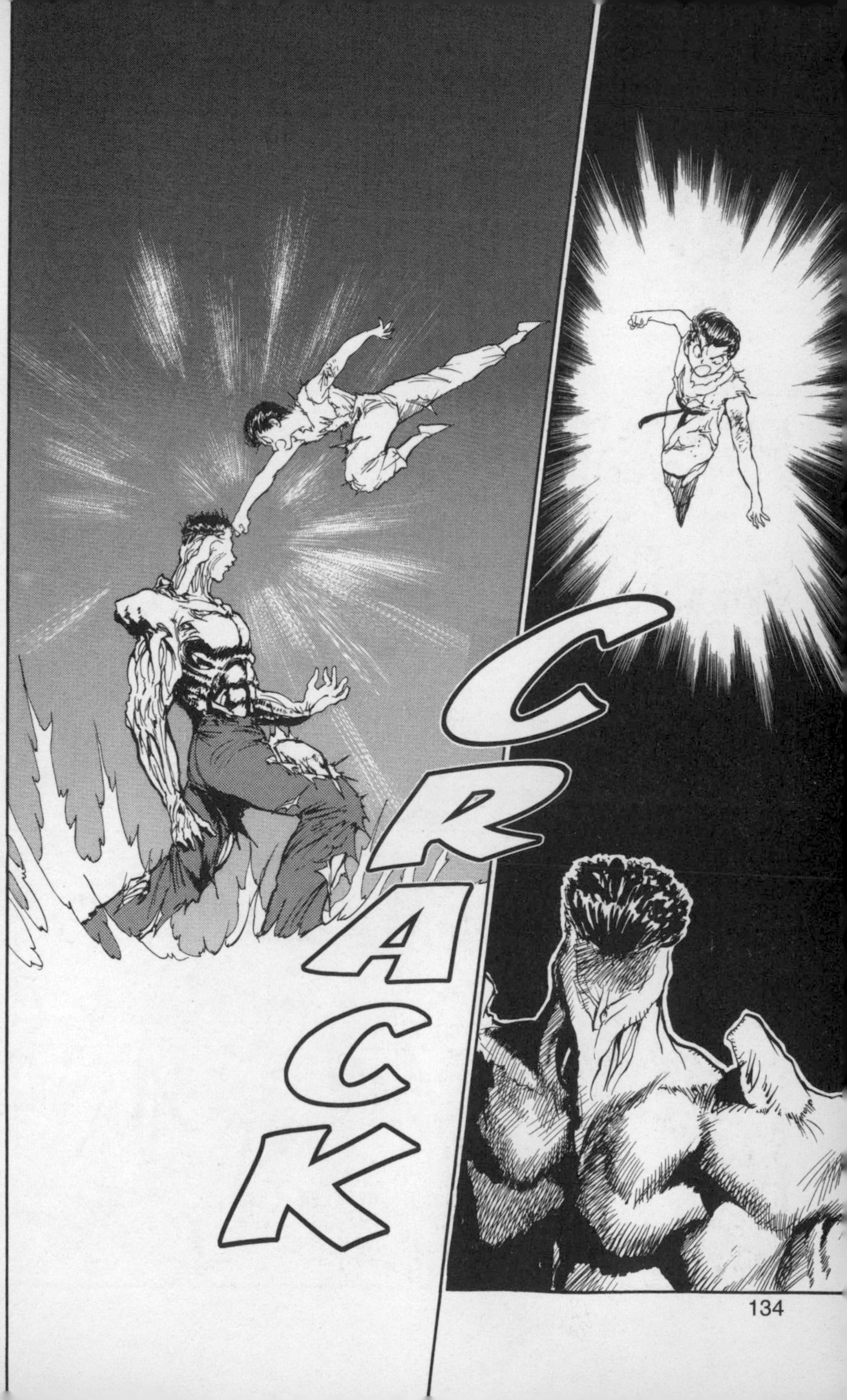
CRACK

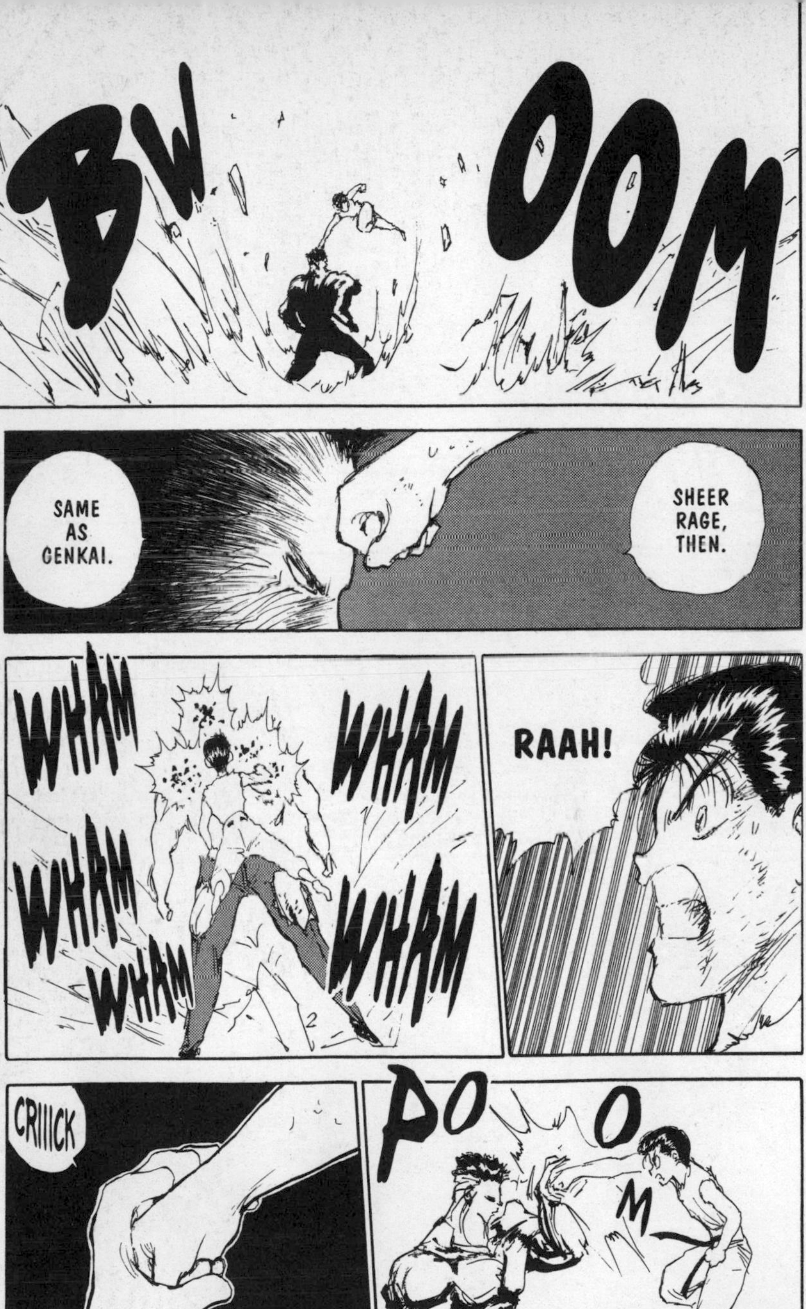
BW
OOM
SHEER RAGE, THEN.
SAME AS GENKAI.
RAAH!
WHRM
WHRM
WHRM
WHRM
WHRM
PO
O
M
CRIIICK

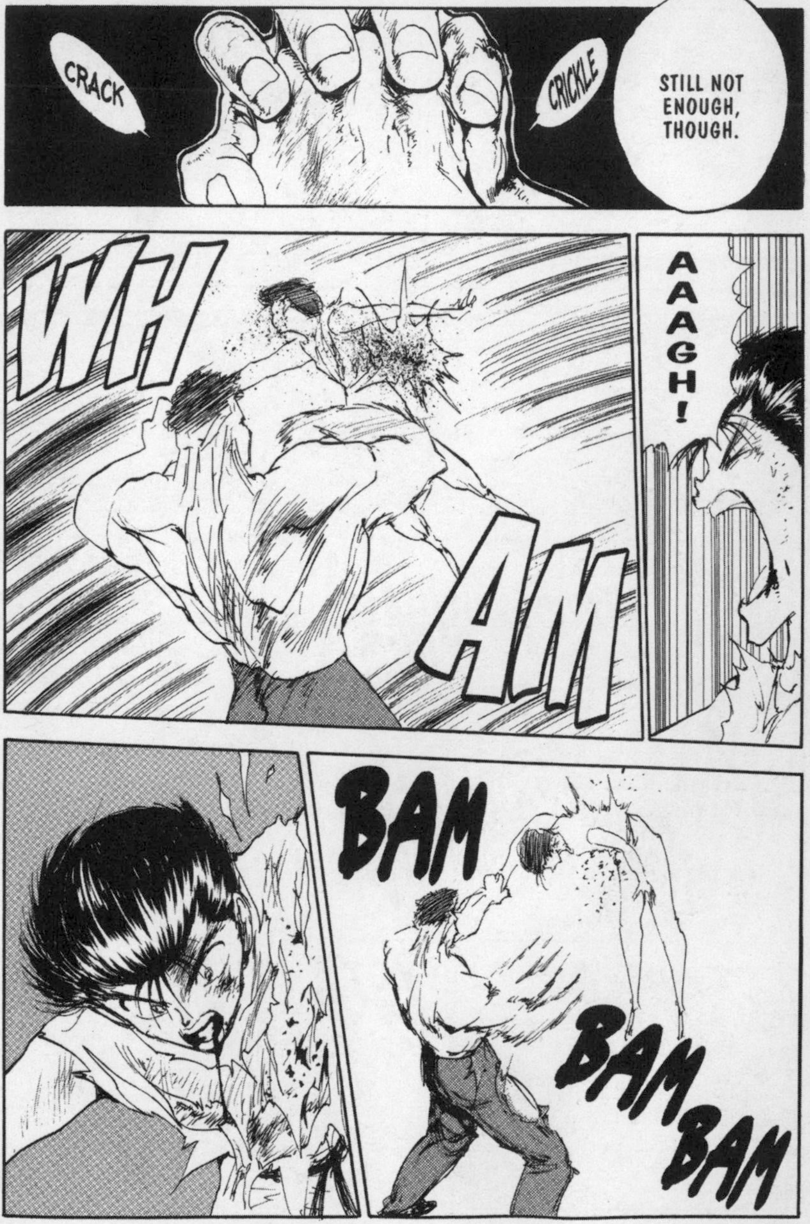
STILL NOT ENOUGH, THOUGH.
CRICKLE
CRACK
AAAAGH!
WH
AM
BAM
BAM
BAM
BAM

READ THIS WAY

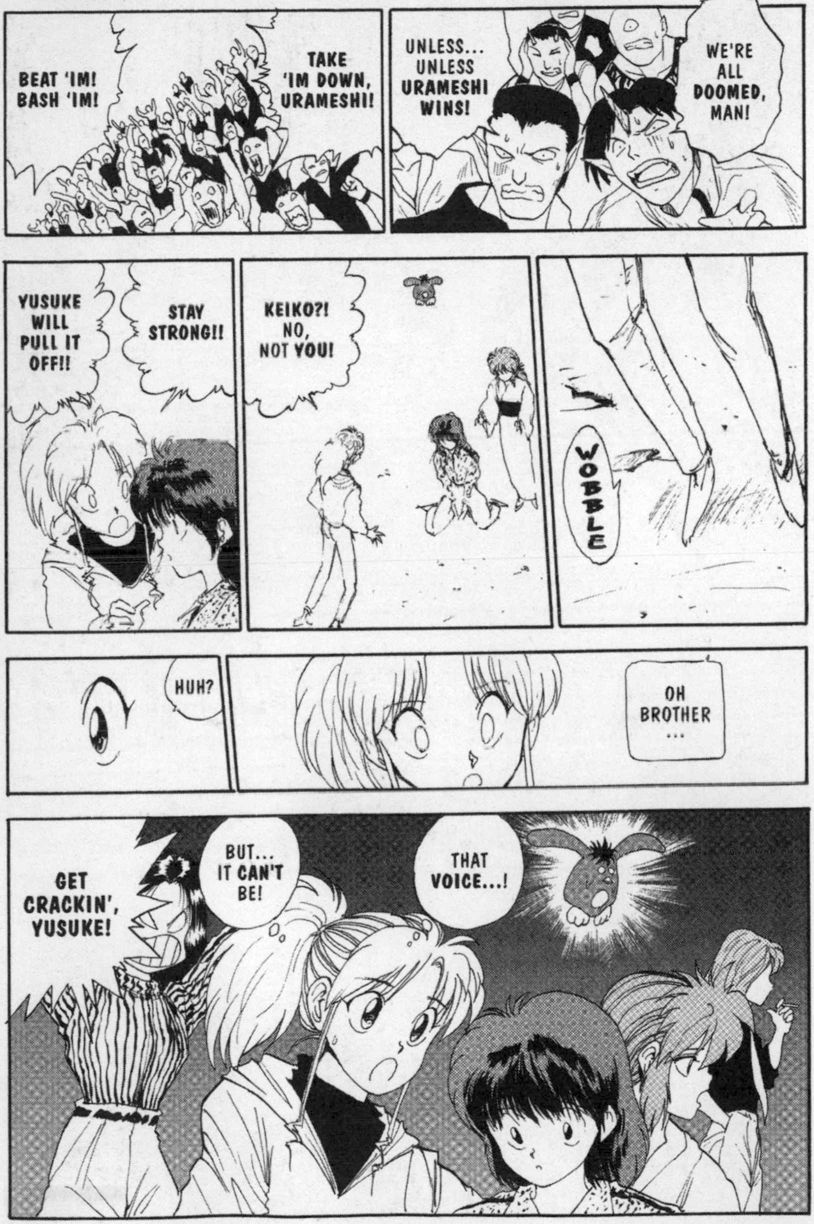
WE'RE ALL DOOMED, MAN!
UNLESS... UNLESS URAMESHI WINS!
TAKE 'IM DOWN, URAMESHI!
BEAT 'IM! BASH 'IM!
WOBBLE
KEIKO?! NO, NOT YOU!
STAY STRONG!!
YUSUKE WILL PULL IT OFF!!
OH BROTHER ...
HUH?
THAT VOICE...!
BUT... IT CAN'T BE!
GET CRACKIN', YUSUKE!

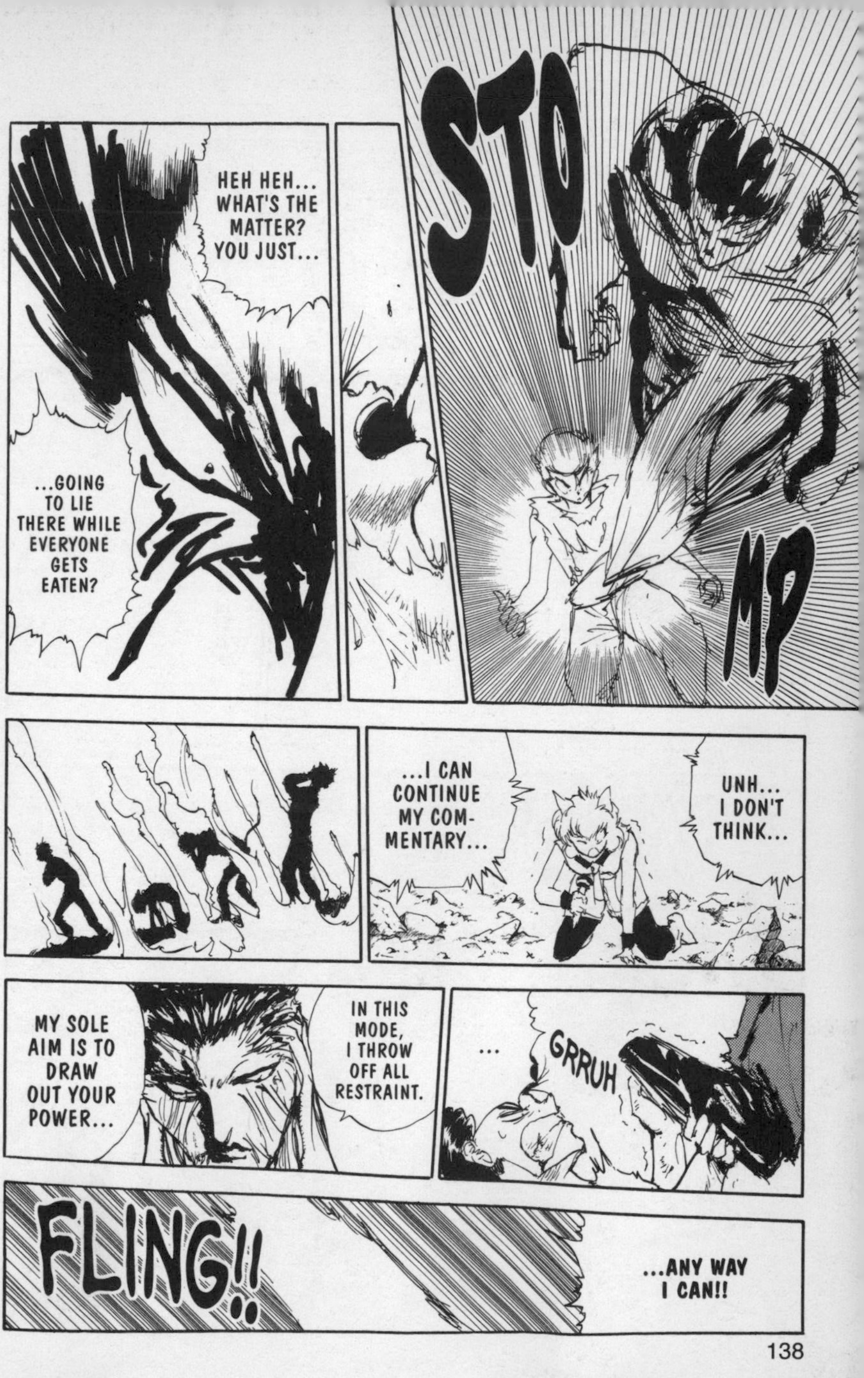
STO
MP
HEH HEH... WHAT'S THE MATTER? YOU JUST...
...GOING TO LIE THERE WHILE EVERYONE GETS EATEN?
UNH... I DON'T THINK...
...I CAN CONTINUE MY COMMENTARY...
GRRUH
...
IN THIS MODE, I THROW OFF ALL RESTRAINT.
MY SOLE AIM IS TO DRAW OUT YOUR POWER...
...ANY WAY I CAN!!
FLING!!

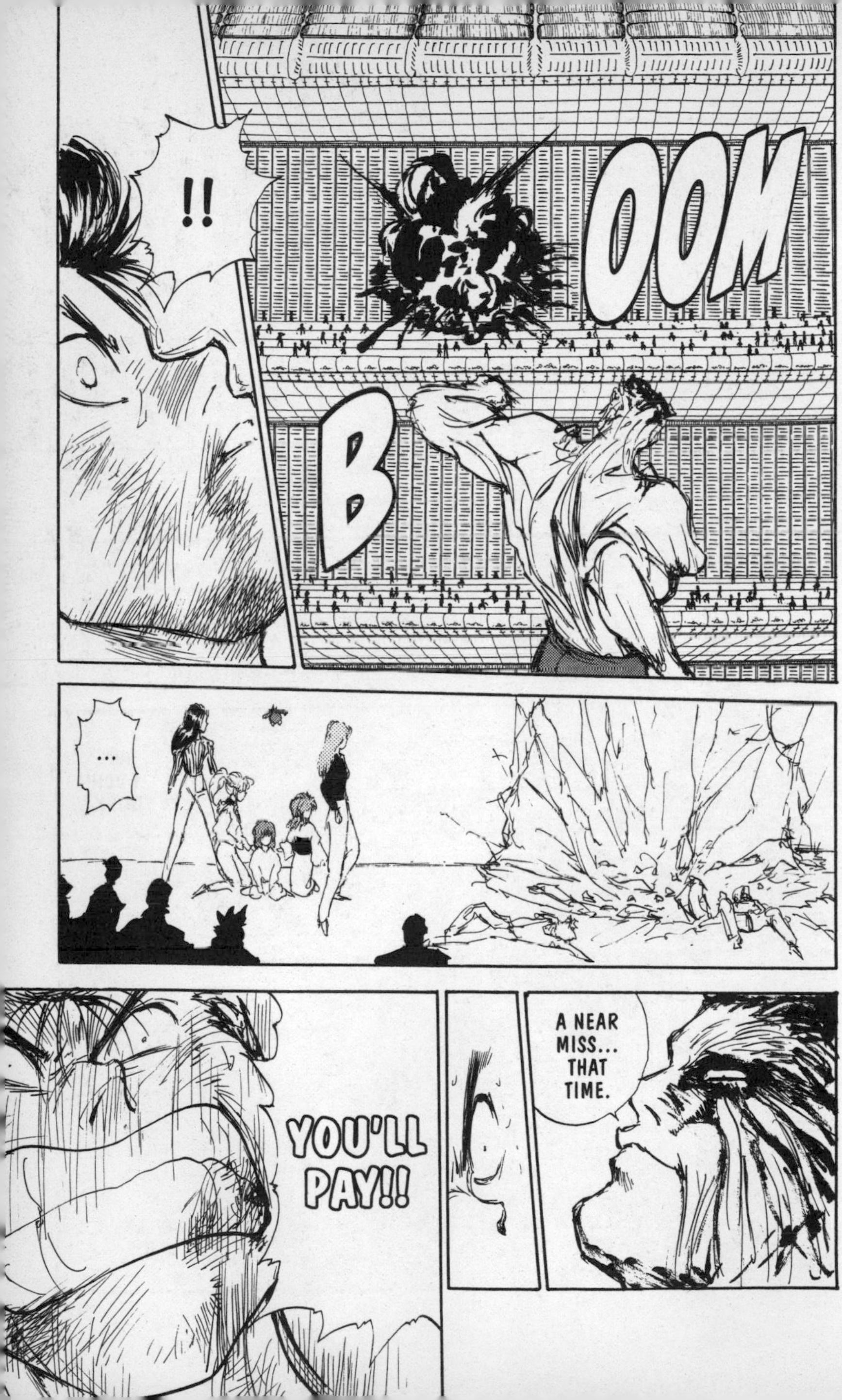

BOOM
!!
...
A NEAR MISS... THAT TIME.
YOU'LL PAY!!

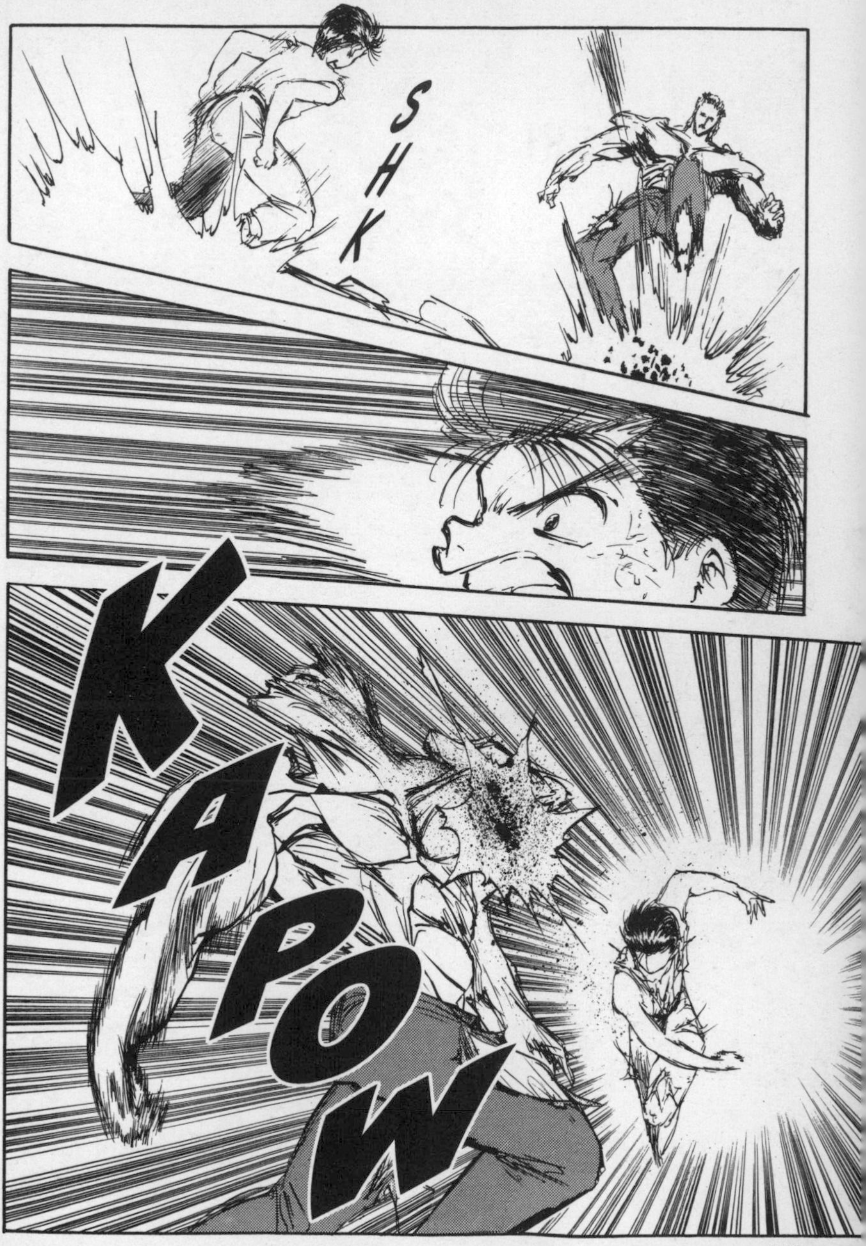
SHK
KAPOW

READ THIS WAY

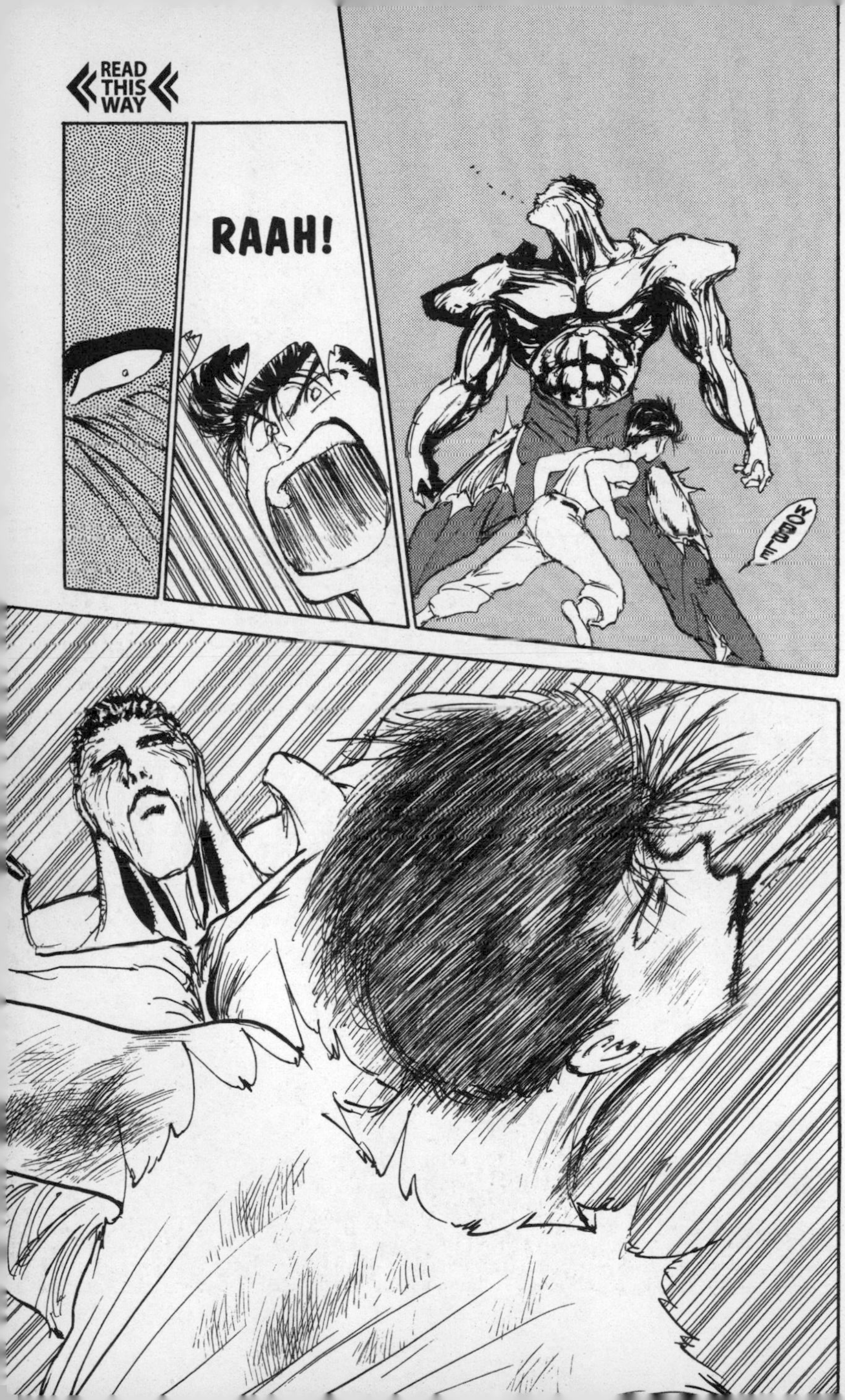
WOBBLE
RAAH!

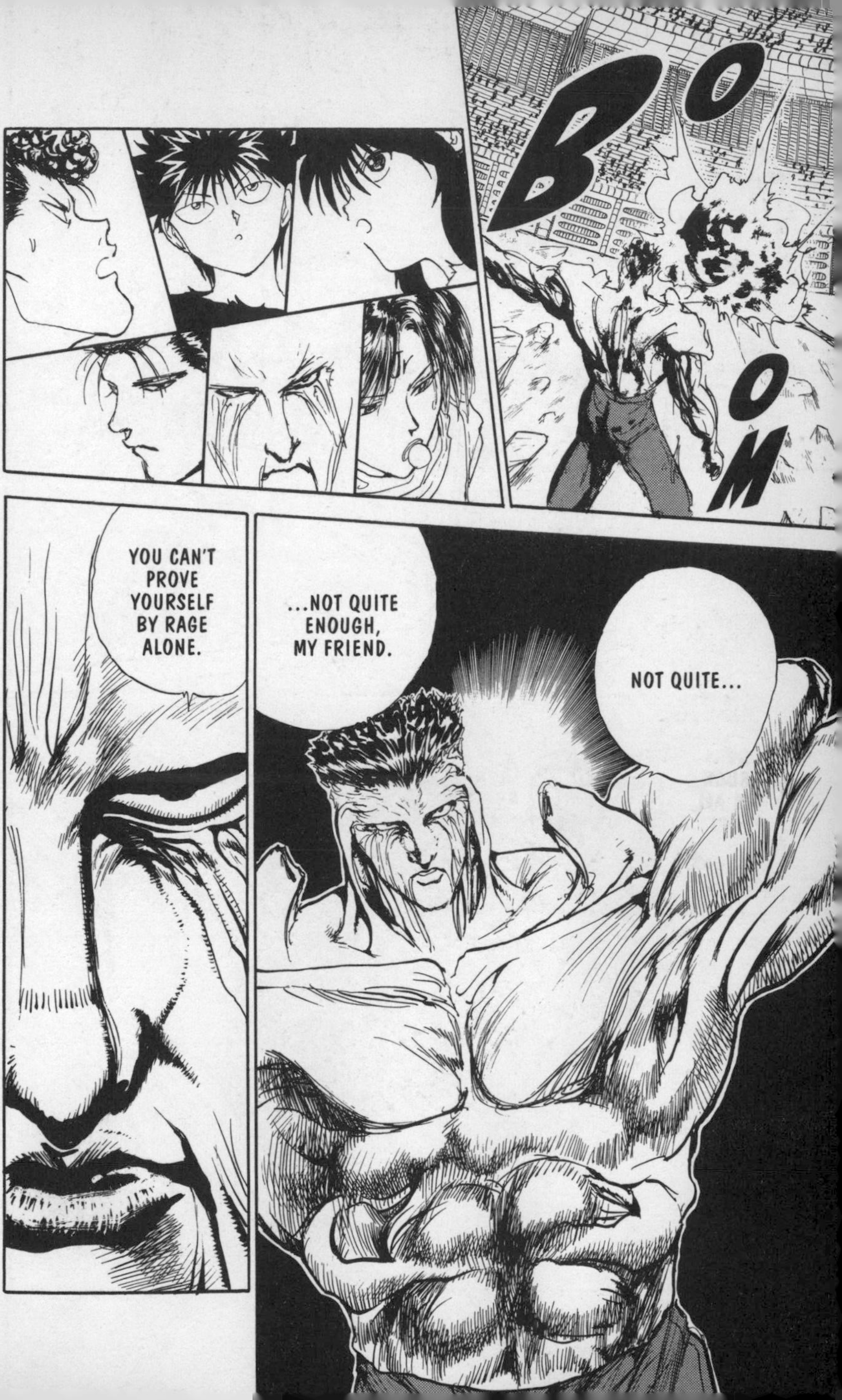
BOOM
NOT QUITE...
...NOT QUITE ENOUGH, MY FRIEND.
YOU CAN'T PROVE YOURSELF BY RAGE ALONE.

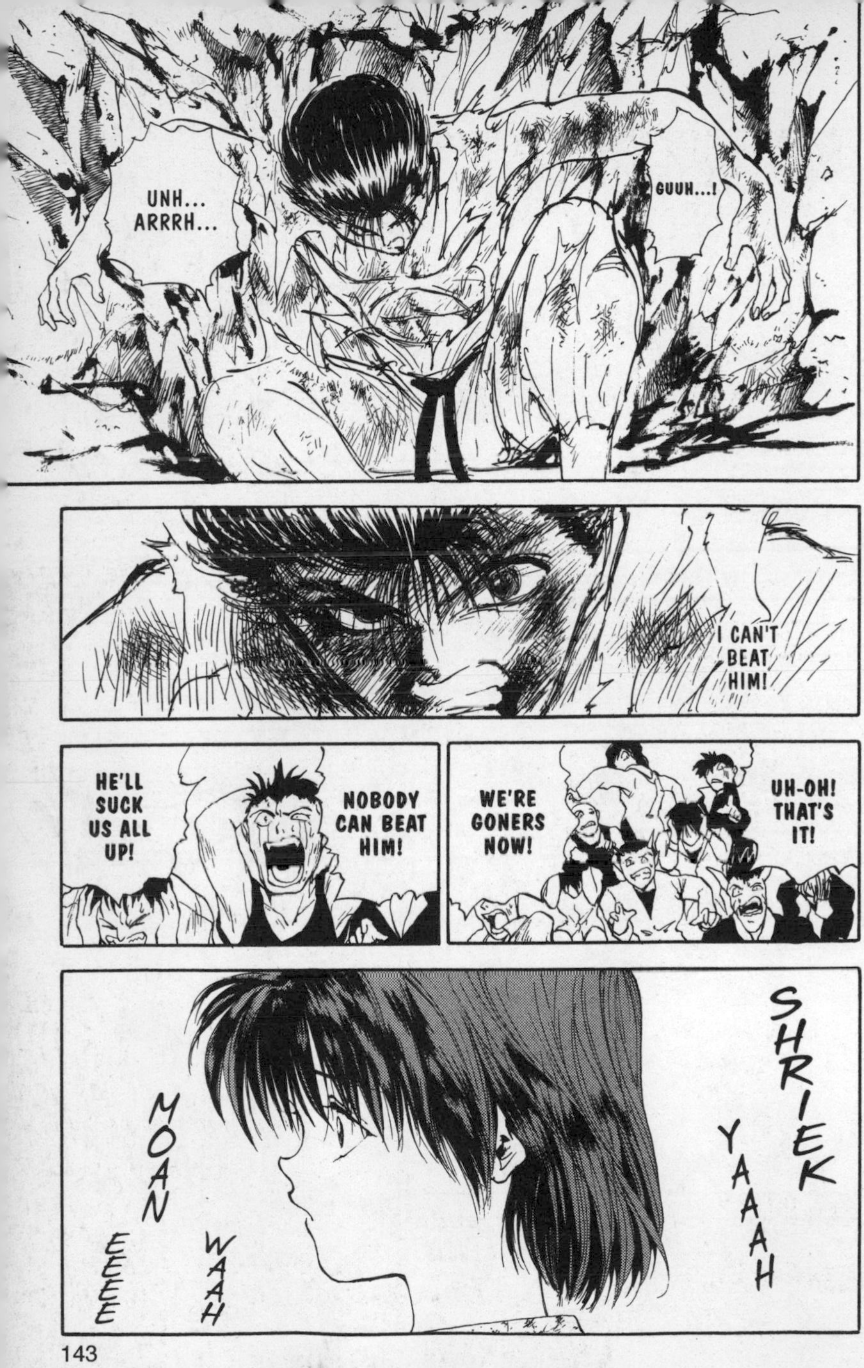
GUUH...!
UNH... ARRRH...
I CAN'T BEAT HIM!
UH-OH! THAT'S IT!
WE'RE GONERS NOW!
NOBODY CAN BEAT HIM!
HE'LL SUCK US ALL UP!
SHRIEK
YAAAH
WAAH
MOAN
EEEE

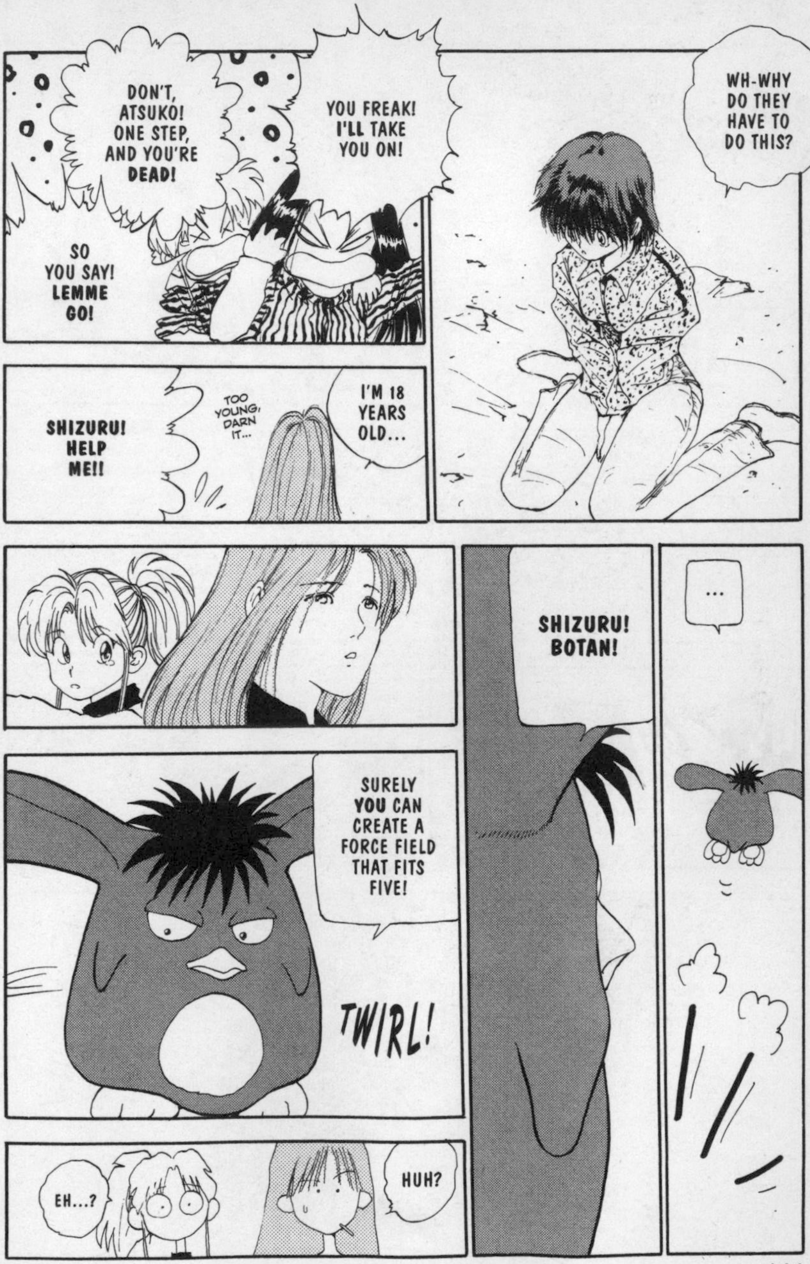
WH-WHY DO THEY HAVE TO DO THIS?
YOU FREAK! I'LL TAKE YOU ON!
DON'T, ATSUKO! ONE STEP, AND YOU'RE DEAD!
SO YOU SAY! LEMME GO!
I'M 18 YEARS OLD...
TOO YOUNG, DARN IT...
SHIZURU! HELP ME!!
...
SHIZURU! BOTAN!
SURELY YOU CAN CREATE A FORCE FIELD THAT FITS FIVE!
TWIRL!
HUH?
EH...?

READ THIS WAY

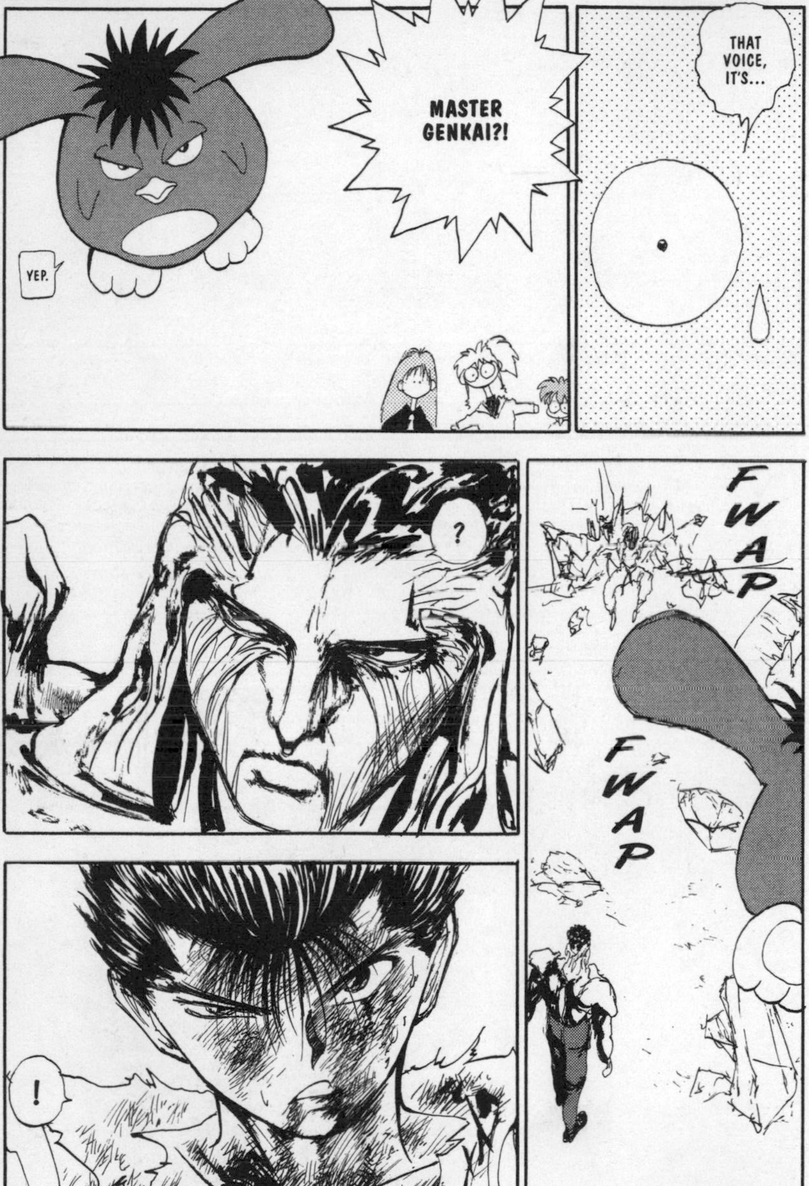
THAT VOICE, IT'S...
MASTER GENKAI?!
YEP.
FWAP
FWAP
?
!

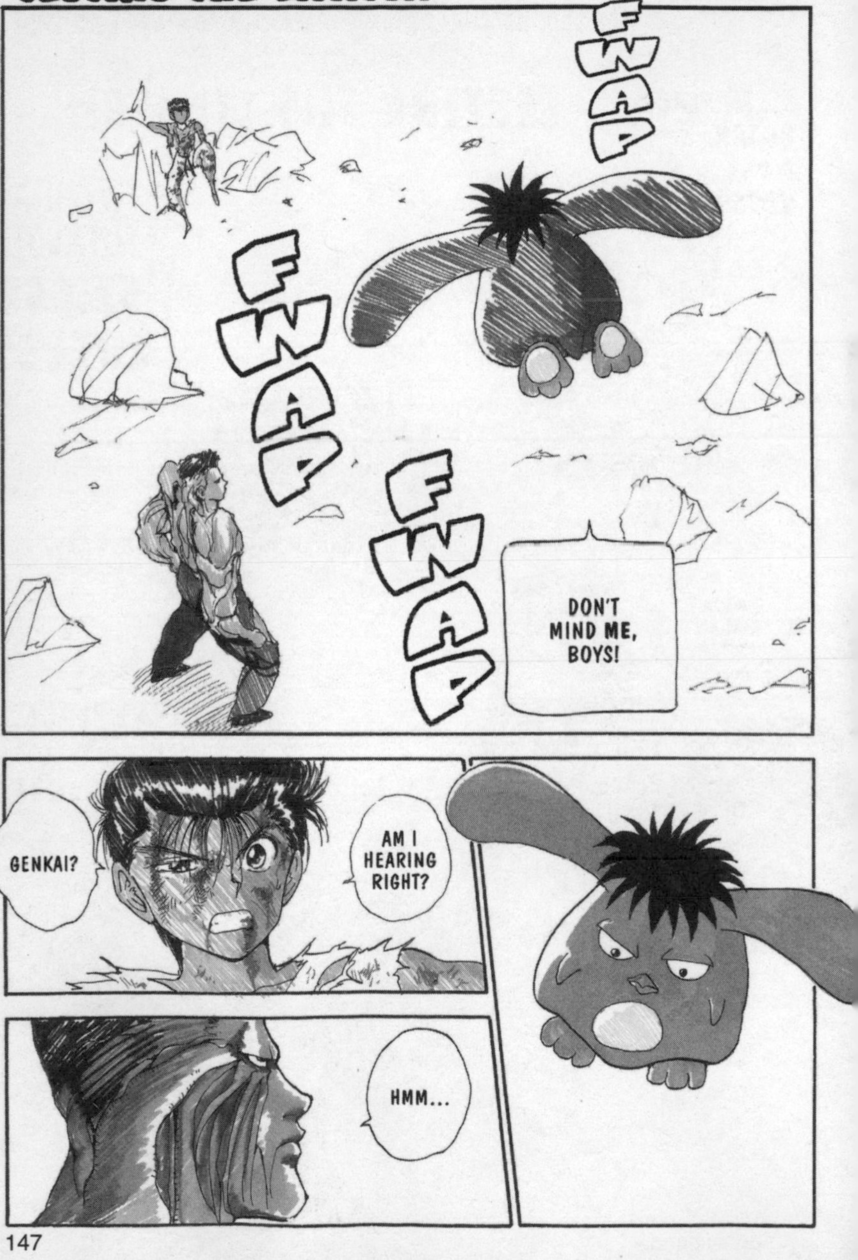
FWAP
FWAP
FWAP
DON'T MIND ME, BOYS!
AM I HEARING RIGHT?
GENKAI?
HMM...

THE SECOND CHARACTER POPULARITY CONTEST RESULTS!!

THIS POLL WAS CONDUCTED IN JAPAN.

TESTING THE LIMITS!!

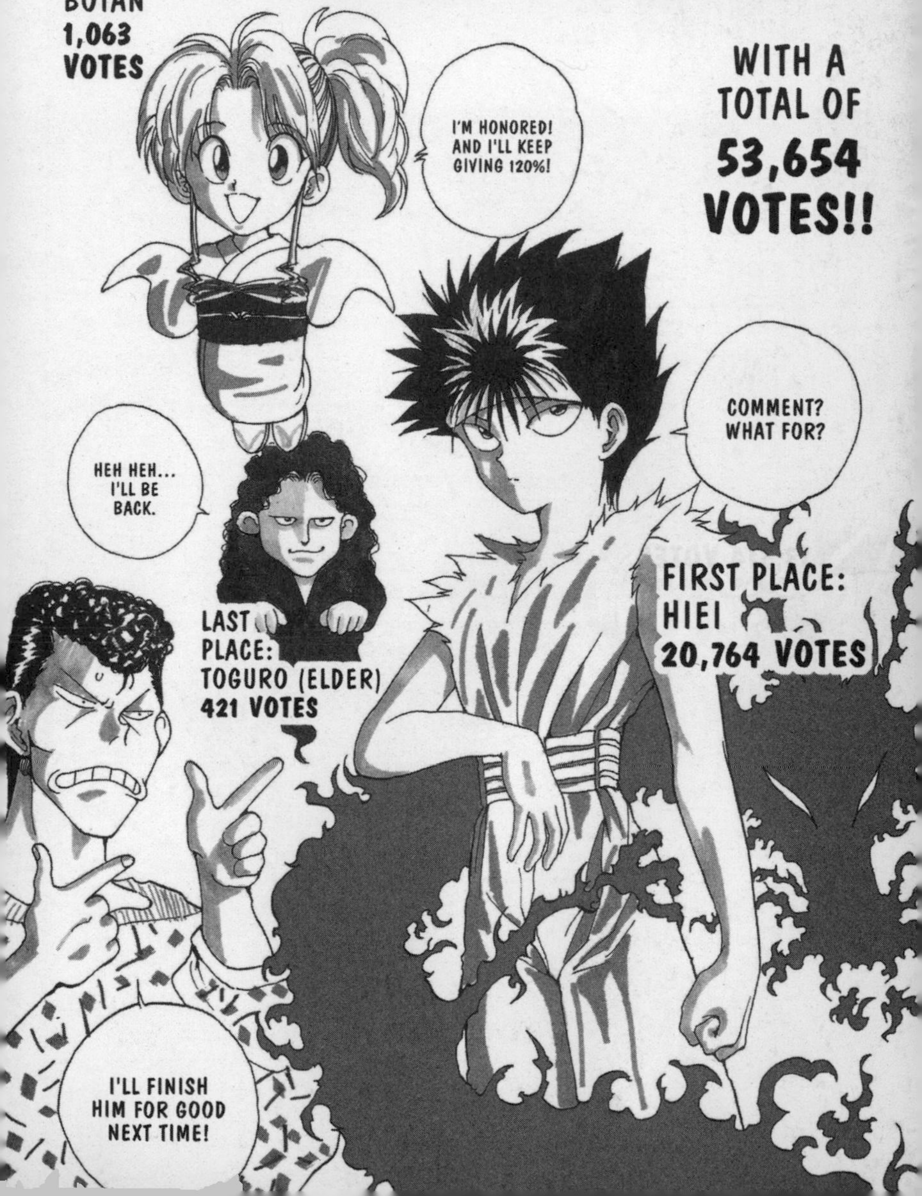
WITH A TOTAL OF 53,654 VOTES!!
I'M HONORED! AND I'LL KEEP GIVING 120%!
SIXTH PLACE: BOTAN 1,063 VOTES
COMMENT? WHAT FOR?
FIRST PLACE: HIEI 20,764 VOTES
HEH HEH... I'LL BE BACK.
LAST PLACE: TOGURO (ELDER) 421 VOTES
I'LL FINISH HIM FOR GOOD NEXT TIME!

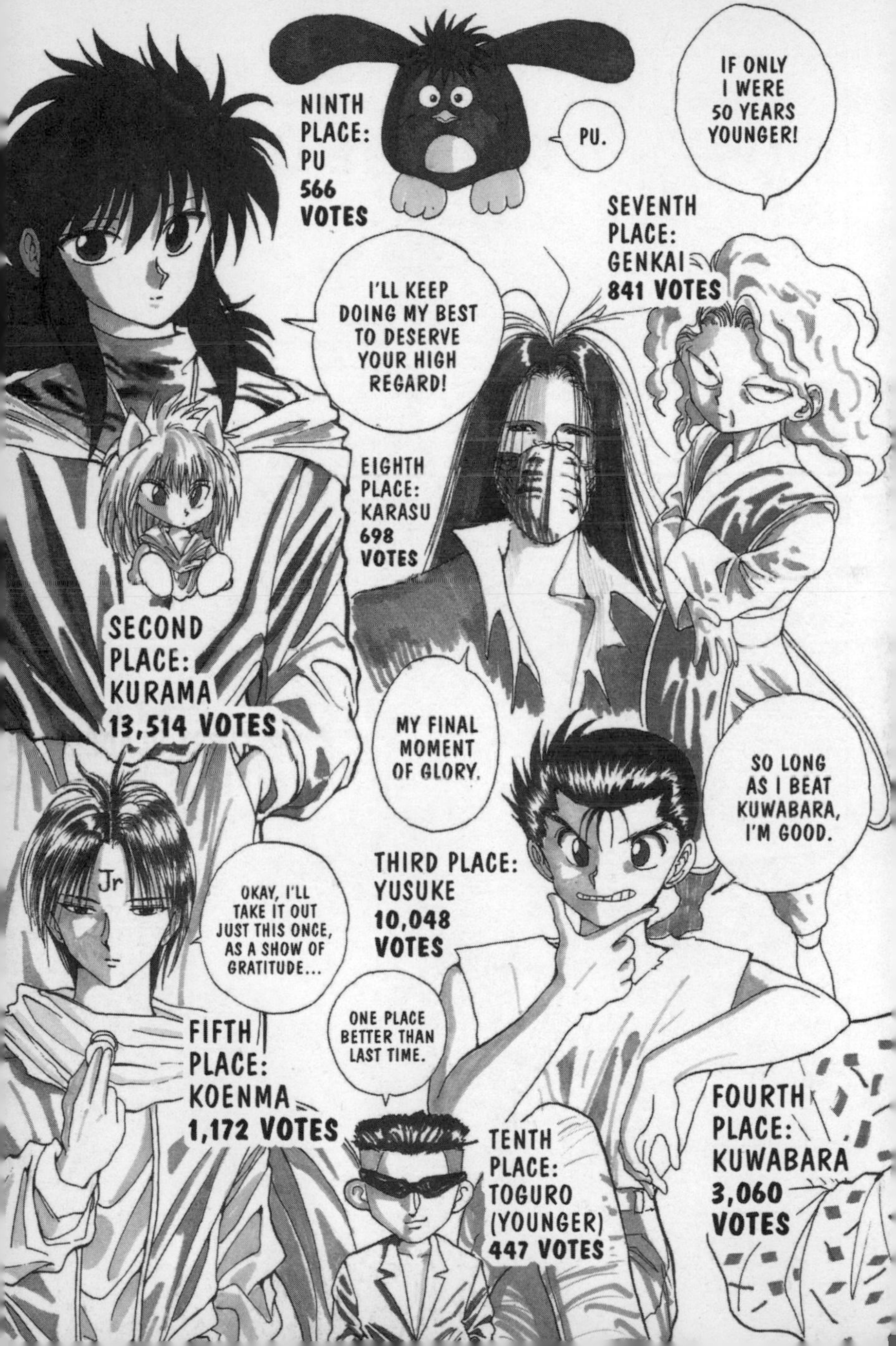
IF ONLY I WERE 50 YEARS YOUNGER!
PU.
NINTH PLACE: PU 566 VOTES
SEVENTH PLACE: GENKAI 841 VOTES
I'LL KEEP DOING MY BEST TO DESERVE YOUR HIGH REGARD!
EIGHTH PLACE: KARASU 698 VOTES
SECOND PLACE: KURAMA 13,514 VOTES
SO LONG AS I BEAT KUWABARA, I'M GOOD.
MY FINAL MOMENT OF GLORY.
THIRD PLACE: YUSUKE 10,048 VOTES
OKAY, I'LL TAKE IT OUT JUST THIS ONCE, AS A SHOW OF GRATITUDE...
FOURTH PLACE: KUWABARA 3,060 VOTES
ONE PLACE BETTER THAN LAST TIME.
TENTH PLACE: TOGURO (YOUNGER) 447 VOTES
FIFTH PLACE: KOENMA 1,172 VOTES

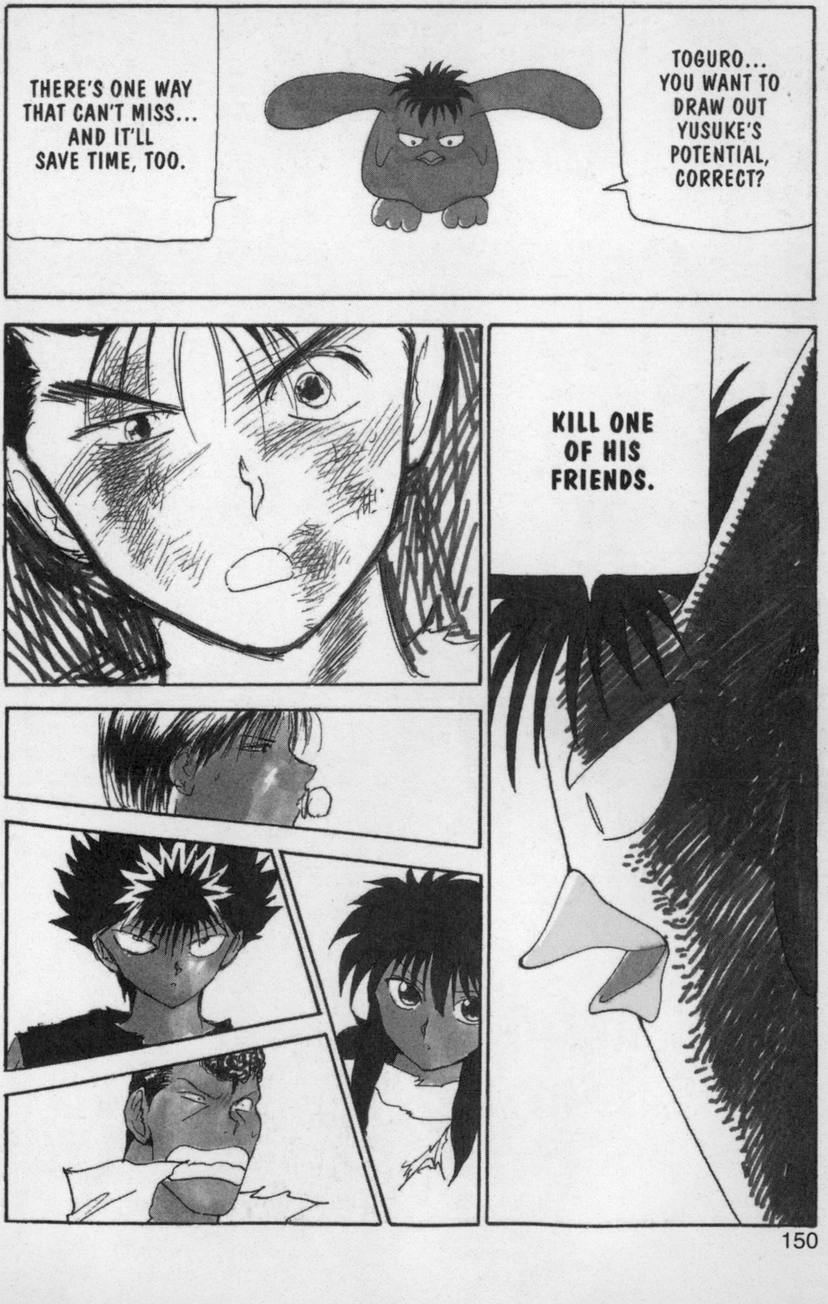
TOGURO... YOU WANT TO DRAW OUT YUSUKE'S POTENTIAL, CORRECT?
THERE'S ONE WAY THAT CAN'T MISS... AND IT'LL SAVE TIME, TOO.
KILL ONE OF HIS FRIENDS.

READ THIS WAY

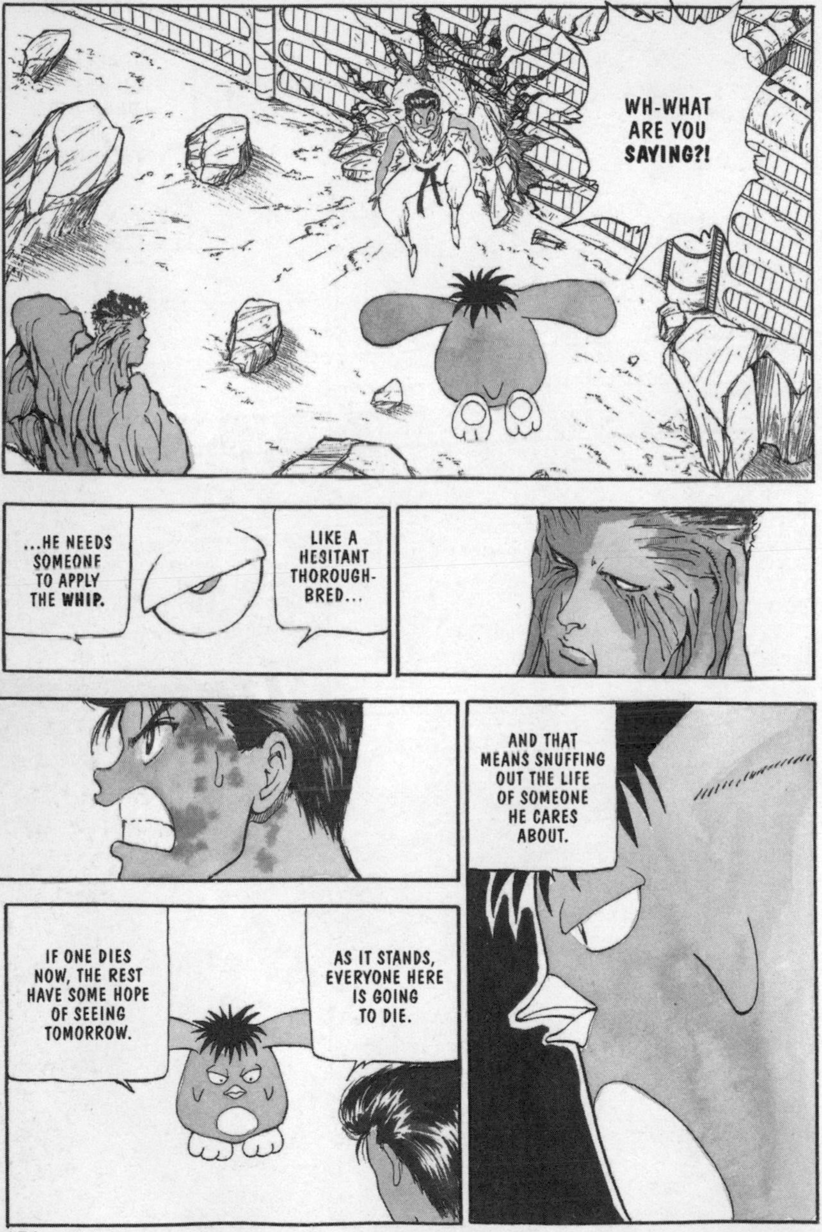

WH-WHAT ARE YOU SAYING?!
LIKE A HESITANT THOROUGH-BRED...
...HE NEEDS SOMEONE TO APPLY THE WHIP.
AND THAT MEANS SNUFFING OUT THE LIFE OF SOMEONE HE CARES ABOUT.
AS IT STANDS, EVERYONE HERE IS GOING TO DIE.
IF ONE DIES NOW, THE REST HAVE SOME HOPE OF SEEING TOMORROW.

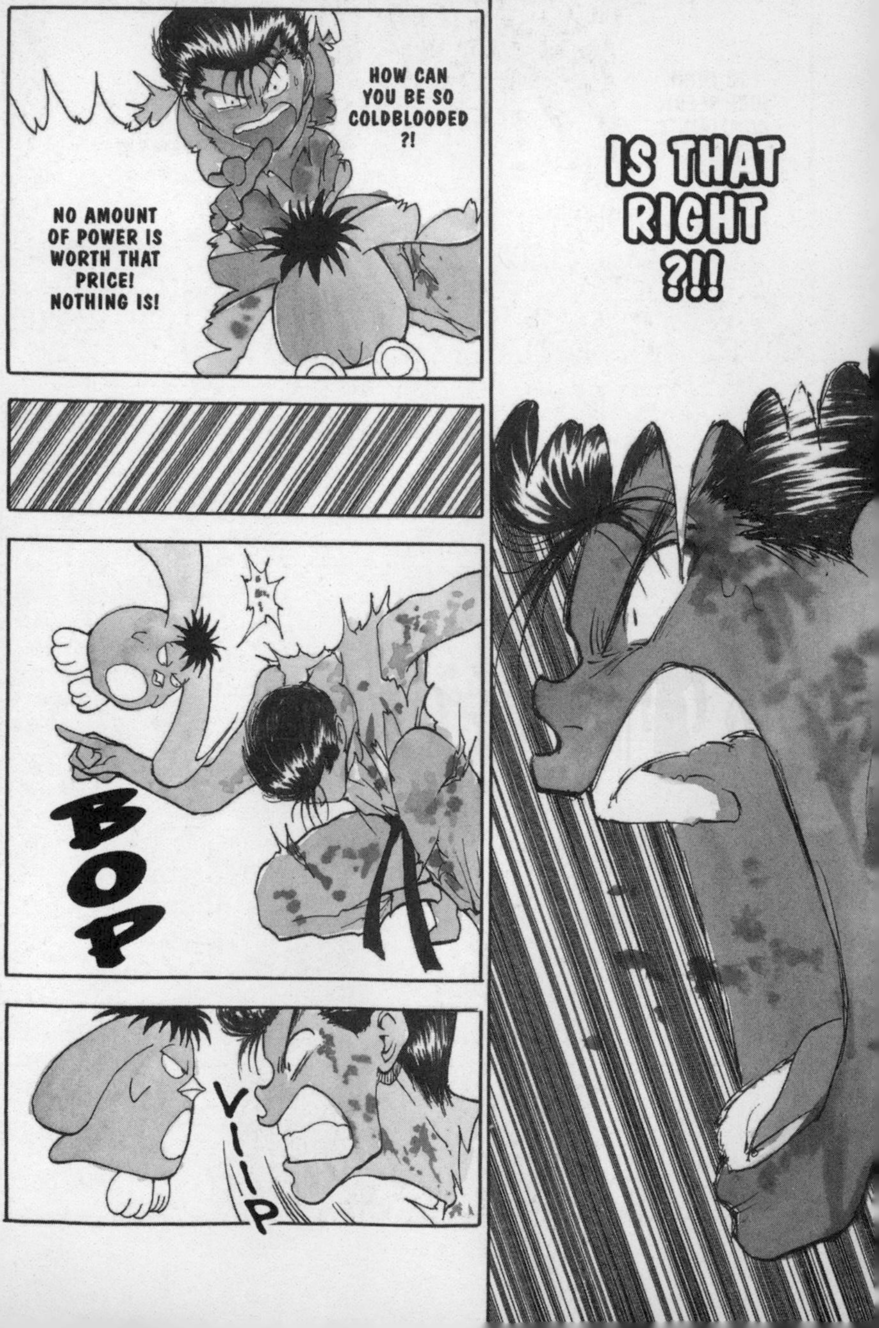
IS THAT RIGHT ?!!
HOW CAN YOU BE SO COLDBLOODED ?!
NO AMOUNT OF POWER IS WORTH THAT PRICE! NOTHING IS!
BOP
VIIP

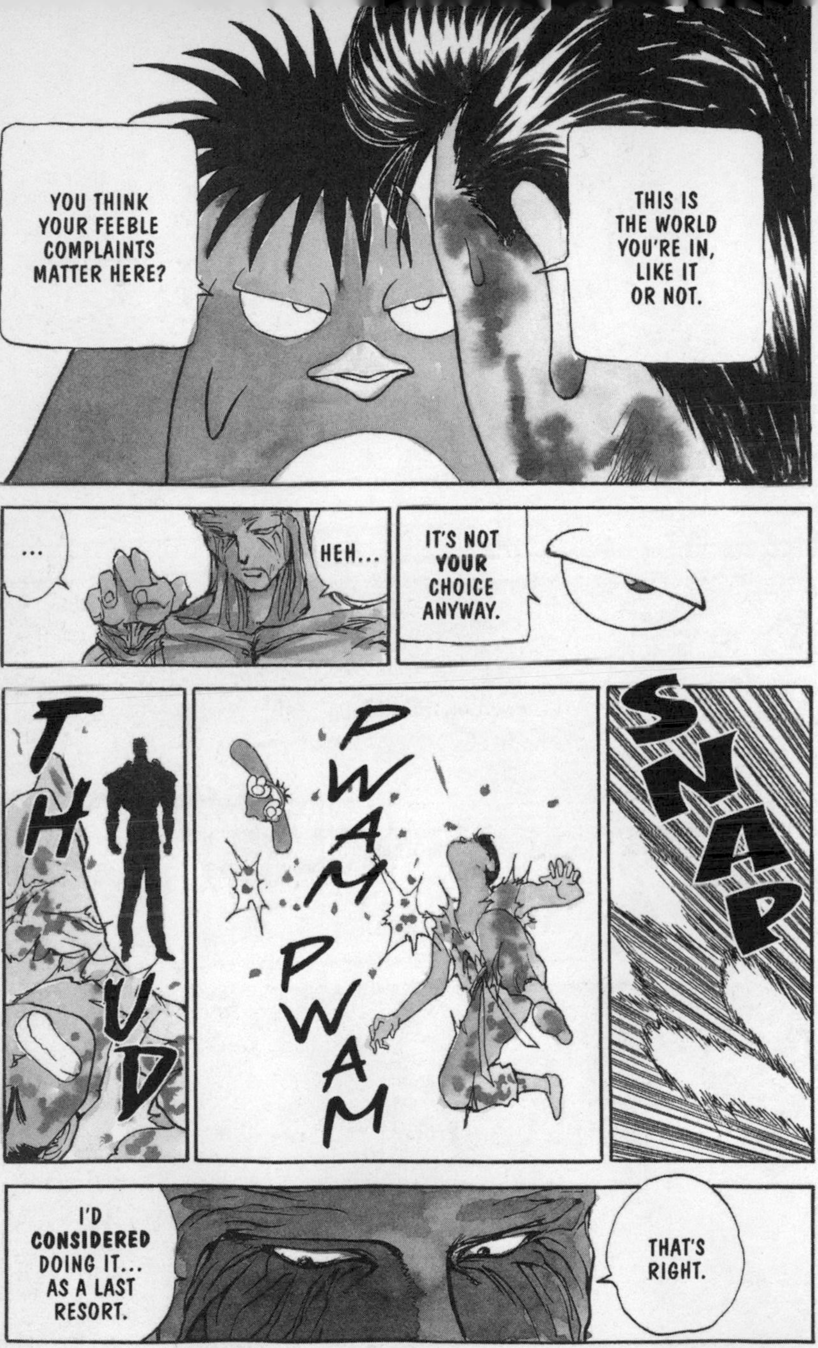
THIS IS THE WORLD YOU'RE IN, LIKE IT OR NOT.
YOU THINK YOUR FEEBLE COMPLAINTS MATTER HERE?
IT'S NOT YOUR CHOICE ANYWAY.
HEH...
...
SNAP
PWAM PWAM
THUD
THAT'S RIGHT.
I'D CONSIDERED DOING IT... AS A LAST RESORT.

UNH!

DON'T...!

SINCE IT APPEARS YOU HAVE LITTLE CONTROL OVER YOUR POWER...

...MY COURSE IS CLEAR.

HMM...

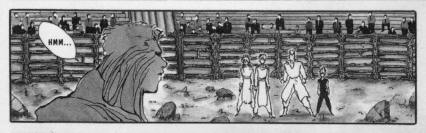

YOU GET TO DIE.

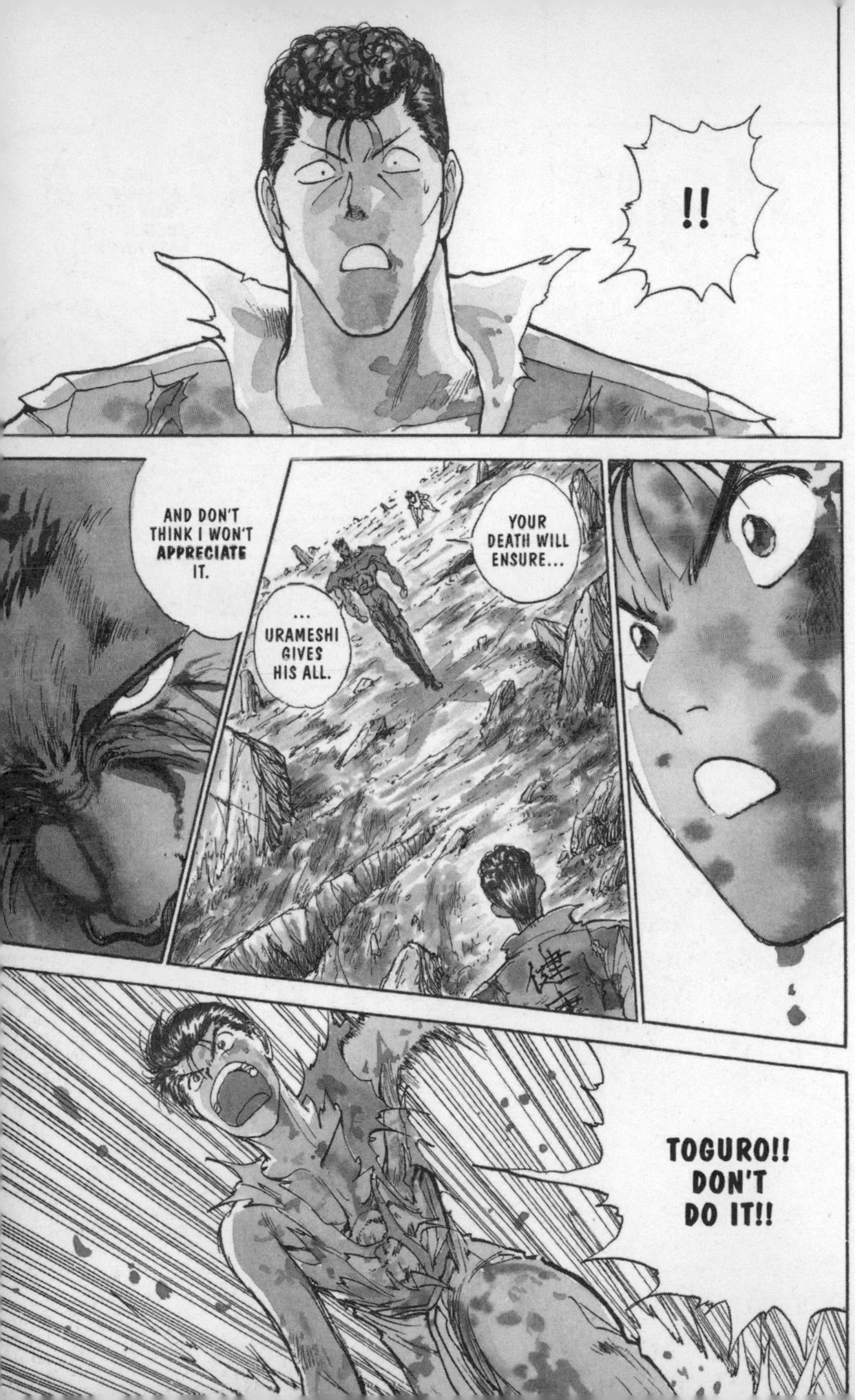
!!
YOUR DEATH WILL ENSURE...
...URAMESHI GIVES HIS ALL.
AND DON'T THINK I WON'T APPRECIATE IT.
TOGURO!! DON'T DO IT!!

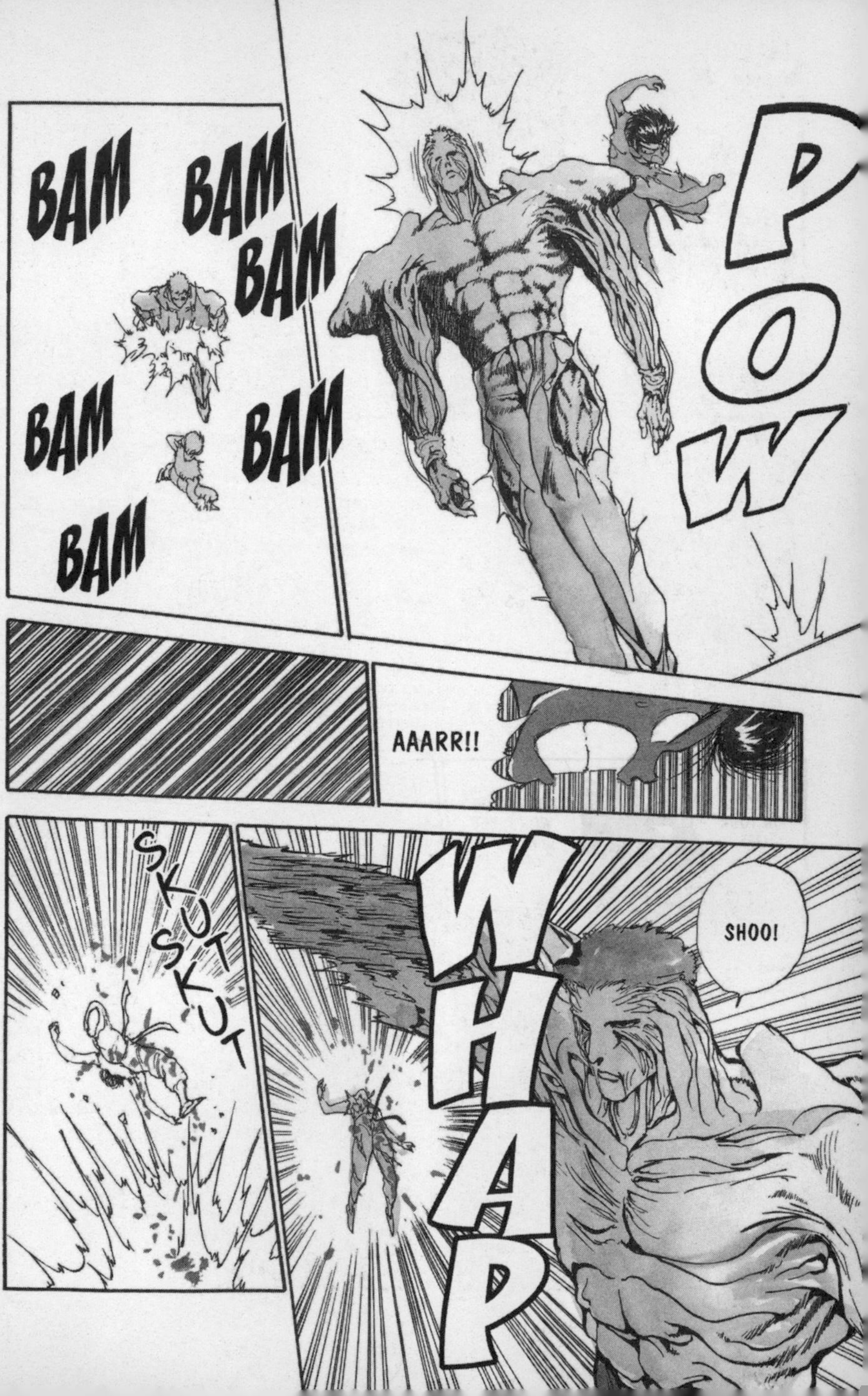
POW
BAM
BAM
BAM
BAM
BAM
BAM
BAM
AAARR!!
SHOO!
WHAP
SKUT
SKUT

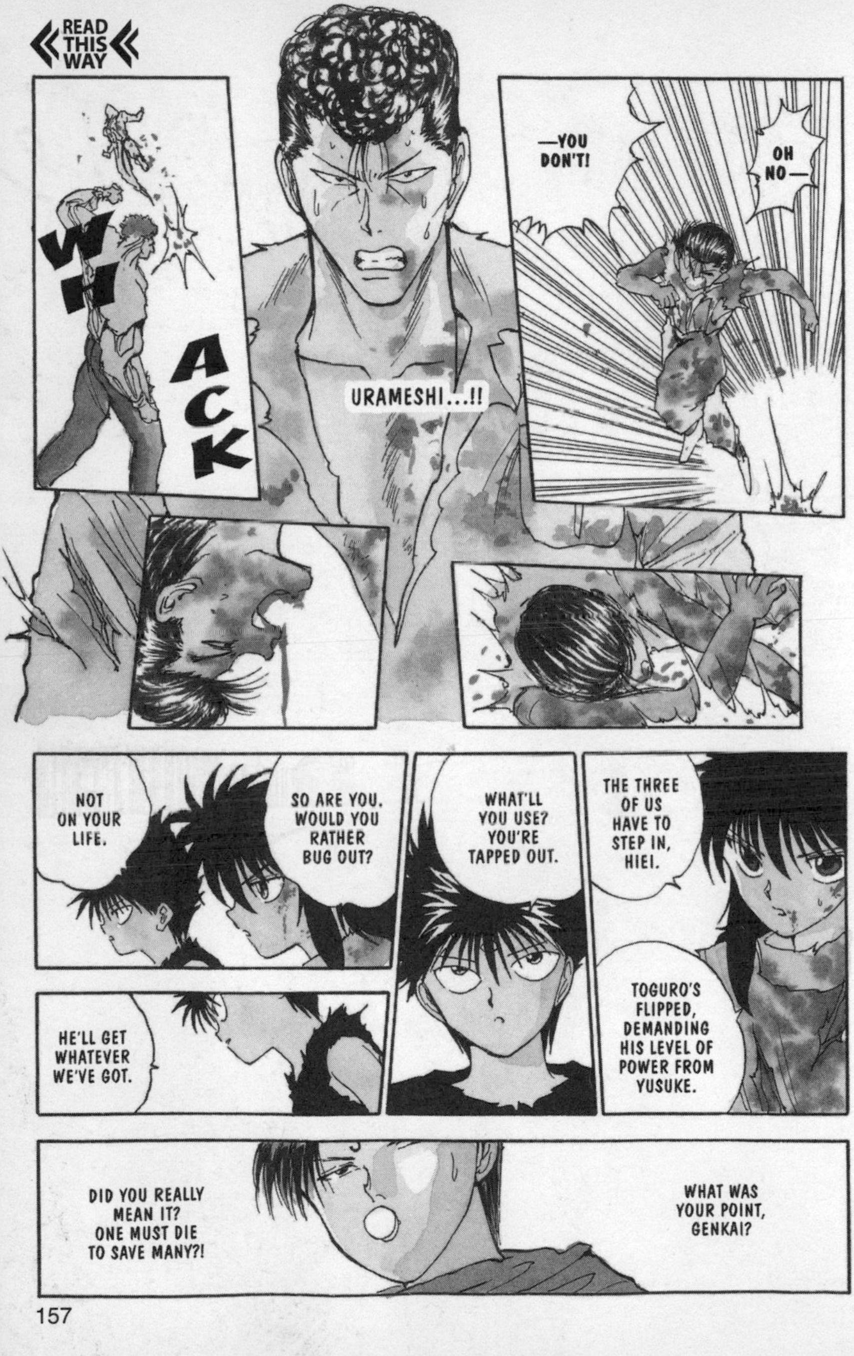
READ THIS WAY
OH NO—
—YOU DON'T!
URAMESHI...!!
WH
ACK
THE THREE OF US HAVE TO STEP IN, HIEI.
TOGURO'S FLIPPED, DEMANDING HIS LEVEL OF POWER FROM YUSUKE.
WHAT'LL YOU USE? YOU'RE TAPPED OUT.
SO ARE YOU. WOULD YOU RATHER BUG OUT?
NOT ON YOUR LIFE.
HE'LL GET WHATEVER WE'VE GOT.
WHAT WAS YOUR POINT, GENKAI?
DID YOU REALLY MEAN IT? ONE MUST DIE TO SAVE MANY?!

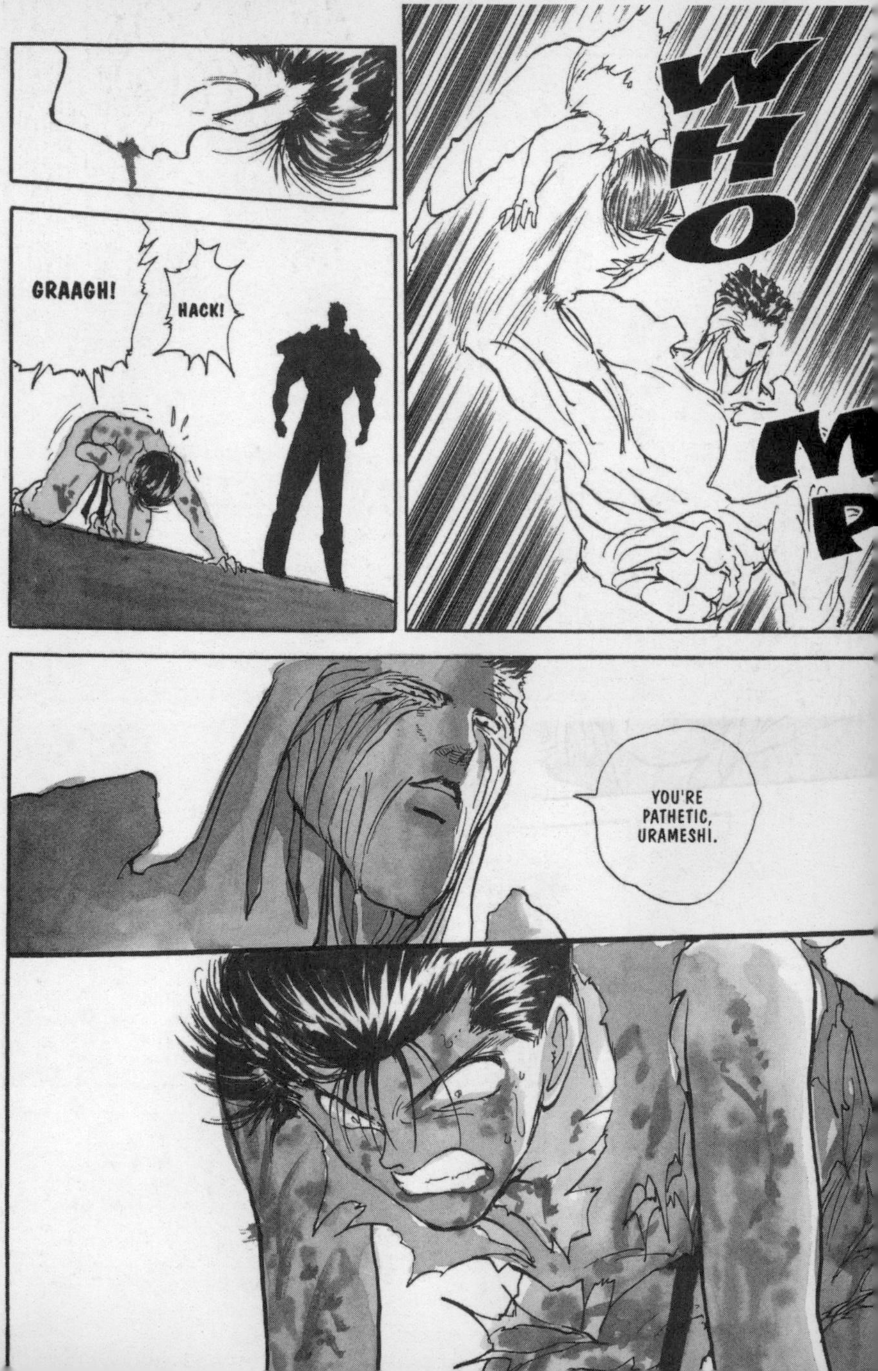
WHOMP
GRAAGH!
HACK!
YOU'RE PATHETIC, URAMESHI.

READ THIS WAY

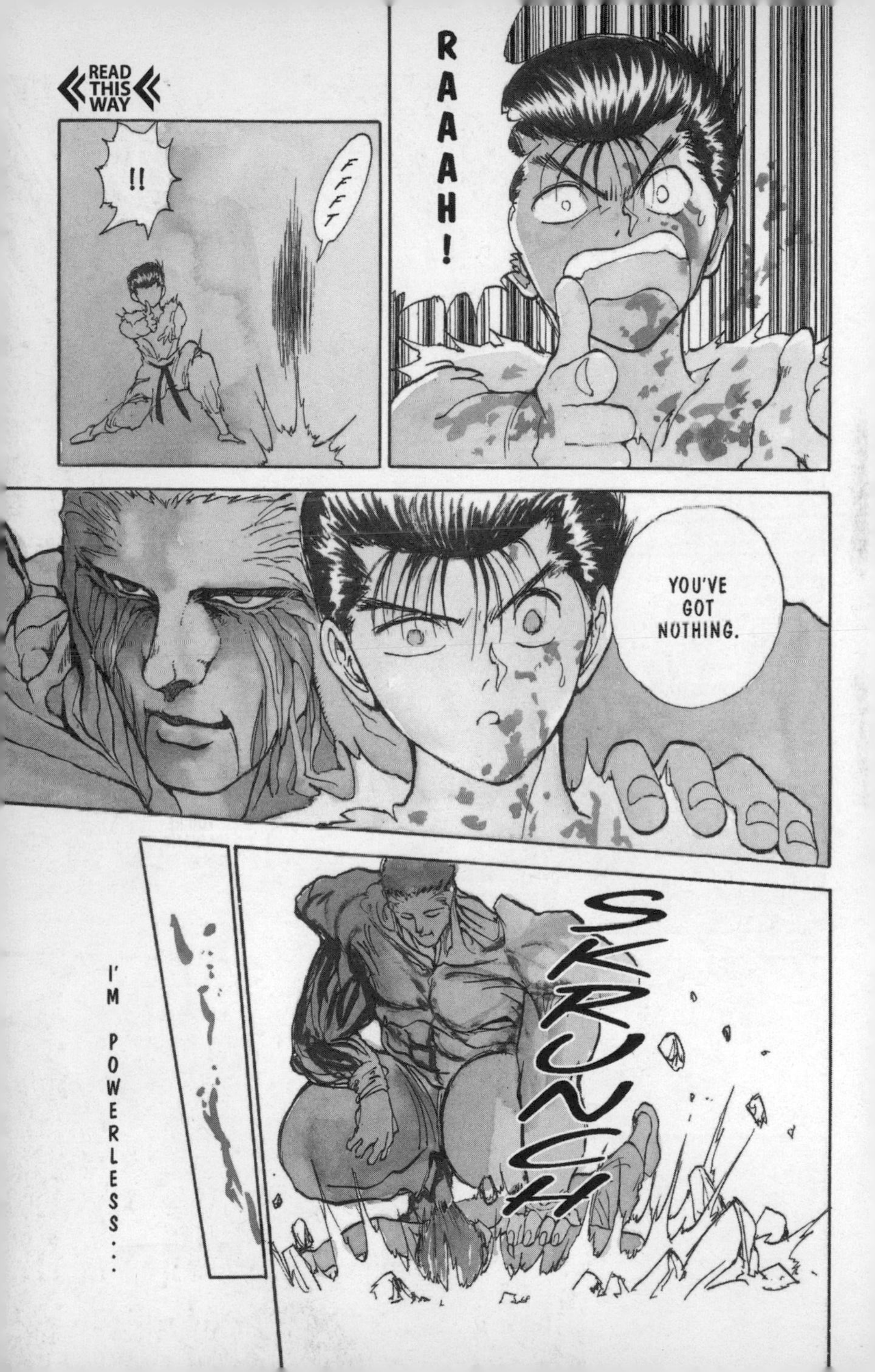
RAAAAH!
FFFT
!!
YOU'VE GOT NOTHING.
SKRUNCH
I'M POWERLESS...

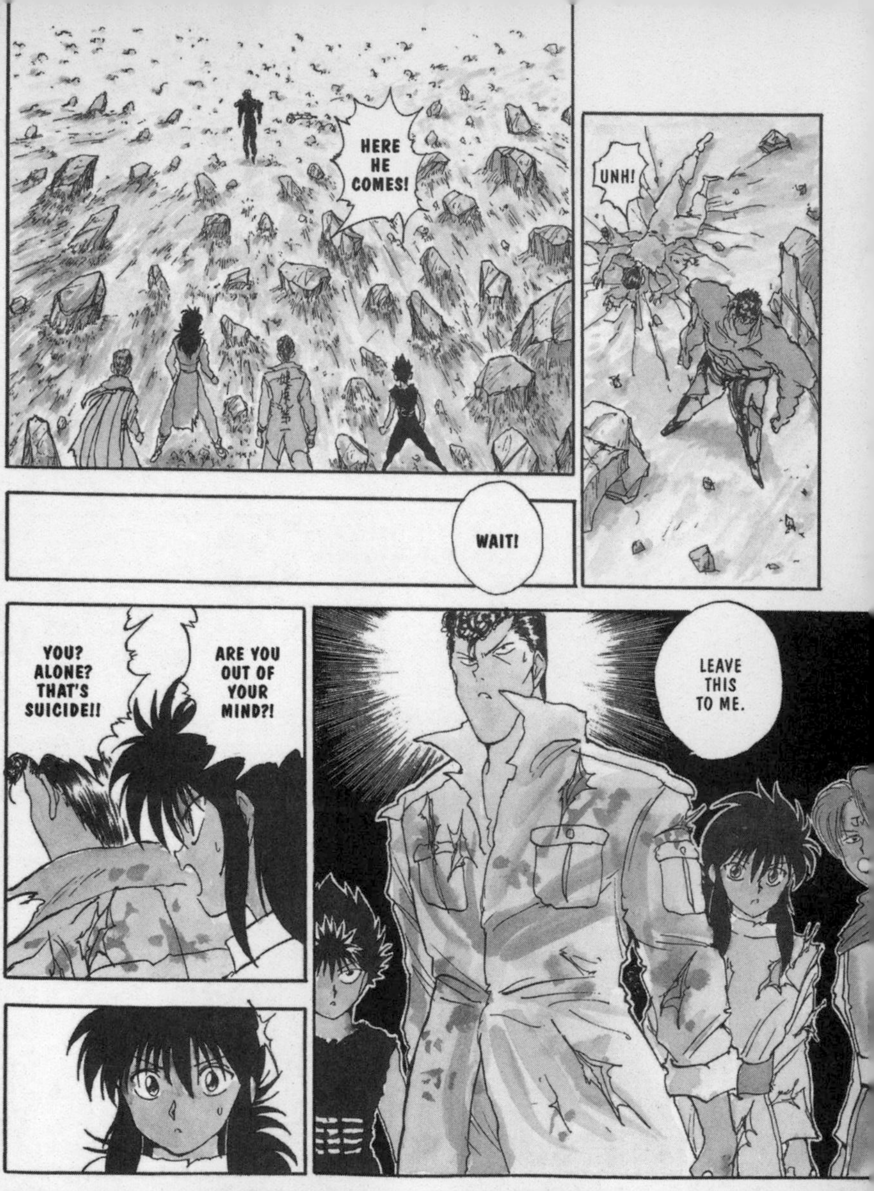
UNH!
HERE HE COMES!
WAIT!
LEAVE THIS TO ME.
ARE YOU OUT OF YOUR MIND?!
YOU? ALONE? THAT'S SUICIDE!!

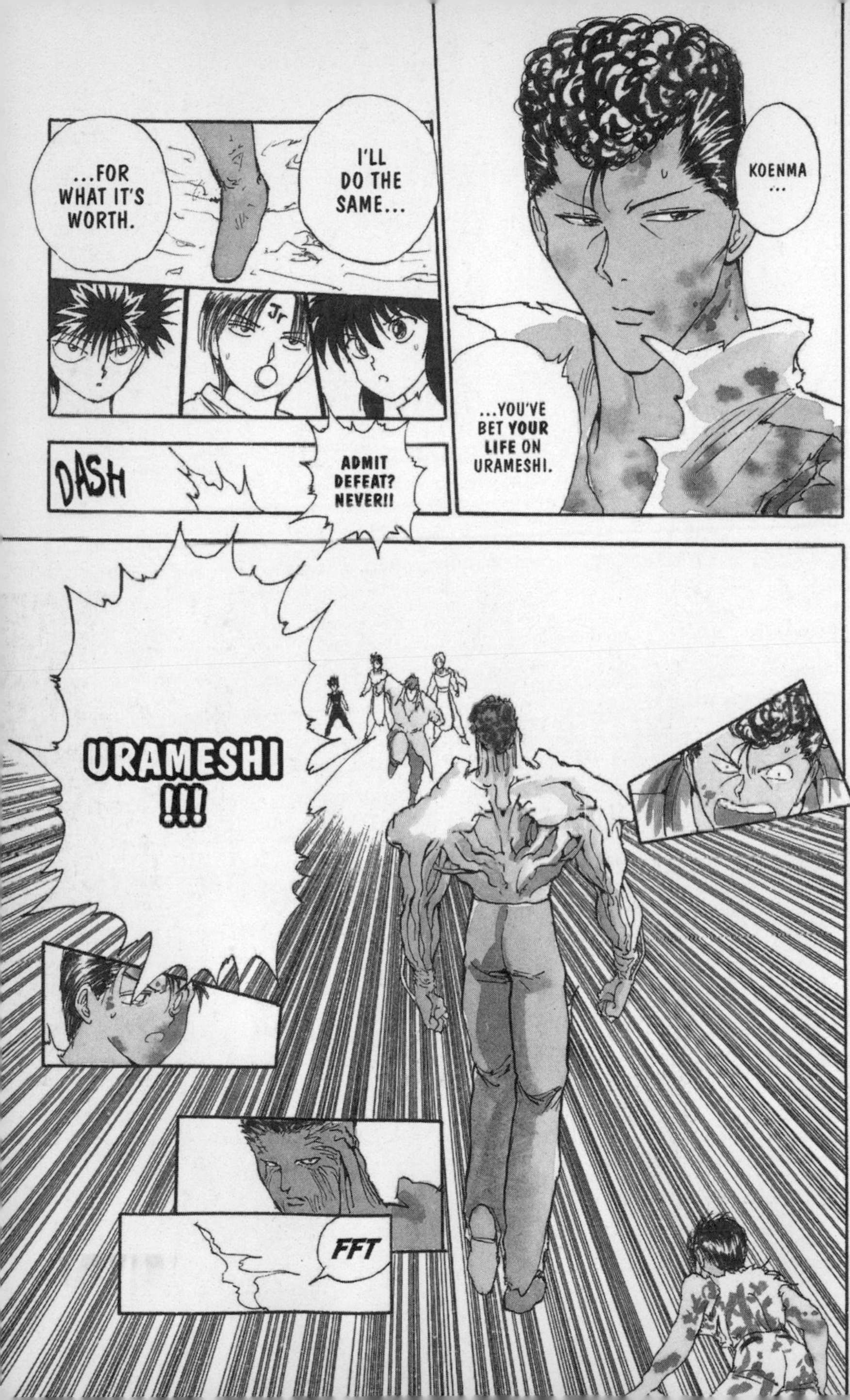
KOENMA ...
...YOU'VE BET YOUR LIFE ON URAMESHI.
I'LL DO THE SAME...
...FOR WHAT IT'S WORTH.
DASH
ADMIT DEFEAT? NEVER!!
URAMESHI !!!
FFT

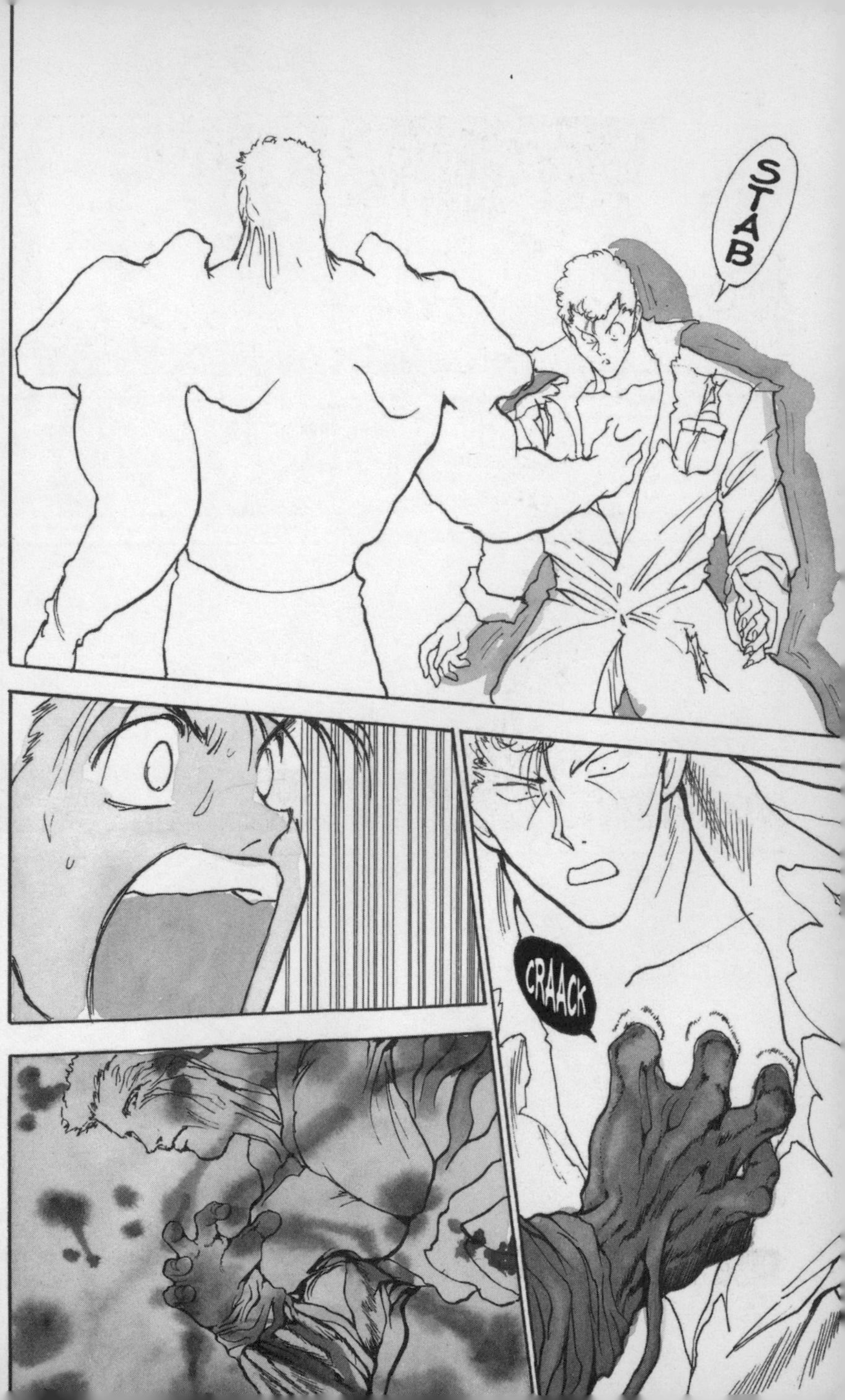
STAB
CRAACK

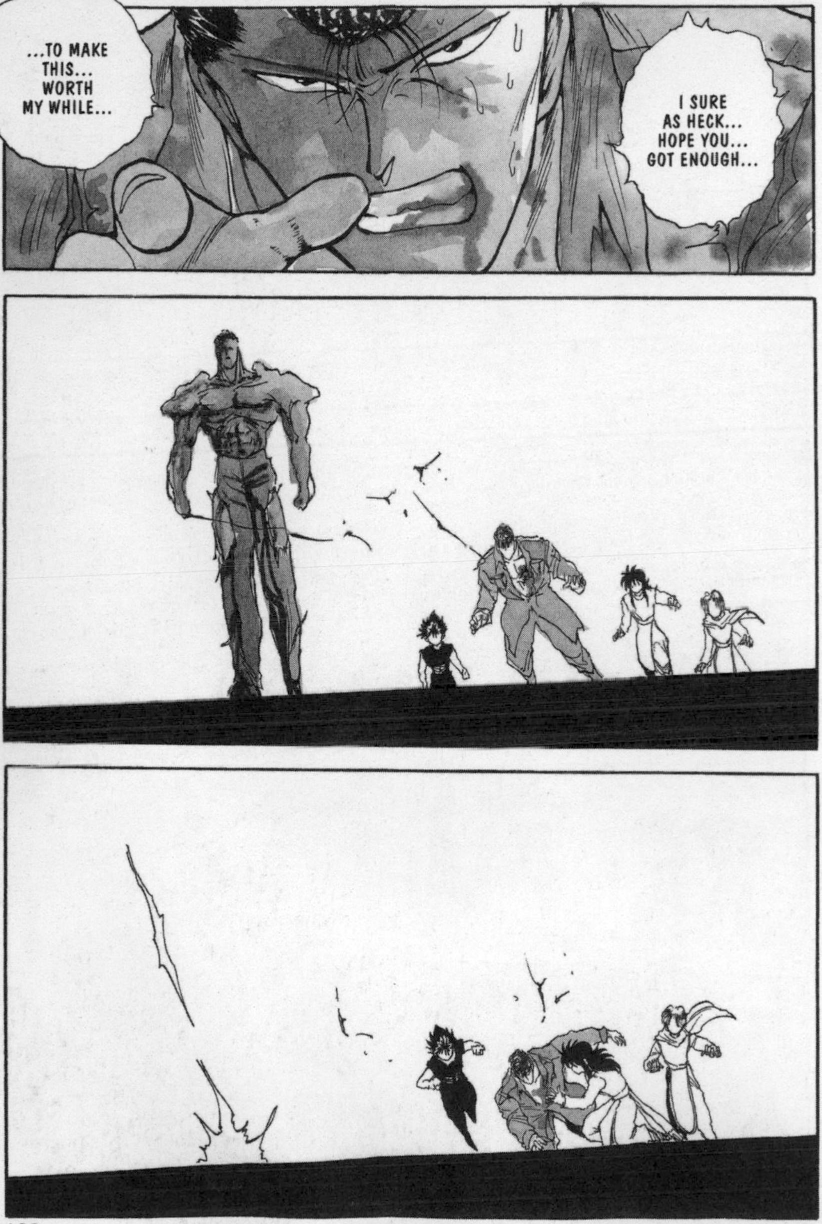
I SURE AS HECK... HOPE YOU... GOT ENOUGH...
...TO MAKE THIS... WORTH MY WHILE...

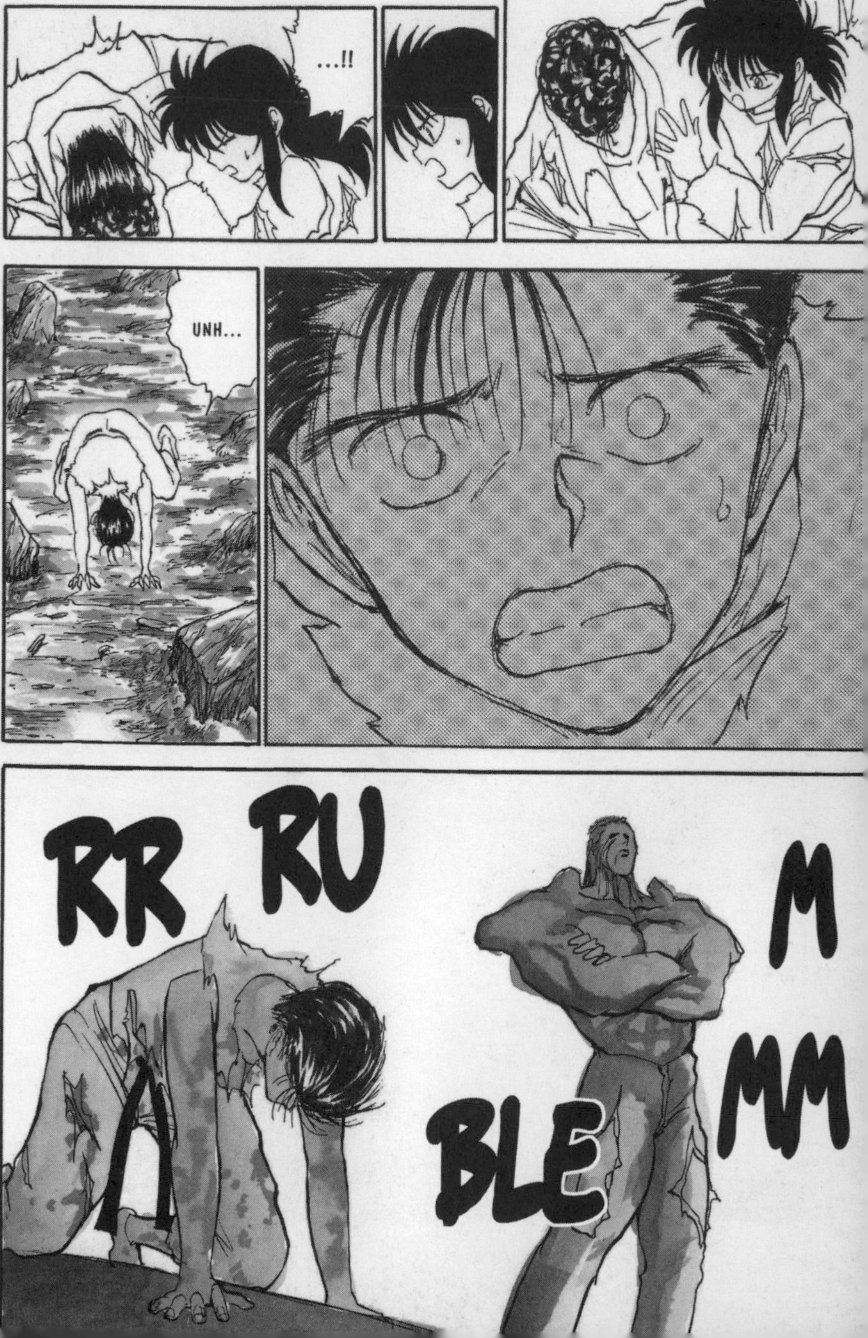
...!!
UNH...
RR
RU
M
MM
BLE

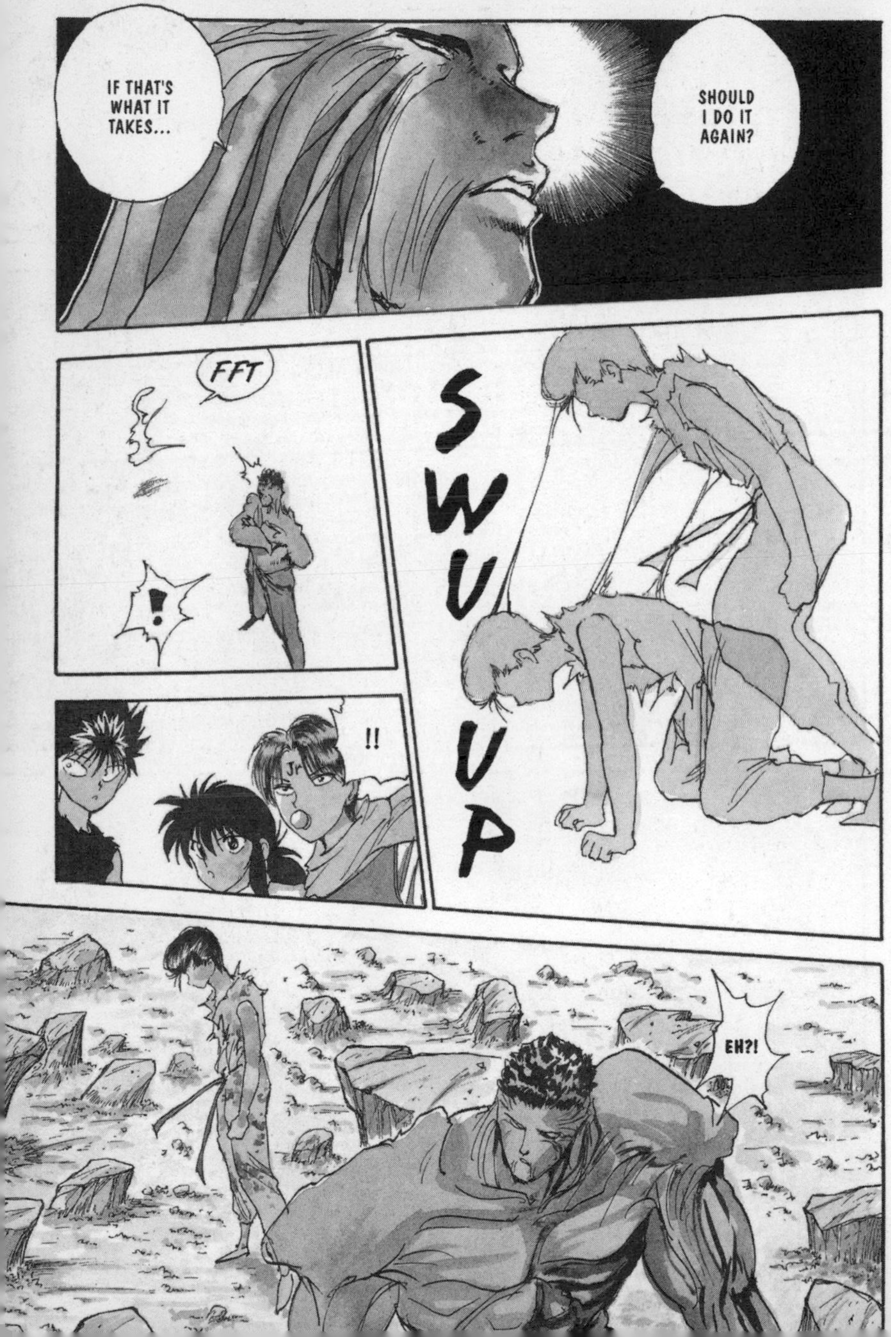
SHOULD I DO IT AGAIN?
IF THAT'S WHAT IT TAKES...
SWUP
FFT
!
!!
EH?!

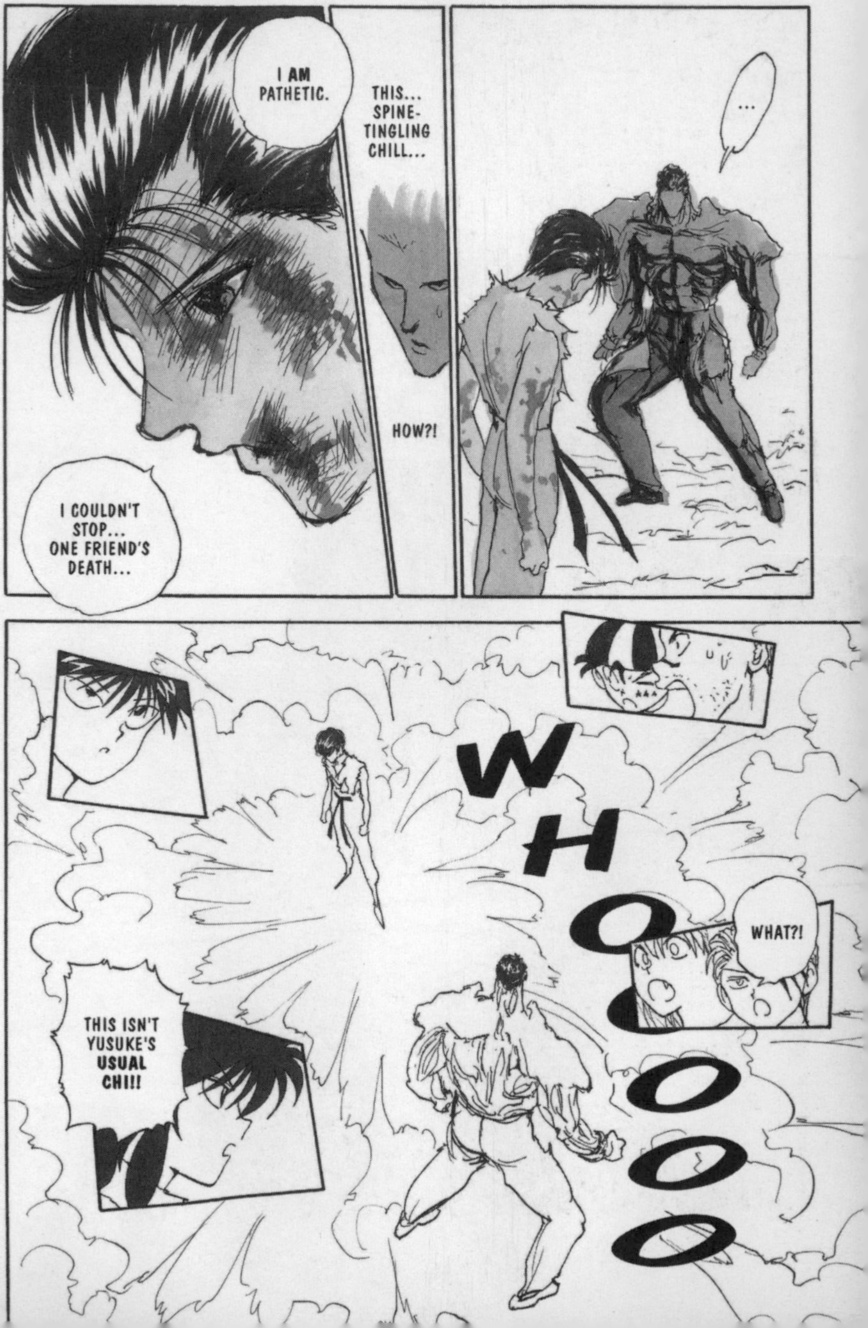
...
THIS... SPINE-TINGLING CHILL...
HOW?!
I AM PATHETIC.
I COULDN'T STOP... ONE FRIEND'S DEATH...
WHOOOOOO
WHAT?!
THIS ISN'T YUSUKE'S **USUAL** CHI!!

READ THIS WAY

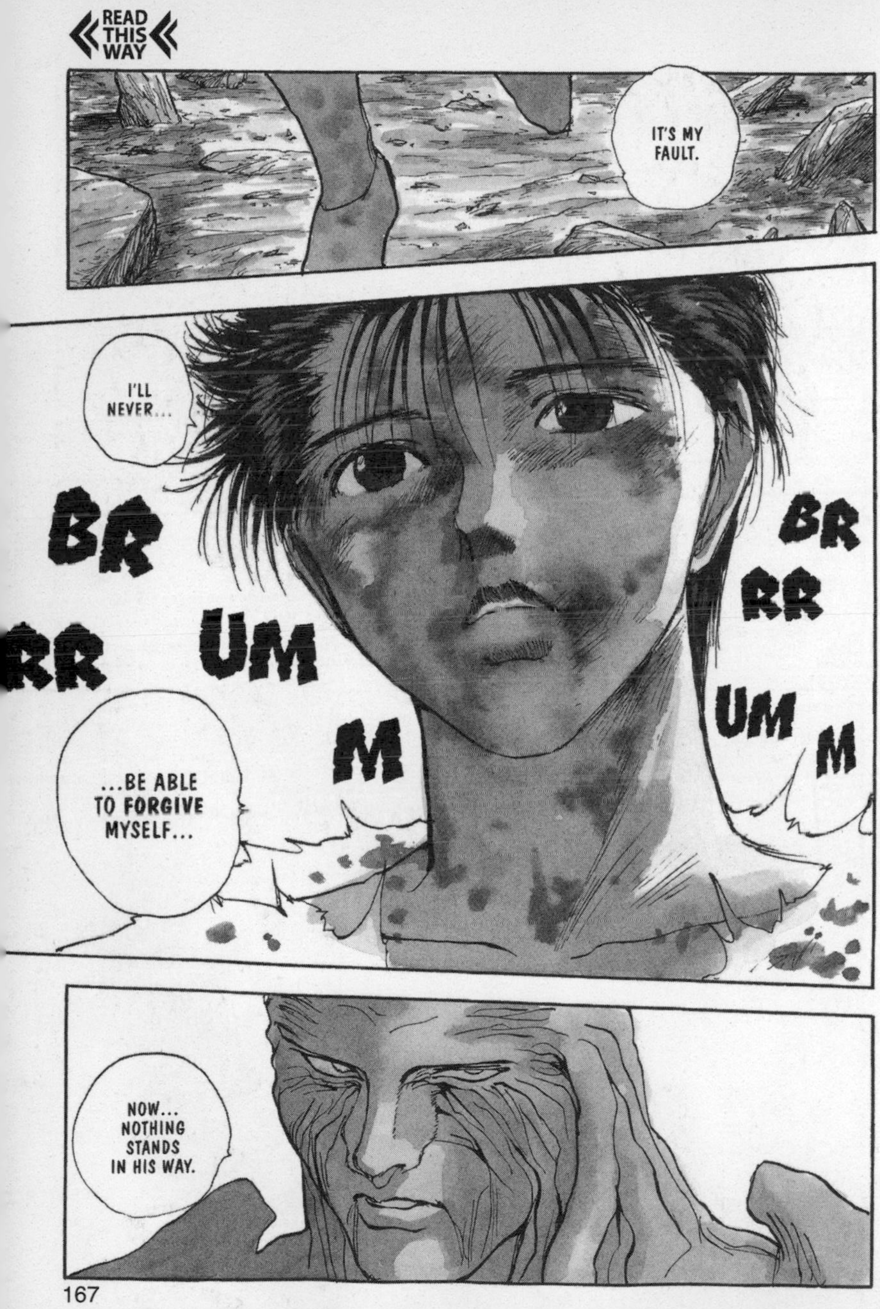
IT'S MY FAULT.
BRRRUMM
I'LL NEVER...
BRRRUMM
...BE ABLE TO FORGIVE MYSELF...
NOW... NOTHING STANDS IN HIS WAY.

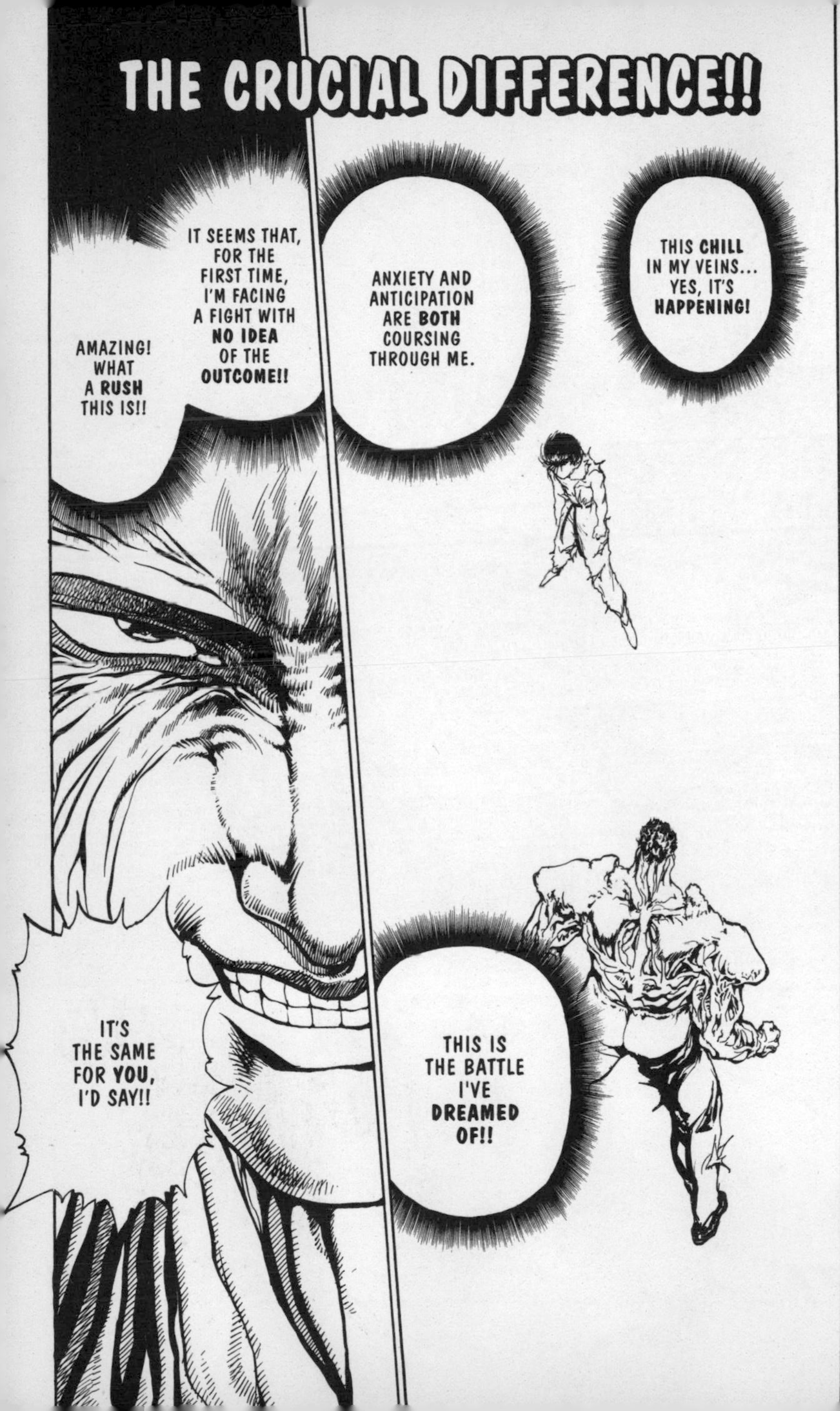
THE CRUCIAL DIFFERENCE!!
THIS CHILL IN MY VEINS... YES, IT'S HAPPENING!
ANXIETY AND ANTICIPATION ARE BOTH COURSING THROUGH ME.
THIS IS THE BATTLE I'VE DREAMED OF!!
IT SEEMS THAT, FOR THE FIRST TIME, I'M FACING A FIGHT WITH NO IDEA OF THE OUTCOME!!
AMAZING! WHAT A RUSH THIS IS!!
IT'S THE SAME FOR YOU, I'D SAY!!

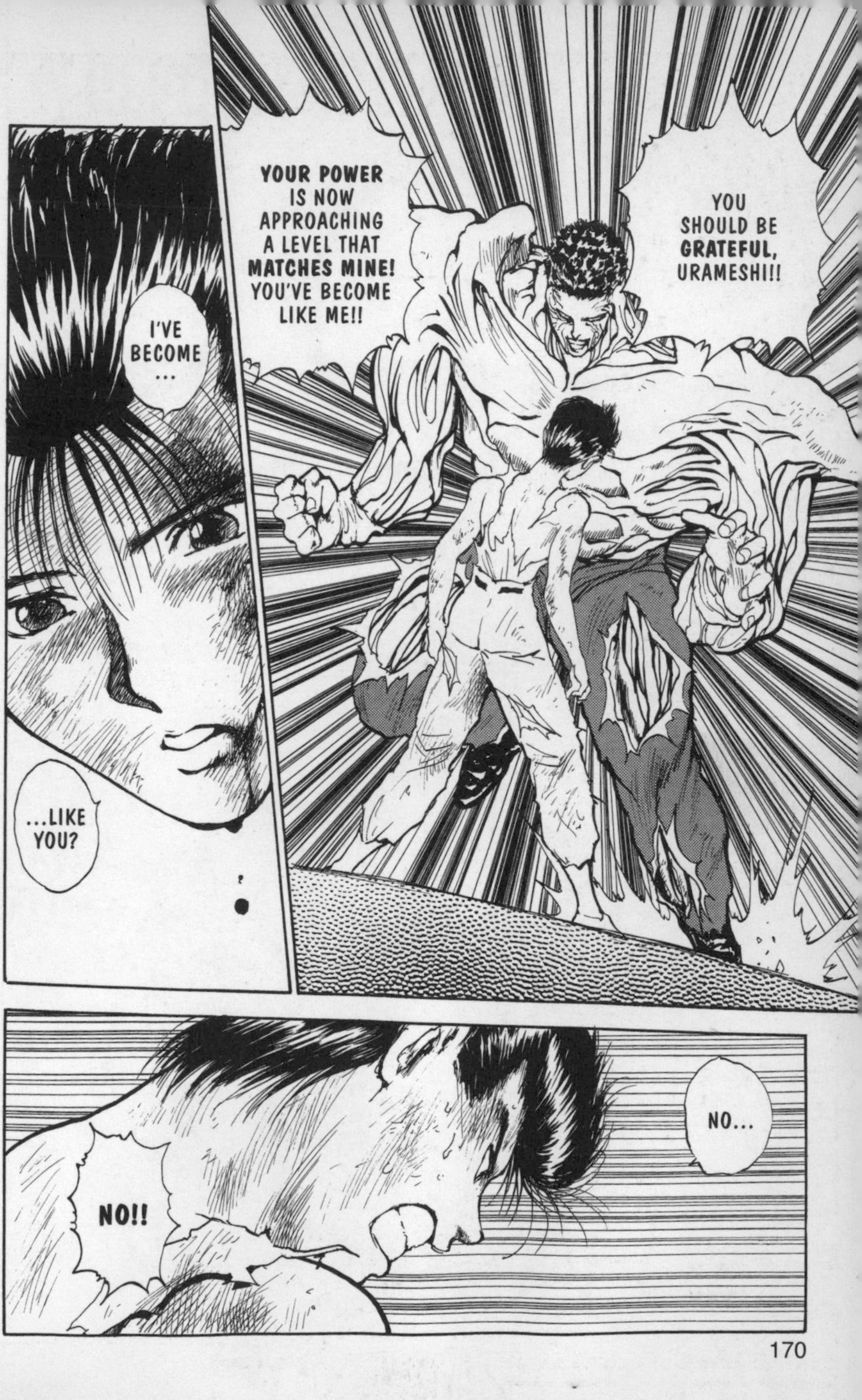
YOU SHOULD BE GRATEFUL, URAMESHI!!
YOUR POWER IS NOW APPROACHING A LEVEL THAT MATCHES MINE! YOU'VE BECOME LIKE ME!!
I'VE BECOME ...
...LIKE YOU?
NO...
NO!!

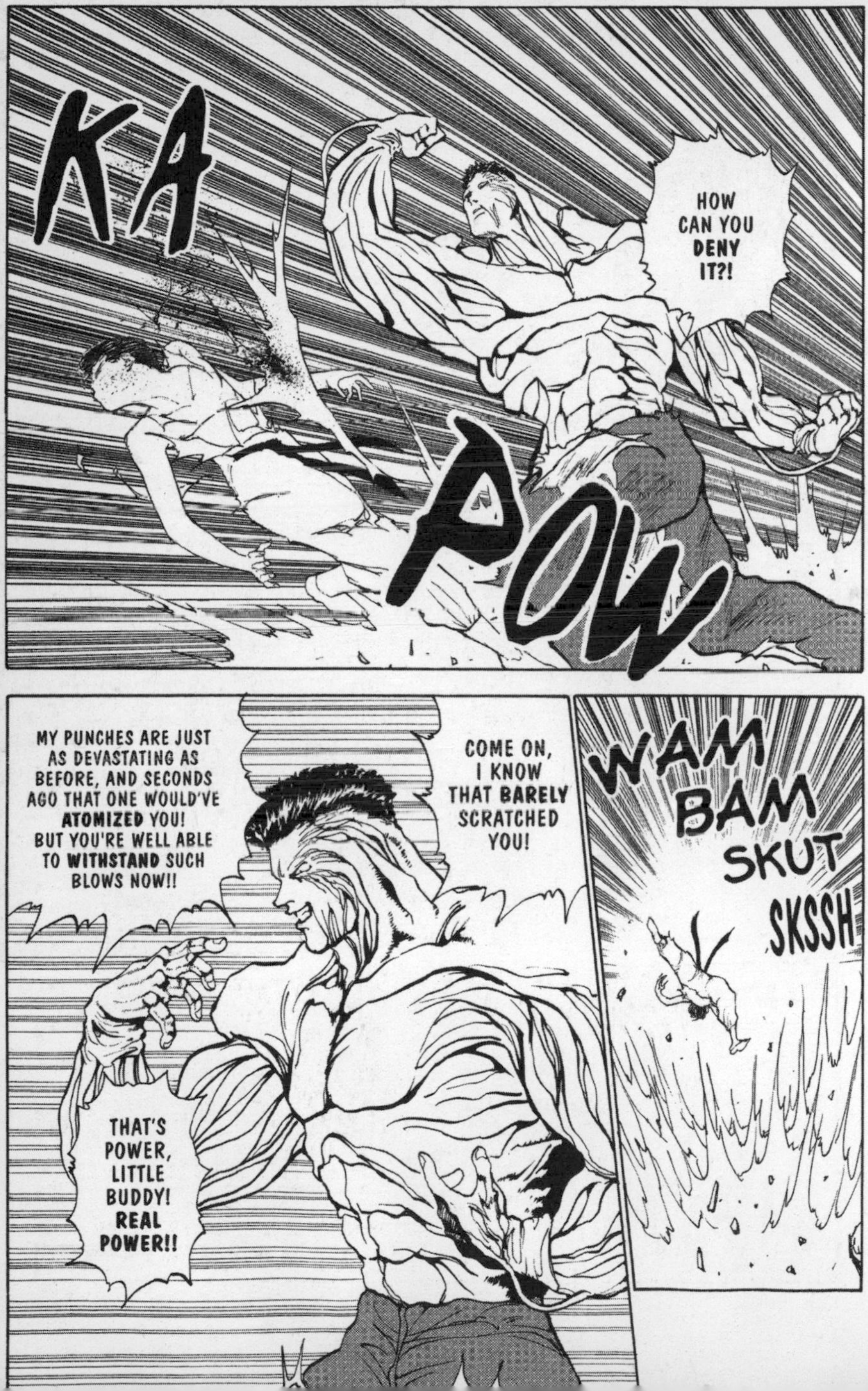
HOW CAN YOU DENY IT?!
KA
POW
WAM BAM SKUT SKSSH
COME ON, I KNOW THAT BARELY SCRATCHED YOU!
MY PUNCHES ARE JUST AS DEVASTATING AS BEFORE, AND SECONDS AGO THAT ONE WOULD'VE ATOMIZED YOU! BUT YOU'RE WELL ABLE TO WITHSTAND SUCH BLOWS NOW!!
THAT'S POWER, LITTLE BUDDY! REAL POWER!!

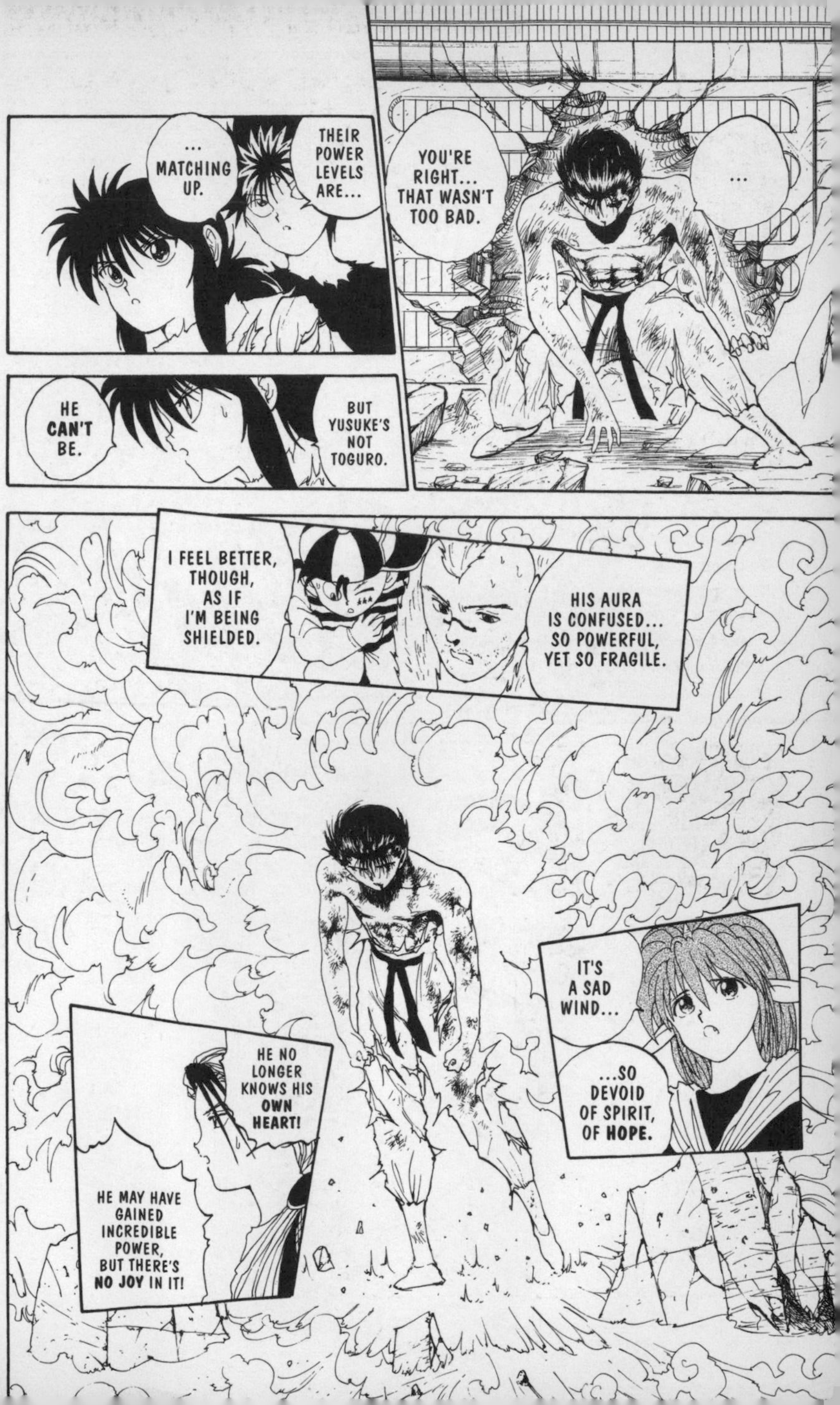
...
YOU'RE RIGHT... THAT WASN'T TOO BAD.
THEIR POWER LEVELS ARE...
... MATCHING UP.
BUT YUSUKE'S NOT TOGURO.
HE CAN'T BE.
HIS AURA IS CONFUSED... SO POWERFUL, YET SO FRAGILE.
I FEEL BETTER, THOUGH, AS IF I'M BEING SHIELDED.
IT'S A SAD WIND...
...SO DEVOID OF SPIRIT, OF HOPE.
HE NO LONGER KNOWS HIS OWN HEART!
HE MAY HAVE GAINED INCREDIBLE POWER, BUT THERE'S NO JOY IN IT!

READ THIS WAY

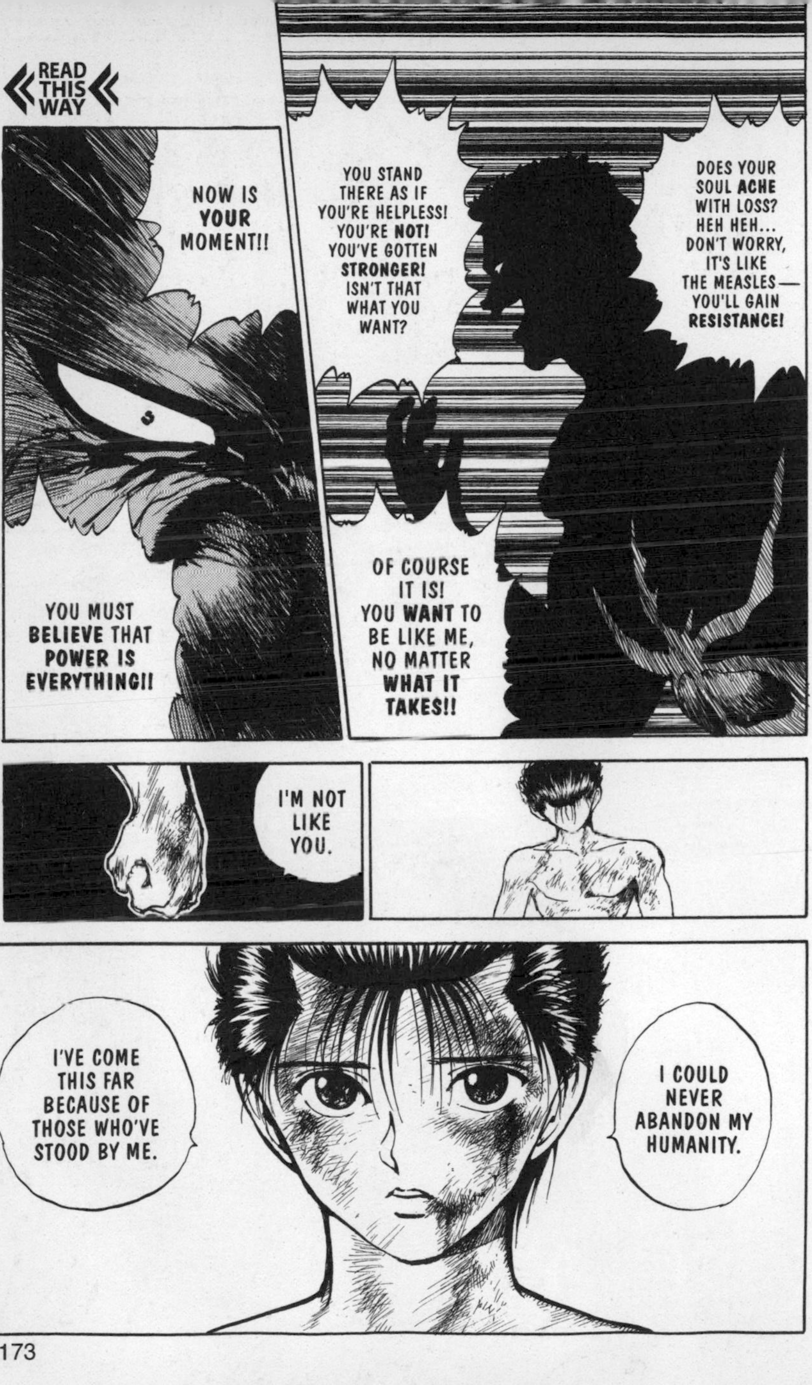
DOES YOUR SOUL ACHE WITH LOSS? HEH HEH... DON'T WORRY, IT'S LIKE THE MEASLES— YOU'LL GAIN RESISTANCE!
YOU STAND THERE AS IF YOU'RE HELPLESS! YOU'RE NOT! YOU'VE GOTTEN STRONGER! ISN'T THAT WHAT YOU WANT?
OF COURSE IT IS! YOU WANT TO BE LIKE ME, NO MATTER WHAT IT TAKES!!
NOW IS YOUR MOMENT!!
YOU MUST BELIEVE THAT POWER IS EVERYTHING!!
I'M NOT LIKE YOU.
I COULD NEVER ABANDON MY HUMANITY.
I'VE COME THIS FAR BECAUSE OF THOSE WHO'VE STOOD BY ME.

THE CRUCIAL DIFFERENCE!!

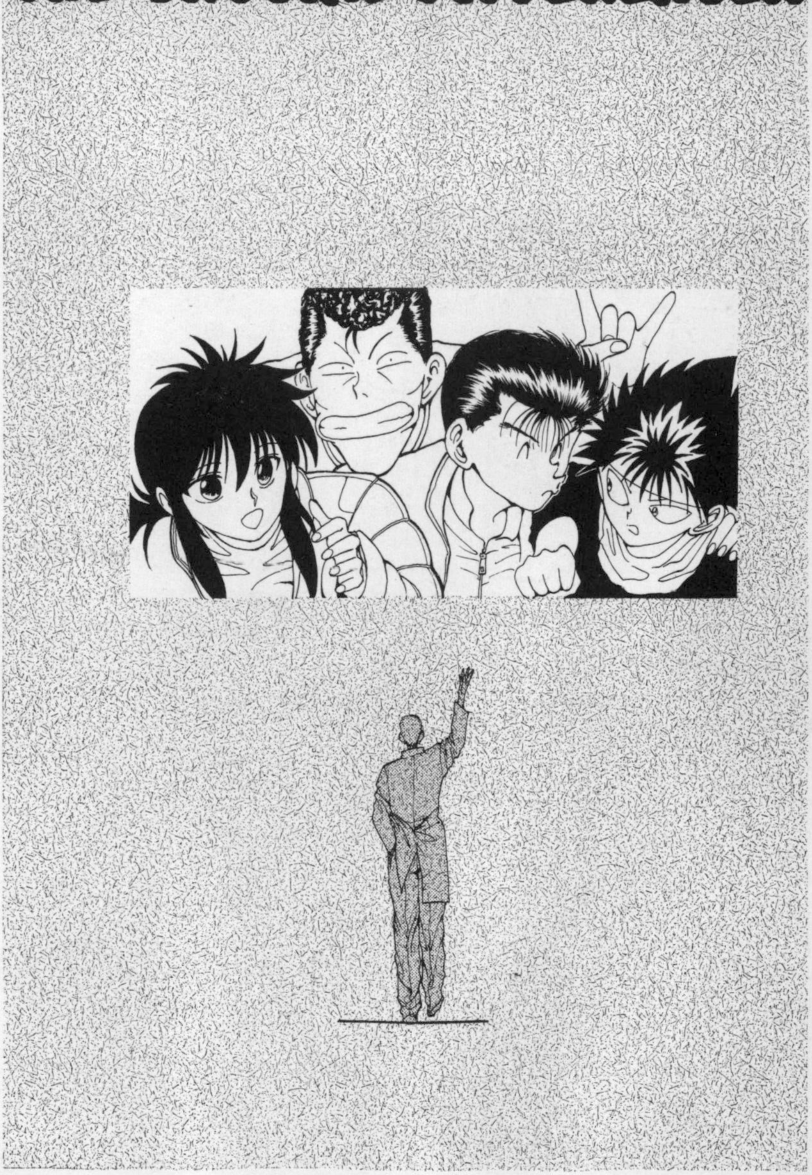

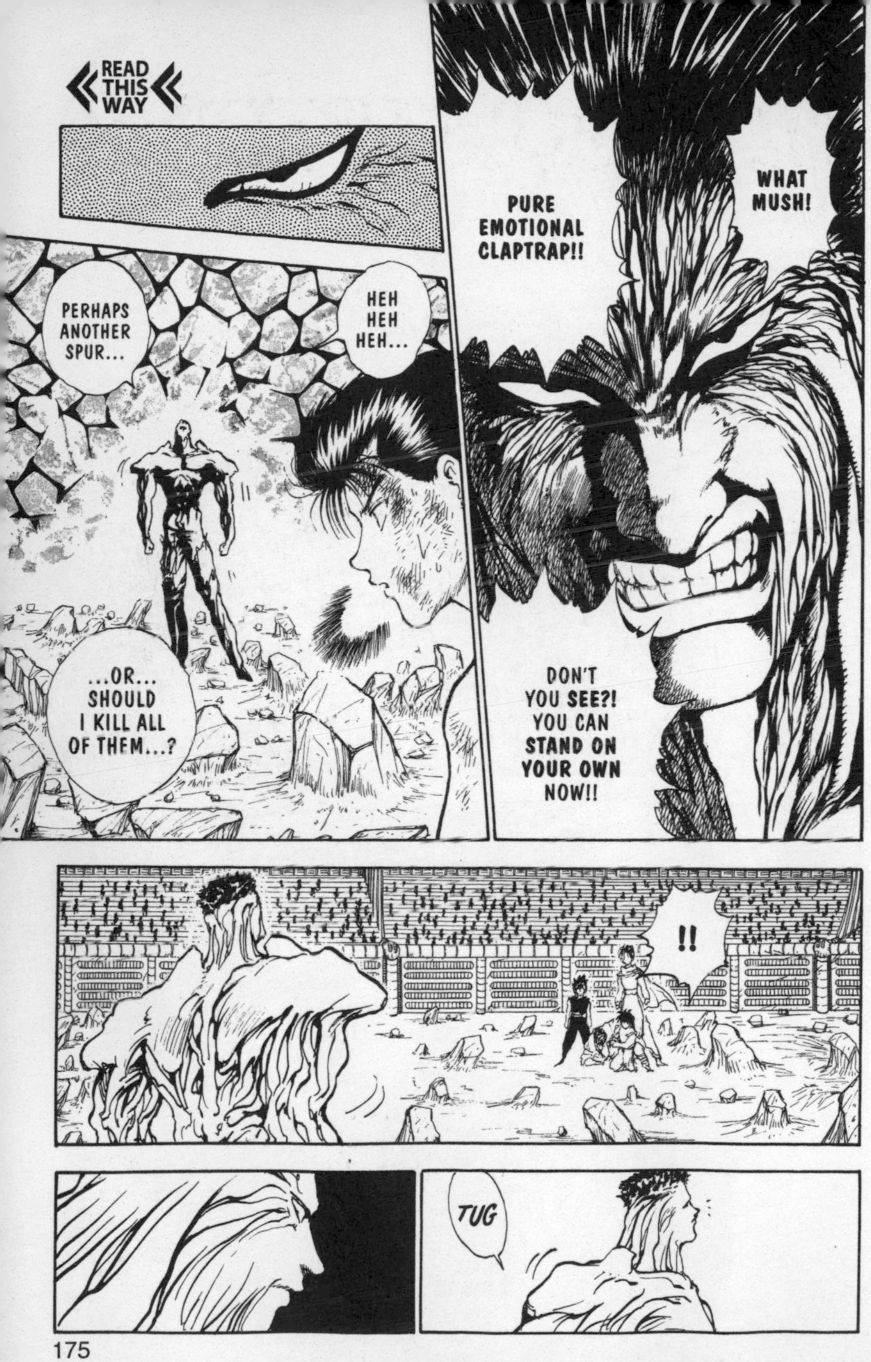
READ THIS WAY
WHAT MUSH!
PURE EMOTIONAL CLAPTRAP!!
DON'T YOU SEE?! YOU CAN STAND ON YOUR OWN NOW!!
HEH HEH HEH...
PERHAPS ANOTHER SPUR...
...OR... SHOULD I KILL ALL OF THEM...?
!!
TUG

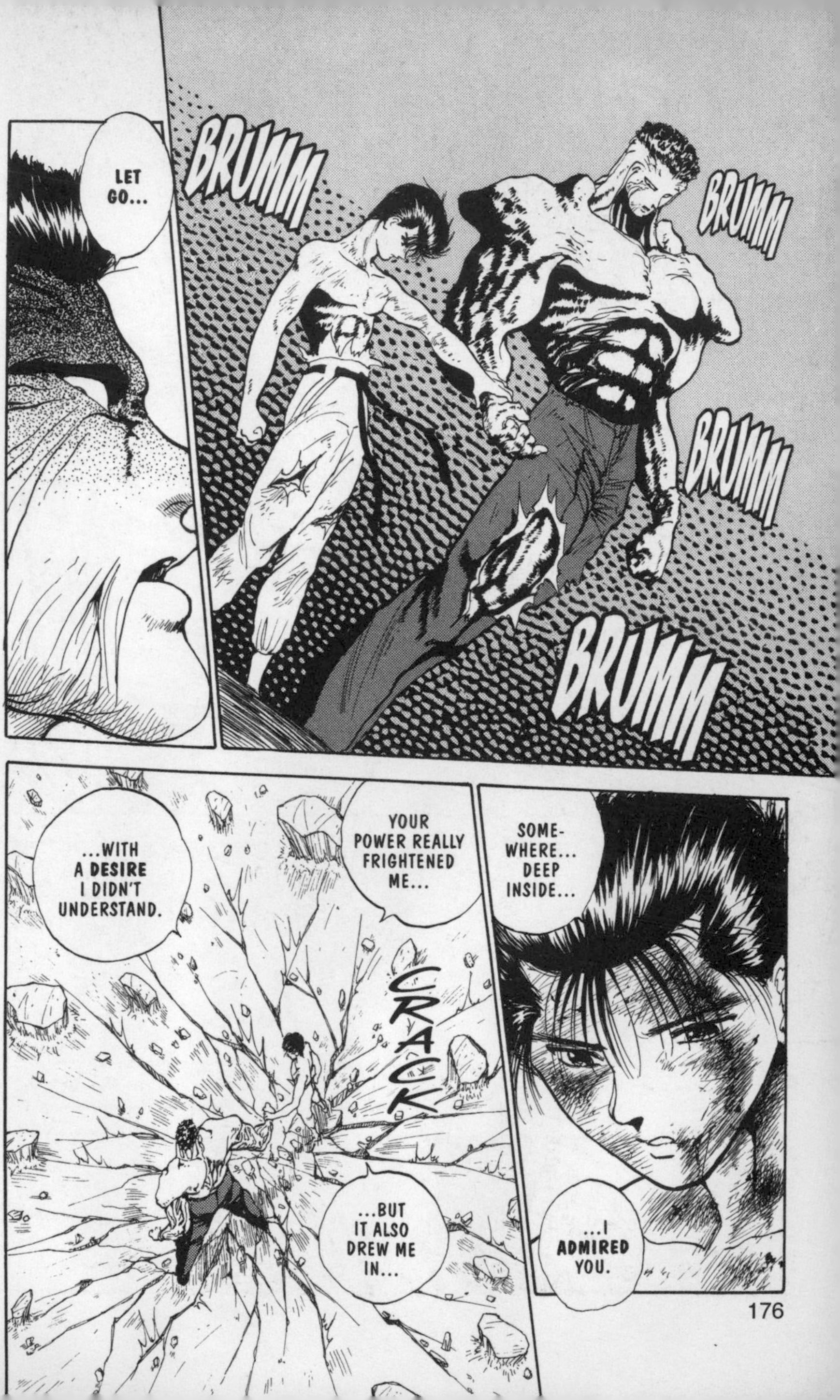
BRUMM
BRUMM
BRUMM
BRUMM
LET GO...
SOME-WHERE... DEEP INSIDE...
...I ADMIRED YOU.
YOUR POWER REALLY FRIGHTENED ME...
...WITH A DESIRE I DIDN'T UNDERSTAND.
CRACK
...BUT IT ALSO DREW ME IN...

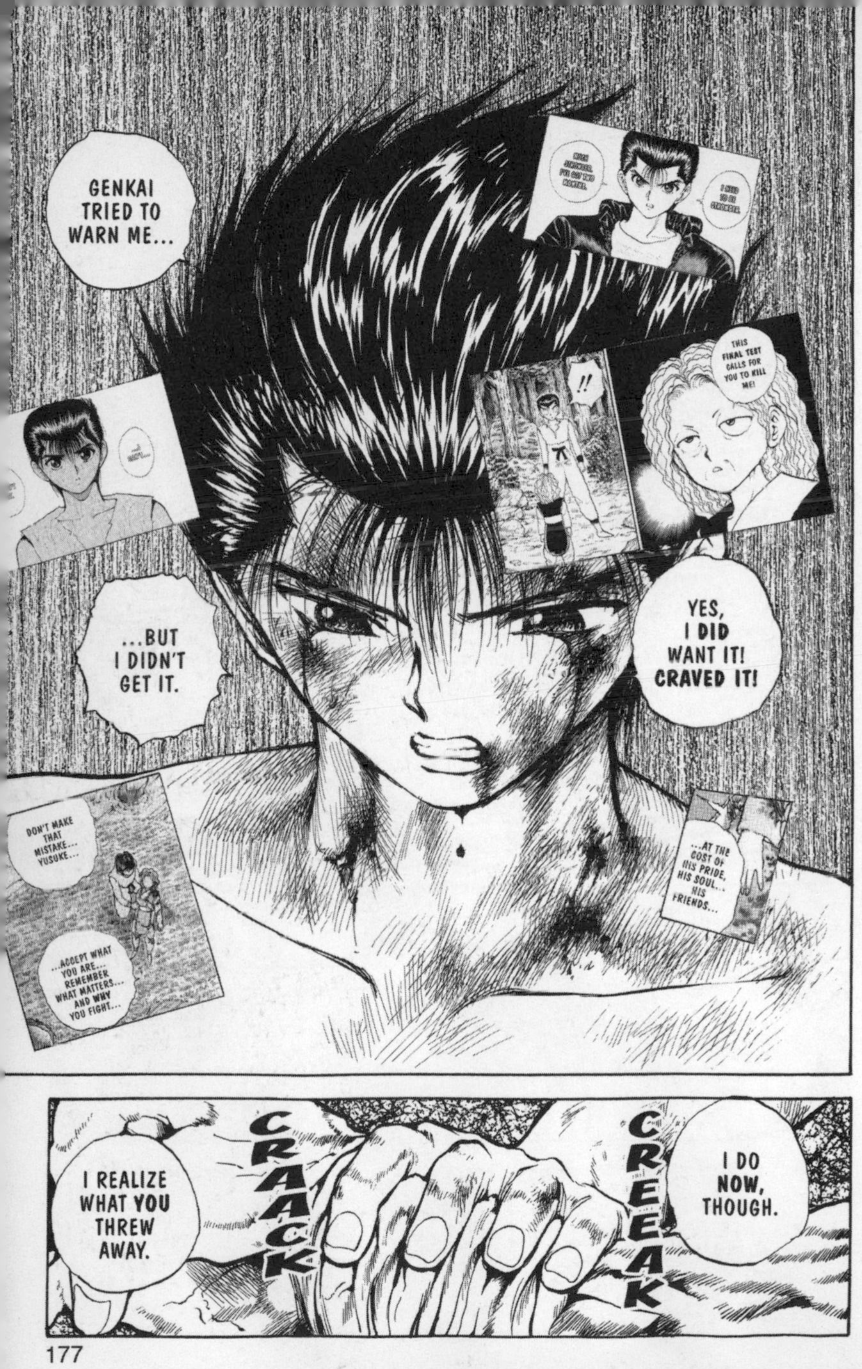
GENKAI TRIED TO WARN ME...
THIS FINAL TEST CALLS FOR YOU TO KILL ME!
!!
...BUT I DIDN'T GET IT.
YES, I DID WANT IT! CRAVED IT!
...AT THE COST OF HIS PRIDE, HIS SOUL... HIS FRIENDS...
DON'T MAKE THAT MISTAKE... YUSUKE...
...ACCEPT WHAT YOU ARE... REMEMBER WHAT MATTERS... AND WHY YOU FIGHT...
I DO NOW, THOUGH.
CREEAK
CRACK
I REALIZE WHAT YOU THREW AWAY.

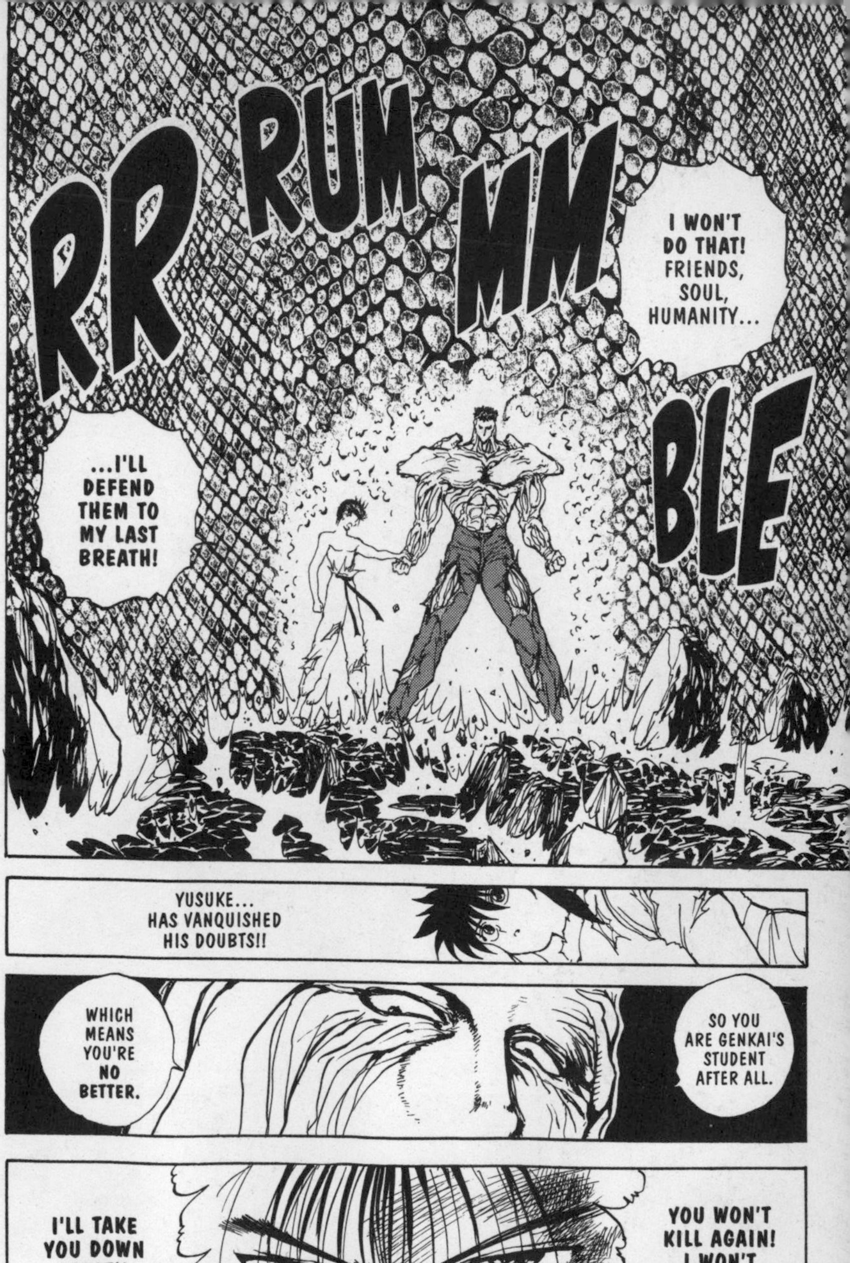
RR RUM MM BLE
I WON'T DO THAT! FRIENDS, SOUL, HUMANITY...
...I'LL DEFEND THEM TO MY LAST BREATH!
YUSUKE... HAS VANQUISHED HIS DOUBTS!!
SO YOU ARE GENKAI'S STUDENT AFTER ALL.
WHICH MEANS YOU'RE NO BETTER.
YOU WON'T KILL AGAIN! I WON'T ALLOW IT!
I'LL TAKE YOU DOWN FIRST!!

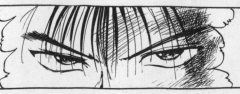

READ THIS WAY

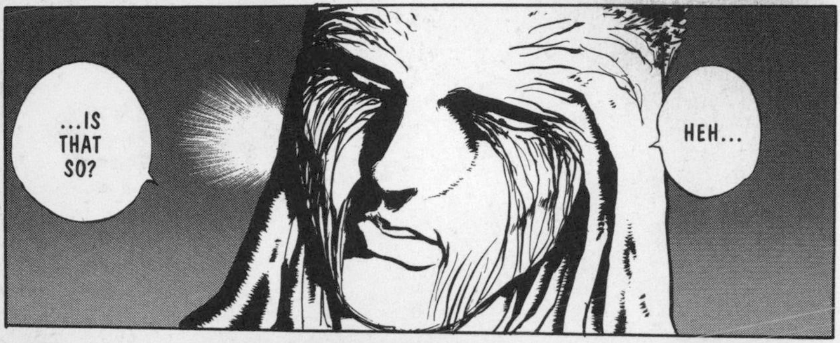
HEH...
...IS THAT SO?

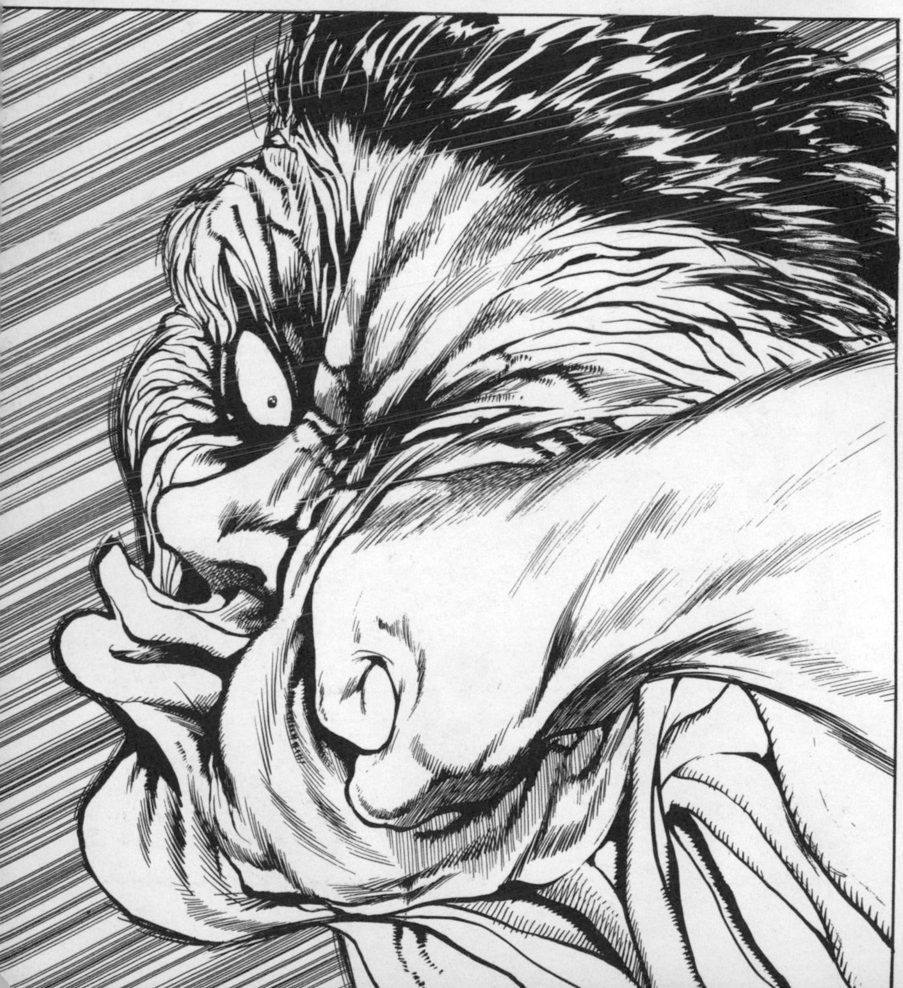

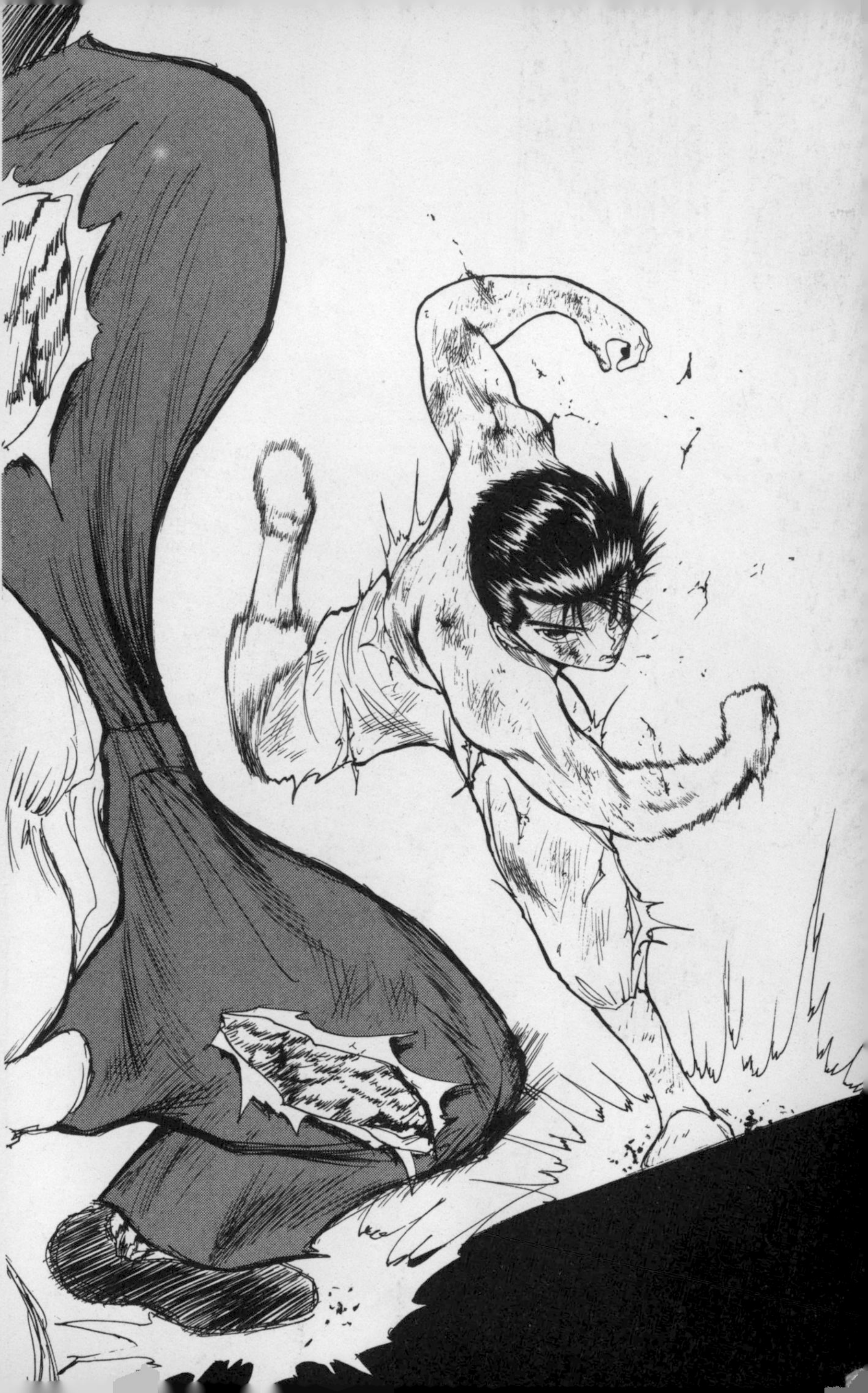

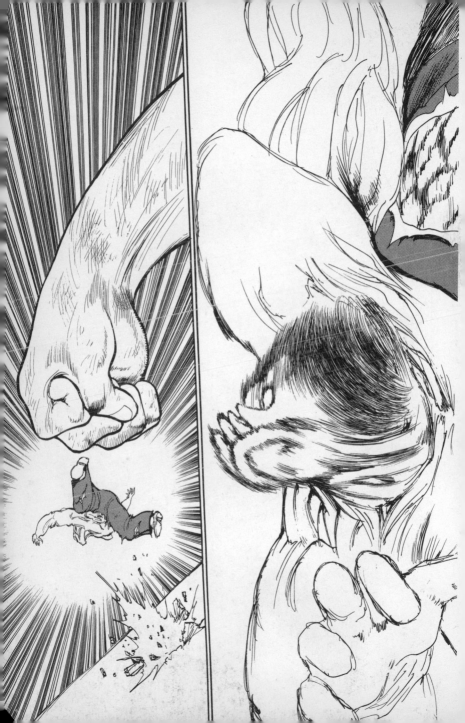

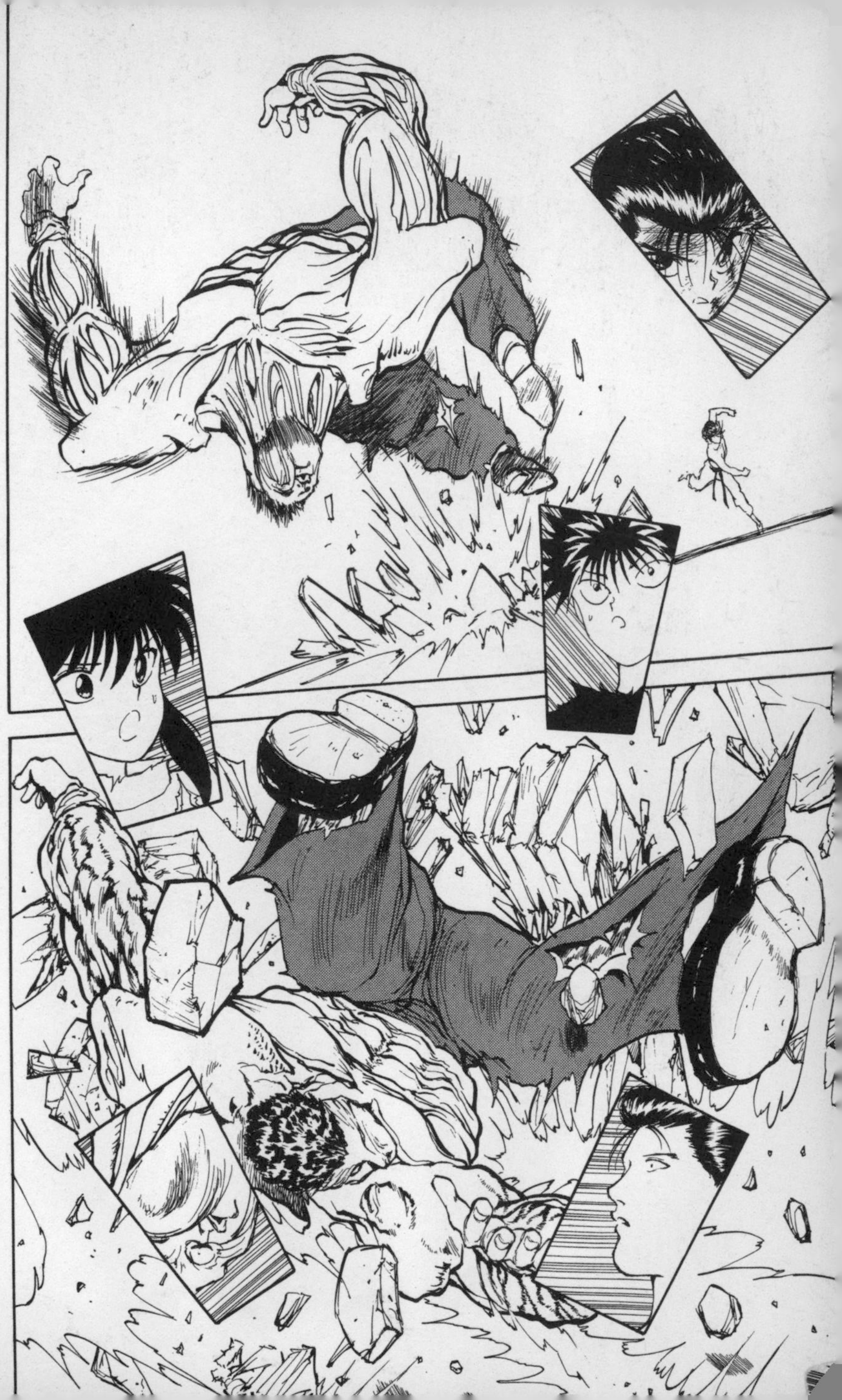

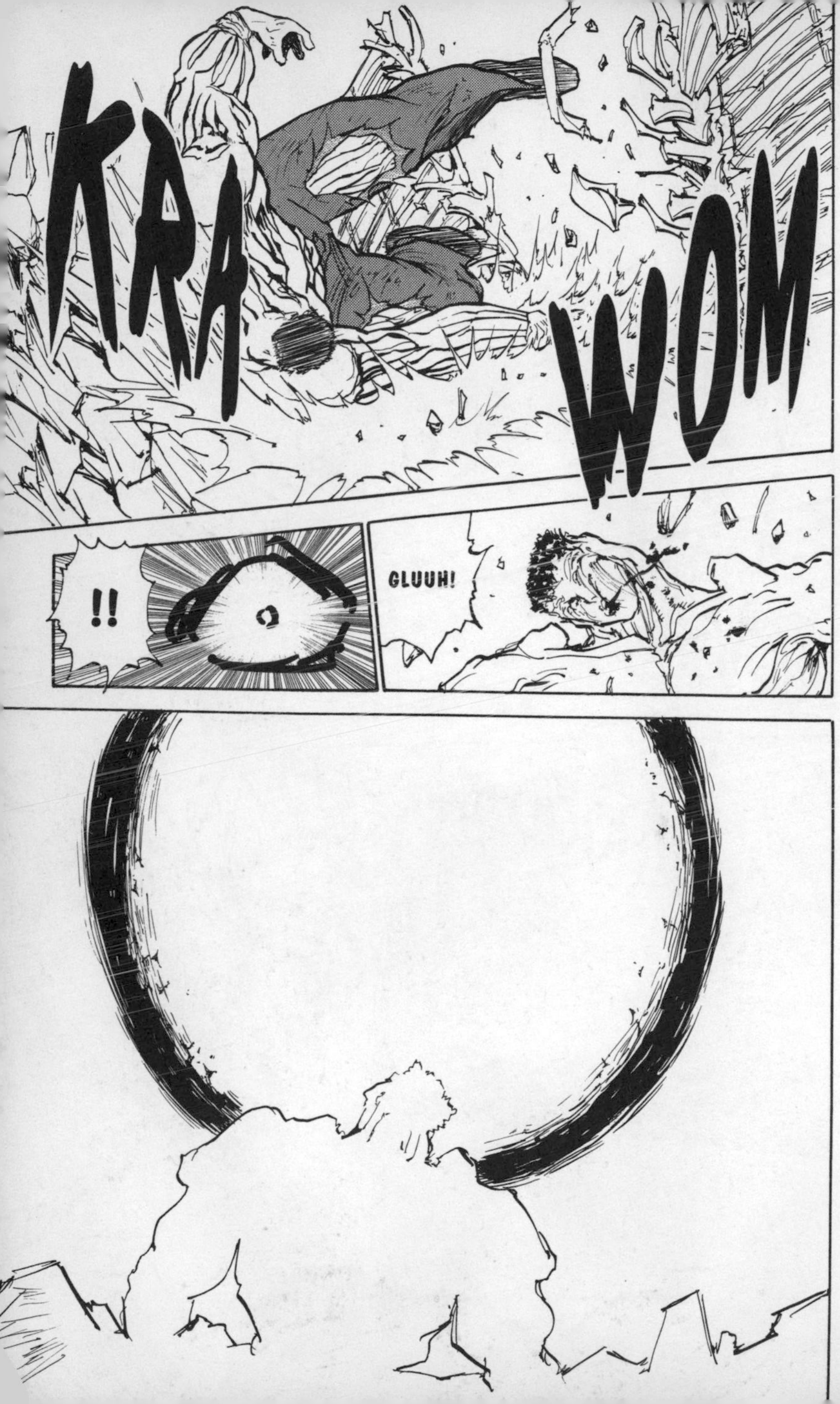
KRA
WOM
GLUUH!
!!

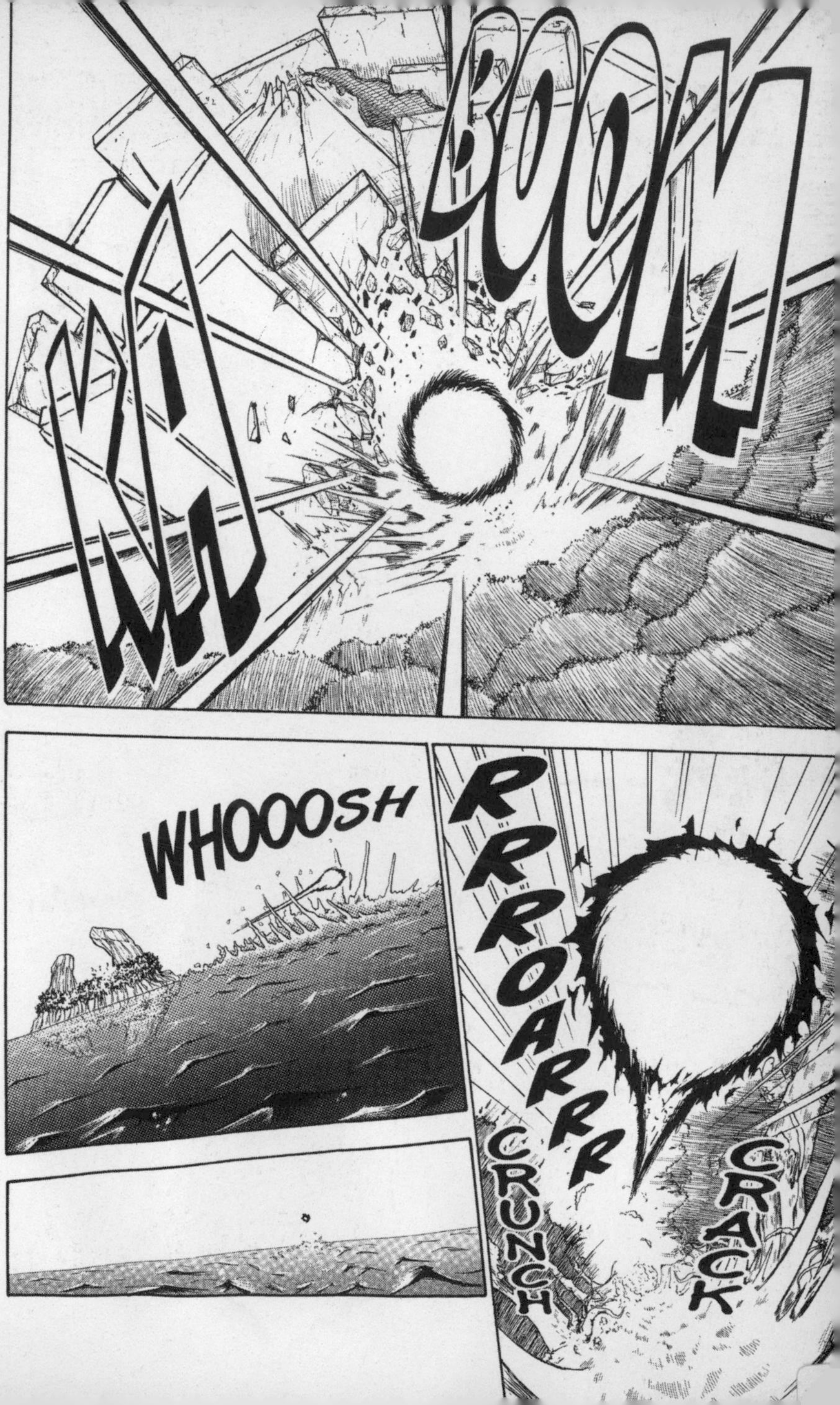
BOOM
RRRROARRR
CRACK
CRUNCH
WHOOOSH

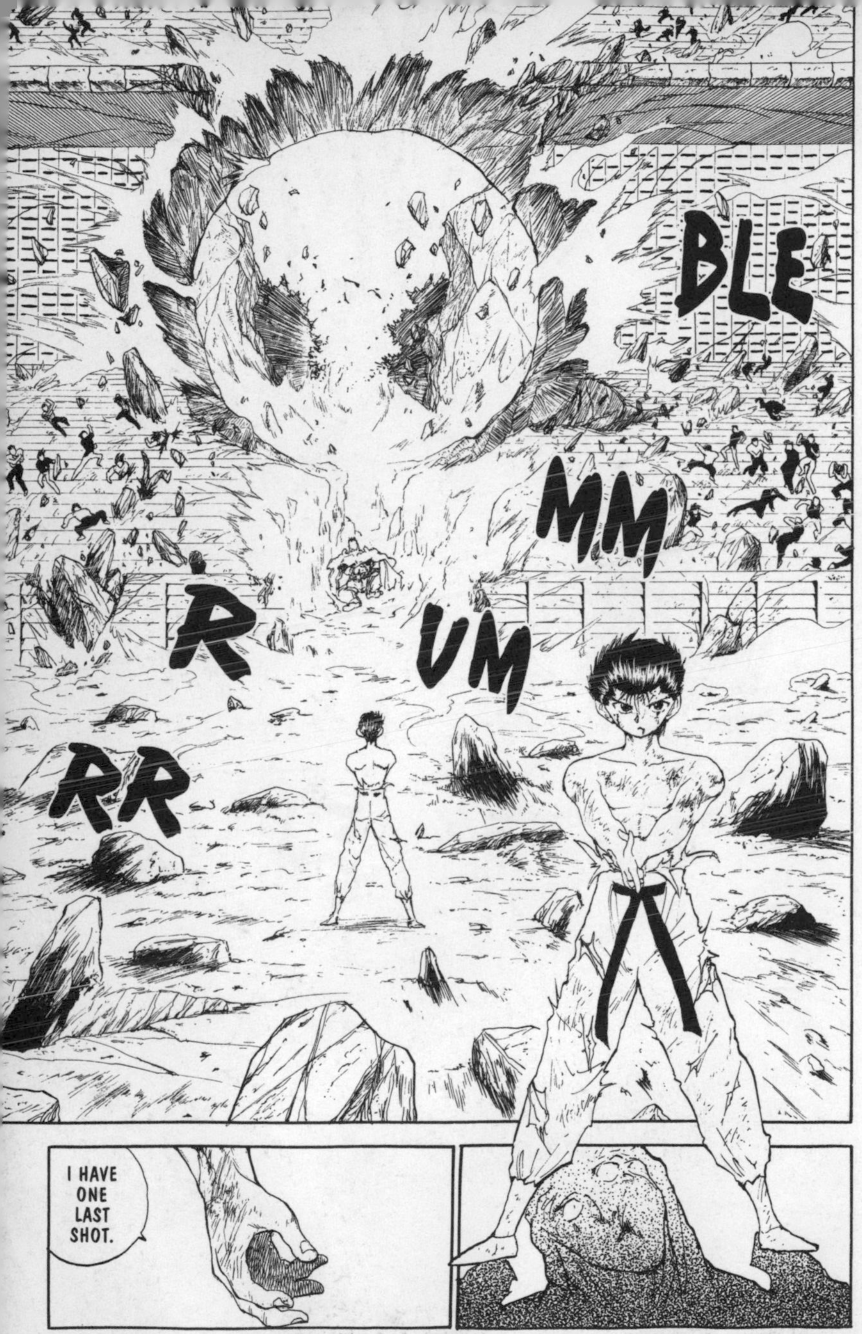
RR
R
UM
MM
BLE
I HAVE ONE LAST SHOT.

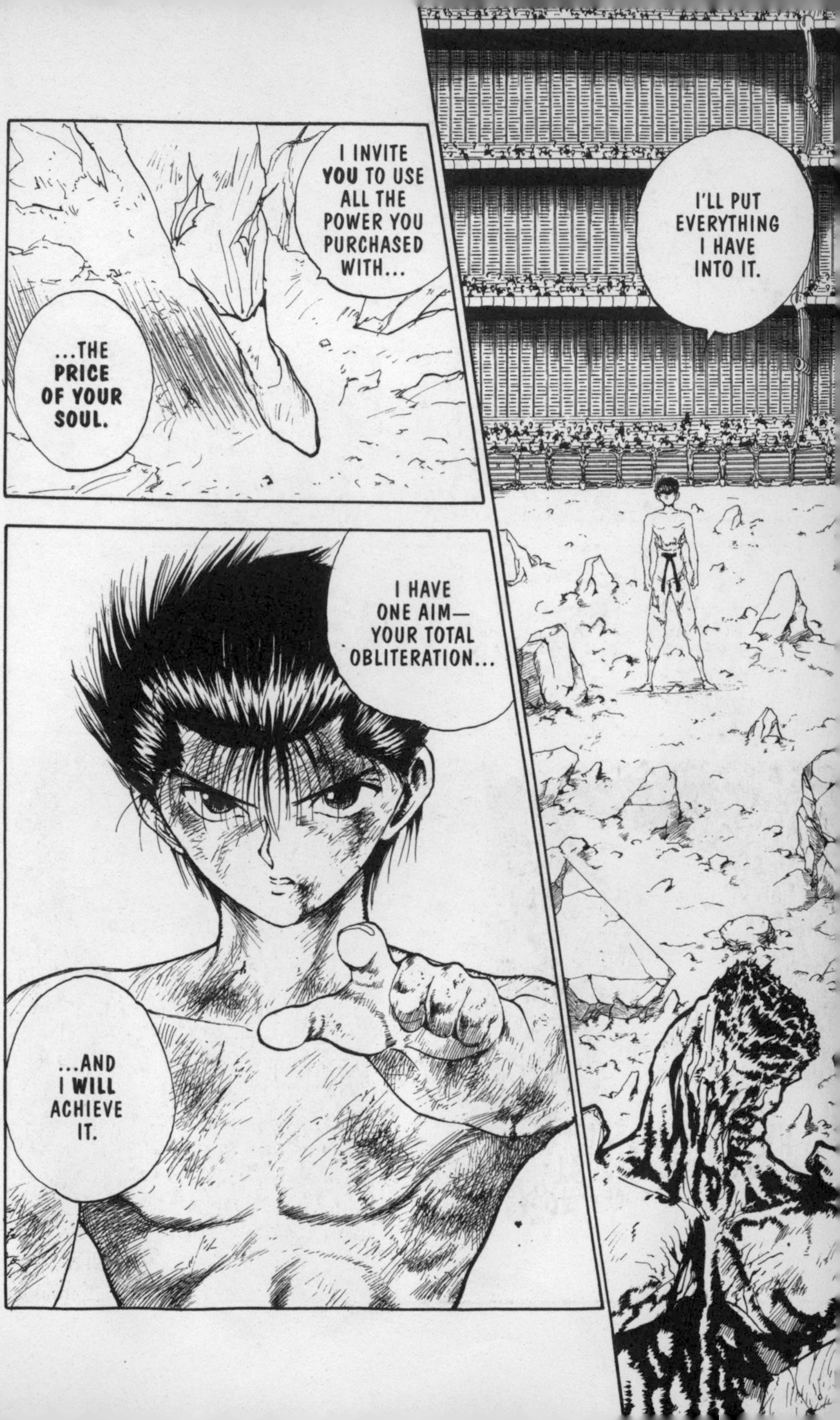
I'LL PUT EVERYTHING I HAVE INTO IT.
I INVITE YOU TO USE ALL THE POWER YOU PURCHASED WITH...
...THE PRICE OF YOUR SOUL.
I HAVE ONE AIM— YOUR TOTAL OBLITERATION...
...AND I WILL ACHIEVE IT.

READ THIS WAY

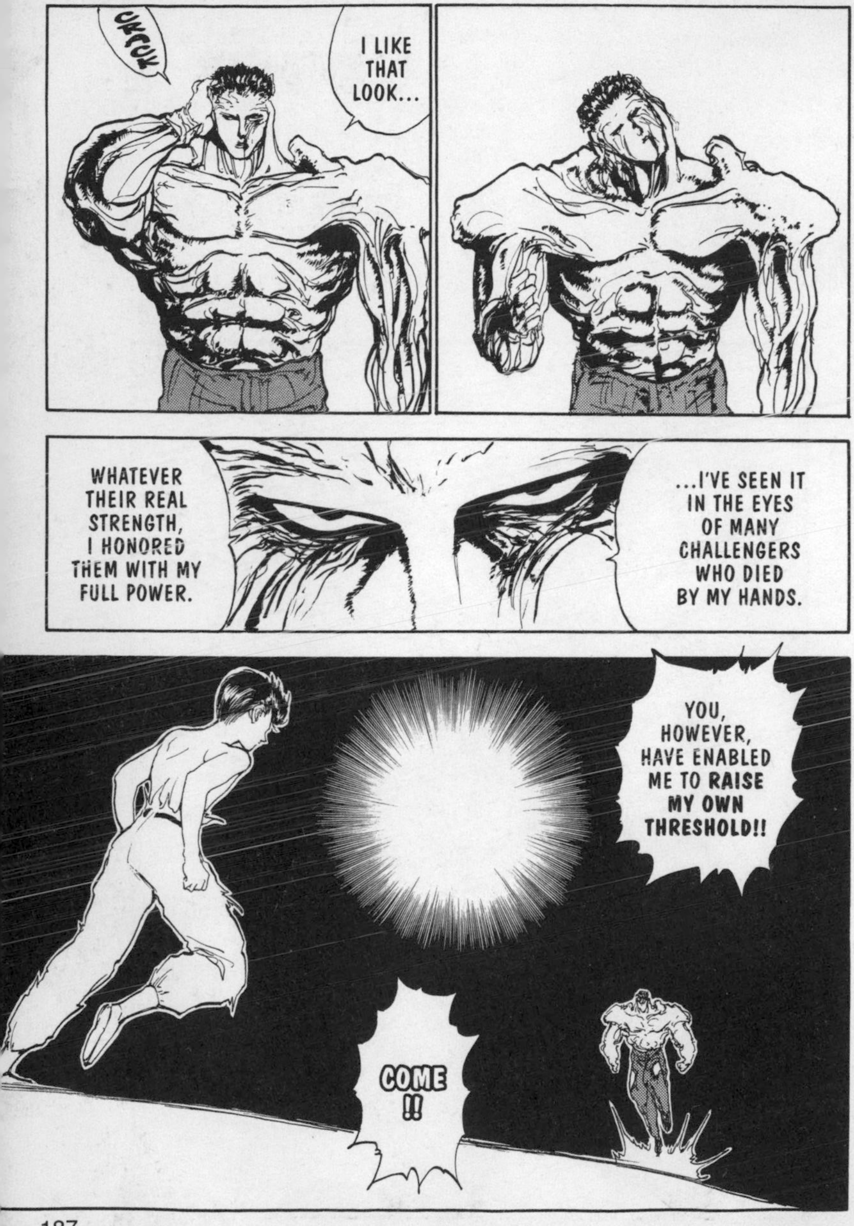
I LIKE THAT LOOK...
CRACK
...I'VE SEEN IT IN THE EYES OF MANY CHALLENGERS WHO DIED BY MY HANDS.
WHATEVER THEIR REAL STRENGTH, I HONORED THEM WITH MY FULL POWER.
YOU, HOWEVER, HAVE ENABLED ME TO RAISE MY OWN THRESHOLD!!
COME !!

COMING NEXT VOLUME...

The stunning conclusion of the long and bloody Dark Tournament! Who will win? Toguro taps into the full extent of his powers as does Yusuke. They're both giving it everything they've got. It's a do-or-die, make-it-or-break-it ending you won't wanna miss!

Coming October 2007!
Read it first in *SHONEN JUMP* magazine!

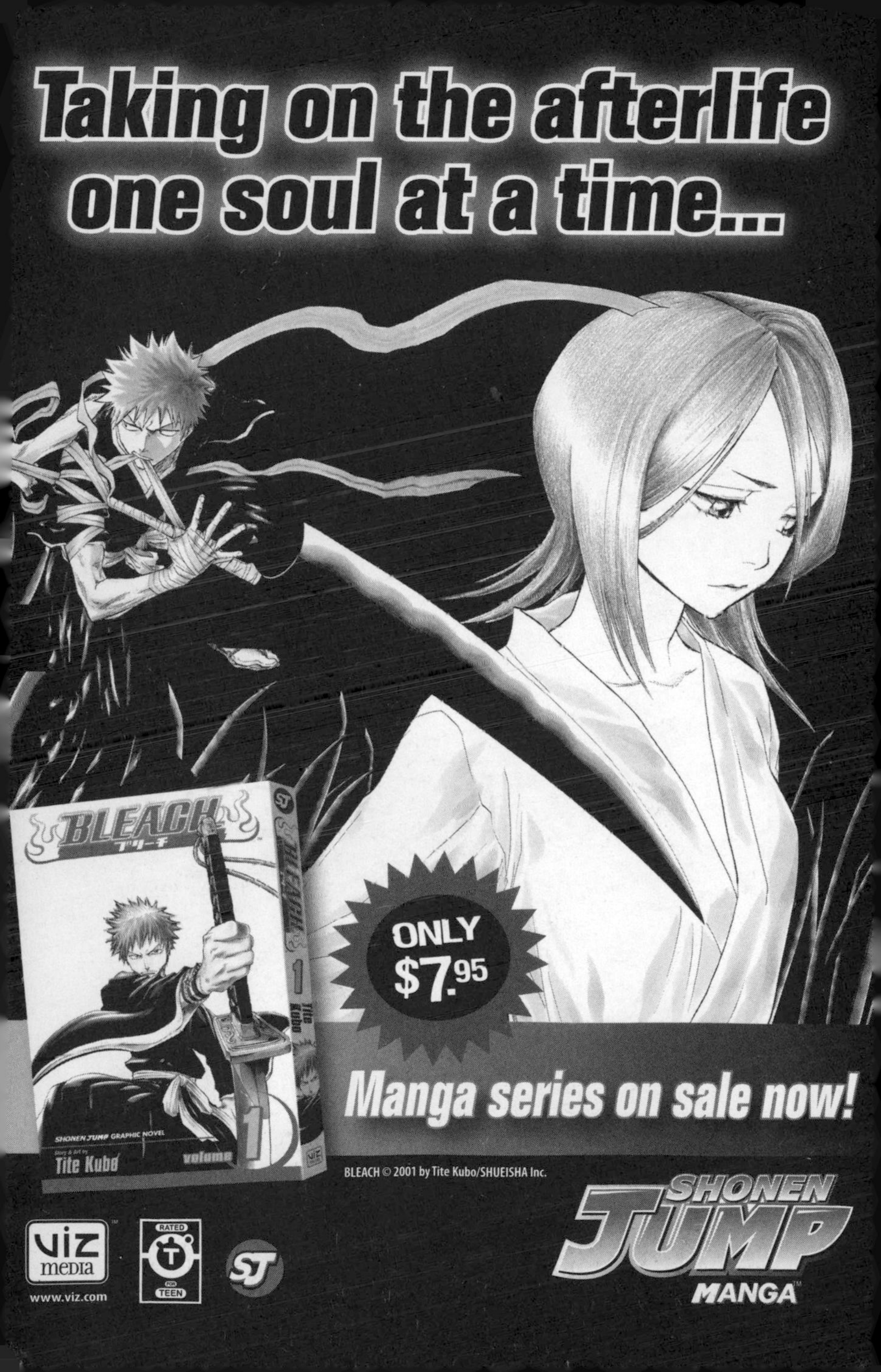
Taking on the afterlife one soul at a time...
BLEACH
ONLY $7.95
Manga series on sale now!
SHONEN JUMP GRAPHIC NOVEL
Story & Art by Tite Kubo
volume 1
BLEACH © 2001 by Tite Kubo/SHUEISHA Inc.
SHONEN JUMP MANGA
viz media
www.viz.com
RATED T FOR TEEN

Tell us what you think about SHONEN JUMP manga!

Our survey is now available online.
Go to: www.SHONENJUMP.com/mangasurvey

Help us make our product offering better!

THE REAL ACTION STARTS IN...

SHONEN JUMP
THE WORLD'S MOST POPULAR MANGA
www.shonenjump.com

ADVANCED

VIZ media